EVER͏   ͏ itical o͏͏   ͏ of the

The United States in World Affairs 1967

The United States
in World Affairs
1967

Richard P. Stebbins

Published for the COUNCIL ON FOREIGN RELATIONS

by SIMON AND SCHUSTER, New York, 1968

The Council on Foreign Relations is a non-profit institution devoted
to the study of political, economic, and strategic problems as related
to American foreign policy. It takes no stand, expressed or implied,
on American policy.

The authors of books published under the auspices of the Council
are responsible for their statements of fact and expressions of opinion.
The Council is responsible only for determining that they should be
presented to the public.

For a partial list of Council publications see pages 463-464.

THE UNITED STATES IN WORLD AFFAIRS, 1967
Copyright © 1968 by Council on Foreign Relations, Inc.
Printed in the United States of America
All rights reserved, including the right to reproduce
this book or any portion thereof in any form.
For information, address
Simon and Schuster, Inc., Rockefeller Center
630 Fifth Avenue, New York, N.Y. 10020

FIRST EDITION

Library of Congress Catalog Card Number: 32-26065

HUGH STEPHENS LIBRARY
STEPHENS COLLEGE
COLUMBIA, MISSOURI

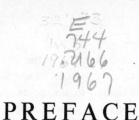

PREFACE

Continuing the series of annual foreign policy surveys initiated by the Council on Foreign Relations in 1931, this volume offers a concise account of the international experience of the United States in 1967. As the title implies, it endeavors to trace the development of American foreign relations in their global context and emphasizes the broad movement of international affairs rather than the minutiae of relations with individual countries. The aim throughout has been to present a balanced and objective narrative that takes account of differing points of view but leaves the reader free to draw his own conclusions from the evidence presented.

The plan of the volume comprises a general survey of the international situation at the outset of 1967 which is followed by a series of regional and topical chapters of a more detailed character. The continuing war in Vietnam and the explosion of hostilities in the Middle East inevitably claim priority attention, and the chapters devoted to these events are necessarily somewhat more voluminous than those concerned with developments in the East-West relationship, the Western community, the countries of the "third world," the United Nations, and the United States itself. The Chronology of Major Events at the end of the volume provides details of elections, changes of government, U.N. resolutions, and other relevant matters.

Except as otherwise noted, direct quotations appearing in the text

120396

have been taken from the official transcripts and edited only for uniformity of spelling and capitalization. The sources of quotations, and of other statements where appropriate, are indicated in the notes. A broad selection from the relevant source material is reproduced in the parallel Council on Foreign Relations volume, *Documents on American Foreign Relation, 1967* (New York: Simon & Schuster, 1968), to which reference has been made in the notes wherever appropriate. Other references are confined where practicable to such standard publications as the U.S. *Department of State Bulletin,* the *U.N. Monthly Chronicle,* and *The New York Times.*

As always, the author is conscious of many obligations and feels a special indebtedness to the Officers and Directors of the Council on Foreign Relations; to President Grayson Kirk and the members of the Council's Committee on Studies; and to Hamilton Fish Armstrong, George S. Franklin, Jr., and other colleagues. David W. MacEachron, the Council's Deputy Executive Director, kindly undertook to read and comment on the entire manuscript, and several other readers made valuable suggestions. Elaine P. Adam provided indispensable assistance in every phase of the undertaking. The staff of the Foreign Relations Library, headed by Donald Wasson, Librarian, and Janet Rigney, Assistant Librarian, were unfailingly helpful, as were Grace Darling, Publications Promotion Manager; Joseph Cucolo, Reproduction Supervisor; Carol Kahn, index specialist; and E. D. Weldon, cartographer.

For permission to reprint cartoons the Council is indebted to Herbert L. Block and to the editors and cartoonists of *The Baltimore Sun,* the *Chicago Sun-Times, The Newark News, The Philadelphia Inquirer,* and *The Washington Star. The New York Times, The Current Digest of the Soviet Press,* and Grove Press, Inc. have kindly authorized the use of certain quotations as indicated in the notes.

In gratefully acknowledging the assistance provided him from so many directions, the author in no way diminishes his personal responsibility for all parts of the volume.

R. P. S.

June 1968

CONTENTS

MAPS

CARTOONS

The United States
in World Affairs
1 9 6 7

1 : Introducing 1967

Americans are fated to remember 1967 as a year of disconcerting violence in both domestic and foreign affairs. Despairing, it seemed, of any improvement of their condition through the slow-moving techniques of reform and orderly progress, masses of underprivileged people at home as well as abroad increasingly sought the momentary, if spurious, release afforded by direct and violent action. Nowhere was the year's predominant mood more strikingly reflected than in the attention accorded a political tract by a dead author—Frantz Fanon's *The Wretched of the Earth*—which explicitly rejected the complacencies of the liberal, middle-class, Western outlook and identified the path of violence as the sole road to liberation for the world's oppressed masses. For Fanon, who died in 1961, violence had been not only a necessary political technique but a moral value in itself. "At the level of individuals," he had written, "violence is a cleansing force. It frees the native from his inferiority complex and from his despair and inaction; it makes him fearless and restores his self-respect."[1] This insight, acquired in the course of the anticolonial struggles which had been Fanon's major concern, seemed equally pertinent to the political and military conflicts still raging in Vietnam, Africa, the Middle East, and Latin America and to the large-scale racial disturbances that shook the equanimity of the United States in the summer of 1967.

From a wholly different point of view, U Thant of the United Nations bore witness to the same trend. "The conflict in Vietnam and the recent fighting in the Middle East have inevitably affected the whole climate of international relations," the Secretary-General wrote in the introduction to his annual report on the work of the United Nations, released in September 1967. ". . . What worries me . . . is the continuing and possibly increasing tendency which colors so much of international relations and of human life in general today—the recourse to violence and threats of violence throughout the world. It is all too clear that the civilized and reasonable approach to international disputes . . . cannot long survive if there is increasingly a resort to violent solutions and to more and more widespread exhortations to violence in the name of one cause or another. . . . When unbridled use of force is accepted and intimidation and threats go unchallenged, the hopes of a world order such as the one outlined in the Charter become dim and hollow. When prejudice and hatred dominate the relations of nations or groups of nations, the whole world takes a step backward towards the dark ages. When violence is highlighted and even glamorized by mass media, thus instilling in society, and particularly in the young, an appetite for solving problems by force, the turbulences of today are dangerously fanned and the seeds of larger and deeper troubles at national and international levels are sown for the future."[2]

1 : Farewell to "Foreign Affairs"

For the people of the United States, the fourth full year of Lyndon B. Johnson's presidency may also have marked the final erasure of the traditional boundary between domestic and foreign affairs, merging both aspects of the national concern within the swiftly flowing currents of universal history. The violent explosion of disillusionment and desperation that occurred in the Negro ghettoes of Detroit and other large American cities in July 1967 went far to fuse two hitherto separate branches of the national policy, one aimed at checking hostile influences in the world outside while the other had sought with intermittent zeal to repair the accumulated injustice and neglect of a century's domestic history. About the magnitude of the shock experienced by the American nation in July of 1967 there can be no room for disagreement. "We have endured a week such as no nation should live through," said President Johnson on July 27 as Detroit began to recover from an orgy of racial violence which had cost 39 lives, left 500 homeless, and inflicted an estimated $500 million in property damage. Among the effects of this harrowing week was a sharply heightened national awareness of the interrelations between the swelling agony of the domestic scene and the travail of American world policy.

Even before the July outbreaks, a consciousness of these interrelations had been noticeably on the increase. President Johnson himself had called attention to the interdependence of domestic and foreign affairs in a 1966 address in which he had defined American foreign policy as an attempt to apply in international relations the same enlightened social and political principles proclaimed by his administration at home.[3] Other responsible Americans, in these years of growing national involvement in Southeast Asia, acknowledged the connection between domestic and foreign affairs but subjected it to a less roseate interpretation. For some at least among the critics of the Johnson administration, the salient feature of American foreign policy in the mid-1960's was not so much the support of freedom and progress in the world at large as the attempt to impose and maintain a particular type of anti-Communist political regime—even, if necessary, by force of arms—in countries that were geographically remote from the United States and in some instances showed scant enthusiasm for their American-supported rulers.

The classical instance of this tendency was found, of course, in South Vietnam. There, the local, anti-Communist government of the Republic of Vietnam had for years been waging open war against internal and external enemies while the United States, which had begun by providing military assistance and advice on a limited scale, had by the mid-1960's become the senior belligerent and was itself engaged in an elaborate and bloody war involving heavy American and Vietnamese casualties, expenditures of some $20 billion a year, persistent, massive bombing of both North and South Vietnam, and an admitted risk of hostilities with Communist China, the Soviet Union, or both.

However earnestly the Johnson administration defended its course of action in Vietnam—and President Johnson, Secretary of State Dean Rusk, and others repeatedly insisted that there was no other way of safeguarding essential Vietnamese, American, and international interests—Americans in growing numbers had come to feel that the price was too high to pay and that their own duty was not to support their government's policy in Southeast Asia but to question, denounce, or even obstruct it. The overt critics of the Vietnam venture, though apparently representing only a rather small minority of the public at large, had been sufficiently active and articulate to keep the nation in a state of effervescence and, if administration spokesmen were to be believed, to encourage the Communist regime in North Vietnam to persevere in its attempts to overthrow the American-supported regime in the South. It was, at any rate, undeniable that the activities of the American "peace" movement had been fulsomely commended by North Vietnamese President Ho Chi Minh and were regularly cited in the Communist press as evidence that America's "imperialist" policy in Southeast Asia lacked the support of the American people.

American objection to the war in Vietnam, meanwhile, had increasingly tended to merge with the movement in behalf of Negro civil rights that had united white and Negro activists in a (thus far) nonviolent struggle against discrimination and segregation in southern school and voting districts and in northern cities. It was precisely here, moreover, that the link between domestic and foreign concerns had become most clearly evident. Civil rights protagonists, often more distinguished for generosity of feeling than for familiarity with the foreign scene, were uniformly opposed to the war in Vietnam—not merely because of its cruelty and ugliness, or because it consumed resources which they felt could be better applied at home, but because it seemed to them a manifestation of the very same obtuseness and brutality they were combating in other forms on the domestic front. "Racism" and "militarism" went hand in hand, declared the Reverend Dr. Martin Luther King, the most prominent among the moderate civil rights leaders, in April 1967. Many Negroes, Dr. King asserted, were becoming convinced that "the two problems, the two issues, are inextricably bound together and that you can't really have freedom without justice, you can't have peace without justice, and you can't have justice without peace."[4] A similar association of ideas was plainly evident in the ranks of white civil rights advocates and antiwar agitators.

Few recognized civil rights leaders were willing, at that time, to go along with Dr. King's further development of his theme: his characterization of the American Government as "the greatest purveyor of violence in the world today"; his contention that the United States was on the wrong side of the revolutionary movement of oppressed peoples throughout the world; or his suggestion that the time might come when the war in Vietnam would have to be resisted by a massive civil disobedience campaign.[5] Abroad, however, an equally unflattering view of the American role in world affairs had long been current; and in recent years it had been eagerly absorbed by more radical American Negro leaders, among them the West Indian-born Stokely Carmichael and other "black power" advocates who were now coming to the fore and beginning to challenge the historic civil rights leadership. Rejecting the whole idea of racial integration and interracial collaboration, these leaders preached a doctrine of racial antagonism more closely attuned to the philosophy of violence espoused by Fanon and his disciples. To their oversimplified vision, the war in Vietnam was simply one more manifestation of white racism in a world where the white man was outnumbered but still powerful. Noting the high proportion of Negro soldiers and casualties in the U.S. forces in Vietnam, they could even portray the war as an instrument of Negro "genocide" forged by America's white masters.

Extravagant as such views might seem, the events of July 1967 in Newark, Minneapolis, Detroit, Washington, Milwaukee, Buffalo, and other urban centers suggested that the emotional climate in which they had developed was more pervasive than most observers had realized. Whether acting spontaneously or guided by more experienced hands, the looters, snipers, and incendiaries of those harrowing days were obviously responding to a sense of alienation within American society, a feeling that they, too, had nothing to lose except their "inferiority complex . . . despair and inaction"—that they, too, in Fanon's phrase, belonged to "the wretched of the earth" for whom violence was the road to freedom or, at least, to fearlessness and self-respect. Not only did the events of July 1967 tend to obscure the solid progress in race relations that had been accomplished in many areas of the national life within the past few years. They bred a climate of fear that augured badly for future progress and militated against a coherent attack on the conditions in which the malady had grown.

Unfriendly foreign critics were not slow to draw the lesson of the July events and to interpret them in an anti-American sense. By an interesting coincidence, the July riots occurred in the midst of the preparations in nearby Havana for the first conference of the Organization of Latin American Solidarity, a gathering of left-wing and revolutionary groups that was masterminded by Cuban Premier Fidel Castro and strongly impregnated with the philosophy expounded by Fanon and further developed, with special reference to the Americas, by such figures as Ernesto (Ché) Guevara and Régis Debray. Hailing the so-called "liberation struggle" of American Negroes, Premier Castro made haste to link it with the violent political and social revolution he himself was endeavoring to promote in Latin America. Stokely Carmichael, a guest of the conference, was acclaimed with an adulation that belied his limited influence at home. Like Castro, he unequivocally associated the North American Negroes with the "oppressed masses" in Latin America and prophesied an early recourse to guerrilla warfare within the United States to disrupt the existing power structure from within.[6]

Such manifestations were not taken with complete seriousness by many Americans of any race. Yet they did suggest that the world was beginning to interest itself in America's business as intimately, and as critically, as America had long interested itself in the business of other countries. America's internal conflicts, it appeared, were no longer regarded as something remote and sacrosanct but as part and parcel of the struggles going forward in other parts of the world. Stokely Carmichael, continuing his unauthorized travels to North Vietnam and other anti-American centers, might be shrugged off at home by whites and Negroes alike; but there were other countries in both hemispheres that were prepared to welcome him as an authentic hero. Nor was it without significance that revolution within the United States was being fervently preached from an island which, only five years earlier, had served for the emplacement of hostile, nuclear-capable missiles and bombers supplied by the Soviet Union.

If few Americans were greatly excited by the tirades in Havana, a great many were moved by the events of July 1967 to take a harder look at the war in Vietnam and the network of international commitments from which it had evolved. The question of "national priorities," which had caused intermittent concern since the beginnings of large-scale American involvement in Southeast Asia, suddenly took on a burning urgency. Whatever else the July riots accomplished, they glaringly illuminated the conditions of urban overcrowding, impoverishment, unemployment and neglect on which existing anti-poverty and "Great Society" programs had thus far exerted a minimal impact. To many sober observers they dramatized the need for massive, multibillion dollar programs of urban renewal, education and vocational training, and the like—not simply as a hedge against further violence but as a matter of elementary national self-preservation.

Yet how could the nation embark on programs of this magnitude when it was already having difficulty in sustaining the costs of the Vietnam venture? Was not this a further argument for hurrying the war in Vietnam to a conclusion, either by a compromise peace or— as one influential group of Americans had persistently advocated— by stronger military action? Above and beyond the Vietnam issue, it was also demanded, was it not time to review the whole range of the nation's foreign commitments with a view to bringing them more nearly into line with its real capabilities? Such questions, in the air for months, were now asked with a new insistency.

Sensitive though he was to all the currents of national opinion, President Johnson showed no disposition to embrace this particular line of reasoning. His contention, over the years, had been that the nation was capable of doing whatever needed to be done on both domestic and foreign fronts. While recognizing the need for increased efforts in such fields as urban renewal, the President did not, during the balance of 1967, propose new domestic programs on anything like the scale that some within his own party were advocating. Indeed, the tendency appeared increasingly to be setting in the opposite direction as domestic outlays were trimmed in the interests of meeting the spiraling costs of Vietnam and securing congressional assent to the accompanying fiscal measures.[7]

In this approach the President undoubtedly took account of majority sentiment in Congress, which even the July riots had not sufficed to imbue with any enthusiasm for increased domestic expenditure at a time of such heavy military demands. For the President himself, moreover, the issues at stake in Vietnam still seemed to outweigh all other considerations—the more so, apparently, because he had been given reason to hope that the gradual intensification of American military pressure in North and South Vietnam might well induce the North Vietnamese regime to discontinue its support of the insurrection before another year was out. The next twelve months would be a specially critical time for the United States because of the presidential election that was to be held in November 1968, and the

President would have been less than human had he not reasoned that his prospects of reelection would be greatly enhanced if the war had meanwhile been successfully terminated. The first priority, so far as the administration was concerned, thus remained as before—to persevere in Vietnam, avoiding incautious "escalation" moves but gradually increasing the pressure until such time as the North Vietnamese "aggressors" desisted and the people of South Vietnam were enabled to live in peace under a government of their own choosing.

This in itself would be a sufficiently hazardous undertaking, given the tenacity of the Vietcong insurgents and their North Vietnamese supporters, the growing aid accorded them from Soviet and Chinese sources, the political inexperience of the South Vietnamese, the clamor of American "hawks" and "doves" who wanted the war "escalated" or "deescalated," and the blasts of criticism that buffeted the United States from friendly as well as hostile quarters around the world. While the war in Vietnam persisted, there could be little hope of forging more stable relationships with the Soviet Union or taming the nuclear peril which had grown to such frightening proportions over the past two decades. In addition, every American effort on the international plane would henceforth be overhung by the great unanswered question of how the United States was to meet the challenge of its own internal problems—which, it now appeared, were themselves a part of the world environment in which it was constrained to operate.

Some experienced observers appeared to doubt that such disparate endeavors could be combined at all. "President Johnson keeps on saying that the United States is big enough and rich enough to pay for the war in Vietnam and at the same time for the Great Society at home," wrote Walter Lippmann. ". . . His willingness to believe that a democracy can have two overwhelming preoccupations at the same time is the mark of an amateur."[8] Both preoccupations, at any rate, were clearly destined to persist for some considerable time. Together they would largely shape the role of the United States in world affairs in 1967 and, presumably, in later years as well.

2 : Transition—to What?

Violence and the preaching of violence are but one of the interlacing strands that make up the global history of 1967. By focusing attention on more favorable aspects of the world scene—the progress of science and technology, the growing resort to international solutions for problems of larger-than-national dimensions, the easing of some historic antagonisms even while others were intensifying—it was possible to reach conclusions that were by no means unrelievedly pessimistic. The mere fact that the specter of World War III had somehow been held at bay through all the perilous changes of the past two decades appeared to justify the hope that humanity might still achieve a new basis for its common existence without destroying itself in the process. What was beyond dispute, as man entered the last third of his pilgrimage through the twentieth century, was the fact that the familiar patterns and relationships of former decades were irrevocably disappearing and that the new age would be unlike anything known in the past.

President Johnson, as was his wont, had offered a relatively optimistic appraisal of world trends in the annual message on the State of the Union which he delivered to a joint session of the Congress—and, by television, to the nation and the world—on January 10, 1967. "We are in the midst of a great transition," the President said, "—a transition from narrow nationalism to international partnership; from the harsh spirit of the cold war to the hopeful spirit of common humanity on a troubled and a threatened planet." There was a risk in change, abroad as at home, Mr. Johnson conceded; but there was a greater risk in standing still. "No part of our foreign policy is so sacred that it ever remains beyond review," he said. "We shall be flexible where conditions in the world change—and where man's efforts can change them for the better."[9]

What was the nature of these changing world conditions to which the United States, like other nations, had somehow to adapt itself? At bottom, they seemed to be part of a world-wide process that had been going forward with accelerating momentum since the beginning of the century: a process of adjustment, sometimes pleasant but more often painful, to the new conditions created by science and technology in a world which had, for the most part, been singularly ill prepared to cope with them. Thanks largely to the uneven progress of the industrial revolution in the decades before 1900, not all the different branches of mankind had been equally well placed to assimilate the scientific and technical advances of the twentieth century. On the contrary, these advances had burst upon a world whose peoples had stood at very different levels of development and were divided every whichway by profound geographic, ethnic, cultural, economic, and political cleavages: between "advanced" and "underdeveloped" nations, between "master" and "subject" races, between "exploiting" and "exploited" classes, between "privileged" and "unprivileged" groups within the same society. All of these differences had had their effect on the way in which the new possibilities were absorbed, utilized, and fought over by nations and by different groups within each nation.

In the course of this prolonged and varied process of assimilation, there had occurred not only the First and Second World Wars but also the so-called "second industrial revolution" of the mid-twentieth century—a process of yet more radical innovation which had arisen from the systematic application of new scientific discoveries and had included among its fruits the atomic and hydrogen bombs, the space satellite, and the electronic computer. Accompanied by equally radical changes in such fields as agriculture, medicine, and communications, this new surge of human inventiveness appeared to hold undreamed-of possibilities for human betterment—or, if misused, for human catastrophe. The critical task confronting the human race, and the governments that claimed to speak for it, was to find ways of exploiting these beneficent new possibilities and at the same time averting their potentially disastrous effects. The problem had been made even more difficult by the determination of most of the governments concerned to minimize the price paid in terms of the relinquishment of national sovereignty or the surrender of established political attitudes. Superimposed upon a dense tangle of preexisting rivalries and animosities at every level of human organization, this problem in its varied aspects had made up most of the substance of international affairs throughout the postwar period.

Preeminent among these global concerns in all the years since 1945 —and in 1967 no less than at earlier times—had been the attempt to exorcise the most dramatic and conspicuous threat to the human future by subjecting the power of the atom to international control and, if possible, confining it entirely to peaceful industrial and scientific uses. Self-evident as the need appeared, the development of such measures had been largely blocked by the persistence of traditional national rivalries and suspicions—above all, the basic ideological and political antagonism between the Soviet Union, with its ingrained revolutionary zeal and hostility to the "imperialist" world, and the United States together with its moderate-minded partners of the West. Apart from a treaty concluded in 1963 prohibiting nuclear weapon tests in the atmosphere, in outer space, and under water—which had itself been unacceptable to two of the nuclear powers, France and Communist China—no serious restriction had yet been placed on the growth of the world's nuclear arsenals, which by the 1960's possessed sufficient deliverable explosive force to destroy the principal nations many times over. In recent years, the war in Vietnam had weighed upon the search for nuclear disarmament as it had weighed on every other aspect of international affairs. Despite this adverse influence, however, there was hope at the beginning of 1967 that agreement might soon be reached on a treaty to prevent the further spread or "proliferation" of nuclear weapons and thus, at least, to limit their availability to the five nations that already possessed them.

Questions of a comparable magnitude and importance had been presented to postwar governments by the condition of those sections of the world, populated mainly by peoples of non-European race, that had been bypassed by the first industrial revolution and had remained in a state of economic underdevelopment and, in most instances, colonial subjection. In the course of the first two postwar decades, over 50 nations with a combined population in excess of one billion had advanced from colonial status to formal independence, thus reversing the global political relations established during four centuries of European colonization and creating a record that will undoubtedly rank among the most striking accomplishments of the twentieth century. In only a few regions, notably in the southern part of Africa, did the persistence of colonial rule and of the related phenomena of racial discrimination or *apartheid* continue to raise international issues of outstanding importance, although the ex-colonial countries still manifested great uneasiness about alleged "neo-colonialist" practices by members of the formerly dominant races who had remained on hand to assist in meeting their problems.

For the winning of political independence had not in itself sufficed to overcome the poverty and unpreparedness which had been the lot of most colonial territories. Apart from their frequent lack of political and administrative experience, nearly all of the latter belonged to the numerous class of economically "underdeveloped" or, at best "developing" countries which, by 1967, made up approximately two-thirds of the 122-nation membership of the United Nations. Efforts to raise the economic level of the less developed countries to a point where they could begin to share the general advance of world prosperity had been a major concern of international policy ever since World War II, undertaken from a variety of motives but never pursued with sufficient energy to forestall a continuous widening of the gap between richer and poorer nations. Production and living standards had improved to some extent in many of the latter group; yet most experts during the 1960's insisted that their rate of growth remained wholly inadequate and that the rich-poor gap continued to widen because the prosperity of the advanced industrial countries was still growing at a rate the poorer countries could not hope to emulate. Yet despite these warnings and despite their own experience of the unwholesome political and social effects of massive poverty in the developing nations, the United States and other "wealthy" countries had in recent years seemed more inclined to reduce their proportionate contribution to overseas economic development than to expand it.

Among the salient causes of the unsatisfactory rate of economic development in most countries of Asia, Africa, and Latin America was the explosive growth of population they were experiencing as improved medical and public health measures reduced the rates of infant and adult mortality while the already high birth rates continued virtually unchecked. One result was a vast increase in the number of young persons competing for the available educational and employment opportunities; another, a steady increase in the population as a whole which went far to offset the gradual increase in agricultural and industrial production and thus precluded any marked gain in individual consumption. This already alarming state of affairs threatened to assume really catastrophic dimensions within the next twenty or thirty years as world population, particularly in the developing countries, began to outdistance the foreseeable world food supplies. In the absence of effective measures for increasing food production as well as checking the rate of population growth, a substantial part of the human race seemed destined to face a threat as terrible in its way as that of the atomic bomb itself.

A third preoccupation of the international community, and hence of American foreign policy, had been the need to cope with a wide variety of national, racial, social, and ideological antagonisms that not only threatened to explode in open conflict but stood in the way of any effectual attack on the deeper problems of human survival. "To save succeeding generations from the scourge of war" had been the major purpose in establishing the United Nations. Yet the world of the mid-1960's exhibited a disheartening spectacle of animosity, distrust, and strife that belied the concepts of human brotherhood underlying the U.N. Charter. Though somewhat attenuated in recent years, the fundamental antagonism between the Soviet Union and its allies on one side and the adherents of the Western tradition on the other continued to impede agreement on arms control and other essential matters and to exacerbate the numerous conflicts arising in other parts of the world. Communist China had increasingly become a focus of hostility not only toward the United States and the "free world" but toward China's erstwhile allies of the Soviet camp. Hostility and latent strife persisted between the Arab states and Israel, between India and Pakistan, and between countless other nations and tribal groups throughout non-Communist Asia and Africa. Despite the disappearance of most of the old colonial empires, the United States and its allies were still widely viewed as "imperialist" or "colonial" countries and were under more or less constant attack by a coalition of "anticolonial" nations drawn from Africa, Asia, and Latin America and regularly supported by the U.S.S.R. and its Communist cohorts. As noted, the more extreme adherents of this group, including Communist China as well as the Castro regime in Cuba, were even beginning to interject themselves into American internal problems and telling American Negroes to join in attacking the existing order rather than trying to better their own position within it.

The increasing prominence of racial issues in the international politics of the later 1960's is a further indication of the way the general climate of world affairs was changing even while the basic problems remained unsolved. In many respects the world of 1967 was a very different planet from that of four or five years earlier, when the East-West "cold war" had reached its apogee in the Cuban missile confrontation of 1962. No longer, as in the days of President John F. Kennedy and Soviet Premier Nikita S. Khrushchev, did the world exhibit a comparatively stable tripartite pattern of Communist, Western, and nonaligned states. The patterns confronting President Johnson and his Soviet counterparts, Premier Aleksei N. Kosygin and Communist Party Secretary Leonid I. Brezhnev, were more complex and elusive. Indeed, the contemporary observer was sometimes tempted to ask whether there *was* a pattern or only a welter of shifting elements that eluded any new consolidation.

The old "Sino-Soviet bloc," once the most solid-looking structure on the international scene, had altered almost beyond recognition and, in the process, lost at least a part of its former awe-inspiring quality. Fifty years after the Bolshevik Revolution of 1917, the Soviet Union seemed clearly to have entered upon that "mellowing" process to which some Americans had long looked hopefully forward. Without renouncing either its revolutionary goals or the expansion of its already formidable military power, the U.S.S.R. was plainly giving increased attention to its internal affairs and, at the moment, showed no eagerness for further armed confrontations with its capitalist opponents. Equally encouraging trends could be observed in the increasingly independent nations of Communist-ruled Eastern Europe. Indeed, the major Communist threat to world peace now seemed to emanate not so much from the Soviet Union as from Communist China, a much weaker yet far more bellicose power which explicitly repudiated the Soviet doctrine of "peaceful coexistence" with non-Communist countries, insisted on the inevitability of violent conflict with "imperialism," and had displayed a quarrelsomeness in its relations with both neighboring and distant countries that was perhaps unmatched in modern history. Yet even the Communist Chinese, since their armed attack on India in 1962, had displayed a reluctance to get involved in actual hostilities despite the violence of their general demeanor. Within the past year, China's weight in international affairs had been further reduced by the effects of the so-called "Great Proletarian Cultural Revolution," an ideological and power struggle within the Chinese Communist organization which had baffled outside observers but had plainly produced chaotic internal conditions verging at times on civil war.

The changes in the West had been less sensational but hardly less far-reaching. Materially, the Western nations were now prospering as never before. Politically, on the other hand, they had suffered a definite loss of momentum and now gave evidence of widespread uncertainty and disorientation. The sense of a common Western purpose and destiny, which had at one time produced such landmark institutions as the North Atlantic Treaty Organization (NATO) and the six-nation European communities, had waned with the apparent diminution of the military threat from the East and the concurrent revival of traditional nationalist sentiments in the West, particularly in the France of President Charles de Gaulle. The obstructive attitude of the French Government with respect to all forms of "supranational" cooperation had not only limited the development of the six-nation community (to say nothing of its enlargement through the accession of Great Britain and other states), but had forced a far-reaching reorientation—if not a fatal weakening—of Western collective defense arrangements by virtue of the French withdrawal from NATO's integrated defense system. The concept of an "Atlantic partnership" between the United States and Western Europe, put forward by President Kennedy as recently as 1962,[10] seemed to most observers to have died in infancy. Observing the disarray affecting the Western community as a whole, a cynic might have suggested that the only thing that held the other Western nations together was their shared antipathy to the United States and its policies.

This widespread discontent with the United States was only partially motivated by distaste for America's unpopular course in Vietnam. In a larger sense, it was part of a growing, world-wide reaction against the constantly increasing and (as many thought) unwholesome American participation in every branch of world affairs at both official and unofficial levels. General de Gaulle was not alone in his belief that the United States, even without conscious design, was moving toward some kind of world "hegemony" through its sheer size and power and its increasing, sometimes unintended influence in every aspect of the world's concerns. The phenomenal expansion of American business enterprise in Canada, in Europe, and in other overseas areas had for years been a source of alarm as well as increasing prosperity to some of the countries affected. More recently, the "brain drain" which drew scientists and professional experts from Europe and the developing countries to better-paying jobs and better working facilities in the United States had come to be as widely resented as the saturation of the postwar world with American soft drinks and popular culture. The so-called "technological gap" between the advanced United States and supposedly backward Europe had become a cause of ever-increasing complaint on the European side and had even been made a subject of formal inquiry in NATO.

The year 1967 was to bring still further evidence of the extent to which America and Americans were making their influence felt in every continent, not only in economic and cultural affairs but even, in some instances, through such underworld activities as gambling, narcotics smuggling, and gun running. Particularly shocking to many observers, at home as well as abroad, was the disclosure in February 1967 that the U.S. Central Intelligence Agency, in addition to other unlauded activities, had for years engaged in the clandestine financing of student and labor organizations on both a national and an international plane. While there were those who found something to say in defense of this activity,[11] the net effect was to strengthen the international revulsion against American foreign policy as lately manifested in Vietnam, in the Dominican Republic, and elsewhere. Revelations of some things the United States had done in the past would make it easier to blame it for still other things which it had not done but for which it could nevertheless serve as a convenient scapegoat.

Many, though not all, in the countries of Asia, Africa, and Latin America had already adopted an attitude of almost habitual animosity toward the United States in view of its allegedly dangerous and reactionary course in Vietnam, its alleged support of "colonialism," particularly in Africa, and its supposed arrogance and insensibility to their grievances. The fact that many of these complaints were either unfounded or greatly exaggerated did not diminish their vehemence. Aside from Vietnam, two issues in particular had of late years bred extreme resentment against the United States and its Western partners and offered a characteristic opportunity for the Communist states to pose as the true friends of the emergent countries. One of these was the limited success of the anticolonial forces in their crusade against the remaining bastions of "colonialism and racial discrimination" in southern Africa—in Rhodesia, in South and South West Africa, and in the Portuguese territories of Angola and Mozambique. The other was the unsatisfactory state of the poorer countries' efforts at economic development, the comparative paucity of outside aid in the form of new investment capital from other than private sources, and their inability to obtain more remunerative terms for their trade with the advanced countries.

Each of these adverse trends had been aggravated in some degree by the war in Vietnam, which, as U Thant and others had pointed out, had damaged the whole climate of international relations even as it heightened the danger of wider hostilities. Resistance to the "Communist aggression" in Vietnam might be an inescapable American obligation, as President Johnson continued to insist; but there could be little doubt that the United States, the world, and Vietnam itself were being heavily penalized in the process. Over and above the human suffering, the loss of life, the diversion of economic resources, and the deepened divisions among the American people, the war had by this time virtually isolated the United States within the international community. Aside from a handful of countries in the Pacific and Far East which happened to share the official American viewpoint, the United States had a thousand critics for every defender of its Vietnam policy. While the war in Vietnam continued, there seemed little prospect that a basis of understanding with the nations of the West or the "third world" would be restored.

So long as the war in Vietnam continued, moreover, there seemed scant prospect of significant improvement in American relations with the countries of the Communist world—particularly the Soviet Union, whose leaders had repeatedly declared that while they desired better relations with the United States, they could not possibly move in this direction while the United States was waging war against "the Vietnamese people." Within the United States itself, there were powerful members of Congress who had set their faces against any measures of accommodation with Communist countries so long as the latter supported North Vietnam's cause. Other Western nations, including even the German Federal Republic under its new Chancellor, Kurt Georg Kiesinger, were striving with might and main to "normalize" their economic and political relations with the countries of the Soviet bloc; but the hands of the United States appeared to be virtually tied by its commitment in Vietnam.

More alarming than the prospect of mere stagnation in U.S.-Soviet relations was the growing threat of a disturbance in the strategic balance between the two powers, of a sort that might undo past progress toward disarmament and start them on still another round in their perennial and costly arms race. Particularly disconcerting had been a series of recent indications that the U.S.S.R., in addition to stepping up its production and deployment of intercontinental ballistic missiles in a way that might threaten the existing American strategic predominance, was commencing the deployment of a limited defensive system aimed at destroying any missiles fired by the United States before they could reach their targets. Within the United States, a clamor had promptly been raised for the deployment of a comparable antimissile defense system—notwithstanding the judgment of the responsible authorities that such a step, in addition to its cost and doubtful effectiveness, would almost certainly prod the U.S.S.R. into more extensive armament. Before venturing onto these slippery slopes, the Johnson administration was determined to explore the matter with the Soviet Government and see whether both powers could not agree to forego a step which, in the view of the Defense Department at least, could add little to the security of either.

3 : Policy for the New Year

It was President Johnson who gave the first official indication of his administration's thinking on the antiballistic missile problem in a rather cryptic passage of his January 10 address on the State of the Union. "The Soviet Union has in the past year increased its long-range missile capabilities," the President confirmed. "It has begun to place near Moscow a limited antimissile defense." (Defense Department authorities spoke also of "another type of defensive missile" which was being deployed "elsewhere in the Soviet Union.") [12] In these circumstances, President Johnson emphasized, his first responsibility was "to assure that no nation can ever find it rational to launch a nuclear attack or to use its nuclear power as a credible threat against us or against our allies." This responsibility, he implied, would be met under all circumstances. But, the President continued, beyond this elementary obligation the United States and the U.S.S.R. had also "the solemn duty to slow down the arms race between us, if that is at all possible, in both conventional and nuclear weapons and defenses." "I thought," the President went on, "that we were making some progress in that direction the first few months I was in office. I realize that any additional race would impose on our peoples, and on all mankind, for that matter, an additional waste of resources with no gain in security to either side. I expect in the days ahead to closely consult and seek the advice of Congress about the possibilities of international agreements bearing directly upon this problem." [13]

Just what the President had in mind was more clearly explained with the submission on January 24 of his Budget for the fiscal year 1967-68, which confirmed the intention to initiate discussions with the U.S.S.R. on a possible mutual limitation on the deployment of antiballistic missile defenses. Pending the result of these discussions, it was disclosed, the United States would continue with the intensive development of its own embryonic antimissile system, known as Nike-X, but would for the time being refrain from actually deploying it. Nevertheless it would reserve the option of reconsidering this decision in the event that the discussions with the U.S.S.R. proved unsuccessful. To provide for actions that might be required at that time, approximately $375 million was allocated in the new budget "for the production of Nike-X for such purposes as defense of our offensive weapon systems"—though not, as yet, for any large-scale deployment such as would surely be needed if major population centers were to be afforded protection against missile attack.[14]

In the meantime, President Johnson had prepared a message to be delivered to Premier Kosygin by the new U.S. Ambassador in Moscow, Llewellyn E. Thompson, expressing the hope that agreement could be reached between the two powers both on this and on other U.S.-Soviet issues.[15] The determination to pursue accommodation with the U.S.S.R. as far as circumstances would permit was heavily underlined in the President's State of the Union message, in which Mr. Johnson cited a number of recent actions aimed at easing East-West tension—notably the negotiation at the United Nations of a new treaty on the peaceful uses of outer space—and particularly urged congressional approval of an East-West trade bill and of a pending U.S.-Soviet consular convention. Relations with the Soviet Union and Eastern Europe, Mr. Johnson emphasized, were currently in a state of transition, and the United States was doing what it could to improve them. "We have avoided both the acts and the rhetoric of the cold war," the President recalled. "When we have differed with the Soviet Union, or other nations, for that matter, I have tried to differ quietly and with courtesy, and without venom. Our objective is not to continue the cold war, but to end it."

Yet an ending of the cold war remained difficult to envisage unless there was also to be an end of the war in Vietnam, in which the United States and the Soviet Union were not only supporting opposite sides but professed to see a test of the Soviet theory that such "wars of national liberation" spelled the eventual world-wide defeat of "imperialism." Though President Johnson had frequently insisted that the discharge of American obligations in Vietnam ought not to interfere with an improvement of U.S.-Soviet relations, the Soviet leaders had expressly repudiated this reasoning. If the United States desired improved relations, they had said, it must first desist from its "aggression" in Vietnam and leave that country to the "Vietnamese." The President, for his part, had shown no interest in abandoning South Vietnam to probable Communist conquest for the sake of agreement with the U.S.S.R. on other matters.

Thus it was the war in Vietnam, rather than the prospect of accommodation with the Soviet Union, that dominated American foreign policy calculations at the beginning of 1967 as it had dominated the life of the United States for many months past. Rehearsing once again the reasons which, in his view, made it imperative for the United States to persevere in Vietnam until "aggression" had been checked, Mr. Johnson offered the nation no hope of an early termination of hostilities. "I wish I could report to you that the conflict is almost over," he said in the State of the Union message. "This I cannot do. We face more cost, more loss, and more agony. For the end is not yet. I cannot promise you that it will come this year—or come next year. . . . How long it will take I cannot prophesy."

Disappointing the hopes expressed in many quarters in the United States and elsewhere, the President offered no new "peace gesture" at the outset of 1967 to match the twice-repeated suspensions of American bombing in North Vietnam which had taken place in 1965 and 1966. The United States, Mr. Johnson emphasized, "will support all appropriate initiatives by the United Nations, and others, which can bring the several parties together for unconditional discussions of peace—anywhere, any time. And we will continue to take every possible initiative ourselves to constantly probe for peace." (Although the President did not mention it, the United States was even then engaged in opening up new channels of communication with the Communist regime in Hanoi.)[16] But in view of the adversary's apparent belief "that he can go on fighting longer than we can, and longer than we and our allies will be prepared to stand up and resist," President Johnson seemed to place little immediate hope in peace endeavors. "Until such [peace] efforts succeed, or until the infiltration ceases, or until the conflict subsides," he said, "I think the course of wisdom for this country is that we must firmly pursue our present course. We will stand firm in Vietnam."

Budgetary policy was already being shaped in accordance with these expectations. With 380,000 men in Vietnam itself and nearly 120,000 more engaged in war-related activities in Southeast Asia, the financial cost of the war had mounted precipitiously, from $0.1 billion in the fiscal year 1965 to $5.8 billion in fiscal 1966 and an estimated $19.4 billion in the fiscal year ending June 30, 1967. In preparing its budget for the new fiscal year, running from July 1, 1967 to June 30, 1968, the administration did not repeat an earlier planning error of assuming that the war would end on a particular date. On the contrary, the budget for fiscal year 1968 expressly provided for "the possibility of an extension of combat beyond the end of the fiscal year." While purporting to "provide our forces in Vietnam with all the weapons and supplies they need," it also did not appear to envisage any great expansion in the level of military operations. Total expenditures for the war (excluding military aid to South Vietnam) were estimated at $21.9 billion, only slightly above the expenditure in 1967.[17]

Such a figure, however, was substantial enough in itself to exert a powerful impact on the nation's economic life and compel a fresh appraisal of other programs and goals. A year before, the President had taken the position that the already heavy costs of American overseas policy need entail no retrenchment in the far-reaching domestic programs associated with the "Great Society" concept—that the nation, in journalistic parlance, could afford both "guns and butter." In 1967, faced with the mounting costs of the Vietnam effort, Mr. Johnson offered a more qualified statement which one columnist described as "guns and margarine."[18] Great Society programs were to continue, but at "a controlled and reasoned pace," the President indicated. "I wish, of course, that we could do all that should be done—and that we could do it now. But the Nation has many commitments and responsibilities which make heavy demands upon our total resources. . . . So let us resolve, now, to do all that we can, with what we have— knowing that it is far, far more than we have ever done before, and far, far less than our problems will ultimately require."

To pay for the war in Vietnam, together with a moderated Great Society program and the normal costs of defense, space exploration, foreign aid, and general government, would in any event cost a great deal of money. From a projected figure of $126.7 billion in fiscal year

1967, the President estimated that total expenditures in the so-called administrative budget, the most familiar measure of government operations, would increase in fiscal 1968 to $135 billion and would exceed foreseeable revenues by around $8.1 billion—somewhat less than the $9.7 billion deficit foreseen for fiscal 1967. (Alternative figures expressed in terms of the "national income accounts," which included various government trust fund operations and were held to present a more accurate picture of the over-all economic impact of the budget, showed total 1968 expenditures of $169.2 billion and a deficit of only $2.1 billion.)

Of the total administrative expenditures of $135 billion, national defense programs—including the $21.9 billion allocated to Vietnam—would account for $76.8 billion or well over half. This largest "peacetime" defense budget in history would exceed by $5.5 billion the already substantial defense expenditure anticipated in fiscal year 1967. Great Society programs, in contrast, were to rise in the new year by a more modest $1.9 billion. Space exploration, at an estimated expenditure level of $5.3 billion, would be reduced from $5.6 billion in 1967. Foreign economic assistance through the Agency for International Development was estimated at a modest $2.4 billion, approximately unchanged from 1967, while "Food for Freedom" expenditures were expected to climb slightly from $1.7 billion to $1.8 billion.

To help finance these varied expenditures and limit the accompanying deficit, the President proposed to spread the burden of financial sacrifice—if Congress approved—by imposing a 6 per cent surcharge on corporate and individual income taxes for a period of two years "or for so long as the unusual expenditures associated with our effort in Vietnam continue." This recommendation, the fruit of many months of inconclusive discussion about the economic merits of a tax increase, failed to awaken enthusiasm among the public, in Congress, or even among professional economists. Although the new budget purported "to meet responsibly the needs of an expanding economy" and assumed a continuation of the rapid growth in national output which had been going on since 1961, actual economic prospects at the beginning of 1967 were somewhat clouded as the economy, already suffering from a loss of momentum dring the later months of 1966, appeared to hesitate between renewed expansion and further decline. With expert economic opinion divided, the question of a tax increase was put off while Congress directed its scrutiny to other aspects of the nation's affairs.

Two other economic issues to which the administration attached particular importance would also remain in suspense for the time being. Prospects for remedying the chronic deficit in the balance of international payments, aggravated of late by the added overseas expenditures associated with Vietnam, would be largely dependent on the performance of American exporters in the coming months and on the success of a set of voluntary "guidelines" designed to limit American investment abroad which the administration had promulgated late in 1966.[19] New steps in international trade policy, meanwhile, would have to await the results of the Kennedy Round of multilateral tariff negotiations, in progress at Geneva for several years and now entering a climactic phase whose outcome would particularly affect the economic relations between the United States and its partners of the industrialized West.[20]

A more immediate, if intangible, concern as America confronted the new year was the climate of disillusionment, dissension and distrust that already overhung the nation and its capital six months before the July riots. Tolerance, respect, and mutual confidence as between citizens, and between citizens and their government, appeared at times to have all but vanished amid the rising clamor of "hawks" and "doves," segregationists and "black power" advocates, youths and older people, "hippies" and "squares." Public opinion polls revealed a marked decline in popular approval of the President, particularly his handling of the Vietnam situation. The so-called "credibility gap" between the administration's optimistic pronouncements on Vietnam and the ugly realities reported from other sources had substantially impaired belief in the government's veracity, including its proclaimed desire for peace. The approach of the 1968 elections had the further effect of ensuring that every pronouncement by anyone in a prominent public position would henceforth be scrutinized as much for its possible political motivations as for its intrinsic merit.

This mood of cynicism, anxiety, and dissent revealed itself in various connections and at widely varied intellectual levels. In Congress, it found its primary expression in a running debate between "hawks" and "doves"—between those legislators, many though not all of them associated with the Republican leadership, who thought the war in Vietnam should be fought more energetically, and those, largely identified with the President's own party, who wanted altogether less emphasis on prosecuting the war and more emphasis on trying to end it.

Beyond the debate over Vietnam, there was evidence of more basic disagreement with American foreign policy as it had developed in recent years. The mediocre success of some recent American initiatives, coupled with the obvious lack of international appreciation for most phases of American policy, had engendered an uneasy feeling that the nation was "overextended" or "overcommitted" in international affairs and should seriously consider curtailing its efforts. "Hawks" as well as "doves" tended to agree on this proposition. Senator Everett McKinley Dirksen, the Senate minority leader and a long-time supporter of vigorous measures in Vietnam, urged "more attention to the conservation of our own strength and resources and less to those nations of the world who regard us as an amiable, vulnerable, jolly Santa Claus who can be slurred at will and cuffed with impunity."[21] Senator Mike Mansfield, the Democratic majority leader and a persistent advocate of negotiations to end the Vietnam conflict, had broken with the administration to promote a resolution calling for a substantial reduction of U.S. military forces in Europe.[22] Senator J. William Fulbright, the Democratic Chairman of the Foreign Relations Committee and a strong advocate of "deescalation" in Vietnam, had announced a series of hearings on "the responsibilities of the United States as a great power," aimed at finding out whether the United States had assumed commitments that went beyond its capabilities and whether its policy was unduly influenced by outworn concepts, as Senator Fulbright himself appeared to feel.[23]

Such manifestations fell short of the "reversion to isolationism" that had from time to time been prophesied in earlier years, partly at least as a means of persuading other governments to accommodate themselves to American wishes. The United States, in 1967, was far too deeply engaged in every aspect of the world's affairs to contemplate a retreat within its own boundaries, even had that been its desire. The real question as 1967 began was whether its future participation in world affairs was to be fruitful and constructive, as had on the whole been true in the past, or whether the effectiveness of American action was to be perverted and nullified by divided counsels at home and by the failure to maintain a due sense of proportion—and, possibly, of human obligation—in the exercise of the many responsibilities confronting the world's most powerful nation.

" – AND NOW A DASH OF THIS – "

Bruce Shanks in *Buffalo Evening News*

4 : A Forward Glance

Such was the divided and rather irascible frame of mind in which the
people of the United States, nearly 200,000,000 in number, looked
forward to the fateful decisions of 1967—above all, the decision
(which admittedly would not lie entirely in American hands) as to
whether the war in Vietnam was to expand, continue, or contract. The
details of that and other critical developments in Asia, the Middle

East, and elsewhere will be recounted in the chapters that follow. Although the struggle in Vietnam continued with increased intensity, it was presently overlapped and, for a time, relegated to second place by the outbreak of a new conflict between the Arab states and Israel— a conflict in which the Arab states enjoyed the clamorous support of the Soviet Union while American sympathies inclined strongly to the Israeli side. Although the danger of a full-scale East-West confrontation was lessened by the rapidity of Israel's military victory in the six-day war of early June, the episode developed in a way that not only earned the United States the deep hostility of the Arab governments but reinstated the Middle East as a second major theater of "cold war" or East-West political competition side by side with the existing theater in Southeast Asia.

The dangerous implications of this enlargement of the East-West rivalry were only partially alleviated by a pair of meetings between President Johnson and Premier Kosygin which took place at Glassboro, New Jersey, on June 23 and 25 as a by-product of the Soviet Premier's visit to New York to denounce the United States and Israel before the United Nations. In confirming their basic differences over Vietnam and the Middle East, the American and Soviet leaders would nevertheless appear to have established a measure of personal rapport that may have assisted in preventing a still further deterioration of the international situation in subsequent months.

2 : Vietnam: The Permanent War?

Had the United States done well in trying to rescue the Republic of Vietnam and devoting such large resources to shoring up a shaky government and an inequitable social system? There can be no satisfactory reply to such a question. To answer it, one would need to know what would have happened had the United States withheld its aid and allowed events in Southeast Asia to take their course. Any reasonable estimate of the American performance in Vietnam must attempt to balance the palpable ills that flowed from the U.S. intervention—some few of which have been touched upon in the preceding chapter—against the unknown but presumably substantial evils the intervention served to avert. From the standpoint of U.S. foreign policy, the tragedy of Vietnam lies in the fact that the situation there at no time offered a choice between "right" and "wrong" courses, but only among a variety of hazardous alternatives.

Had the United States declined to assist the Saigon regime in its attempts to combat a rising Communist insurgency, domestically based but vigorously supported from outside, it seems hardly open to doubt that South Vietnam would within a relatively short time have lapsed under Communist control—as, indeed, it had almost done at the time of the French defeat in Indochina in 1954. The possibility of successful resistance to Communist inroads in such neighboring countries as Laos, Cambodia, Thailand, and Indonesia would have been immensely weakened, and the chances for an eventual consolidation of Southeast Asia on a non-Communist basis, such as appeared to be occurring in 1966 and 1967, would have virtually disappeared. Through its increasingly active intervention in South Vietnam from 1961 onward, the United States had managed not only to prevent that country's political submergence but, presumably, to check the advance of Communism over a much wider area of Asia. Yet this had been accomplished at an incalculable cost in human suffering and life, in damage to America's own domestic tranquility and international standing, and at the risk of wider disasters affecting the peace of the world.

Dismayed by the rising ferocity of the struggle, some Americans were prone to assert that the whole idea of a Communist threat to South Vietnam was a figment of overheated brains in Washington. Others maintained that the threat, even if real, was none of America's business; still others, that the threat was real but should be dealt with by more forthright means and with less regard for consequences. Almost unheard amid the clamor of dissentient voices were those who appeared to understand and sympathize with the official strategy of employing only that measure of force that might be necessary to halt the North Vietnamese "aggression." No one could be sure, in 1967, just how the whole unprecedented venture was going to turn out, or how the eventual results would measure up against the possible consequences of a different course of action. It was, however, still possible to recognize that however widely and indiscriminately condemned, American action in Vietnam was not the product of mere blind frivolity but represented a serious—even if perhaps misguided —attempt to cope with real and fateful problems.

5 : Points of Argument

The international atmosphere of 1967 was one in which even the most elementary features of the Vietnam situation were subject to sharp dispute and virtually no statement could pass unchallenged by adherents of a different viewpoint. Even those who considered that the United States had had an inescapable duty to intervene in support of the Saigon government did not necessarily feel called upon to defend the forms the intervention had taken, particularly the bombing

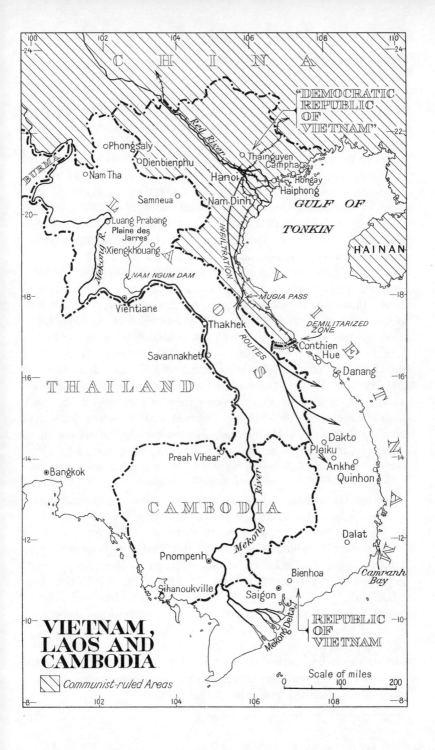

VIETNAM, LAOS AND CAMBODIA

of North Vietnam and the massive deployment of American troops that had begun in 1965 at a time when a Communist victory in South Vietnam had seemed dangerously close. The strategy and tactics of the conflict will undoubtedly remain a subject of hot debate for years to come. Nor is it surprising, in view of the heavy losses sustained by Americans as well as Vietnamese—6,731 Americans killed and 38,217 wounded in action from 1961 through 1966, with the expectation of much heavier casualties to come—that many Americans as well as foreigners should have sickened of the enterprise and clamored ever more insistently for negotiations to end the fighting. To move the conflict from the battlefield to the conference table seemed to most people the obvious way—indeed, the only sane and civilized way—of settling the issues and stemming the attendant bloodshed.

What the advocates of negotiations seemed often to overlook, however, was the fact that negotiation can be fruitful only when the parties involved are pursuing more or less compatible objectives—or, alternatively, when one party is prepared to renounce at the conference table the very objectives for which it has been fighting on the battlefield. In Vietnam, up to the beginning of 1967, this essential condition had clearly not obtained. To anyone who took the trouble to examine the situation, it was all too evident that the purposes of the main contestants, with their various supporters and cobelligerents, were diametrically opposed. Each side insisted that the other party had been the "aggressor." Neither side evinced the slightest readiness to indulge its opponents—or the desires of an anxious world—by abandoning its own aims. Whether these aims were good or bad, they were so directly in conflict as to be mutually exclusive.

On the Communist side there were two major elements, the insurgent military and political organization within South Vietnam and the supporting government of North Vietnam. With several years of fighting already behind it, the "Vietcong" military organization in South Vietnam was believed in the winter of 1966-67 to comprise some 62,000 "main force" fighters, 110,000 local and district guerrillas, and 58,000 political and administrative cadres and support troops. With its political organ, the so-called National Liberation Front of South Vietnam (N.L.F.), the Vietcong claimed control of half the population of South Vietnam's villages and hamlets and was admitted by allied authorities to control at least 17 per cent of the entire Southern population and to be in a position to contest the control of areas inhabited by another 28 per cent.

Closely associated with, if not in actual control of, the insurgent organization was the Communist government of the Northern "Democratic Republic of Vietnam" (D.R.V.) with its capital at Hanoi. In addition to providing the insurgents with material support and strategic guidance over a period of years, the D.R.V. had infiltrated as many as 45,000 of its own troops into South Vietnam and, in the winter of 1966-67, was known to be concentrating much larger forces just above the North-South military demarcation line at the 17th parallel. According to American authorities, a North Vietnamese general named Nguyen Chi Thanh directed the entire military effort in the South up to the time of his death in the summer of 1967.

Even if they occasionally differed in matters of emphasis and tactics, the Hanoi regime in the North and the N.L.F. in the South seemed basically in accord about the objectives for which they were jointly fighting. Despite a certain amount of calculated ambiguity, the nature of their common goal was clearly evidenced by their public statements,[1] particularly when these were examined in the light of actual Communist practice in Vietnam and elsewhere. What both Hanoi and the leaders of the N.L.F. were unmistakably aiming at was to oust the Americans from South Vietnam, get rid of the "puppet" government in Saigon, substitute a "popular" regime in which Communists would wield essential control, and move from there to bring about the reunification of North and South Vietnam under a Communist regime. No one who studied their programs and actions in the light of Communist performance as observed in other parts of the world could reasonably doubt that the ultimate aim was the establishment of a Communist Vietnam encompassing both North and South.

Nor was there any reason for surprise that such a program should have been unacceptable not only to South Vietnam's military leaders but, so far as could be judged, to the great majority of the people under their jurisdiction. The government in Saigon, whose uniformed military forces had thus far borne the brunt of the fighting, had never enjoyed much popularity in the country at large. The military regime headed since June 1965 by Premier Nguyen Cao Ky and Chief of State Nguyen Van Thieu was not much more highly regarded than the earlier regime of President Ngo Dinh Diem, terminated by a *coup d'état* in 1963. As recently as 1966, adherents of the militant wing of the Buddhist movement centered in the northern cities of Danang and Hué had spearheaded a serious attempt to overthrow the ruling military junta. Widely as the Saigon government was detested, however, there had never been any evidence that even its most bitter opponents wanted to be ruled by the Vietcong or the Communists. True, the Vietcong had somehow managed to recruit new members in South Vietnam at a rate exceeding its substantial losses from military operations and desertion. On the other hand, it had quite failed to prevent the holding in September 1966 of elections to a South Vietnamese constituent assembly which was intended to prepare the way for the adoption of a constitution, the holding of legislative elections, and a return to civilian government.

It goes without saying that the United States Government was no more sympathetic to the Communist program for South Vietnam than were the South Vietnamese themselves. Disclaiming any selfish ambitions of its own, the United States had been unequivocally opposed to letting the country fall under Communist control. Its overriding objective had been authoritatively defined by President Johnson in a speech of April 7, 1965, as the assurance of "an independent South Vietnam —securely guaranteed and able to shape its own relationships to all others—free from outside interference—tied to no alliance—a military base for no other country." The United States, the President had emphasized on this and other occasions, sought no advantages for itself and had no intention of trying to overthrow the North Vietnamese government. Once the war was ended, he had said, it was even ready to include North Vietnam in a massive program for regional development in Southeast Asia as a whole. At the same time, Mr. Johnson had warned, the United States was ready to do whatever might be necessary to ensure "the independence of South Vietnam and its freedom from attack"; and, he had added, it did not intend to "withdraw, either openly or under the cloak of a meaningless agreement."[2]

So long as this basic opposition of purposes persisted, it was difficult to see how negotiations, even if they could be brought about, could put an end to the conflict. More probably they would provide only a temporary respite which both sides would employ in strengthening their respective military positions. Authorities in Hanoi and Washington displayed a firmer grasp of this reality than did the innumerable men of good will, from U Thant down, who had ceaselessly exhorted the parties to bring their dispute to the conference table. Some advocates of negotiations had urged the reconvening of the Geneva Conference of 1954, which had sanctioned the partition of former French Indochina and had been reassembled in 1961-62 to deal with the problem of Laos. Others favored a commencement of negotiations on some other basis, possibly as a result of action through the United Nations. The essential thing, in the opinion of most of those not directly involved, was to get the parties to stop fighting and start talking.

Without overlooking the force of this peace sentiment, both Washington and Hanoi had tended thus far to treat the idea of negotiations more as an aspect of political warfare than as an immediately practicable goal. The United States had long since made known its readiness for "unconditional discussions" with the interested governments (its attitude about discussions with the N.L.F. itself remained somewhat ambiguous), and had also signified its acceptance of the Geneva agreements as an adequate basis for peace[3]—not a small concession in view of the failure of those agreements to assure peace in the past. In addition, the President and Ambassador Arthur J. Goldberg, the U.S. Representative to the United Nations, had repeatedly urged the U.N. to focus its own resources on the search for peace.[4] At the same time, Washington had continued to make clear its determination to ensure South Vietnam's right to live in peace and decide its own destinies—in other words, to remain free from the Communist domination the other side was trying to impose upon it.

The government of North Vietnam had linked its attitude on negotiations even more closely to the exigencies of its war effort. As far back as April 1965, North Vietnamese Premier Pham Van Dong had put forward a four-point statement which said that while United Nations intervention in Vietnam was unacceptable under any circumstances, a Geneva-type conference could be reconvened provided the United States would, among other things, undertake to withdraw completely from South Vietnam, desist from all acts of war against North Vietnam, and allow South Vietnam's affairs to be settled in accordance with the program of the N.L.F.[5] To responsible Americans, this seemed another way of saying that the United States must renounce its whole purpose in South Vietnam before a conference could even meet. But others who were less concerned about long-term Communist aims appeared to feel that North Vietnam was being quite magnanimous in offering to negotiate even on these one-sided terms.

More recently, Hanoi had sought to capitalize on the growing international distaste for American policy, particularly the bombing of North Vietnamese territory, by introducing still another preliminary condition. If the United States really wanted a peaceful settlement, said North Vietnamese President Ho Chi Minh in January 1966, it must not only accept Pham Van Dong's four-point program, and prove its acceptance "by actual deeds"; it must, in addition, "end unconditionally and for good all bombing raids and other war acts" against North Vietnam.[6]

The raising of this second condition seemed hardly to bespeak great eagerness for negotiations. On the contrary, it would make the opening of negotiations that much the more difficult. Nevertheless, the demand for termination of the bombing had since stood out more and more prominently as the months went by and the air offensive continued. Stop the bombing, Hanoi had seemed to say, and you can have negotiations; continue it, and you will never get them. Since the bombing was, in any case, being widely condemned on humanitarian grounds and even its military efficacy had been sharply questioned in some quarters, this demand quite naturally heightened domestic and international pressure for its discontinuance. "A powerful nation like the United States," U Thant had said in one of the milder expressions of the prevailing sentiment, "should take the initiative in the quest for peace and show an enlightened and humanitarian spirit."[7]

This, however, was not an argument that commended itself to responsible American authorities. It was quite unfair to ask one party to tie its hands militarily while the other kept both hands free, American officials maintained. In Secretary Rusk's eyes, such a plan would involve stopping "half the war" while letting the other half continue. President Johnson had more than once declared that he could not ask American troops to fight under such inequitable conditions.[8] American authorities, moreover, were by no means assured that Hanoi's insistence on a halt in bombing was motivated by a genuine interest in peace negotiations. Already, Washington recalled, there had been two "pauses" in the bombing, the first from May 13 to 18, 1965 and the second from December 24, 1965 to January 31, 1966. On neither occasion had Hanoi shown any readiness to engage in peace talks. Its current agitation of the issue, Washington surmised, was inspired either by a desire to embarrass the United States or, perhaps, by the hope of actually gaining relief from the bombing without making any concessions of its own.

Though nominally directed only against carefully selected military targets, it was apparent by late 1966 that the American air attacks had been causing increasing civilian casualties as well as increasing disruption of North Vietnamese supply systems and the like. Yet those few Americans who were able to visit North Vietnam in late 1966 and early 1967 gained the impression that the bombing had in no way dampened the fighting spirit of the population but, if anything, had strengthened the determination to go on fighting until North Vietnam's aims were realized.[9] Even if the bombing were to be stopped, there was no certainty that North Vietnam would actually come to the peace table. Nor did Washington overlook the fact that in its insistence on a bombing halt Hanoi had in no sense withdrawn its earlier, basically unacceptable conditions for ending the conflict.

What Washington *had* appeared willing and even eager to consider was the possibility of *reciprocal* steps, involving both the United States and North Vietnam, which would serve to moderate the conflict without putting either side at a military disadvantage. Ambassador Goldberg had made an explicit offer along these lines in an address to the U.N. General Assembly on September 22, 1966. "We are prepared," he had said, "to order a cessation of all bombing of North Vietnam the moment we are assured, privately or otherwise, that this step will be answered promptly by a corresponding and appropriate deescalation on the other side."[10] Hanoi, however, had shown nothing but scorn for this proposal, and neither U Thant nor any of the other advocates of a bombing halt had been able to promise that American action would be followed by any corresponding action on North Vietnam's part. So long as Hanoi insisted on a unilateral cessation of bombing and the United States insisted on reciprocity, the fighting seemed destined to continue and the desire for peace talks to remain unappeased.

So far as the conduct of the war was concerned, each side had important assets and significant weaknesses. From a condition of extreme danger in early 1965, U.S. authorities maintained that the military situation had by now improved to a point where allied forces were stronger than ever before and the adversary could no longer have any hope of conquering South Vietnam or driving out its defenders. Side by side with the South Vietnamese forces of 623,000 stood an American force of 380,000 which was being rapidly augmented and was expected to reach perhaps 480,000 within the next twelve months.

"PRACTICALLY EVERYBODY HERE BUT HANOI!"

Canfield in *The Newark News*

With the addition of 45,000 combat troops from South Korea and smaller contingents totaling around 7,000 from Australia, New Zealand, and the Philippines, allied ground strength had reached a point at which not one but several large-scale operations could be carried on simultaneously and the Vietcong could be kept on the run as never before. At the same time, it was conceded that the bombing of supply lines and communications facilities in North Vietnam had failed to halt the infiltration of men and material from North to South. Nor had the adversary as yet shown any sign of adopting President Johnson's view "that the war he started is costing him more than he can ever gain."[11] In the words of Henry Cabot Lodge, the U.S. Ambassador in Saigon, "We are in a condition where they cannot win, we cannot be defeated, but we have not won yet."[12]

Similarly, U.S. authorities professed a definite though qualified satisfaction over the progress of civilian affairs in South Vietnam. Although the "pacification" program designed to bring security to the countryside still lagged distressingly, developments in government-controlled areas appeared to justify a degree of optimism. A dangerous inflation had been checked, foundations for a transition to civilian government were being laid, and the existing military leadership had promised to devote increased attention to its programs of nation-building and social reform or "revolutionary development." At a meeting in Manila in October 1966, this resolve had been formally endorsed by President Johnson and the leaders of the five Far Eastern and Pacific nations that had joined the United States in supporting South Vietnam's fight for survival: the Republic of Korea, Australia, New Zealand, the Philippines, and Thailand, which had provided air bases to the United States for the bombing of North Vietnam. At their Manila meeting, the leaders of the allied governments had also made a collective if somewhat ambiguous commitment to withdraw their forces from Vietnam within six months after the end of the war.[12a]

Meanwhile the American strategy of gradually increasing military pressure had come under growing attack from two opposite directions. On one side were the "doves" in the United States and abroad who regarded the American presence in Vietnam as unjustified and clamored for an end of the bombing and a liquidation of the war. Hanoi had given the impression that it counted heavily on pressure from this quarter to force a reversal of U.S. policy by the time of the 1968 presidential elections if not before. At times, indeed, domestic and international criticism of the bombing policy seemed actually to be having some effect on U.S. strategic decisions. Largely because of the world-wide furor touched off by a pair of U.S. raids on the Hanoi area in mid-December of 1966, the North Vietnamese capital was exempted from further air attack until January 16, 1967, although this respite turned out to be wholly temporary.

A more immediate challenge to the existing strategy was presented by the limited but articulate company of "hawks," both military and civilian, who disagreed with the whole idea of fighting a limited war, demanded an easing of the restrictions that had thus far safeguarded many North Vietnamese targets against American air attack, and particularly called for action against the port of Haiphong and the jet bases in the Hanoi-Haiphong area which formed the core of North Vietnam's air defense system. This, too, was a viewpoint whose influence could not be lightly disregarded. Thus far, however, President Johnson had resisted most demands for further intensification of the bombing. Like Defense Secretary Robert S. McNamara, the President appeared to feel that the additional damage that might be inflicted on Hanoi's war effort was less important than the risk of complications with the U.S.S.R. and Communist China, North Vietnam's friends and sponsors.

Locked as they were in fierce competition for the leadership of the Communist world, the U.S.S.R. and China had vied with each other in pledges of support for Vietnam's Communists and, from time to time, had freely hinted at possible retaliation for U.S. military moves against North Vietnam. The U.S.S.R., in addition to strongly backing Hanoi's diplomatic position and refusing to employ its own influence in favor of peace negotiations, had been assisting the North Vietnamese war effort on a large scale and furnished Hanoi with dozens of MIG aircraft as well as antiaircraft guns and rockets and other types of modern military equipment. Though Moscow had seemed anxious not to involve itself in any direct confrontation with the United States over Vietnam, authorities in Washington could not be sure how sharply it would react in case of air raids or blockade measures that might affect Soviet personnel or vessels.

The possibility of Chinese intervention in the conflict had at times appeared a more immediate danger, not only because of China's proximity to Vietnam and obvious sensitivity about developments there but also because of the somewhat erratic behavior of the Chinese Communist leadership. Communist China, too, was providing North Vietnam with material support, technical assistance in such fields as transportation, and diplomatic backing and advice. Unlike the U.S.S.R., which had been doing nothing to encourage peace negotiations, Communist China had been actively discouraging them and had repeatedly warned Hanoi against the danger of falling into an American "trap." The likelihood of outright Chinese intervention had, however, appeared to wane in the course of 1966, thanks in part to American assurances that the United States had no intention of endangering Chinese security interests, and in part to China's own absorption in the ups and downs of its "Cultural Revolution." Still, U.S. authorities saw no advantage in creating avoidable incidents. U.S. ground units had been carefully restrained from entering North Vietnamese territory, and U.S. aircraft were normally barred from operating over Vietnamese areas close to the Chinese frontier. How long these restrictions would continue in effect would depend both on the course of developments in Vietnam and on the success of U.S. military authorities and other advocates of an extended air offensive in converting the President to their point of view.

Aside from the overt backing of the Communist countries, Hanoi could count on at least the moral support of a broad segment of international opinion in Asia and Africa, in Western Erope, at the United Nations, and in the United States itself. U Thant, for one, had become an outspoken critic of U.S. actions and a tireless advocate of a halt in bombing. More cautiously, Pope Paul VI appeared to incline in the same direction. President de Gaulle had lost no opportunity to castigate the policy of the United States and to insist on the necessity for its withdrawal from Southeast Asia. Equally harsh indictments of American policy, mingled in some cases with expressions of active sympathy for Hanoi, emanated from the antiwar ranks within the United States itself.

Even those Americans who deplored the "excesses" of the antiwar agitators tended to be deeply distressed not only by the bombing but by the whole character of the war, with its heavy toll of troops and civilians, its masses of refugees, and the atrocities attributed to both sides and frequently recorded by the television cameras. Faced by so abhorrent a picture, many were inclined to discount official assertions that the war was necessary to protect South Vietnam's right to self-determination, to redeem America's pledges of assistance, or to permit a stabilization of Southeast Asia. Though seldom founded on detailed analysis, this world-wide emotional revulsion against the war could easily come to rank with the military operations themselves as an influence on the outcome of the conflict.

6 : A Hope That Failed

By the winter of 1966-67 it was widely believed that the war had reached a critical turning point and could not continue much longer at its current level of intensity. Either the contestants would have to be dragged to the conference table, it was felt, or the conflict would in all probability be "escalated" to a new pitch of violence and perhaps draw still other nations into its vortex. Considering the damage inflicted on North Vietnam in recent months, moreover, it was not difficult to imagine that Hanoi might be a good deal more interested in peace talks than its formal stand would indicate. The North Vietnamese leaders themselves may not have been averse to exploiting this assumption, if only to intensify the pressure on the United States to halt the bombing. At all events, a series of ambiguous statements by North Vietnamese spokesmen at the beginning of 1967 sufficed to open a new round of peace speculation and thus reactivate an already familiar cycle of hope and disappointment.

Premier Pham Van Dong began the process on January 3 in an interview with a current visitor to Hanoi, Harrison E. Salisbury of *The New York Times.* His famous four-point statement of 1965, the North Vietnamese Premier now explained, did not embody "conditions" for the holding of peace talks, as might have been supposed from its language; it merely set forth a "basis of settlement."[13] While this subtle distinction was being analyzed, another apparent signal was given out in Paris by Mai Van Bo, Hanoi's principal diplomatic representative in France. Reiterating the necessity that the bombing of North Vietnam be halted "definitely and unconditionally," this spokesman suggested on January 5 that if such a step were taken, his government would be willing to consider an American proposal for "contacts."[14] U Thant, who had been exploring the North Vietnamese and Vietcong attitude with U.S. encouragement, found nothing new in the Dong and Bo statements, but reaffirmed his own conviction "that there will be no move towards peace so long as the bombing of North Vietnam is going on."[15] Other interpreters of Hanoi's position laid equal stress on this point. Two private American visitors to North Vietnam, William Baggs and Harry S. Ashmore, reported to the State Department on a conversation with Ho Chi Minh in which, according to the Department's version, the North Vietnamese President "had insisted that there could be no talks between the United States and Hanoi unless the bombing were stopped, and unless also the United States stopped all reinforcements during the period of the talks." President Ho, the two Americans further reported, had been "adamant against any reciprocal military restraint by North Vietnam."[16]

Such news could scarcely encourage official hopes of a constructive change in the North Vietnamese position. At the same time, authorities in Washington were convinced that Hanoi *ought* by this time to be seeking peace, and that even the most unpromising leads must be followed up if only to forestall later charges that the United States had been negligent in the pursuit of peace. This was all the more true at the moment because peace sentiment was continuing to build up in connection with plans for the observance of a four-day military truce in early February on the occasion of Tet, the Lunar New Year, under a proposal put forward by South Vietnam and accepted with qualifications by the Vietcong.

It was in the midst of these discussions that the United States, apparently in early January, took the initiative in establishing a direct, confidential channel for communication with North Vietnamese representatives in Moscow. John C. Guthrie, Minister-Counselor of the U.S. Embassy in the Soviet capital, served as the intermediary in this series of "exchanges," which continued through January and early February. According to information later released by the State Department, the channel was employed on four separate occasions to transmit proposals which "called attention to the upcoming Tet cease-fire and urged direct talks aimed at resolving this Vietnam conflict." The only response from the North Vietnamese, however, was "a diatribe against the United States" delivered on January 27.[17] (In a later elaboration, the State Department said that "a wide variety of proposals was put before Hanoi in these Moscow contacts, without at any time producing any useful response.")[18] In a more public demonstration of the American interest in peace, the State Department also took occasion during this period to "elaborate" and bring up to date the "Fourteen Points for Peace in Southeast Asia" which had served for the past year as a compendium of American views on questions relating to negotiations and peace terms.[19]

While these secret exchanges in Moscow were going forward, the

North Vietnamese peace rocket was given another boost by means of an interview accorded by North Vietnamese Foreign Minister Nguyen Duy Trinh to a sympathetic newsman, the Australian Wilfred Burchett, on January 28. On the surface, it is true, Trinh's remarks seemed the reverse of conciliatory. He stated flatly that it was "only after the unconditional cessation of U.S. bombing and all other acts of war against the D.R.V. that there could be talks between the D.R.V. and the United States." Insisting that the "four points" were still the basis of Hanoi's position, he further declared that the "Vietnamese people" were still "determined to fight until total victory to defend the North, liberate the South, achieve the peaceful reunification of the fatherland, and contribute to the maintenance of peace in this area and in the world."[20]

Uncompromising as it sounded, however, this declaration was described by Mr. Burchett and other sources close to the North Vietnamese government as nothing less than a "good-will" gesture. In contrast to earlier statements, it did not say that the bombing must be halted "finally and unconditionally," but only "unconditionally." Once this was done and all other acts of war were halted, according to Trinh, there "could" be talks with the United States. Trivial as these verbal differences appeared, it began to seem as though even a temporary halt in the bombing and "other warlike acts" might under certain circumstances be viewed in Hanoi as an acceptable basis for peace talks.

"As of this moment, I cannot report that there are any serious indications that the other side is ready to stop the war," President Johnson observed on February 2. He himself, the President emphasized, was eager to consider any proposal the North Vietnamese might make; indeed, he virtually pleaded with them to take "just almost any step" along the lines of "reciprocal action" that would enable him to suspend the bombing.[21] As the Tet truce set for February 8-12 approached, peace talk continued to swell. Presidential assistant Walt W. Rostow hinted that negotiations might be imminent. Senator Robert F. Kennedy, emerging from a conference with the President, denied but failed to quash persistent reports that he had received a "peace feeler" during a visit to Paris.[22] Messrs. Baggs and Ashmore, with the approval of the State Department, mailed a letter to Ho Chi Minh describing the U.S. position as they understood it.[23]

Not even the opening of a new U.S. ground offensive on February

6, two days before the scheduled commencement of the Tet cease-fire, could slacken the peace momentum. On February 7, Pope Paul VI addressed an emotional appeal to President Johnson, Chief of State Thieu, and President Ho to express his hope that the forthcoming suspension of hostilities would open the way to peace negotiations.[24] Also on February 7, Soviet Premier Kosygin arrived in London for talks with British Prime Minister Harold Wilson. In a speech next day that was widely assumed to reflect the views of the Hanoi regime, Kosygin lauded the recent Trinh statement and echoed its message. "The unconditional cessation of American bombing and all other aggressive acts against the Democratic Republic of Vietnam," Kosygin reiterated, ". . . is necessary in order to enable talks . . . to take place."[25] Although he did not say that talks actually *would* take place if the bombing stopped, the implication seemed clear.

President Johnson also took two important actions on February 8. In a reply to the Pope's message, he "devoutly" echoed the wish for an extension of the Tet truce and a commencement of negotiations—adding, however, the familiar qualification that he was sure the Pope "would not expect us to reduce military action unless the other side is willing to do likewise."[26] More sensationally, the President undertook to make the same point in a secret and personal communication to Ho Chi Minh, dispatched via Moscow in time to reach the North Vietnamese leader on February 10. In this tactfully worded communication, which was later described by the State Department as reaffirming proposals already laid before North Vietnamese representatives in Moscow, the President stressed his hope for "serious and private discussions leading toward an early peace" and suggested that the Tet truce presented a favorable opportunity for an immediate start. He could not, Mr. Johnson repeated, give orders for a unilateral cessation of bombing and other military actions against North Vietnam, since such a step might confuse world opinion as well as handing North Vietnam an unduly tempting military opportunity. As an alternative, however, the President offered a suggestion which he described as going "even further." "I am prepared," he wrote, "to order a cessation of bombing against your country and the stopping of further augmentation of U.S. forces in South Vietnam as soon as I am assured that infiltration into South Vietnam by land and by sea has stopped."[27]

If this is what the United States had been proposing in its earlier exchanges with the North Vietnamese, the lack of a favorable response from Hanoi is not surprising. It is true that the United States was offering something new—not only "a cessation of bombing," but also "the stopping of further augmentation of U.S. forces in South Vietnam"—and this at a time when the military build-up, which had already brought total U.S. strength to over 400,000, was still going forward at top speed. In return for this concession, however, the United States was also asking for something new—something which appeared to suggest that its price for a suspension of the bombing had actually gone up. No longer was it soliciting "just almost any step" to permit an end of the bombing, as President Johnson had seemed to do on February 2.[28] On the contrary, it was in effect giving notice that the bombing would be continued until the President was assured that "infiltration into South Vietnam by land and by sea" had actually stopped—in other words, until he had evidence that North Vietnam had ceased supporting the Vietcong and its own troops in South Vietnam and was, in effect, leaving them to their fate.

Though President Ho's reply to this communication was not received until February 15, developments in the intervening days gave little reason to suppose that Hanoi was going to accept it. Few military incidents marred the four-day Tet cease-fire period; but the lull in fighting was actively exploited by Hanoi in what Prime Minister Wilson was to describe as a "massive southward movement of troops and supplies"—or, in the President's own phrase, a "major resupply effort of their troops in South Vietnam."[29] Notwithstanding these unfavorable portents, the United States did not immediately resume bombing when the truce expired on February 12. Resumption of bombing was delayed for almost two additional days—not, apparently, because the President was still awaiting a reply from Ho Chi Minh, but because Kosygin was still in London and the United States did not wish its actions to be "misconstrued"[30] at a time when the British were desperately trying to elicit some indication that North Vietnam would at least reduce its infiltration if the bombing ceased.

So near were these efforts to success, Mr. Wilson later insisted, that peace had been "almost within our grasp." "One single simple act of trust"—he did not say by whom—was all that would have been needed to continue the truce "until the parties were around the conference table." Though bombs were again falling as he spoke, the British Prime Minister still seemed convinced that North Vietnam genuinely wanted peace and that only "a very, very small movement" would be needed "to activate all the complicated machinery which would bring us to peace negotiations."[31]

American authorities were not so sanguine. The conclusive proof of Hanoi's attitude, in their view, had been the publication on February 13 of a letter from Ho Chi Minh to the Pope which had amounted to little more than a truculent-sounding restatement of Pham Van Dong's "four points."[32] The North Vietnamese leader's subsequent letter to President Johnson, received February 15, merely added the further point that the "Vietnamese people" would "never accept conversation under the clear threat of bombs." If the United States really wanted talks, Ho declared once again, "it must first halt unconditionally [he did not say "permanently"] the bombings and all other acts of war against the Democratic Republic of Vietnam."[33]

In announcing the resumption of bombing on February 13 (U.S. time), President Johnson again emphasized that "the door to peace is, and will remain, open, and we are prepared at any time to go more than half way to meet any equitable overture from the other side."[34] Hanoi, however, seemed to think it had already made overtures enough. Once the letter to President Johnson had been delivered, it "broke off the Moscow channel"[35] and took no further action in the matter except for its unilateral publication of the Johnson-Ho exchange some weeks later.[36] Though there would be no lack of new peace proposals in the weeks ahead, the decisive actions in the immediate future seemed fated to occur on the battlefield.

7 : Guam to Glassboro

Experience had shown that when peace hopes failed, military escalation was likely to follow in spite of Washington's dislike for the use of that term to describe American actions. As on similar occasions in the past, intensification of the war and a further heightening of pressure on the Communist adversary were the unmistakable sequel to the February peace probe. A whole series of novel actions bespoke the United States' determination to prosecute the war with increased vigor, exploit the growing possibility of large-scale ground actions, and prosecute the air offensive with a somewhat diminished regard for international sensibilities.

A major new ground offensive, Operation Junction City, was launched on February 23 in the hope of locating and wiping out a Vietcong headquarters in the area close to the Cambodian frontier. Next day it was revealed that North Vietnam was for the first time being brought under artillery fire as well as aerial bombardment in an attempt to silence antiaircraft positions in and beyond the six-mile-wide Demilitarized Zone between North and South Vietnam. On February 25, two North Vietnamese power plants were attacked by air in the first such strikes since the previous September.

Two further steps were disclosed on February 26. One was an authorization to U.S. warships to enter North Vietnamese territorial waters for the purpose of shelling coastal supply routes; the other, the partial mining from the air of certain North Vietnamese rivers in order to impede operations by sampans and junks while avoiding danger to Soviet vessels or other deep-water traffic. In still another move to "increase the price" exacted for Hanoi's obstinacy, the President authorized the first in a long series of air attacks on North Vietnam's principal industrial center, the Thainguyen iron and steel complex some 50 miles north of the capital. While it obviously played a key part in North Vietnam's war effort, Thainguyen differed from other major targets in that it was not directly involved in the infiltration of men and supplies.[37]

Such measures inevitably inspired new outcries against U.S. tactics, accentuated a running argument in the halls of Congress, and challenged anew the ingenuity of those who still sought means of bringing the adversaries to the peace table. Senator Robert Kennedy, whose disagreements with the President had begun to fascinate the entire nation, called on March 2 for a halt in bombing as part of a new, three-point peace plan which, however, was promptly dismissed by Secretary Rusk as substantially duplicating proposals already rejected by Hanoi.[38] U Thant, returning from a visit to Burma on which he had spoken with North Vietnamese representatives, reiterated once again his view that a cessation of bombing was a necessary preliminary to useful and meaningful talks.[39]

Though recently quoted as saying that "all the king's horses and all the king's men are not going to move us out of our position,"[40] President Johnson also insisted that the United States was always ready for negotiations on a basis of "equity and fairness." Again he pleaded for "just almost any reciprocal action on their part" that

would justify a bombing halt.[41] "Reciprocity must be the fundamental principle of any reduction in hostilities," the President reiterated on March 15 in a major address at Nashville, Tennessee in
which he again emphasized that America's determination to pursue
every chance of peace was as unshakable as its determination to
"stay the course" in association with the Republic of Vietnam.[42]

Consistent with this demand for reciprocity was Washington's
favorable response to a new, confidential peace plan put forward by
U Thant on March 14. Momentarily bypassing the question of a
bombing halt, the Secretary-General now advanced the idea of a
"general stand-still truce"—in other words, a cessation of military
operations by both sides—as a step toward direct talks and a reconvening of the Geneva Conference. Not only the United States but
South Vietnam indicated general acceptance of this equitable-sound-
ing proposal; it was Hanoi that scorned it on the ground that it failed
to distinguish "between the aggressors and the victims of aggression."[43] Admitting that "the positions of the parties have never been
so far apart," U Thant promptly reaffirmed his earlier insistence
that a bombing halt by the United States was the key to early talks
and the only realistic alternative to "a very prolonged and bloody
war" that might easily spread to areas not yet involved.[44]

That the war was due for still further intensification seemed wholly
evident from events that had occurred while the Thant plan was
under discussion. During this period, President Johnson and his principal advisers had devoted three exhausting days, March 19-21, to a
journey to the Pacific island of Guam for conferences with Ambassador Lodge, General William C. Westmoreland, the top U.S. commander in Vietnam, and Messrs. Ky and Thieu, who had insisted on
being present. The main significance of this back-breaking excursion
appeared to lie not so much in any specific business to be transacted
as in a pervasive emphasis on the need to achieve more rapid and
decisive results in both the military and the civilian phases of the war
—in the campaign against the Vietcong and in the internal evolution
of South Vietnam itself. Some observers went so far as to interpret
the Guam meeting as the opening move in a campaign to finish the
war before the 1968 U.S. election.

President Johnson exuded optimism as the Guam conference convened on March 20. "There are many signs that we are at a favorable
turning point," he told the South Vietnamese leaders. "Your fighting

men, aided by your allies, now hold the initiative and are striking heavy blows against the strongholds and refuges of the Vietcong and their North Vietnamese masters. And in the villages the medicine of the revolutionary development program is already beginning to take effect. The Vietcong are turning sharply against that program's administration. I think that is very solid tribute to its effectiveness."[45] Mr. Johnson particularly lauded the completion by South Vietnam's Constituent Assembly of the draft constitution that was to serve as the basis for the return to a constitutional regime. Though modified in important respects to ensure acceptance by the military junta, the constitutional draft as approved on the eve of the Guam meeting retained sufficient democratic features to be extolled by the American President as "the foundation stone of a freely and popularly elected government."[46]

The Guam conference served also to underline a number of impending personnel changes. Ambassador Lodge, it was explained, would shortly be returning to Washington and would be replaced in Saigon by Ambassador Ellsworth Bunker, who had won diplomatic laurels by his work in adjusting crises in West Irian and the Dominican Republic and currently bore the title of Ambassador at Large. Ambassador Eugene Locke, in turn, would become Deputy Ambassador as successor to William J. Porter. Robert W. Komer, a presidential assistant who was also a specialist on South Vietnam's "pacification" or "revolutionary development" program, would also be setting up a Saigon office in token of an increased emphasis on improving security and stimulating reform at village and hamlet levels.

A rather jarring note in a conference so largely concerned with South Vietnam's internal regeneration was the militant attitude of Premier Ky, who was generally expected to seek the South Vietnamese presidency under the new constitution. The youthful South Vietnamese leader displayed only perfunctory interest in the revolutionary development program and the "national reconciliation" plan for rehabilitating repentant Vietcong elements, another project long pushed by the United States. His principal concern, it appeared, was to see that the pace of military action was further stepped up—primarily by the United States—and to forestall any softening in the U.S. terms for peace negotiations. "How long will we have to wait?" the Premier asked rhetorically as he enumerated the military advantages Hanoi continued to enjoy as the result of Washington's reluctance to sanction all-out hostilities.[47]

A number of the restrictions Premier Ky complained about were destined to be lifted within the next few months, although no new military decisions were taken at the Guam meeting itself and even the responsibility for the revolutionary development program was not precisely fixed pending further study by Ambassador Bunker. (Early in May the new Ambassador decided that the U.S. role in the program should be centralized under General Westmoreland's headquarters, with Mr. Komer serving as the General's deputy.)[48] "I would sum up the whole conference by saying I think it has been a very constructive exchange," the President reported on March 21 in what seemed a striking letdown from the exuberance of the day before. "I think we have a difficult, serious, long, drawn-out, agonizing problem that we do not yet have the answer for," Mr. Johnson added. ". . . It is going to take a lot of extra effort and a good deal more time."[49]

The Guam meeting, in other words, had brought no essential changes; nor was the situation significantly altered by Hanoi's unexpected publication of the Johnson-Ho Chi Minh letters during the hours when the President was flying back to the United States. The war, to all appearances, was about to settle back into its familiar, gradually expanding pattern as fresh U.S. troops arrived in Vietnam —by late March, their number had swelled to 425,000—and the scale of operations relentlessly increased. Almost every day there was some new development that seemed to suggest an accelerated pursuit of military success and a gradual tightening of the ring around North Vietnam. On March 22, it was disclosed that a part of the force of B-52 bombers that had been regularly flying in from Guam, primarily to bomb suspected Vietcong concentrations in the South, would in future operate from much closer bases in Thailand. Five days later, Navy attack bombers from the nuclear-powered carrier *Enterprise* struck within five miles of the port of Haiphong. The immunity of Haiphong itself, thus far assured by Washington's reluctance to invite complications with the U.S.S.R., was not to last much longer. Plans for a Navy air attack on two power plants within the city's perimeter, carried out on April 20, were approved by the President several weeks in advance.

In the meantime, additional peace initiatives streaked across the skies amid the tension and anxiety engendered by Marshal Ky's militancy, by new battles and rising casualty rates, and by reports that downed American fliers were being humiliated and mistreated by their North Vietnamese captors.[50] Hanoi's rejection of the U Thant plan for a "general stand-still truce" had promptly given rise to a suggestion by Democratic Senator Joseph S. Clark of Pennsylvania—strongly backed by U Thant himself, though just as strongly discouraged in U.S. administration quarters—that the United States should drop its demand for reciprocity and simply cease fire unilaterally.[51] This idea was scarcely launched before a proposal from Saigon for a new, 24-hour truce on May 23 in commemoration of the birth of Buddha inspired a new if delusive hope for a longer, mutual cease-fire.

More sophisticated—and basically reciprocal in its provisions—was an elaborate four-stage plan advanced by Canadian Foreign Minister Paul Martin on April 11. Its purpose was to bring about a military "disengagement" and a cessation of hostilities preparatory to a restoration of the cease-fire negotiated in 1954. Hanoi's decisive rejection of this overture—on the familiar ground that it made no distinction between "aggressors" and their victims—did not totally discourage the Canadians. Saigon accepted the plan, and the United States displayed its interest by suggesting an amendment involving a mutual, supervised withdrawal of the opposing military forces to a distance of ten miles north and south of the Demilitarized Zone.[52]

Since an effective neutralization of the border area between North and South would obviously reduce the infiltration of men and supplies into the South, the United States would presumably have favored such a measure at any time. In April of 1967 it had special reasons for wishing the area around the Demilitarized Zone could be taken out of the war, for the military situation in that sector had taken a sudden turn for the worse in the few weeks since the Guam conference. An upsurge of Vietcong activity in northern South Vietnam, plus a concentration of strong North Vietnamese forces in and beyond the Demilitarized Zone, had already necessitated the flying in of 7,500 Army troops to reinforce what had hitherto been an area of exclusive Marine responsibility. North Vietnam, it was suggested, might even be getting ready to pour its own forces southward in an attempt to cut off and smother the U.S. and South Vietnamese defenders below the D.M.Z. This northward shift in the war's center of gravity, which

HUGH STEPHENS LIBRARY
STEPHENS COLLEGE
COLUMBIA, MISSOURI

was to become increasingly marked as the season advanced, was to accentuate the strain on U.S. manpower in Vietnam and provide new arguments for increasing U.S. forces even beyond the strengths already authorized.

In the meantime, the air war underwent a further intensification with the attack on Haiphong of April 20—at a cost of over 100 civilian casualties, according to Hanoi's unverifiable complaint—and the resumption a few days later of bombing of objectives in and around Hanoi itself. Two of North Vietnam's four jet airfields were also attacked for the first time on April 24 in response to what was described as increased activity by North Vietnamese fighter planes. These measures elicited the usual outcries from Hanoi, Peking, and Moscow; yet they brought no sign that either China or the U.S.S.R. intended to intervene in the conflict, notwithstanding a recent success in ironing out their mutual differences concerning the transit of Soviet military supplies across China to North Vietnam.[53]

The United States, meanwhile, could note with satisfaction a renewed endorsement of its general policy in Vietnam by three separate but overlapping groups of allied nations whose representatives had been meeting in Washington. The first of these was the eight-nation Southeast Asia Treaty Organization (SEATO), whose policy-making Council held its twelfth session—without the participation of France—on April 18-20 and reaffirmed the necessity of defeating the Communist aggression in Vietnam.[54] Next came the representatives of the "Manila powers," the seven Asian and Pacific nations contributing troops to the allied war effort, who met on April 20-21 to hail the progress supposedly achieved since the Manila meeting in October 1966.[55] Finally, the three-nation ANZUS Council, representing Australia, New Zealand, and the United States, held its annual meeting on April 21-22 and reaffirmed the hope that North Vietnam would "reverse its intransigent stand."[56]

These diplomatic developments passed almost unheeded by the American public amid the furor occasioned by General Westmoreland's visit to the United States in late April on a kind of administration-sponsored barnstorming tour, apparently aimed at mobilizing public support for the administration's policy and preparing the ground for any troop increases that might be thought necessary. In contrast to General Douglas MacArthur's practice during the Korean war, the commander of U.S. forces in Vietnam did not in any way

120396

challenge the strategic directives he was receiving from Washington. Still less did he offer any encouragement to those who had seen him as a possible presidential candidate. He did, however, offer strong support of the administration's war policy in an address to an Associated Press luncheon in New York on April 24 and an appearance before a joint session of Congress on April 28.[57]

General Westmoreland's description of American policy as one of "unrelenting but discriminating military, political, and psychological pressure on [the enemy's] whole structure at all levels" could not have been expected to awaken universal enthusiasm in the superheated home front atmosphere of 1967. Nor did the military picture he painted afford much cause for rejoicing. In predicting "some of the bitterest fighting of the war" in the days and months ahead, the General was felt by many to be contradicting his own expressions of optimism about the general course of military operations. Thousands were troubled by his avowed dislike of cease-fire proposals as "a military advantage to the enemy and a detriment to our side"; while his expression of dismay at "recent unpatriotic acts here at home" was widely construed as both an affront to the "peace" movement and a challenge to freedom of expression and the right of dissent.

The most troubling aspect of the Westmoreland visit, however, was the almost universal assumption that the General had come home to plead that more American troops be sent to Vietnam to join the 440,000 already there. Just what reinforcements the General thought necessary was not publicly disclosed, and he later denied that he had ever asked for a specific figure; but the published estimates of his requirements now ran from 525,000 to as high as 600,000. Though President Johnson denied that any new decision on a further troop build-up was imminent,[58] the overtones of the visit were such as to encourage a general impression that the conflict had reached a stage at which old restrictions were falling by the wayside and the whole concept of a "limited" war might soon become obsolete.

Various new developments helped to sustain this feeling in the following weeks. There were new raids and heavy air battles in and around the Hanoi area; fierce fighting in the region just south of the Demilitarized Zone; new casualty reports which showed that over 3,000 Americans had been killed since the beginning of 1967 alone; new instances in which downed American pilots were placed on public exhibition by their North Vietnamese captors; a one-sided condemnation of U.S. war policies by the unofficial "International

War Crimes Tribunal" sponsored by Bertrand Russell in Stockholm; two seemingly deliberate "bumpings" of American destroyers by Soviet warships in the Sea of Japan; and a warning by U Thant that the world might be witnessing "the initial phase of World War III."[59]

Admitting the inevitability of "heartaches, . . . frustration, and . . . dissent," the President insisted on May 18 that there had been no change in American objectives, that he perceived no "great fluctuation" in the pace of the war, and that he, at any rate, did not share the feeling that matters were getting out of control or moving toward a wider collision.[60] But an incalculable new factor was now entering the situation with the rapid development of the international crisis in the Middle East and a concurrent deterioration in many aspects of the relationship between the United States and the Soviet Union. Local flare-ups were also beginning to occur in such places as Hong Kong and along the armistice line between North and South Korea, thus suggesting a possibility that U.S. and allied interests around the globe might be subjected to coordinated Communist pressure as had happened in some past international crises.

Anxiety was heightened by a harsh Soviet note, received in Washington on June 2, complaining that a Soviet merchant ship had just been bombed and two of its crewmen injured in an American air attack on the North Vietnamese port of Campha, 50 miles north of Haiphong. Although the United States initially disclaimed responsibility for this mishap, it later conceded—after a second Soviet note asserting that one crewman had died and several had been injured—that the vessel might have been hit by "suppressive fire" directed by U.S. aircraft at a North Vietnamese antiaircraft site.[61]

Had the U.S.S.R. desired to create a major incident over Vietnam at this juncture, the opportunity was clearly there. But by this time Moscow's own international policy was being thrown into disarray by the onset of war in the Middle East and the rapid defeat by Israel of the Arab air forces and armies. Under these disturbing conditions, Moscow offered no further challenge to the extension of the U.S. air attacks on North Vietnamese objectives, which continued throughout the following weeks but seemed to develop of their own momentum without any direct relation to the sensational events that were taking place in the Middle East.

If the startling diplomatic upsets of June 1967 did nothing to sharpen Soviet opposition to the U.S. role in Vietnam, they also failed to overcome Moscow's evident reluctance to work for a negotiated peace. The continued inflexibility of the Soviet position on Vietnam was one of the most disappointing revelations of the Johnson-Kosygin "summit" meetings which took place at Glassboro, New Jersey, on June 23 and 25—the result, as already noted, of Kosygin's presence in New York for an emergency U.N. session on the Middle East. So far as Vietnam was concerned, Kosygin apparently repeated at Glassboro what he and others had been intimating all along: that talks with North Vietnam could be started promptly—within three or four weeks, according to some accounts—if the United States would make the preliminary gesture of stopping the bombing. But Kosygin's public statement after his meeting with the President showed no apparent change in the basic Communist terms for ending the war. "It was emphasized on the Soviet side," Kosygin said, "that a settlement of the Vietnamese problem is possible only on the condition of an end to the bombing of the territory of the Democratic Republic of Vietnam and the withdrawal of United States forces from South Vietnam."[62]

Confronted with these well-known demands, President Johnson undoubtedly explained to Kosygin his objections to stopping "only half the war" as well as his determination to "match and . . . outmatch every step to peace that others may be ready to take." The area of agreement on Vietnam, the President admitted after the conference had closed, was even smaller than on the Middle East. "It is defined," he said, "by the fact that the dangers and the difficulties of any one area must never be allowed to become a cause of wider conflict."[63] What these words appeared to mean was that the war in Vietnam, like the war in the Middle East, must be prevented from bringing on direct hostilities between the United States and the Soviet Union. If this was an accurate reflection of the Soviet views as well, it would be a precious reassurance to the United States in the difficult episodes of war that still lay ahead.

8 : The Fever Mounts

While it had often seemed that the struggle over Vietnam had already reached a point of maximum intensity and intolerable nervous strain, the months that followed the Glassboro confrontation were to bring yet a further intensification of the anxieties and debates that accompanied each new phase of military operations. The search for peace, in contrast, appeared to undergo a temporary loss of momentum in spite of a campaign by Senator Mansfield and others aimed at engaging the United Nations in an active peace effort. With Hanoi and Washington still at an impasse over the matter of a halt in the bombing, the opportunities for constructive diplomatic action by the U.N. or anyone else were painfully limited. U Thant, who no longer disguised his sympathy for what he described as the "national independence" movement in South Vietnam,[64] announced that he personally was desisting from further peace efforts until the United States stopped bombing the North.[65] A cessation of bombing in the North, however, was the very last thing the American administration appeared to contemplate. Indeed, it was on the verge of ordering a further and far-reaching extension of the bombing operations.

Through the spring, President Johnson and his advisers had also been struggling with the problem of the ground war as placed on their agenda by General Westmoreland's April visit. Early in July, Defense Secretary McNamara undertook one of his periodic visits to South Vietnam to confer with the military leaders and appraise their needs on the spot. In contrast to the reports of military "stalemate" so prevalent at home, Mr. McNamara professed to find gratifying and even spectacular progress in almost every phase of the war effort. The only marked exception, he indicated, was the pacification program in liberated areas, which seemed to be held back mainly by the inability of the South Vietnamese forces to provide adequate security against renewed Vietcong attack.

So far as the demand for more American troops was concerned, Mr. McNamara noted that the forces in Vietnam would soon be reaching their currently authorized strength of 480,000 through the arrival of some 20,000 or 30,000 more men within the next 90 days. Some further additions even beyond that level would undoubtedly be necessary, the Secretary of Defense conceded; but he also suggested that there was room for more effective utilization of the forces already on hand, only about one-third of which represented "combat units" in the strict sense of the term. Additions beyond the 480,000 level, he indicated, would not be large enough to necessitate any call-up of Reserves such as the Joint Chiefs of Staff had been urging.[66] President Johnson, after conferring with Secretary McNamara and

General Westmoreland in Washington, was equally indefinite. "We realize that some additional troops are going to be needed and are going to be supplied," he said on July 13.

Before fixing any new ceiling, the President seemed anxious to find out what further contributions might be expected from "the other allies" involved in the Vietnam fighting. South Vietnam itself, with an estimated 700,000 men now under arms in its military, paramilitary, and police forces, would obviously continue to bear the heaviest burden. Other allied contributions, according to Mr. McNamara's offhand calculation, now included about 45,000 Koreans, 6,500 Australians, 200 New Zealanders, 2,200 Filipinos, and 2,500 Thais who had recently been designated for Vietnam service.[67] To the extent that these contingents could be increased, the strain on U.S. uniformed manpower would obviously be lessened. Two special presidential envoys, General Maxwell D. Taylor, former Ambassador to the Republic of Vietnam, and Clark Clifford, a long-time presidential adviser who was serving as Chairman of the Foreign Intelligence Advisory Board and would later be named successor to Secretary McNamara at the Defense Department, were dispatched on a quick tour of Pacific capitals to explore the question of troop levels as well as other matters of common interest.

However convinced of the need to defeat the Communist aggression in Vietnam, none of the allied countries exhibited much enthusiasm about devoting additional armed forces to the endeavor. President Ferdinand E. Marcos of the Philippines, who had gone through a bruising political fight to win congressional authorization for the engineer battalion already in Vietnam, declined to receive the new American mission at all. President Chung Hee Park of the Republic of Korea saw no possibility of sending more combat troops, although he apparently undertook to make available a total of 15,000 reservists over a period of time in order to free more of the Korean troops already in Vietnam for combat duty. South Vietnam itself announced a 65,000-man increase in the ceiling on its uniformed forces, from 735,000 to 800,000. Australia and New Zealand made no promises, but later in the year announced increases of 1,700 and 170 in their respective contingents, while Thailand subsequently let it be known that its contribution of combat troops would eventually be increased to a full division of 10,000 or more.[68]

Against these rather modest prospects the President had also to balance the mounting financial cost of the war, already running well beyond his January estimates, as well as a sharply inflationary trend in the domestic economy and a surge of demands for new domestic projects in the wake of the July riots in U.S. cities. For Americans of Senator Fulbright's persuasion,[69] such factors were an added argument for limiting any expansion of the Vietnam commitment; but there were other considerations, domestic and international, that still spoke for going forward. The President's conclusion, announced in a special message to Congress on August 3, seemed to follow a middle course. What had been decided, he said, was to authorize a rather limited increase of "at least 45,000" in the number of men to be sent to Vietnam in the fiscal year ending June 30, 1968. The authorized ceiling, in other words, would be increased from the current 480,000 to 525,000 or, possibly, even more. In announcing this decision, the President also called for utmost economy in defense and other governmental expenditure and renewed his January appeal for a tax surcharge—now set at 10 per cent, rather than 6 per cent—on individual and corporate incomes.[70]

It was apparently at about this time that the President also decided to accept the advice of his uniformed advisers and authorize a further relaxation in the restrictions on bombing in North Vietnam. Since the Campha raid on June 2, the attacks on barracks, communications facilities, and selected industrial objectives had gone forward amid loud domestic argument but with only one minor international incident when a second Soviet vessel was struck in Haiphong harbor, this time without casualties, on June 29.[71] Far more dismaying to most Americans had been the disastrous fire that swept the aircraft carrier *Forrestal* in the Gulf of Tonkin on July 29, causing the death of 129 crewmen (together with 64 injured and 3 missing) and briefly curtailing the air offensive until another carrier could be brought into position.

These events had naturally heightened the revulsion of some Americans against the whole policy of bombing in the North. They had not, however, diminished the belief of the responsible military chiefs that more decisive results could be obtained if only the bombing campaign were freed of the limitations which still precluded the full use of American air power in the Hanoi and Haiphong areas and, in addition, practically barred American aircraft from a buffer zone 25 to 30 miles wide along the Chinese frontier. Pressure to ease these restrictions had lately been building up in connection with the scheduling of special hearings on the matter by the Preparedness Investigating Subcommittee of the Senate Armed Services Committee, headed by Democratic Senator John Stennis of Mississippi and known for the "hawkish" convictions of most of its membership. Quite aside from congressional considerations, moreover, the administration presumably found the moment a suitable one to review its air strategy and ensure its coordination with the latest decisions affecting the ground war.

It was apparently on August 8 that Admiral U.S. Grant Sharp, who as U.S. Commander-in-Chief in the Pacific was responsible for coordinating the bombing offensive, was given a list of sixteen newly approved targets in North Vietnam that went a considerable way toward meeting the demands advanced by the military chiefs. Among the new targets was a vital link in the North Vietnamese communications network, the Longbien (Paul Doumer) bridge spanning the Red River at a distance of 1.7 miles from the center of Hanoi.[72] This objective was attacked for the first time on August 11, one span of the bridge being cut. (It was later completely demolished.) Civilian casualties in the raid, according to Moscow's report, exceeded 100.

More startling were the events of August 13, when U.S. fighter-bombers struck at four points along the rail and highway route running northeast from Hanoi and constituting North Vietnam's principal supply line from Communist China. Two of the targets were situated only ten miles from the Chinese border; and next day there was a second raid at approximately the same distance. The danger here, of course, was that Communist China might take retaliatory measures or even enter the war; but administration spokesmen, responding to the cries of alarm that were promptly raised within the United States, insisted that such attacks did not constitute "escalation" or a widening of the war. "We think that these targets are directly related to the enemy's capacity to move material into South Vietnam to kill American boys," President Johnson explained; but, he said, the attacks were in no wise "intended as any threat to Communist China." "We believe," the President added, "that Peking knows that the United States does not seek to widen the war in Vietnam."[73]

It was true that the Chinese had from time to time been given private assurances that the United States had no intention of attacking their territory or, for that matter, sending ground forces into

North Vietnam. One such assurance, according to report, had been conveyed as recently as June 14 at one of the periodic meetings of the U.S. and Chinese Ambassadors in Warsaw. But would the Chinese continue to rely on these assurances when U.S. planes were bombing only ten miles from their frontier? Anxiety was redoubled on August 21 when it was learned that two U.S. jets had actually been shot down over Chinese territory while taking evasive action after a bombing raid near Hanoi. "With all precautions taken, you are going to have incidents like this one," said White House Press Secretary George Christian. But, he repeated, "We're confident Peking is aware that the United States does not seek involvement of Red China."[74]

Communist China did not, in fact, show any great alarm about the new bombing extensions. Its attention was engaged at the moment in a serious crisis with Great Britain over developments in Hong Kong;[75] and its description of the latest "U.S. air violations" as "blatant provocation against the Chinese people" was dismissed in Washington as no more than "routine squawking."[76] The Soviet Union, too, seemed disinclined to modify its stand in any significant way. A harshly critical statement disseminated by the Tass agency[77] spoke vaguely of eventual "retaliatory steps" but seemed to have been issued primarily for the record. The official newspaper *Izvestia* asserted that the United States and China were actually operating on the basis of a tacit understanding: "Do not interfere with us in Vietnam and we will not touch you."[78]

At all events, bombing near Communist China was rapidly establishing itself as a recognized element in U.S. strategy, and new targets were added to the approved list even as the internal debate about the morality, diplomatic expediency, and military effectiveness of the air war was rising to new heights of intensity. Throughout the month of August, a parade of military figures which included Admiral Sharp, General Earle G. Wheeler, the Chairman of the Joint Chiefs of Staff, and the uniformed heads of the Army, Navy, Marine Corps, and Air Force went before the Stennis subcommittee to extol the air offensive and urge its extension to still other "lucrative" targets. Their recommendations were warmly echoed in a formal report of the subcommittee, issued on August 31, which bitterly complained of past restraints, demanded that the air offensive be pressed "in the most effective way possible," and specifically called for "closing the port of Haiphong, isolating it from the rest of the country, striking all meaningful targets with a military significance and increasing the interdiction of the lines of communication from Red China."[79]

More noteworthy than this reiteration of familiar views was the disclosure that they were not shared but, in part at least, were strongly opposed by the Secretary of Defense. With his analytical and statistical approach to military problems, Mr. McNamara seemed far less convinced than the military chiefs concerning the potentialities of the bombing offensive. The bombing of the North, he assured the Stennis subcommittee on August 25, was no substitute for an effective "counterinsurgency campaign" in the South. Admittedly it had made infiltration from the North more difficult, hurt the North's warmaking capacity, and "put a high price tag" on its continued aggression. Beyond this, in Mr. McNamara's opinion, there was not much the bombing could accomplish even if existing restrictions were lifted, harbors mined, ports bombed, and the risks of confrontation with the U.S.S.R. or China disregarded. Short of a direct attack on North Vietnam's population, which no one was advocating, Mr. McNamara seemed to feel that no amount of bombing would force Ho Chi Minh's regime into submission, compel it to come to the negotiating table, or even cut off the infiltration of men and supplies into South Vietnam.[80]

Though President Johnson insisted that there was no "deep division" among his advisers on bombing policy,[81] most observers gained the impression that Secretary McNamara had already lost his anti-bombing argument within the councils of the administration. Military developments in the following weeks would tend to bear out this impression. But Mr. McNamara's apparent dissent was mild indeed compared with that of Senators Fulbright, Mansfield, Robert Kennedy, and others, both Democratic and Republican, who were increasingly questioning not only the air war but the whole course of U.S. involvement in Vietnam. Particularly objectionable to Senator Fulbright and others had been the President's frequent citation of the so-called Tonkin Gulf Resolution of 1964,[82] adopted as an expression of congressional solidarity at a particularly critical moment of the war, as a justification for his whole subsequent line of action. A series of Foreign Relations Committee hearings initiated by Senator Fulbright in mid-August with a view to redefining the term "national commitment"[83] had served as a running counterattraction to the Stennis hearings and a sounding board for the expression of "dovish" sentiments which made up in earnestness for anything they might lack in novelty.

The debate in Congress and the nation during these August weeks had been further embittered by conflicting views with respect to South Vietnam's political evolution and the presidential and senatorial elections that were now scheduled to be held in that country on September 3. The prospect that a genuinely democratic regime could emerge from this process of "nation-building" had never been rated very highly by unofficial observers, given the distracted state of the country and the entrenched position of the military junta. Some influential Americans, Ambassador Lodge among them, had maintained that it would be a positive mistake to exclude the military from authority in the midst of a war for national survival. The military, in any case, were still in control and seemed bound to exercise a great if not predominant influence on the outcome of the elections. In addition, Marshal Ky's announced intention of running for the presidency had appeared to many observers virtually to ensure his election and, with it, the perpetuation of military rule.

South Vietnam's military leaders were not, however, united among themselves. Months earlier, there had developed the possibility of a dangerous split within the ruling group with the disclosure that Chief of State Thieu was also harboring presidential ambitions and was even prepared to run against Marshal Ky, his own Prime Minister. Under strong pressure from his military colleagues—supplemented, perhaps, by advice from the U.S. Embassy—Marshal Ky eventually agreed to step aside, leave the presidential candidacy to General Thieu, and himself become a candidate for Vice-President on General Thieu's ticket. But the military authorities were less considerate of challengers from outside their own group. On their orders, two of the most prominent (and least bellicose) presidential candidates were disqualified in July by the Constituent Assembly, which had remained in session during the transitional period. One of these was the exiled General Duong Van Minh ("Big Minh"), who had led the coup against the late President Diem in 1963 and still retained considerable popularity in the country. The other was Au Truong Thanh, a respected economist and declared "peace" candidate who disclaimed Communist sympathies but had urged a halt in bombing, a cease-fire, and negotiations to end the conflict, thus convincing the junta of his unsuitability. Although all candidates, including Thieu and Ky, were expressing themselves as favoring peace negotiations under varying conditions, Thanh's program had been by far the most specific in this regard.

With unorthodox opinions denied an effective outlet, the election campaign increasingly took on the appearance of a one-sided contest between the military, as represented by Thieu and Ky, and a disorganized opposition that seemed predestined to scatter its votes among ten different presidential candidates, some of them old-line politicians and others comparative unknowns. Since the government controlled the news and had maintained censorship of the press in defiance of the new constitution, it was difficult to see how Thieu and Ky could lose even if the conduct of the elections was technically unexceptionable—and even if they consented to meet their civilian opponents in open debate, as they refused to do until the closing days of the campaign. The result of the whole process, it seemed to most observers, would be merely a continuation of military rule behind a new institutional façade.

An electoral campaign conducted under such conditions was naturally viewed abroad with a cynicism that bordered on despair. Critics of U.S. policy found confirmation of their darkest assumptions; even administration supporters were inclined to ask anew what kind of regime the United States was really fighting for. The prevailing pessimism was scarcely lessened by reports of White House admonitions to Ky and Thieu or by assurances from Ambassador Bunker and others that the campaign was proceeding without major irregularities. Nevertheless a group of governors and other prominent Americans agreed to go to South Vietnam and observe the elections under the guidance of former Ambassador Lodge. Twenty-three other nations also sent observers on South Vietnam's invitation, although U Thant declined to act on a request for official U.N. observation.

For an election held under such dismaying auguries, the outcome of the September 3 voting disclosed a number of encouraging features. Polling was necessarily limited to secure areas, yet no fewer than 56 per cent of South Vietnam's eligible voting population of 8.5 million went to the polls in spite of a concerted campaign of Vietcong terrorism. To most of the official U.S. observers, the actual voting seemed fair enough and even comparable to elections in the United States. Other foreign observers, according to a State Department summary, also considered that the election had been "con-

ducted remarkably smoothly and fairly in light of the wartime conditions and Vietcong harassment," that the Saigon government "made
every attempt to hold an honest and free election, and that voting
officials had demonstrated a high level of efficiency."[84]

As expected, Thieu and Ky emerged as the winning candidates,
though with only one-third of the popular vote. The major surprise
of the election was the second-place showing of another peace advocate, Truong Dinh Dzu, whose 17.2 per cent of the total was enough
to convince most observers that peace sentiment within the country
would have to be more fully taken into account by any future government. Despite the clean bill of health issued in Washington, Mr.
Dzu and other defeated candidates were quick to condemn the elections as fraudulent, and it was only under further military pressure
that the Assembly later validated the election results. Some eyebrows
were also raised by the make-up of the new 60-man Senate, in which
the disciplined Roman Catholic electorate captured some 27 seats
despite the fact that they represented only 10 per cent of the country's population. The implications of this phenomenon could be
better assessed after the election of a House of Representatives and
the installation of the newly elected President and Vice-President,
scheduled for later in the year. Meanwhile it could at least be acknowledged that the people of South Vietnam had acquitted themselves with dignity in difficult circumstances.

Whatever might be said in criticism of the elections, moreover,
they clearly represented no triumph for the Vietcong and did nothing
to further that group's political ambitions. Although it seemed to be
maintaining its strength in the field, there could be little doubt that
the Vietcong had suffered heavily in the past months and that some
of its individual members, if not the leadership, had become seriously
discouraged. The rate of defections had doubled since 1966.

A further hint of changing enemy attitudes could be found in a
new political program drawn up in August by the South Vietnamese
National Liberation Front and later given wide circulation.[85] While
reaffirming the determination to overthrow the "U.S. puppet regime"
and drive out "the cruel U.S. aggressors," it also stressed the Front's
intention of holding "free general elections" and setting up a broadly
representative "national unity democratic government." This change
of emphasis seemed not to affect the essence of the Communist program but could conceivably make it easier to include the N.L.F. in

future peace arrangements. Meanwhile, there was no indication whatever that the insurgency was about to collapse; yet there did remain a question as to how long it could be maintained in view of its apparent failure to win broad support and the relentless punishment to which it was being subjected.

9 : The San Antonio Formula

The question of ability to hold out under punishment was also not without application to the United States. If Hanoi and the N.L.F. had scorned the opportunity to negotiate a disadvantageous peace, it was presumably because they hoped that a failure of American will would eventually open the way to an advantageous one. Most observers, indeed, had by this time concluded that Hanoi and its associates would hold on at least until the U.S. election of 1968 before resigning themselves to any fundamental reassessment of their position. In the meantime, developments on the American scene seemed calculated to sustain a belief that American resolve might weaken decisively in 1968 or possibly even in 1967.

For the United States had also suffered both morally and materially in recent land, air, and sea combats. By September, American casualties sustained in 1967 exceeded those of all the previous six years. As autumn approached, the ground war was heating up once more and the Marines at Conthien and other outposts below the Demilitarized Zone were coming under murderous fire from North Vietnamese positions across the border. American opinion, which thus far had broadly sustained the President's policy in spite of loud dissent at the extremes, appeared increasingly impatient with the whole philosophy of limited war and graduated pressure. "Win or get out" was the slogan that now began to gain increasing currency.

The administration, which plainly had no intention of "getting out," still appeared in two minds about adopting a full-scale "win" policy of the sort the Stennis subcommittee had urged. Secretary McNamara, preoccupied as ever with the infiltration of manpower from North to South, disclosed plans to construct an electronic barrier or warning system below the Demilitarized Zone to make the North-South passage more difficult. At the same time, however, the air assault on North Vietnam was further intensified in what seemed a sharp deviation from Mr. McNamara's views. In authorizing a further series of attacks on the rail and road communications leading from China, the administration admittedly took a calculated risk so far as the Chinese reaction was concerned. While he could offer no "gold-plated guarantees" about Chinese conduct, Secretary Rusk observed, the United States had "no designs on China" and it was his opinion that Peking would be "most ill-advised" to come into the war.[86]

In addition to continued bombing of the land routes from China, the United States now undertook to strike directly at North Vietnam's maritime supply routes through the bombing of port installations and communications. Here again it plainly deviated from the views of Secretary McNamara, who had told the Stennis subcommittee that most of North Vietnam's imported military equipment actually came by land and that even the closure of the three major ports of Haiphong, Hongay, and Campha would not prevent it from maintaining the level of military operations in the South. Nevertheless, U.S. planes returned to Campha on September 10 for their first attack on the port installations as such. Two days later came the opening of a series of attacks on the Haiphong area which focused on the bridges between docks and mainland and seemed to aim at isolating the port in exactly the way the Stennis group had recommended. Early in October, U.S. planes attacked another of North Vietnam's MIG airfields in apparent disregard of warnings that the elimination of suitable bases within Vietnam might force the MIG's to operate out of China, thus multiplying the risk of incidents.

Midway in this intensified bombing offensive, the U.N. General Assembly opened its 22nd Regular Session in New York amid an almost universal demand that the United States stop bombing altogether before the situation became even more dangerous. U Thant, citing unconfirmed reports of an agreement by "some of its sympathizers" to supply North Vietnam with volunteer airmen and other technicians, insisted afresh that if the United States would only stop bombing unconditionally, meaningful talks could begin within three or four weeks.[87] Such an assurance, however, still remained much too indefinite for the United States. The real question, as Ambassador Goldberg pointed out in addressing the Assembly on September 21, was not whether there "could" but whether there actually "would" be negotiations if the bombing were halted. What exactly would

Hanoi do, and what would its friends do, to advance the cause of peace if the bombing stopped?[88] Conciliatory in tone and obviously the product of much deliberation in Washington, Mr. Goldberg's address stopped well short of offering the unilateral halt in bombing that most U.N. delegations regarded as the only meaningful gesture the United States could make.

Nothing had really changed in the U.S. position, Soviet Foreign Minister Andrei A. Gromyko told the Assembly next day; and his further statement that peace in Vietnam depended on the withdrawal of the "aggressors"[89] indicated that nothing had changed in the Soviet position either. Western statesmen who conferred with Gromyko during his days in New York found him less than ever inclined to lend a hand in reconvening the Geneva Conference or exerting a peaceful influence in Hanoi. There, the Goldberg speech was unceremoniously dismissed as a "new American-style trick."[90]

Mr. Goldberg had said nothing definite in his speech about the precise conditions on which the United States would insist in connection with any cessation of the bombing. There is evidence, however, that Washington had by this time receded from the far-reaching demands incorporated in the President's February letter to Ho Chi Minh. At that time, Mr. Johnson had taken the position that the bombing could stop only when he was assured that the infiltration into South Vietnam had ceased.[91] More recently, the United States had apparently indicated to Hanoi that it would not hold out for a cessation of infiltration but would be satisfied if Hanoi would refrain from taking advantage of a bombing halt to increase the level of its military effort.

According to some accounts, this proposition had been formally put to Hanoi as early as August 25, in the midst of the newly intensified air offensive, and had been further emphasized by several brief interruptions in the bombing.[92] This exercise having yielded no positive result, a version of the new U.S. terms was now made public by the President himself in an important address delivered on September 29 to the National Legislative Conference in San Antonio, Texas. Mr. Johnson's defense of U.S. policy in Vietnam was no less resolute than on earlier occasions; but he also took the opportunity to restate his conditions for a bombing halt in language that seemed deliberately less precise, and therefore less uncompromising, than he had hitherto employed. "The United States," the President said in what was later to become known as the San Antonio formula, "is willing to stop all aerial and naval bombardment of North Vietnam when this will lead promptly to productive discussions. We, of course, assume that while discussions proceed, North Vietnam would not take advantage of the bombing cessation or limitation."[93]

In San Antonio, this might seem a rather generous assumption. It was not so regarded in Hanoi. The use of "vague terms and circuitous contentions" did not make U.S. intentions any the less "threadbare," said *Nhan Dan,* Hanoi's Communist Party newspaper. The United States, *Nhan Dan* insisted, had no right to ask North Vietnam for any conditions whatsoever, but must itself "put an unconditional end to all war acts" in North Vietnam. From the tone of its commentaries it seemed only too clear that despite the obvious pain inflicted by U.S. bombing, Hanoi still held firmly to its basic demand that the United States not only stop the bombing but get out of Vietnam and turn the southern half of the country over to the National Liberation Front.[94]

Yet even the harshest restatements of the North Vietnamese attitude could not discourage the widespread assumption that a halt in the bombing would pave the way for talks—or the further, even more questionable assumption that talks, if held, would lead to useful results. Within the United States itself, support for the administration's Vietnam policy appeared to be dwindling from day to day. While congressmen raised their voices to demand a far-reaching redefinition of U.S. objectives, administration spokesmen like Secretary Rusk and Vice-President Humphrey insisted more vehemently than ever that Vietnam was vital to America's own security as well as to world peace. Perseverence in Vietnam, Mr. Rusk implied, was an essential element in meeting the foreseeable threat of "a billion Chinese . . . armed with nuclear weapons." To call in question the reliability of American commitments, he warned, could mean "mortal danger" for the United States and "catastrophe for all mankind."[95]

As official tempers mounted, unofficial protest against the war also moved toward a new climax. On the weekend of October 21-22, National Guardsmen and regular Army paratroops were called to Washington to face an assemblage of some 35,000 to 50,000 peace demonstrators who had announced their intention of immobilizing the Pentagon, although they were eventually persuaded to limit themselves to non-violent protest.

10 : No Peace in Sight

To the extent that they aimed at bringing about a reduction in the violence of conflict, the activities of American peace demonstrators during the autumn of 1967 must be accounted a signal failure. They did not shake, and may even have fortified, the administration's conviction that the only way to achieve a satisfactory peace was to intensify the military pressure until Hanoi stopped fighting. Still less could such manifestations have been expected to weaken Hanoi's apparent determination to persevere, no matter how heavy the sacrifice, in the hope of an eventual reversal of American policy. With both sides still intent on seeking a solution by force of arms, the conflict was to reach still greater heights of ferocity as the year moved toward its close.

Disregarding the national and international clamor for a halt in the bombing, the United States further stepped up its air offensive in the Hanoi-Haiphong area in the last days of October, multiplying its attacks on jet bases, power plants, shipyards, and other targets until the November rains began to interfere with bombing operations. Concurrently, the enemy initiated a series of savage attacks on U.S. positions at Locninh, Dakto, and other points in the Central Highlands. With unprecedented fury and a disregard of casualties that recalled the fanaticism of North Korean troops in 1950-51, North Vietnamese and Vietcong units attacked again and again in what Hanoi was soon acclaiming as the commencement of a great new "winter-spring offensive." Although U.S. military authorities were prompt to declare the offensive a failure, they could not ignore the heavy casualties sustained by their own forces or the weakened defense of coastal areas as troops were drawn inland to meet the new challenge.

Fighting around Dakto was still in full swing in mid-November when General Westmoreland and Ambassador Bunker returned to Washington for another round of high-level strategy conferences. To the surprise of many baffled citizens, the visitors breathed no word of discouragement but reported gratifying progress in almost every sector of the war effort, always excepting the still lagging pacification program. The adversary, General Westmoreland conceded, had not yet realized the impossibility of winning. Nevertheless, he asserted, the infiltration rate had been reduced, enemy ranks were thinning, and "the end begins to come into view." Estimates of total Communist strength, according to General Westmoreland, had been reduced from 285,000 to 242,000, exclusive of political cadres. If the bombing continued, he suggested, the United States might even be able to begin token withdrawals of its own forces within another two years.[96]

A significant by-product of these discussions was an authoritative indication that there would be no further increase in American forces once the authorized level of 525,000 had been reached. (Current U.S. strength in Vietnam was about 468,000.) At his November 17 news conference, the President tersely disclosed that he and General Westmoreland had discussed the question of troop levels at some length and that the General anticipated no increase above the levels already approved. As though to prevent any misinterpretation of this announcement, the President went on to reaffirm the U.S. commitment to South Vietnam, insisted once again that the United States would hold out for an "honorable peace," and warned Hanoi against gambling on the outcome of the 1968 elections or imagining that it would be easier to "make an inside deal" with another President.[97]

A conspicuous element in the "success stories" proliferating in Washington in connection with the Bunker-Westmoreland visit was the reported progress of "nation-building" as registered in South Vietnam's most recent elections and subsequent transition to constitutional government. As in the military field, however, administration optimism concerning the political picture in South Vietnam contrasted sharply with the assessments of unofficial observers. There had been no serious complaint about the elections to the House of Representatives, which had been carried out without major incident on October 22 and produced a somewhat more balanced membership than that of the new Senate. But much more serious reservations were already being expressed about the new, nominally civilian administration which had assumed office on October 31 with the swearing in of President Thieu as chief executive and the relegation of Marshal Ky to the comparative obscurity of the vice-presidency. To most Americans whose judgment was unhampered by official responsibility, the new team in Saigon looked neither very progressive nor especially receptive toward peace opportunities. The make-up of the new cabinet headed by Premier Nguyen Van Loc was uncomfortably reminiscent of the military government it was ostensibly replacing. Any hope that the cause of "revolutionary development" would receive a decisive impetus from the advent of a civilian regime was already evaporating.

Nor did the change of administration in Saigon seem likely to contribute anything substantial toward political conciliation, either within South Vietnam or between North and South. To be sure, President Thieu had promised in his inaugural address to "open widely the door of peace" and urge Hanoi to join him at the conference table.[98] The tone of Thieu's remarks, however, was nothing if not militant. He obviously did not share the widely held view that a pause in bombing could be a useful prelude to peace negotiations. Although he had talked vaguely in the past about a readiness to confer with emissaries of the National Liberation Front,[99] he seemed to entertain no serious thought of entering into discussion with his government's adversaries.

In Washington, this stand was now becoming a source of embarrassment. The National Liberation Front, since the release of its new political program at the beginning of September, had been showing increased interest in bringing its ideas to world attention, asserting its independence of Hanoi, and publicizing its proposals looking toward the formation of a coalition government in South Vietnam. In the course of September, the N.L.F. had even raised the question of sending representatives to the U.N. Assembly in order to maintain informal contact with national delegations there. This idea, it is true, had found no favor with the United States. Official Washington continued to look upon the N.L.F. as a mere Communist "front" and interpreted the coalition idea as a typical Communist device for misleading public opinion in order to gain power. At a later stage, it would cite captured documents purporting to substantiate its view.[100]

Nevertheless, the growing prominence of the N.L.F. in current peace discussions would seem to have contributed to a further relaxation of the U.S. attitude with respect to the role that organization might play not only in peace talks but, ultimately, in a pacified South Vietnam. After originally opposing any Vietcong role in peace talks, the United States had long since indicated that it would have no objection if N.L.F. representatives were included in a North Vietnamese peace delegation. An indication of a still further shift in the American position was offered by Ambassador Goldberg when he appeared before the Senate Foreign Relations Committee on November 2 to testify on a pending resolution, sponsored by Senator Mansfield, which asked the administration to consider bringing the Vietnam question before the U.N. Security Council.

Despite past disappointments, Mr. Goldberg disclosed, the United

States was already circulating among Security Council members a draft resolution that called for an international conference aimed at establishing a permanent peace in Southeast Asia on the principles of the Geneva agreements. Disappointingly, the U.S. Representative reported, his consultations had disclosed "a general unwillingness" for the Security Council to involve itself with the Vietnam question in this or any other form. But Mr. Goldberg also stated in response to questions that the United States would be prepared to support participation by the National Liberation Front in any discussion that might be held by the Security Council. Further, he implied, it would not object to N.L.F. participation in an actual peace conference if that was the wish of the conference itself.[101] This stand was publicly endorsed next day by the State Department.[102]

While Senators pondered these words, administration spokesmen continued to insist that their readiness for peace negotiations was equaled only by their determination to continue the war as long as might be necessary to protect the security of Southeast Asia and the United States. President Johnson, speaking aboard the carrier *Enterprise* off the California coast on November 11, created a momentary sensation by suggesting that peace talks could even take place on "a neutral ship on a neutral sea."[103] Though obviously skeptical about the prospects for action through the United Nations, the President offered no formal objection to the Mansfield resolution, which the Senate unanimously endorsed on November 30 in an unusual display of harmony between administration critics and supporters.[104]

Ambassador Goldberg thereupon resumed his consultations at the United Nations while awaiting instructions from Washington to request a formal meeting of the Security Council. As anticipated, however, the outlook for such a meeting continued anything but favorable. Hanoi continued to deny the competence of the U.N. to deal with the question at all. The Soviet Union and France were definitely opposed to Security Council consideration, and U Thant did not disguise his own doubts about the usefulness of trying to involve the world organization. On December 20, Mr. Goldberg indicated that his efforts were being abandoned in view of what he called the "intransigence" of "certain members" of the Security Council.[105]

Not peace negotiations, but a fiercer and wider war appeared to be in prospect as the holiday season approached amid the usual conflicting announcements concerning the belligerents' plans for brief, unsupervised truces at Christmas and New Year's. The news that Secretary McNamara would soon be leaving the Pentagon, announced in the wake of the Westmoreland-Bunker visit, was widely interpreted as a sign that the United States intended to cast off all restraints in the conduct of its air and ground operations. A week-long series of raids on the Hanoi-Haiphong area, initiated during a break in the weather in mid-December, appeared to bear out this interpretation; indeed, there were reports that the United States not only had relaxed previous restrictions on its pilots but had consciously adopted an air strategy aimed at breaking the enemy's will rather than merely interdicting the flow of supplies.[106]

Ground operations were also intensifying beyond previous experience, though here the initiative lay with an adversary whose offensive spirit and indifference to casualties were frankly baffling to U.S. military authorities. A sense of urgency, not to say desperation, appeared to have infected the enemy battalions. To some it seemed that they must be on the verge of collapse and were making a last violent effort before resigning themselves to peace negotiations; others read their behavior as a maximum bid to influence U.S. opinion against the war in advance of the 1968 election campaign. Enemy strength, in any case, seemed not to have been reduced to nearly the extent that General Westmoreland had supposed. Revised estimates made public on December 19 placed total enemy manpower in the range of 418,000 to 483,000[107]—almost exactly equal to the 486,000 U.S. troops who would be in Vietnam by the years' end.

An additional worry during these weeks was the prospect that the ground war might spill over into Cambodia and perhaps into Laos and North Vietnam, all areas where allied ground forces had thus far been forbidden to operate. Despite Cambodian denials, there seemed no doubt that Vietcong and North Vietnamese forces were freely moving in and out of Cambodian territory and using it as a "sanctuary" where they could rest and regroup without fear of allied attack. Former President Eisenhower and President Thieu, among others, had expressed themselves as strongly in favor of "hot pursuit" of enemy units across the Cambodian frontier.[108] Responsible U.S. authorities were known to be giving serious thought to this possibility, and even to be considering a "quarantine" of Cambodian territory to prevent supplies from reaching the enemy across its territory. There was also talk of moving into Laos in an attempt to cut off infiltration over the so-called "Ho Chi Minh trail," a step that was strongly opposed by the Laotian Government despite the cooperation it was providing in air operations against the infiltration routes. Finally, voices were being raised in favor of dropping the restrictions against ground operations north of the 17th parallel, where enemy concentrations in and north of the Demilitarized Zone continued to present a serious hazard to U.S. units just to the south.

Such discussions inevitably raised again the old question as to what the Communist powers would do if the war were to be expanded beyond its previous territorial limits. Already Communist China had promised "staunch backing" to Cambodia if the United States extended the war to its soil. A Soviet statement of December 10 warned harshly against extending the war into Laos and Cambodia.[109] To American diplomatic overtures aimed at forestalling such an eventuality, Cambodia's Prince Norodom Sihanouk hotly responded by predicting an American invasion and promising to fight it with the support of the Communist countries. Only at the end of the year did an apparent modification of the Prince's attitude give hope that the Cambodian phase of the problem could be adjusted by strengthening the international machinery set up by the Geneva Conference to safeguard Cambodia's neutrality.[110]

In addition, the United States was now engaged in growing difficulty with its own allies in South Vietnam, principally because of the differing approaches of the two governments to the problem of the Vietcong and the N.L.F. Neither Washington nor Saigon felt any special tenderness for the Vietcong, whose calculated cruelty was demonstrated afresh on December 6 in an attack on a peaceful hamlet with flame throwers and grenades that killed some 200 "montagnard" refugees. But while the United States now seemed inclined to overlook the Vietcong's moral shortcomings to the extent of admitting it to participation in peace talks and even, perhaps, to a governmental role, the Saigon government remained grimly opposed to a trend in which it undoubtedly perceived a serious threat to its own position. On one recent occasion, it had even arrested a "middle-level" Vietcong representative who was trying to get in touch with Ambassador Bunker.[111]

These differences were sharpened by the increased attention being given the Vietcong and the N.L.F. in connection with the continuing peace initiatives at the U.N. and elsewhere. Even U.S. Government quarters appeared to be engaged in a far-reaching reappraisal. "The

N.L.F. is not all Communist," Vice-President Humphrey stated in a December 7 radio interview. "Some of the non-Communist members," the Vice-President speculated, might even split off and enter a coalition government. To quiet Saigon's understandable dismay at such a prospect, the State Department promptly declared that American policy with respect to the N.L.F. was unchanged. At the same time, it implied that the United States would indeed favor any South Vietnamese initiatives looking toward direct contact with N.L.F. elements.[112]

President Johnson bore down even more heavily on this point in a television interview presented on December 19, at a moment when the N.L.F. was receiving increased publicity thanks to the recent circulation of its program to all members of the United Nations.[113] Peacemaking, President Johnson now emphasized, was essentially a task for the leadership and people of South Vietnam, rather than for outside parties. The war, he suggested, could be ended in "weeks" or even "days" if only the other side would face "five simple facts." All "the other side" really needed to do, the President indicated, was to (1) respect the Demilitarized Zone, (2) allow the unity of Vietnam to be settled by negotiation, (3) get out of Laos, (4) stop infiltrating Laos, and (5) permit the South Vietnamese to work out their own future on the basis of "a one-man, one-vote constitutional system."[114]

Like earlier statements of U.S. peace aims, the President's five-point plan appeared to call for rather heavy sacrifices by the adversary —substantially, the abandonment of virtually everything the Communists professed to be fighting for. Hanoi, characteristically enough, was to dismiss the Johnson program as a mere cloak for further intensification of the war.[115] The significant point, however, was not so much the content of the new, five-point peace program as the President's emphasis on the technique of peacemaking. The correct procedure, Mr. Johnson suggested, had been indicated by President Thieu himself in his supposed expression of readiness to engage in "informal talks with members of the N.L.F." A favorable response to the Vietnamese President's "statesmanlike . . . suggestions," Mr. Johnson implied, would work wonders. Presumably, the American President was referring to a broadcast interview of September 10 in which the then President-elect Thieu had said that while he would never negotiate directly with the Vietcong as a political entity, he would be glad to talk with anyone from the N.L.F. "at lower level or at high level."[116] But this random comment, made more than three months earlier, was scarcely the well-pondered initiative that President Johnson now chose to make of it.

In view of President Thieu's repeatedly expressed abhorrence of the N.L.F. and all its works, the South Vietnamese leader was not unjustified in feeling that his position that had been misrepresented in the December 19 broadcast. President Johnson had made a mistake, Mr. Thieu implied next day in conversation with newsmen. The only N.L.F. people to whom he would consider talking were former N.L.F. members who had "come over to our side"[117]—in other words, defected. But since such individuals would obviously not be qualified to speak for the N.L.F., it was difficult to see how such discussions could advance the cause of peace in the way that President Johnson now seemed to envisage.

The danger of an open split between Saigon and Washington was lessened by the fact that the two Presidents were about to meet in Australia at memorial services for the late Prime Minister Harold Holt, which were also attended by the heads of all the other allied governments with troops in Vietnam.[118] In conversations in the Australian capital on December 21, Messrs. Johnson and Thieu were able to agree on an ambiguous joint statement that gave equal weight to their respective views even if it failed to reconcile them completely. In a sense, they agreed, the question was academic. Perceiving "no sign that North Vietnam was prepared to take any of the many avenues to peace that had been opened," the two leaders could at least agree that their governments had "no alternative to continuing appropriate military actions."[119]

Military action was clearly uppermost in President Johnson's mind as he flew from Australia to Thailand and thence to Camranh Bay, South Vietnam, on December 23. In the course of a brief visit with American troops, the President reaffirmed the American commitment more vigorously, not to say militantly, then ever before. The enemy, he declared, was "holding desperately . . . trying to buy time—hoping that our nation's will does not match his will." "We are not going to yield," the President insisted. "We are not going to shimmy. We are going to wind up with a peace with honor which all Americans seek."[120]

Still on December 23, the President flew across South Asia, with a quick stop in Pakistan, and on to Italy for an exchange of greetings with Italian leaders and a hastily arranged conference with Pope Paul VI at the Vatican. Increasingly critical of the attitude of both sides in the conflict, the Pope apparently took the opportunity to renew his plea for a halt in the bombing of North Vietnam. The President, on his part, not only asked for papal intercession on behalf of American prisoners of war but explained again his insistence on reciprocity (or, in the Pope's phrase, "mutual restraining") in any steps to scale down the conflict. Clearly there was no meeting of minds on this vital point, but the President would seem at least to have offered profuse assurances "that the disappointments we had known in the past would not deter us from trying any reasonable route to negotiations."[121]

Yet the number of "reasonable" routes to negotiation appeared sadly limited. Ambassador Goldberg's soundings with regard to a Security Council discussion had come to nothing; so had the President's attempt to encourage direct discussions between Saigon and the N.L.F. A third possibility, an extension of the *pro forma* Christmas and New Year cease-fires as a point of departure for peace negotiations, aroused far less hope than in earlier years. No such extensions were in fact arranged, and the actual cease-fire periods were marred by more than the usual number of incidents in which Vietcong or North Vietnamese units apparently failed to heed the orders issued by superior commands.

Conceivably the obstacles to negotiation might still be reduced by the spontaneous action of one or both Vietnamese governments. President Thieu had promised during the campaign to submit a direct proposal to Hanoi; and South Vietnamese Foreign Minister Tran Van Do, passing through Paris in late December, reported that his government was in fact transmitting a proposal involving a return to the Geneva arrangements and a "regrouping" of the fighting forces on either side of the 17th parallel[122]—in other words, an enemy evacuation. Hanoi made no immediate comment on this rather disadvantageous proposition. It did, however, choose this moment to restate its demand for a halt in U.S. bombing in terms that seemed to clear up at least one of the uncertainties that had subsisted throughout the past year and could thus be interpreted as a step toward negotiations.

"The U.S. Government," North Vietnamese Foreign Minister

Trinh observed on December 29, "has unceasingly claimed that it wants to talk with Hanoi but has received no response. If the U.S. Government truly wants to talk, it must . . . first of all stop unconditionally the bombing and all other acts of war against the D.R.V. After the United States has ended unconditionally the bombing and all other acts of war against the D.R.V., the D.R.V. will hold talks with the United States on questions concerned."[123] Trinh did not say how soon such talks would start, nor what "questions concerned" they would cover. But he did unequivocally state, for the first time, that if the bombing stopped there would—rather than could—be talks. This minor verbal change would be sufficient in itself to start a new wave of hope—and of demands for a cessation of bombing—as 1968 began.

What the Trinh statement emphatically did *not* promise was a modification of basic Communist aims. On the contrary, the North Vietnamese Foreign Minister specifically reaffirmed Hanoi's repeated promise to "fight the U.S. aggressors in order to defend the North, liberate the South and advance toward the peaceful unification of the country."[124] So long as Hanoi persisted in its proclaimed intention of determining the political future of South Vietnam—for that was what "liberation" obviously meant in the North Vietnamese vocabulary—it was difficult to see how talks with the United States could do more than confirm the basic opposition of purposes that had animated the struggle from the beginning.

Some U.S. authorities did believe that Hanoi was under growing pressure to moderate its aims in consequence of the punishment it was taking in the air war and the increasingly heavy strain on its own armed forces as well as those of the Vietcong. Yet despite extremely heavy losses in recent months, the Vietcong and North Vietnamese units showed no sign of slackening the rhythm of their "winter-spring offensive," and there were indications as the year ended of an ominous concentration of fresh forces in northern areas near the Laotian frontier. While American military quarters urged more decisive action against enemy "sanctuaries" in Cambodia, Laos, and north of the Demilitarized Zone, political authorities still seemed hopeful that the use of such areas could be curbed by diplomatic means. Developments in this critical matter, one State Department authority observed, were "somewhat more in the laps of the North Vietnamese than . . . of ourselves."[125]

Whatever the future might bring, year-end statistical calculations provided a sobering insight into the price already exacted from Vietnamese and Americans alike. American losses from 1961 through 1967 were listed as 15,997 killed in action and 99,742 wounded, of whom 59,972 had required hospitalization. Americans killed in 1967 alone came to 9,353. Enemy killed since the beginning of the war exceeded 250,000, according to U.S. estimates. Within the past year, Secretary McNamara reported, the opposing forces had lost about 165,000 effectives, including about 88,000 killed in action, 30,000 dead or disabled by wounds, 6,000 taken prisoner, almost 18,000 defectors, and about 25,000 disabled by disease or lost through desertion or other causes.[126]

Reviewing the year's achievements, Secretary McNamara would also report a marked improvement in the security of the South Vietnamese countryside, with 67 per cent of the population now living under allied military protection and some form of continuing administration under the authority of the Republic of Vietnam. But any gains in rural security had also been bought at a heavy price. Within the past twelve months, Vietcong terrorists were said to have killed 3,820 civilians and kidnaped 5,368. Total civilian casualties in South Vietnam in 1967 were estimated at 24,000 killed and 76,000 wounded. Estimates of the number of refugees in South Vietnam, many of them uprooted by American military action, varied from 409,000 to nearly twice that number.

In themselves, such figures conveyed little impression of the human suffering involved, nor did they include the toll exacted by the air war in the North. They did suggest that if the principles at stake in Vietnam were great, the cost of defending them was not less so.

3 : Flames in the Middle East

America's involvement in the postwar Middle East was rooted in considerations not wholly dissimilar to those that had so deeply immersed it in the struggle over Southeast Asia. Here, too, the basic concern of American policy had been to promote the peaceful development of the area's emerging nations and, as an integral part of this endeavor, to check the intrusion of hostile outside influences that might prove inimical to both local and American interests. The existence in the Middle East of special preoccupations like the safety and well-being of the state of Israel and the assurance of an uninterrupted flow of oil supplies had if anything accentuated U.S. sensitivity to the wider dangers that were felt to overhang the area as a whole. The principal outside threat to Middle Eastern security and stability had, not surprisingly, been seen in the expansionist outlook attributed to the U.S.S.R., whose apparent ambitions for preponderance in the area beyond its southern frontiers had been intermittently manifested both during the Stalin era and subsequently.

The United States had not, on the whole, been notably successful in its attempts to encourage orderly development within the Middle East or to maintain effective barriers against Communist penetration. The advance of Communism, it is true, had been a great deal more limited than in the Far East. Although the Russians had established an influential position in the United Arab Republic, Syria, Iraq, and

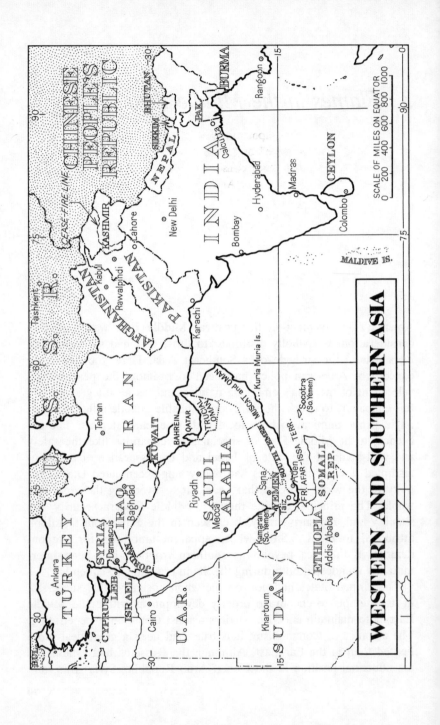

WESTERN AND SOUTHERN ASIA

Algeria, no Middle Eastern or Arab state had actually fallen under Soviet or Communist control. In the main, the issue of Communist penetration had been overshadowed by quarrels and rivalries indigenous to the region. In addition to the long-standing and seemingly immitigable hostility between the Arab states and Israel, the Arab countries themselves had been divided by all manner of jealousies and conflicts, the most important of which had been a growing rift between such "progressive" or "revolutionary" states as the U.A.R., Syria, and Algeria and more conservative, monarchical governments like those of Jordan and Saudi Arabia.

Mainly because the danger of overt Communist takeovers in the Middle East had at most times seemed comparatively remote, the United States had not felt it necessary to intervene in Middle Eastern affairs on the same scale or with the same persistence as in the Far East. The postwar withdrawal of French and British power had left it as the principal representative of Western interests in the region, with a particularly heavy stake in the development and exploitation of its oil resources; but such influence as it possessed had been exerted mainly through diplomatic and economic rather than military channels. While attempting so far as possible to remain on good terms with all the countries of the area, Washington had concentrated since the mid-1950's on three main lines of action.

First had come the attempt to maintain a northern barrier against Soviet penetration, mainly through sponsorship and support of the Central Treaty Organization or CENTO pact linking Great Britain, Turkey, Iran, and Pakistan.

Second had been the attempt to prevent disturbance of the tenuous political order and military balance between Israel and the Arab states—combined, however, with a degree of emotional attachment to Israel which found expression is an evident unwillingness to permit that country to be destroyed by its Arab neighbors as the latter had repeatedly threatened.

Third, and scarcely less important in recent years, had been the support extended to the more conservative Arab governments, particularly Jordan and Saudi Arabia, in their resistance to threats and pressure from the U.A.R. and other "revolutionary" Arab states.

Each of these three lines of action had involved at least implicit opposition to the policies of the Soviet Union as well as the more "progressive" or "revolutionary" forces in the Arab world. The "progressive" Arab mentality, as articulated by President Gamal Abdel Nasser of the U.A.R. and others, was intensely nationalistic and anti-imperialist and therefore characterized by strong hostility to the West as well as to Israel. Appeals to this negative side of the Arab outlook had proved extremely useful to the U.S.S.R. in consolidating the influence gained through assistance on important economic projects—among them the famous Aswan High Dam—and its generous aid in tanks, MIG's, and other modern weapons to the U.A.R., Syria, Iraq, and Algeria.

The United States, by the mid-1960's, had thus begun to find itself at odds with a combination of Arab and Communist governments on virtually every Middle Eastern issue. The CENTO pact, an overt defensive alliance against the Soviet Union, had never been popular in the Arab world, and some of its regional members, like Iran, were on less than friendly terms with their Arab neighbors. In the Arab-Israeli quarrel, American efforts to be fair to both sides had collided with the increasingly anti-Israel position adopted by the U.S.S.R. in its attempt to curry favor with the Arab states. In the quarrel between conservative and revolutionary Arab governments, similarly, the United States had become increasingly alienated from the U.A.R., Syria, and the other countries under Soviet patronage and increasingly identified with active support for Jordan and Saudi Arabia, whose relations with the U.S.S.R. were marked by coolness and mistrust on both sides.

Apart from sporadic military clashes on the frontiers between Israel and its neighbors, this hardening of Middle Eastern alignments had been mainly confined to the levels of political maneuver and competitive arms shipments. Though anxious not to become a "major arms supplier" in the Middle East, the United States had in recent years considered it necessary to supplement the efforts of other Western governments in furnishing modern arms to Israel, Jordan, and Saudi Arabia as a means of balancing the "massive" Soviet arms shipments to the U.A.R., Syria, and other "revolutionary" countries. Yet even such small-scale arms races would tend to increase the scope and intensity of fighting if major hostilities should again break out in the Middle East; and there were, at the beginning of 1967, at least two danger zones where a conflagration could all too easily develop. One of these was the region of the military demarcation lines between Israel and its Arab neighbors, particularly Jordan and Syria, which had become the scene of increasingly serious military clashes in the course of 1966. The other was the remote and turbulent land of Yemen, where civil war had been going on since 1962 and had recurrently threatened to become a cause of hostilities between the U.A.R. and Saudi Arabia, long-standing rivals that had become the partisans of opposite Yemeni factions.

The dangers of this situation were sufficiently evident to anyone who remembered how World War I had developed out of the interplay of Balkan rivalries and great-power alliances. Let a really serious incident occur between any two Middle Eastern states, and their patrons in Washington and Moscow might well be forced to consider whether to back them up at the risk of a confrontation with the other great power. A U.S.-Soviet confrontation over the Middle East could quite conceivably result in global war, as the confrontation over Cuba had very nearly done in 1962. On the other hand, a failure by either power to stand up for the particular interests it had espoused within the region would compromise its prestige both locally and around the world and, in all probability, vastly increase the prestige and influence of the other party.

On the whole, the danger of an all-out confrontation over the Middle East had not appeared particularly acute in recent years in view of the rather cautious attitude in foreign policy that had characterized the Soviet Government since the advent of Brezhnev and Kosygin in 1964. Moscow's behavior on the Vietnam issue had seemed to reflect a strong desire to avoid a clash with the United States, despite its unequivocal support of North Vietnam and the Vietcong. Yet there could obviously be no guarantee that the U.S.S.R. would always refrain from playing with fire, either in the Far East or in the Middle East. Indeed, its encouragement of the "revolutionary" Arab governments had at certain recent periods seemed downright inflammatory, as though the "cold war," restrained in Europe and the Far East, might still be given free rein in the in-between regions.

There had also been signs that Communist China, always on the lookout for opportunities to press its revolutionary offensive against "imperialism," had been seeking to ingratiate itself with extremist Arab elements such as those that centered around the revolutionary government of Syria and the so-called Palestine Liberation Organization headed by Ahmed Shukairy in Cairo. Given the bitter Sino-Soviet rivalry for leadership of the world's revolutionary forces, a Chinese bid for influence in the Middle East might easily act as a spur to the Soviet Union and lead it to display even less caution than might have been true had its own position been less open to challenge.

11 : The Fire Is Laid

These were not the only aspects of the Middle Eastern situation that justified a measure of American uneasiness as 1967 began. CENTO, the "northern tier" alliance erected by Secretary of State John Foster Dulles in the mid-1950's in the hope of sealing off the whole Middle East against Soviet penetration, also looked shakier than at any time since its formation.

Both Soviet and Western policies shared in the responsibility for CENTO's anemic appearance. The U.S.S.R., which had outflanked or "leapfrogged" the northern barrier in the 1950's to gain a lodgment in the Arab states to the south, had proceeded in the 1960's to attack the moral foundations of CENTO itself by ostentatious displays of friendliness, rather than hostility, toward Turkey, Iran, and Pakistan, the alliance's three regional members. Those countries, meanwhile, had grown increasingly disillusioned at the failure of their Western partners, Great Britain and the United States (which was an active participant in the pact, though technically not a member) to support their special interests more vigorously. Turkey had been particularly incensed by the alleged inadequacy of American support for its defense contribution in CENTO and NATO, as well as the U.S. refusal to take its side in the Cyprus dispute with Greece. Pakistan was furious with both the United States and Britain because of their nonsupport in its quarrel with India, which had led to open war in the Subcontinent in 1965. So thoroughly alienated was the Pakistani Government led by Marshal Muhammad Ayub Khan that it now seemed to enjoy closer and more confident relations with Communist China than with its own allies.

Iran, for its part, was gnawed by perpetual dissatisfaction over the scale of the U.S. military aid programs devised for its benefit. By no means inconsiderable by American standards—they totaled in the neighborhood of $1 billion—these programs had remained wholly inadequate to Iran's defense needs as seen by its energetic ruler,

Muhammad Reza Shah. The measure of Iranian discontent was revealed in February 1967 by the disclosure that the Tehran government had turned to the Soviet Union and concluded a large-scale industrial and arms deal whereby Iran would receive some $110 million worth of Soviet-made antiaircraft guns, military trucks, armored troop carriers, and the like as well as a steel mill complex and machine tool factory. In return, Iranian natural gas was to be shipped to the Soviet Union via a specially constructed pipeline.[1] Official reaffirmations of Iran's pledge to CENTO did not disguise the fact that such a deal ran counter to CENTO's whole philosophy, exemplifying the same methods the U.S.S.R. had previously employed with such success in drawing various Arab countries toward its orbit.

Conditions in the Arab world, meanwhile, offered a spectacle of general disorganization and episodic violence that presented continuing opportunities for Soviet maneuver. During the later months of 1966, the U.S.S.R. had greatly increased its popularity in the Arab countries by uncompromisingly supporting the Arab position in a series of U.N. debates growing out of clashes along the Israeli frontiers. The most important of these had been a large-scale Israeli retaliatory raid on the Jordanian village of Es Samu (al-Samu) on November 13 which had, indeed, evoked the censure of all members of the Security Council, including the United States.[2] Concurrently, the U.S.S.R. had moved to undercut the United States and strengthen its own influence in the U.A.R. President Abdel Nasser's improvident financial policies, hostility to Israel, and public denunciations of the United States had created widespread resentment in Washington and become an increasingly serious barrier to the provision of food and other types of American economic aid. While Washington hesitated over Cairo's most recent request for assistance, the U.S.S.R. had come forward with a timely promise to meet one-fourth of the U.A.R.'s wheat requirements in the coming year.[3]

President Abdel Nasser, however, was a man who cherished his own and his country's independence and had gone to some lengths to make it clear that he would never play the role of "stooge" for any foreign power, Soviet or Western. If his government had become increasingly dependent on Soviet military and economic assistance, this was partly because the U.A.R. President had been too ready to antagonize the United States and other Western countries and partly because his concept of a personal role in history had engaged him in a series of far-flung enterprises that far transcended the U.A.R.'s own resources. Not only had the Egyptian leader recurrently attempted to unify the whole of the Arab world under his banner and rid it of such "reactionary" influences as those of King Faisal of Saudi Arabia and King Hussein of Jordan. In addition, he had cast himself as leader of a general crusade against "imperialism" and "colonialism" throughout the Middle East and Africa and, with President Tito of Yugoslavia and the late Prime Minister Jawaharlal Nehru of India, had been a leading exponent of the policy of nonalignment in world affairs—although his concept of nonalignment had impressed most Americans as being heavily weighted in favor of the Soviet Union and against the West.

While his political attitude had never lacked dynamism, Abdel Nasser had not in recent years been particularly bellicose in his attitude toward Israel. He clearly shared the universal Arab view that Israel was a noxious product of "imperialism and Zionism" which must some day be eliminated. For the time being, however, he had seemed not too discontented with the existing situation under which the Suez Canal was closed to Israeli vessels (contrary to a U.N. Security Council resolution of September 1, 1951)[4] and a U.N. Emergency Force was deployed along the U.A.R.-Israeli armistice line to discourage terrorist raids and other belligerent activities in either direction. While endeavoring to keep a step or two ahead of Israel in the race for modern weapons, Abdel Nasser had publicly taken the position that the Arab states were too disunited among themselves to contemplate an early military showdown with their common enemy.[5]

Contrasting with this relative caution toward Israel had been Abdel Nasser's deepening involvement in the affairs of the Arabian peninsula. To a long-standing animosity toward Saudi Arabia and its traditional regime he had of late years added a heavy commitment in support of the new republican government of Yemen, established with Egyptian assistance in 1962 but still under challenge by royalist adherents of the old regime who continued to hold out in the back country with Saudi Arabian support. Even the dispatch of some 70,000 Egyptian troops—more recently reduced to around 50,000—had not sufficed to put down this monarchist resistance movement, although it had helped to ensure that President Abdallah al-Salal and the other authorities of the Yemeni republican government in Sana would do nothing inconsistent with Abdel Nasser's wishes.

Beyond Yemen lay the British-ruled territories of Aden and the Federation of South Arabia, a loosely organized conglomerate of tribal sheikdoms to which Great Britain had announced its intention of granting full independence in 1968. Nationalist and terrorist agitation, openly supported both by Yemen and by the U.A.R. itself, had long been rife in the South Arabian territories and was increasing as the date of independence approached. Although the protagonists of this activity were divided among themselves, the principal nationalist groups were strongly influenced by Nasserist ideas and clearly bent on putting Arab nationalism in the saddle when the British departed. With a little luck, it seemed perfectly conceivable that Abdel Nasser and his partisans might shortly gain full control of both Yemen and South Arabia, thus virtually encircling conservative Saudi Arabia and acquiring a springboard from which they might be able to extend some measure of influence around the Persian Gulf and into Western Africa.

Such possibilities loomed ever more vividly as the Arabian situation boiled and bubbled through the first months of 1967. In Aden, growing anti-British terrorism was aggravated by a three-way fight among rival terrorist groups, the weakest of which supported Saudi Arabia while the other two were identified with the more activist forms of Arab nationalism. A three-man United Nations mission which visited Aden in April, ostensibly to help prepare the transition to independence, found itself caught in the cross fire between these divergent opposition groups and the British-supported government and hastily retired amid a hail of bombs and grenades.[6] The British, already at their wits' end and in no mood to commit their dwindling military resources to another colonial war, intensified the search for some coherent nationalist group to which they could hand power even before their scheduled withdrawal in January 1968.

In Yemen itself, meanwhile, a tenuous cease-fire arrangement which Abdel Nasser and King Faisal had negotiated in 1965 was moving toward complete breakdown as the undefeated royalists prepared to resume full-scale hostilities and the pro-Nasser republicans prepared to meet them. Recurring incidents between the U.A.R. and Saudi Arabia heightened the tension. In January, Abdel Nasser's air force was accused of deliberately attacking a Saudi border town, and the Saudis complained repeatedly of acts of sabotage committed on their territory by infiltrators trained in Yemen by the Egyptians. In addition, Yemeni royalists accused the U.A.R. of carrying out at least two poison gas raids which assertedly caused heavy civilian casualties, although this charge was sharply denied by U.A.R. authorities.

As was its habit, the United States employed such influence as it possessed in encouraging moderation by all the parties concerned in Yemen's affairs. Although the United States had recognized the republican government soon after its establishment, its own position in Yemen remained tenuous and was about to be further impaired by one of the year's more flagrant manifestations of anti-Americanism. A mob attack on the U.S. aid mission in the southern Yemeni city of Taiz on April 26 was followed by the detention of two American aid officials for trial on the surprising charge that they had attempted to destroy the city by firing a bazooka at an ammunition dump. Though quick to deny the charge and withdraw the rest of the aid mission, the United States was obliged to leave the two officials provisionally in Yemini custody. Fear for their lives was increased by further mob scenes and by an atmosphere of growing crisis marked, among other things, by new U.A.R. raids on Saudi Arabian positions. A threatened tragedy was, however, averted when Abdel Nasser himself agreed to intercede with the Yemeni authorities and arrange for the release of the two victims, who were able to leave Yemen on May 17.

This action occurred, surprisingly, at a moment when the Egyptian leader's general attitude had taken on an increasingly disobliging and even defiant character. Throughout the early part of the year, Abdel Nasser's recurrent displays of belligerence had suggested that he was either being driven to desperation by his country's economic problems or, perhaps, hoped to sweep them aside in some bold move on the international front. In a particularly bellicose speech of February 22, apparently inspired by difficulty in meeting his government's indebtedness to the United States and other Western creditors, the Egyptian President had vehemently accused the United States of trying to "strangle" his country through its aid policies. "We shall not repay our debts to anyone who exerts pressure upon us," he thundered.[7] Despite the shouts of approval they invariably elicited from local audiences, such declarations seemed a poor way of securing the additional financial assistance of which the U.A.R. was plainly in need. Further aid from the International Monetary Fund, in particular, had been conditioned on stringent financial reforms which the Cairo government had thus far refused to make even though the Russians themselves had advised it to do so.

These problems were still unsolved at the end of March when Soviet Foreign Minister Gromyko visited Cairo for three days of secret talks. Beyond a published communiqué recording the customary identity of views on Vietnam and other international questions,[8] nothing was revealed concerning the subjects discussed on this occasion or the courses of action that may have been agreed upon. What is known it that six weeks later, on May 13, Abdel Nasser belatedly signified his agreement to the financial reforms demanded by the International Monetary Fund.[9] In other respects, the demeanor of the Egyptian regime in the weeks that followed the Gromyko visit appeared less rather than more conciliatory. In addition to a noticeable truculence in relation to Saudi Arabia, Yemen, and the South Arabian Federation,[10] Abdel Nasser now began to show an intense and increasingly bellicose interest in an alarming situation that had begun to develop between Israel and Syria.

12 : The Match is Held

It was Syria rather than the U.A.R. that had been the prime mover in most of the Arab-Israeli collisions of recent years. Aggressively radical and nationalist even by Arab standards, the military regime nominally headed by Chief of State Nureddin al-Atasi and Premier Yussef Zayen had outdistanced the U.A.R. itself in hostility to the West and the espousal of extremist revolutionary tendencies. Its sponsorship of infiltration and terrorist attacks on Israel, some of them based in Syria itself and others carried out by way of Lebanon or Jordan, had been the principal factor in the succession of frontier clashes that culminated in the Es Samu raid of November 13, 1966. A temporary letup in terrorist activities had followed that occurrence; but by early January of 1967 the frontier raids and bomb attacks had resumed, Israel was again complaining to the Security Council, and Premier Levi Eshkol was warning the Syrians that they courted the danger of fresh retaliatory action.

Secretary-General Thant expressed the view that the local clashes now occurring were essentially a seasonal phenomenon growing out of the activities of Israeli cultivators in the lowlands along the military demarcation line, which Israel claimed as part of its territory. But warnings from General Odd Bull, Chief of Staff of the U.N. Truce

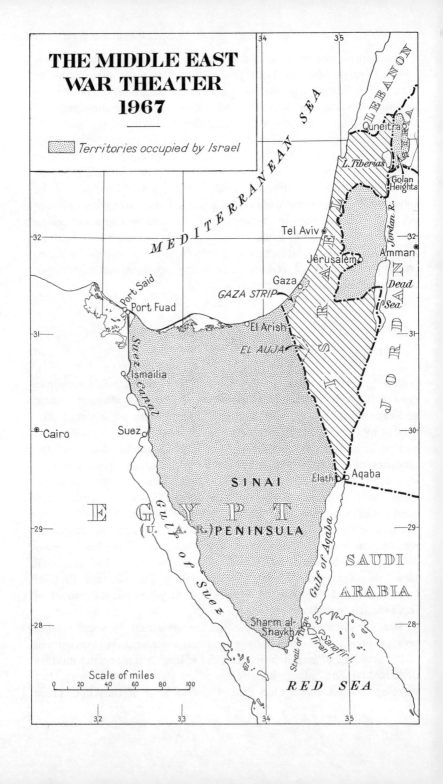

THE MIDDLE EAST WAR THEATER 1967

▨ *Territories occupied by Israel*

MEDITERRANEAN SEA

LEBANON

SYRIA

Quneitra

L. Tiberias

Golan Heights

Tel Aviv

Jordan R.

A'mman

Jerusalem

I S R A E L

Gaza

GAZA STRIP

Dead Sea

Port Said

Port Fuad

El Arish

EL AUJA

Suez Canal

J O R D A N

Ismailia

Cairo

Suez

S I N A I

Elath

Aqaba

E G Y P T

(U. A. R.) PENINSULA

Gulf of Suez

Gulf of Aqaba

SAUDI

ARABIA

Sharm al-Shaykh

Strait of Tiran

Tiran I.

Sanafir I.

Scale of miles

0   20   40   60   80   100

RED SEA

Supervision Organization, concerning the possibility of a large-scale collision prompted the U.N. Secretary-General in mid-January to issue a public appeal for both sides to restrain their forces. This recommendation was warmly echoed next day by Secretary of State Rusk.[11]

In addition, U Thant now took the initiative in calling for an emergency meeting of the U.N.-sponsored Israel-Syria Mixed Armistice Commission, a body set up under the armistice agreement of 1949 but unused in recent years because of disagreements about its jurisdiction. Both Israel and Syria agreed to the convocation of the M.A.C. for the limited purpose of discussing practical arrangements on cultivation, and two meetings were held on the Israeli-Syrian frontier on January 25 and 29. Instead of discussing the agreed agenda, however, Syria used the occasion to insist that Israel withdraw entirely from the demilitarized zones.[12] A third meeting scheduled for early February failed to take place, and instances of infiltration and border clashes were soon occurring as frequently as before.

During these weeks, Israel repeatedly warned that its patience was exhausted and that it would again resort to retaliatory action if the provocations did not cease. This threat was made good on April 7 when Israel's French-built Mirage jets were brought into action to silence Syrian artillery positions from which fire had been directed at Israeli settlements. Not only did Syria lose six of its Soviet-built MIG-21's, but some of the Syrian pilots were pursued to the outskirts of Damascus 60 miles away. Yet border incidents continued to occur as the world began to speculate about the likelihood of another full-scale war like that of 1956.

There had been times in the past when the U.A.R. had seemed to lay a restraining hand on the impetuous Syrians. But no such moderating influence was evident when U.A.R. Premier Muhammad Sidky Soleiman visited Damascus on April 18-23—three weeks after Gromyko's visit to Cairo—and joined his hosts in a declaration of common resolve "to apply joint plans to crush Israeli aggression against Syria."[13] The most noteworthy sequel to this conference was a terrorist incursion five miles into Israeli territory on May 9 which Israel attributed, as usual, to members of the Syrian-trained El Fatah terrorist organization. Syria, commented Premier Eshkol and Foreign Minister Abba Eban, was again approaching the danger point and risking a new taste of Israeli air power.[14]

It is not surprising that a certain militancy should have made itself felt in Israeli statements at this period, the more so since Israel was just then getting ready to celebrate its nineteenth anniversary and had scheduled a military parade in Jerusalem, defying a threatened boycott by Western and other governments on the ground that such a display would constitute a technical violation of the armistice agreements. At the same time, there is no reason to assume that Israel was preparing for anything in the nature of a full-scale military attack on Syria, as was later alleged by Abdel Nasser, Premier Kosygin, and others.

According to Abdel Nasser's later statement, on May 13 his government received "accurate information that Israel was concentrating on the Syrian border huge armed forces of about eleven to thirteen brigades" in preparation for "an aggression against Syria," allegedly timed to occur on May 17. Although he did not specify the source of this information, the U.A.R. President later implied that "an enemy plan to invade Syria" had been amply confirmed from Syrian, U.A.R., and Soviet sources.[15] Premier Kosygin's recollection, as subsequently reported to the U.N. General Assembly, differed both in details of timing and in the precise intentions imputed to Israel. From around May 9 onward, according to the Soviet version, "Israeli troops began concentrating at the Syrian borders, and mobilization was carried out in the country. In those days, the Soviet Government, and I believe others too, began receiving information to the effect that the Israeli Government had timed for the end of May a swift strike at Syria in order to crush it and then carry the fighting over into the territory of the United Arab Republic."[16]

The Israelis, for their part, have insisted that this alleged mobilization for an attack on Syria was nothing but a "monstrous fiction." The nonexistence of the alleged Israeli troop concentrations, according to Foreign Minister Eban, had been certified by Secretary-General Thant as early as May 9 and could equally well have been verified by Syria itself—or by the Soviet Ambassador in Israel—had they availed themselves of the opportunities for on-site inspection of the frontier areas. It was Syria, Mr. Eban recalled, that had caused the trouble by sending terrorists into Israel, bombing Israeli settlements, and thus evoking occasional Israeli responses "limited in scope and time." "All that Syria had to do to insure perfect tranquility on her frontier with Israel," he pointed out, "was to discourage the terrorist war." Instead of doing so, Eban contended, Egypt, Syria, and Jordan, "assisted and incited by more distant Arab states," embarked from May 14 onward on "a policy of immediate and total aggression."[17]

Considering the talent for self-deception disclosed by some of the Arab governments at later stages of the crisis, it is reasonable to suppose that the Israeli stance was in fact a good deal less threatening than Abdel Nasser, the Syrians, and the Russians professed to find it. The U.S.S.R. itself, moreover, would seem to bear a considerable share of the responsibility for failing to point out to the Arabs the dangers of the increasingly bellicose line they were taking. Irrespective of anything Gromyko may have said to Abdel Nasser a few weeks earlier, there was no mistaking the inflammatory tone of a communiqué published in *Pravda* on May 16 which reported the visit of an Egyptian parliamentary delegation to Moscow and gave sweeping endorsement to Abdel Nasser's belligerent attitude both on the Palestine question and on Yemen and Aden.[18]

Whatever the extent of his information or misinformation, it was Abdel Nasser who took the actions that served to escalate the crisis from local to international dimensions. On May 14, according to the U.A.R. President's own statement, he sent word to the Syrians that if Israel attacked, "Egypt would enter the battle from the first minute." At the same time, Egyptian forces were placed on a war footing and, according to Nasser, "began to move in the direction of Sinai to take up normal positions,"[19] thus conveying the impression that the U.A.R. would attack Israel in the rear if Israel did in fact move against Syria.

There was, however, an important obstacle to any U.A.R. military action against Israel. Between these two hostile countries stood the 3,400 blue-uniformed men of the United Nations Emergency Force (UNEF), which, with Abdel Nasser's consent, had been deployed for the past decade along the Egyptian side of the Israeli-Egyptian armistice line. UNEF would clearly have to be got out of the way if Abdel Nasser's military moves were to have their full effect. An informal request for its removal was in fact presented to UNEF headquarters on May 16 and, when this brought no immediate result, repeated in a formal message which was laid before Secretary-General Thant on May 18.[20]

The promptness with which U Thant acceded to this request within a few hours of its receipt has been sharply criticized in many quarters and heatedly defended by the Secretary-General and his aides.[21] UNEF, as U Thant himself reminded the Egyptians, "has been an important factor in maintaining relative quiet in the area of its deployment during the past ten years and . . . its withdrawal may have grave implications for peace." Grave implications for peace it certainly had, and it is conceivable that a different Secretary-General might have found ways of delaying so radical a step until the established organs of the U.N. could be brought into the picture. In the last analysis, however, UNEF had been deployed in the area only because Abdel Nasser had thus far found it useful. If its usefulness to the U.A.R. President had ceased, there was no legal or practical way in which it could remain. (Although UNEF had been highly useful to Israel, too, that country had never permitted and still refused to allow its deployment on the Israeli side of the line.) To make matters more difficult, India and Yugoslavia immediately gave notice that they, at any rate, would withdraw their contingents from UNEF in deference to the Egyptian request. While most of the force was still physically present in the area during the subsequent hostilities and suffered a number of casualties, it took no active part in developments after May 18.

The decision to withdraw the U.N. Emergency Force had implications that went beyond the immediate problems involving Syria, Israel, and the U.A.R. In addition to patrolling the Israeli-U.A.R. armistice line, UNEF had also maintained a small detachment at Sharm al-Shaykh at the entrance to the Gulf of Aqaba for the purpose of ensuring freedom of navigation through the Strait of Tiran, a narrow passage which was considered by the Egyptians to be a part of their territorial waters but was regarded by Israel, the United States, and others as international waters open to "innocent passage" by the shipping of all nations. Since 1957, the UNEF detachment at Sharm al-Shaykh had safeguarded Israel's right of navigation through the Strait of Tiran and the Gulf of Aqaba to the port of Elath at the head of the gulf. Now, it appeared, the detachment was to be removed in consequence of U Thant's agreement to pull out the entire U.N. Force.

For Israel, however, free navigation through the Strait of Tiran was a matter of tremendous psychological importance, all the more so because of Abdel Nasser's closure of the Suez Canal to Israeli shipping. The United States, among others, had recognized the importance of unobstructed access to Israel's "back door" at Elath as early as 1957, when Washington had issued a formal declaration supporting Israel's right of free and innocent passage through the strait.[22] Abdel

Nasser might, of course, intend to respect this right even if the restraining influence of UNEF was removed. Should he fail to do so, he
would not only be attacking an important Israeli interest but would be
risking differences with the United States and other maritime powers
over an important point of international law.

Even before the Egyptian leader's intentions were disclosed, the
announcement of UNEF's withdrawal had led to intensified mobilization measures and mounting war talk both in Israel and in most
countries of the Arab world. U Thant, preparing to fly to Cairo on an
urgent peace mission, found the situation more menacing than at any
time since 1956.[23] The United States, Great Britain, and other governments prepared to deploy their diplomatic resources in a major
effort to safeguard the threatened peace.

In addition to urging moderation on all parties, the United States
apparently made considerable efforts to bring about some form of
collective action by the great powers to head off the impending crisis.
On one side, Washington apparently sought to reinvigorate the so-
called Tripartite Declaration of 1950, in which the United States,
Great Britain, and France had expressed their collective opposition to
any use or threat of force in the Middle East and had pledged prompt
action to prevent any violation of frontiers or armistice lines.[24] Concurrently, an attempt was apparently made to enlist the cooperation
of Premier Kosygin in cooling the ardor of the "revolutionary" Arab
states.[25] Despite their differences, Washington and Moscow had managed to follow parallel policies in the war between India and Pakistan
in 1965. The need for a similar parallelism in the Middle East had
often been pointed out and had rarely seemed more pressing.

Finally, the United States would seem to have made a direct approach to Abdel Nasser's government in the hope of dissuading it
from taking precipitate action. A new U.S. Ambassador, Richard H.
Nolte, arrived in Cairo on May 21 and, according to Egyptian sources,
brought with him a letter from President Johnson containing detailed
proposals relative to Egypt's future conduct. This document, it was
said, not only recommended a mutual withdrawal of U.A.R. and
Israeli military forces from the border region but asked that the
U.A.R. refrain from entering the Gaza sector at the Mediterranean
end of the frontier and, in addition, keep its forces out of Sharm al-
Shaykh until it had officially guaranteed free passage through the
Strait of Tiran. But such proposals, if made, would seem to have been

as unappealing to the recipients as was President Johnson's February letter to Ho Chi Minh. In pronouncing them unacceptable, the U.A.R. Foreign Minister is said to have warned Ambassador Nolte that "If Israel carries out any aggression against any Arab country, we shall consider you as partners."[26]

Abdel Nasser's thoughts, it seemed, were taking the opposite course to what the United States had hoped for. In a bellicose speech of May 22 that gave his own version of how the crisis had developed, the U.A.R. President put an end to any further speculation about his intentions in the Gulf of Aqaba and the Strait of Tiran. "The Aqaba Gulf constitutes Egyptian territorial waters," he declared. "Under no circumstances will we allow the Israeli flag to pass through the Aqaba Gulf." Two days later the Egyptian press reported that the entrance to the Gulf had actually been mined. Announcing in the same speech that a "state of complete mobilization" existed in Gaza and Sinai, Abdel Nasser defied "the Jews" to make war and also poured scorn on what he called the "Islamic alliance" of Saudi Arabia, Jordan, and Iran. The "Arab world," he said, could not possibly coordinate its military plans with anyone who belonged to this imperialist and pro-Zionist combination, although he did hope that Iran would stop sending oil to Israel.[27]

In Washington, President Nasser's declaration regarding the Gulf of Aqaba was felt as a direct rebuff and one that called for a public reply. "The purported closing of the Gulf . . . to Israeli shipping has brought a new and very grave dimension to the crisis," said President Johnson in a broadcast of May 23, in which he reaffirmed the basic U.S. commitment to oppose aggression and support "the political independence and territorial integrity of all the nations of that area." "The United States," the President emphasized, "considers the Gulf to be an international waterway and feels that the blockade of Israeli shipping is illegal and potentially disastrous to the cause of peace. The right of free, innocent passage of the international waterway is a vital interest of the entire international community." Similiar representations were made in Cairo through Ambassador Nolte.[28]

Although the United States did not say what, if anything, it meant to do should Egypt fail to reopen the Gulf, the movement of vessels of the U.S. Sixth Fleet toward the Eastern Mediterranean suggested that it intended to be ready for all eventualities. Yet Washington obviously had no desire to try to break the blockade by force, or even to sanction a forcible move by the Israelis, who claimed to be quite capable of dealing with the supposed mines as well as the position at Sharm al-Shaykh. The Israelis, indeed, were to complain more than once about the delays imposed upon them while the United States cast about for some diplomatic procedure that might serve to get the Gulf reopened.

The most hopeful line of action, originally suggested by the United Kingdom, involved the drafting of an international declaration in favor of freedom of navigation, to be signed by as many governments as possible in the hope of impressing Cairo with the importance of changing its mind. But nothing ultimately came of this project, for which even the British showed only intermittent enthusiasm and which appealed to few other governments. "We were first asked to wait two days," Premier Eshkol later recounted. "Then we sent Abba Eban to the United States—and were asked to wait a further fortnight. President Johnson promised great things. They told us that 40 to 50 maritime powers would sign a guarantee for free passage through the Tiran Strait. We examined the situation and found that it really came down to a dozen and finally to only two countries and then, perhaps, to only one—Israel."[29]

While this effort was being initiated, the general threat to peace had been taken under consideration by the U.N. Security Council. At an initial meeting on May 24, that body heard Ambassador Goldberg urge France, Great Britain, and the U.S.S.R. to join the United States in working for peace either inside or outside the United Nations.[30] Almost simultaneously, France also came out in favor of a four-power approach, though Paris seemed to prefer a more formal "four-power conference" and incidentally took the position that the Tripartite Declaration of 1950 no longer had any relevance to the situation. Great Britain, which likewise had been actively seeking to promote accord among the great powers, showed equal eagerness to enlist Soviet cooperation, preferably through the United Nations.[31]

Even the U.S.S.R., though hesitant to fall in with any specific proposal, seemed not averse to exerting a peaceful influence. Soviet leaders later intimated that they themselves had been taken unawares by Abdel Nasser's action at the Tiran Strait. Though Israel was harshly blamed in Moscow for allegedly stirring up a "war psychosis,"[32] some attempt was apparently made to caution the Egyptian President against further intemperate action. On May 26, Abdel

Nasser later reported, he received separate messages from the United States and the U.S.S.R., both urging that his government "not be the first to open fire."[33] Israel, whose cabinet was by this time debating whether it might not be well advised to go to war immediately, received a similar cautionary message from the Soviet Union on May 27.[34] Kosygin, according to later reports, also wrote President Johnson to suggest that both powers urge restraint on the opposing sides.[35] In fact, a note from President Johnson urging restraint (and hinting at the possibility of Soviet intervention if Israel were to attack) was received by the Israelis early on May 28.[36]

Thanks in part to these conciliatory efforts, tension eased perceptibly over the May 27-28 weekend. U Thant informed the Security Council that Abdel Nasser had disclaimed any intention of initiating offensive action; and the Secretary-General's appeal for a "breathing spell" to let tension subside[37] was warmly supported by the United States and others as the Security Council continued its discussion.[38] But even as the Council deliberated, Abdel Nasser began to display renewed militancy. The Arab states, by this time, were in a fever of warlike enthusiasm. Algeria, Iraq, and others had promised to send troops to support the Arab cause; Iraq was putting pressure on the Western oil companies to deny oil to "aggressors." Even Jordan decided that the time had come to patch up its quarrel with the U.A.R. Visiting Cairo on May 30, King Hussein went so far as to sign a mutual defense pact with Jordan's long-time adversary.

Some writers have singled out the conclusion of the Jordanian-Egyptian pact on May 30 as the critical development that convinced the Israelis they no longer had any choice but to fight. Another event that did nothing to slow the march toward open war was the apparent receipt in Cairo of an encouraging signal from the U.S.S.R., where U.A.R. War Minister Shams-al-Din Badran had just completed three days of talks. "Badran relayed to me a message from Kosygin," Nasser reported on May 29, "saying that the Soviet Union stands with us in this battle and will not allow any country to interfere, so that the state of affairs prevailing before 1956 [i.e., before the opening of the Strait of Tiran to Israeli shipping] may be restored." "Now that we have the situation as it was before 1956," Nasser exulted, "Allah will certainly help us to restore the situation before 1948"—the year of Israel's creation. "Our enemy," the U.A.R. President added, "is not only Israel but also America and Britain, and we shall treat them as enemies."[39]

President Nasser's statements were not denied in Moscow, where Syrian President al-Atasi had also been visiting; and there were other indications that the Soviet Government was shifting to a more out-spokenly pro-Arab line and might even be preparing to convert the crisis into a major East-West confrontation. On May 30 came the startling news that the U.S.S.R. intended to send ten warships of its Black Sea fleet into the Mediterranean to join the fifteen or twenty Soviet vessels already there, one or two of which were dogging the heels of the U.S. Sixth Fleet as it awaited developments in the area of Crete. In Moscow, this might seem no more than a fitting response to the recent eastward movement of U.S. naval vessels; yet such a move was also bound to encourage the Arabs and heighten the tension already prevailing in that part of the world. U.S. naval authorities chose this moment to reveal that harassing maneuvers by Soviet vessels had frequently endangered ships of the Sixth Fleet in the past; and such harrassment was to increase in the following days. In conjunction with the recent bumpings of U.S. naval vessels in the Sea of Japan,[40] it seemed quite possible that the U.S.S.R. was deliberately working to raise the tension even while it remained in diplomatic touch with the United States.

Whatever the relative weight ascribed to these varied influences, from June 1 onward the slide to war became rapid and seemingly irreversible. In Israel, public opinion had become increasingly resentful of diplomatic restraints. A decisive corner was turned on June 1 when Premier Eshkol yielded to popular clamor and turned the Defense Ministry over to Major General Moshe Dayan, the hero of the Suez war and a potent symbol of Israeli militancy. Israel, said the new appointee, could fight alone if diplomacy failed; it would "strike and strike very hard"[41]—an accurate description of the war plan that Israel was to put into effect a few days later.

Israel's apparent determination to defend its existence on the battle-field was not affected by France's brusque announcement on June 2 that it would sign no maritime declaration, considered itself to be in no way committed to any of the states involved in the crisis, and, in fact, would deny its support to any country that took the initiative in resorting to arms.[42] For President de Gaulle, this statement was merely a public reaffirmation of what he had already told Foreign Minister Eban in private: "If Israel is attacked, we shall not allow it to be destroyed, but if you attack, we shall condemn your initiative."[43] Both in Israel and elsewhere, however, the French announcement was read as a public disavowal by the country that had been one of Israel's main supporters for more than a decade and had become its principal source of aircraft and other modern arms. So uncompromising an application of General de Gaulle's concept of national interest was to prove decidedly unpopular in France itself; but it sufficed to define the position to which France would rigidly adhere throughout the coming months.

Hope for a peaceful solution was not entirely abandoned even at this late date. A special American envoy, Charles W. Yost, had gone to Cairo to try to restore diplomatic communication. Prime Minister Wilson was visiting the United States and urging prompt resolution of the Tiran problem. The Security Council was still in session and intermittently discussing a U.S. resolution in support of U Thant's appeal for a "breathing spell."[44] President Johnson was still insisting on America's determination "to preserve the peace" and "preserve the territorial integrity of the nations involved in that area."[45] A further glimmer of optimism appeared with the disclosure on June 4 that President Nasser had agreed to send two high-ranking officials, Vice-President Zakariya Mohieddine and Deputy Premier for Foreign Affairs Mahmoud Fawzi, for discussions in Washington. But this plan, too, was destined to come to nought; and the U.A.R. President did much to cripple it in advance by declaring that he would not only refuse to recognize the proposed maritime declaration but would regard it as "an aggressive act" and "a preliminary to an act of war."[46]

Realistically speaking, there was no "peace plan" that could conceivably have bridged the gap between the contending Middle Eastern countries—unless, perhaps, the great powers had been sufficiently united to subject them to unified and overwhelming pressure. Israel clearly felt that it had been placed in a position where it had no choice but to fight for its very survival; and the Arabs had worked themselves into a state of hysteria in which they undoubtedly felt the same way. Under such circumstances, it may be questioned whether even the most far-reaching steps available to the American Government—an outright guarantee of Israel's territorial integrity, or action to break the blockade at Tiran—would have sufficed to keep the peace. For the Western powers it could at least be said that they had recognized the dangers that might flow from an outbreak of hostilities and had exerted themselves, in however ineffectual and disorganized a way, to prevent an explosion. The U.S.S.R., in contrast, had wavered between moderation and incitement and had seemingly ended by embracing the latter course. The question now before the world was whether the conflict that had by this time become unavoidable would be limited to the immediate contenders or would become a landmark in the wider struggle between East and West.

13 : The Flames Are Lit

If the world was once again to escape the hazards inseparable from any large-scale East-West confrontation in the age of nuclear missiles, a major share of the credit must go to the efficient training, skillful leadership, and outstanding fighting qualities which enabled the Israeli Armed Forces to win a clear-cut and decisive military victory over their combined antagonists in the brief space of six days. Admittedly neither the U.S. nor the U.S.S.R. had any desire to become actively involved in a conflict among Middle Eastern states or to run the risk of a direct clash. Premier Kosygin and President Johnson made haste to reassure each other on this point in an exchange of messages over the Moscow-Washington teletype or "hot line" shortly after hostilities broke out on the morning of Monday, June 5.[47] Yet a prolonged military struggle among closely matched antagonists would surely have placed both powers under heavy pressure to take action in support of their respective favorites. As events fell out, their preference for noninvolvement was abetted by the rapidity and decisiveness of Israel's military victory, which by the end of the week had presented both the belligerents and the great powers with a radically new situation necessitating fundamental policy reappraisals on all sides.

The end results of this process were to be a reaffirmation of the U.S.S.R.'s commitment to the Arab states and a widening of the chasm of incomprehension and hostility that separated the latter from the United States and Britain. In the longer run, such a development might obviously be fraught with serious dangers for the balance of international power and the peace of the world. But for the short run, at least, the Soviet-Arab line-up was to look a good deal less formidable once the Arab belligerents had been defeated in the field, lost the greater part of their Soviet-supplied arms and equipment, and surrendered to Israel a commanding strategic position which the latter, understandably enough, would show no haste to relinquish.

The military events of this third Arab-Israeli war have been well recounted by other writers[48] and require only brief recapitulation. The question of who fired the first shot—a matter on which the belligerents predictably disagreed and which the United Nations, with its limited facilities in the area, was unable to clarify satisfactorily—is of more polemical than historical significance. In Arab minds, there was no doubt that Israel attacked first and thus became the "aggressor." Israel, on the contrary, has maintained that it did not inititate military action until it had evidence that it was itself being attacked by land and in the air. The more important probability is that Israel had stood ready to launch its preclusive attack on June 5 whether or not any enemy aircraft appeared on its radar screens. Having made up its mind that there was no other way of forestalling its own destruction at the hands of its neighbors, Israel was ready and able to seize the initiative and exploit the advantages of strategic surprise.

For all practical purposes, the military outcome of the war was decided in its first hours as waves of Israeli attack planes, flying by circuitous routes to escape radar detection, succeeded in destroying the greater part of the Egyptian Air Force before Abdel Nasser's MIG's had so much as left the ground. This brilliantly successful operation was to have excellent consequences for Israel but very disagreeable ones for the United States and Britain. It either inspired or lent verisimilitude to the Arab allegation, first voiced in Cairo on June 6 and systematically repeated for months thereafter in spite of the most categorical denials,[49] that the two Western powers had actually participated in the air attacks and thus in effect joined Israel in making war on the U.A.R. and other Arab countries.

Such a fiction—which was not echoed by the U.S.S.R.—may perhaps have been psychologically necessary to ease the humiliation of the Arab defeat by a small power like Israel. But the actions based upon it, while decidedly hurtful to Western interests, were to prove even more damaging to the interests of the Arabs themselves. Without stopping to examine the facts, Abdel Nasser promptly invoked a series of drastic "retaliatory" measures which included the closing of the Suez Canal, the breaking of diplomatic relations with the United States (relations with Britain had been broken previously) and an order for the expulsion of all Americans in the U.A.R. Several other Arab governments promptly broke diplomatic relations on their own account, and those in a position to do so also cut off oil supplies to the United States, Great Britain, and Western Germany—for the

Bonn government was likewise accused of excessive partiality for Israel despite its declaration of neutrality on the opening day of the conflict. France alone among the major Western powers was exempted from Arab reprisals, since its repudiation of Israel was already known and its prompt suspension of arms deliveries to the belligerent states was rightly interpreted as far more damaging to Israel than to any of its antagonists.

With the Arab air forces virtually destroyed—for Jordanian and Syrian air bases had also been attacked as soon as it became evident that those countries were determined to enter the war—the way was open for Israel to follow up its advantage on the ground. By Wednesday, June 7, Israeli forces had gained control of most of the Sinai Peninsula, occupied Sharm al-Shaykh, and seized the bulk of the Jordanian territory west of the Jordan River. Politically and psychologically, the major prize of this lightning campaign was the Jordanian-held Old City of Jerusalem, with its religious sites dating from biblical and early Muslim times. "We have returned to the holiest of our holy places, never to depart from it again," General Dayan exulted, apparently forgetting that both Premier Eshkol and he himself had previously disclaimed any ambition for territorial conquest.[50]

Jordan, which had loyally come to the aid of the U.A.R. but had received no effective help from its Arab friends, was in no position to prolong the struggle once its West Bank territories had been overrun. Although an initial cease-fire call adopted by the U.N. Security Council on June 6[51] had gone unheeded by all parties, a second resolution telling the governments concerned to stop fighting by 8:00 P.M., Greenwich Mean Time, on June 7[52] was quickly accepted by both Israel and Jordan. While the Security Council argued about further action, the U.A.R. and Syria sent word next day that they too accepted the cease-fire provided Israel did so.

But the reckoning between Israel and Syria was still to come. Charging wholesale violations of the new cease-fire, Israeli forces smashed into Syria on Friday, June 9, captured the high ground along the border—the Golan Heights—where so much harassment had originated, took the fortress town of al-Quneitra twelve miles inside Syria, and appeared ready to go right on to Damascus. "We should turn the world into a hell in face of the aggressors, and we will win," President al-Atasi insisted. But though the Syrian radio continued to adjure its hearers to "kill, burn and destroy,"[53] Syria's powers of resistance were already broken. A third U.N. cease-fire resolution, unanimously adopted June 9 and demanding that hostilities cease forthwith,[54] was accepted by both sides in the course of June 10 and officially signed the following day.

By its victory in this "six-day war," Israel had not only saved its own life but gained a more favorable territorial and strategic position than at any time in the past. With 679 killed and 2,563 wounded, it had also suffered far less than its adversaries. Casualty figures from the Arab side were notably imprecise, but Jordan appeared to be the hardest hit, with an estimated 15,000 civilian and military dead and with total military casualties reported to number 25,000. The U.A.R. eventually reported 11,500 killed and 5,500 captured, while Syria's official tabulation, reflecting a much briefer period of hostilities, listed 145 dead and 1,590 wounded. Among noncombatant forces, 14 Indian members of UNEF had been killed and 24 wounded, while the United States had sustained the more grievous toll of 34 dead and about twice that number wounded in an inadequately explained Israeli air attack on the communications vessel *Liberty* off the Sinai Peninsula on June 8.

Some of the war's most pitiful victims were among the Arab refugees, officially numbering 1.3 million though probably fewer in reality, whose families had fled from Israel in the earlier war of 1948-49. Some 900,000 of this group who had been eking out a U.N.-supported existence in the Gaza area and western Jordan now found themselves once again under Israeli control. "New" refugees to the number of some hundreds of thousands were also created by the fighting. Of those remaining in Israeli-occupied territory, between 100,000 and 200,000 crossed the Jordan to seek an equally precarious existence under King Hussein's authority. Israel seemed glad to see them go, although it denied putting pressure on them to leave and later readmitted a limited number.

Less publicized, but possibly even more tragic, was the fate of Jewish groups in the U.A.R., Aden, Morocco, and Libya who became the victims of mob attacks and, in the U.A.R. at least, of official "security" measures reflecting the mood of xenophobia attendant on defeat. Numerous Americans residing in the Arab world also suffered hardship as a result of mob violence or official Arab expulsion orders, which ultimately led to the evacuation of at least 26,000 Americans from the Middle East. A ban on American travel to the region, imposed at the outset of hostilities, was only gradually relaxed in the course of the postwar months.

The economic costs to the belligerents and the world defied computation and would clearly extend into the unforeseeable future. The Arab states had lost, among other things, an estimated $1 billion worth of Soviet military equipment, much of which had fallen intact into the hands of the Israelis. Less easily remedied was the damage the Arab states inflicted on themselves and the international community by the various "retaliatory" measures through which they attempted to assuage their own humiliation and punish the Western powers for their supposed involvement in Israel's "aggression." The closure of the Suez Canal, decreed by Abdel Nasser and reinforced by the sinking of five vessels in transit, deprived the tottering Egyptian economy of one of its principal sources of foreign exchange, aggravated the balance-of-payments problems of the United Kingdom, and delayed the shipment of American wheat to hungry India—a country which, ironically, had strongly supported the position of the U.A.R. in relation to Israel. The temporary stoppage of oil exports to the United States and much of Western Europe proved considerably more painful to Iraq, Kuwait, and other oil-producing countries than to the intended victims, who had little difficulty in maintaining their oil stocks through rearrangement of supply sources and transit routes.

It was in the psychological and political realm that the damage appeared most severe and, in all probability, most lasting. Any lingering hope of Arab-Israeli reconciliation appeared to evaporate amid the shame and resentment engendered on the Arab side by this third defeat at Israeli hands in less than twenty years. Paradoxically, it seems not to have occurred to the Arab masses to blame their own leaders for the catastrophe they had suffered. In Egypt, it is true, there was considerable resentment in military circles over the supposed defects of Abdel Nasser's leadership. But when the U.A.R. President announced on June 9 that he accepted full responsibility for what had happened and was tendering his resignation, his gesture provoked such an explosion of popular protest that by the next day he was back in office and, to all appearances, more firmly seated than ever.

The full weight of Arab fury was directed not against those who had preached war with Israel, but rather against Israel itself and its supposed backers among the great powers. Even the U.S.S.R. did not escape criticism for encouraging the Arabs to assert themselves yet doing nothing effective to save them from defeat. Far more intense and less quickly dissipated was the animosity toward Great Britain and particularly the United States, not only in "revolutionary" Arab countries but throughout the Arab East and even in hitherto friendly North African lands like Libya and the Sudan.

A number of shifts in the balance of influence within the Arab world accompanied this psychological readjustment. For the moment, at least, the preeminence and potency of Abdel Nasser and the U.A.R. were severely shaken. Among the consequences of his involvement in war with Israel had been the necessity of withdrawing troops from Yemen and reducing his commitment there. Saudi Arabia, in contrast, had not participated actively in the war, sustained no important military or economic damage, and emerged in a relatively stronger position both locally and in Arab affairs generally. Even more striking was the enhanced prestige of Algeria, whose government had sent troops to aid the U.A.R. and, even after the fighting was stopped, persisted in a violently anti-Israeli and anti-Western posture that contrasted with the rather cautious attitude of President Houari Boumedienne at earlier times. To some observers, Boumedienne's feverish diplomatic activity in the weeks that followed the conflict bespoke an ambition to supplant the U.A.R. as the center of Arab revolutionary energies and a focal point for Arab contacts with the U.S.S.R.

For the most startling aspect of the Arab political upheaval was a still further intensification of psychological, political, and material bonds with Moscow. Despite their mutual disillusionment, both the Arabs and the Soviet Union responded to the crisis in their fortunes not by drawing apart but by drawing even closer together. At first glance, it is true, the defeat of the Soviet-equipped Arab armies appeared to represent a colossal defeat for Soviet policy. Yet if the U.S.S.R. was primarily concerned with advancing its own selfish interests in the area, it could quite reasonably take the view that the Middle Eastern advantages it had failed to gain through an Arab victory were still achievable through the very fact of Arab defeat. Instead of detaching itself from what might have seemed a hopeless cause, Moscow chose to strengthen its identification with Arab aims and to counter the Arabs' inevitable skepticism and disillusionment by new displays of solidarity and support. A brief review of the interplay of Soviet and American diplomacy from the beginning of the war will help to clarify the wider significance of this reaction in the context of continuing competition among the great powers.

14 : New Phase of the East-West Struggle

Premier Kosygin's and President Johnson's mutual assurance that their governments wanted to stay out of the war had in no way meant that their Middle Eastern objectives had become compatible in other respects. On the contrary, each of the two powers continued on and after June 5 to pursue the same general line as before: on the Soviet side, strong support of the Arabs and ferocious animosity toward Israel; on the American side, an attempt to maintain at least formal impartiality while at the same time ensuring that Israel's vital interests were protected. The principal element of novelty, once hostilities had begun, was the fact that both powers appeared to acknowledge an overriding interest in keeping the war from getting out of control. This shared insistence on the need to contain the fighting was reflected in the unanimous votes by which the Security Council, in successive resolutions couched in ever more insistent terms, admonished the belligerents to conclude a cease-fire and desist from military action.[55]

Subject to this basic limitation, however, the United States and the U.S.S.R. quite obviously reserved the right to try to influence developments in a direction favorable to the interests of their respective protégés. The U.S.S.R. lost little time in stepping forth as the defender of Arab interests in face of Israel's alleged "aggression." The Soviet position, for the duration of the war and for long afterward, was set forth in a Soviet Government statement of June 5, the opening day of hostilities, which roundly denounced Israel's "war of aggression," pledged "resolute support" for the Arab states, and demanded that Israel "stop immediately and unconditionally its military actions . . . and pull back its troops beyond the truce line"[56]— thus, of course, sacrificing whatever military advantage it might gain through the progressive defeat of the Arab armies.

The United States, in contrast, did not concede that Israel had been the aggressor; nor did it seem entirely unwilling to give the

Israelis an opportunity to exploit their initial military success. Officially, the U.S. position as defined by the White House and the Secretary of State was that the United States was "not a belligerent" but was determined to carry out its responsibilities under the U.N. Charter, achieve an immediate cease-fire, and "devote all its energies to bring about an end to the fighting and a new beginning of programs to assure the peace and development of the entire area." There is no reason to question the sincerity of these aims. Yet "neutrality," as Secretary Rusk observed, is not the same as "indifference"; and the Secretary of State declined to endorse the sweeping statement of a subordinate official that the United States was "neutral in thought, word, and deed."[57] In fact, the advent of war had touched off a remarkable surge of pro-Israeli feeling in the United States that was presumably not without its effect even in government circles.

These U.S.-Soviet differences were evident throughout the war and the concurrent Security Council discussions looking toward a cease-fire. Quite simply, what Moscow sought was a cease-fire that would be accompanied by a U.N. condemnation of Israel and by the insistence that the latter withdraw behind the armistice lines—in other words, return to the precarious and unsatisfactory *status quo ante*. Although the U.S.S.R. was subsequently to vote for a number of cease-fire resolutions that failed to include the demand for Israeli withdrawal, it was generally assumed that it did so only in the hope of hastening an end of hostilities and thus limiting the scale of the Arab defeat.[58]

The American objective, in contrast, was a cease-fire that could also serve as the basis for a creative effort aimed at establishing conditions of lasting peace. "There is now a real chance for all to turn from the frustrations of the past to the hopes of a peaceful future," said President Johnson on June 7 as he announced that a special committee of the National Security Council, with McGeorge Bundy as executive secretary, would coordinate U.S. efforts to this end.[59] To embark thus early in quest of a "peace of reconciliation" among such violent enemies might seem utopian, but was at least more constructive than the alternative offered by the U.S.S.R. In the meantime, some observers gained the impression that U.S. tactics in the Security Council were helpful in allowing Israel time to win its battle and thus achieve a better negotiating position than it had held in the past.[60]

With the two major powers pursuing such contradictory objectives, the Security Council was in no position to deal with wider issues while the fighting continued. The three resolutions it adopted, all by unanimous vote, during the week of June 5 were limited to calling for a cease-fire "as a first step" and commissioning the Secretary-General to make the necessary arrangements to ensure that the cease-fire was respected. A fourth resolution, unanimously adopted on June 12 in response to further clashes between Israel and Syria, was limited to condemning any and all cease-fire violations and military movements across cease-fire lines.[61]

Only when the fighting had substantially halted could the Security Council turn its attention to longer-range considerations. Still confronting it as the noise of battle abated were two rival proposals, one of Soviet and the other of American origin, which reflected the diametrically opposite views of the two powers. The Soviet draft—a mere "prescription for renewed hostilities," in Ambassador Goldberg's phrase—called once again for condemnation of Israel's "aggressive activities" and withdrawal of Israeli troops behind the armistice lines.[62] The U.S. proposal, in contrast, envisaged a more comprehensive and forward-looking procedure. Its principal feature was a call for "discussions promptly among the parties concerned, using such third party or United Nations assistance as they may wish, looking toward the establishment of viable arrangements encompassing the withdrawal and disengagement of armed personnel, the renunciation of force regardless of its nature, the maintenance of vital international rights and the establishment of a stable and durable peace in the Middle East."[63]

The reference in this American draft to "withdrawal and disengagement of armed personnel" appeared to echo, though in much more qualified fashion, the Soviet view that Israel should not expect to remain in the territories it had wrested from three of its Arab neighbors. This, indeed, was a natural enough position for a government that had so often pledged its support of the U.N. Charter and the political independence and territorial integrity of all the nations of the Middle East. Yet even so qualified a reference to military withdrawal appeared to conflict with the announced views of Israel itself. That country had officially declared as early as June 10 that it "cannot return to the 1949 armistice agreement and boundaries determined by those agreements."[64] Those agreements and boundaries had given Israel no real security in the past, and most Israelis obviously felt that by winning the war they had earned the right to new and more secure frontiers. "Be under no illusion that the State of Israel is prepared to return to the situation that reigned up to a week ago," said Premier Eshkol on June 12. ". . . The position that existed until now shall never again return. The land of Israel shall no longer be a no man's land, wide open to acts of sabotage and murder."[65]

In other respects, the American proposal to the Security Council was more consistent with Israel's views. "The maintenance of vital international rights" was clearly meant to include Israel's right of passage through the Gulf of Aqaba and, presumably, through the Suez Canal as well. The procedure suggested by the United States— discussion among the parties concerned, with optional assistance by the United Nations or other third parties—also leaned toward Israel's declared position, since the Israeli cabinet had already decided that Israel could no longer put up with the uncertainties of the armistice system and must replace it with a definitive peace settlement reached in direct negotiations with the Arab states. The only difficulty with this procedure was that the U.A.R. and the other Arab governments seemed utterly averse to holding peace talks with Israel and, in fact, had already begun to talk of renewing the battle as soon as circumstances permitted.[66]

Neither the Soviet nor the American proposal was approved by the fifteen-member Security Council when a vote was taken on June 14. A paragraph-by-paragraph vote on the Soviet draft disclosed that only four states—the U.S.S.R., Bulgaria, India, and Mali—favored the unqualified condemnation of Israel, and only six—the same four plus Ethiopia and Nigeria—were prepared to vote for the unqualified withdrawal of Israeli forces. But the more constructive U.S. resolution also failed to pass and, indeed, was not even pressed to a vote in view of the fact that several delegations had asked for more time to study the issues involved. All the Security Council could manage immediately was the adoption of one more unanimous resolution that called on Israel to ensure the safety and welfare of inhabitants of the war zones, facilitate the return of refugees, and (with other governments) respect the legal rights of war prisoners and civilians.[67]

By this time it was evident that the Soviet Union and most of its Eastern European allies had determined to redouble their support of the defeated Arabs, both in U.N. debates and propaganda and in more practical ways. As early as June 9, while Israel was opening its offensive on the Syrian front, leaders of seven European Communist nations had met in Moscow and six of them had joined the U.S.S.R. in denouncing Israel's "aggression"—carried out, so they asserted, in collusion with the United States and other "imperialist forces." Demanding a cessation of military action and a withdrawal by Israel behind the truce line, they had further promised that in the event of noncompliance they would "do everything necessary to help the peoples of the Arab countries to administer a resolute rebuff to the aggressor."[68] President Tito of Yugoslavia, a frequent nonconformist in matters of Communist policy, was among the signers of this document; but Nicolae Ceausescu, the Rumanian Communist leader, withheld his signature in a fresh display of Rumania's independent stand within the Soviet bloc.

In the course of their Moscow meeting, the participants apparently took a further decision to reequip the U.A.R.'s shattered Army and Air Force and thus reestablish some semblance of military balance in the Middle East. As many as 200 MIG fighter planes were earmarked for this purpose, it was said, and some planes were apparently dispatched immediately to the U.A.R. by way of Yugoslavia. On June 10, moreover, the U.S.S.R. and most other Soviet bloc states abruptly severed diplomatic relations with Israel in protest against the continuance of military operations in defiance of the U.N. cease-fire resolutions. Unless military actions halted immediately, Moscow warned, it would join with other "peace-loving states" in adopting "sanctions" against Israel.[69] Again, Rumania alone among the Eastern European countries declined to follow the Soviet lead.

A natural consequence of the decision to maintain support of the defeated Arab states was a determination to persevere in the political offensive already initiated by the U.S.S.R. in the Security Council. Even before the defeat of its resolution demanding Israeli withdrawal behind the armistice lines, the U.S.S.R. had given notice that it would if necessary appeal the issue to the General Assembly, where its chances of obtaining a favorable vote would presumably be greater. Though opposed to this move on procedural grounds—for the U.S.S.R. in demanding an emergency session of the Assembly had pointedly ignored the "Uniting for Peace" procedure set up years earlier on American initiative[70]—the United States prepared to bow to the will of the majority of United Nations members and continue the discussion in the larger body.

15 : Search for a New Beginning

Once before, in 1960, the U.S.S.R. had used the General Assembly as a gigantic stage from which to dramatize a political point. On that occasion, Premier Khrushchev had headed the procession of chiefs of state and government who gathered in New York to hear an abortive demand for the reorganization of the United Nations.[71] In 1967, it was the more dignified Premier Kosygin who crossed the Atlantic, followed by the leaders of the other Soviet bloc countries, for the avowed purpose of extracting from an emergency session of the General Assembly the condemnation of Israel that the Security Council had failed to vote. The calculation behind this Soviet move seemed obvious enough. Even if the 122 U.N. member governments should fail to pronounce themselves in favor of Soviet and Arab views, they could at least be made acquainted with those views in the most dramatic and authoritative manner possible. The effect on the Arab countries of such a demonstration of Soviet solidarity would not be lost.

Yet even now there were indications that Soviet policy in Middle Eastern affairs was less firmly established than might have appeared from the uncompromising address Kosygin delivered before the Assembly's Fifth Emergency Special Session on June 19. As expected, the Soviet Premier proposed that the Assembly adopt a resolution condemning Israel's "aggression," demanding its immediate withdrawal from the occupied territories and payment of compensation for damage inflicted on its neighbors, and calling for Security Council measures "to eliminate all the consequences" of the aggression.[72] But while the U.S.S.R. was plainly willing to go all out in seeking a political condemnation of Israel at the United Nations, it was by no means clear that the men in Moscow were prepared to go as far in backing the hopes of revenge that were being voiced in the Arab world—particularly in Syria and Algeria, which were urging the U.A.R. to open a guerrilla war against Israel now that conventional warfare had failed.

Nor was it certain as yet that the Soviet Government was prepared to slam the door on any understanding with the United States on Middle Eastern affairs. On the contrary, Kosygin's mere presence in New York was bound to raise a hope that he might be induced to meet with President Johnson and that the two leaders might come to an understanding not only on the Middle East—perhaps in the form of an agreement to limit the supply of arms to Middle Eastern countries—but also on such issues as Vietnam, a nuclear nonproliferation treaty, and the curbing of the U.S.-Soviet missile race.

There is reason to believe that some aspects of Soviet policy in these matters remained unsettled at the time of Kosygin's trip and were still being debated within the Soviet ruling group. A meeting of the Central Committee of the Soviet Communist party, convened in Moscow on June 20-21 to hear a report on the Middle East crisis by Party Secretary Brezhnev, concluded with the issuance of a declaration approving the actions of the Soviet Government and renewing the promise to do "everything necessary" to help the Arab peoples "administer a resolute rebuff to the aggressor."[73] Apparently, however, it was also decided that the "rebuff" must not have a military character. President Podgorny, who left Moscow in the middle of the meeting on an urgent flight to Cairo, would seem to have assured Abdel Nasser that he would get some arms but to have discouraged any idea of reopening hostilities that might have been germinating in the Egyptian leader's mind. After a brief return to Moscow, Podgorny continued on a similar mission to Syria and Iraq.

The demotion at this same period of two persons high in the Soviet party apparatus served to strengthen the impression that the Central Committee meeting had been the final act in a struggle between Soviet "moderates" of the stamp of Brezhnev, Kosygin, and Podgorny and a more militant group, comprising both Army and party figures, who had apparently favored a more aggressive stand in the Middle East, supplemented, perhaps, by harassing action in Berlin or elsewhere.[74] The apparent victory of the "moderates" did not, presumably, mean that Soviet policy would become more accommodating toward the United States, but only that the previous unaccommodating line had been approved and confirmed and would be maintained in preference to any more bellicose attitude.

This point was to be well illustrated in the course of Kosygin's meetings with President Johnson, which were promptly arranged in the aftermath of the Central Committee meeting and, as already noted, took place at Glassboro, New Jersey on June 23 and 25. As with Vietnam, so with the Middle East: the American and Soviet leaders set forth their respective views, recognized that they were basically at variance, yet managed to place them in the wider perspective of what seemed a common desire for peaceful relations. Kosygin, in his public report on the Glassboro talks, confined himself to stressing once again the urgency of Israeli withdrawal behind the armistice lines.[75] President Johnson, more hopefully, professed to have found "elements . . . of common ground . . . in respect to such simple propositions as that every state has a right to live, that there should be an end to the war in the Middle East, and that in the right circumstances there should be withdrawal of troops." "This is a long way from agreement," the President conceded, "but it is a long way also from total difference."[76]

At the United Nations, however, the difference still appeared total. Anticipating Kosygin's offensive in the General Assembly, the United States had by this time come forward with a major policy statement of its own, developed from its proposals to the Security Council and enunciated by the President in a broadcast of June 19. "Certainly, troops must be withdrawn," Mr. Johnson had conceded; but withdrawal of troops would by itself solve nothing: ". . . there must also be recognized rights of national life, progress in solving the refugee problem, freedom of innocent maritime passage, limitation of the arms race, and respect for political independence and territorial integrity." These, the President declared, were the "five great principles of peace" to which the United States remained committed; and, he emphasized, it stood ready to offer all appropriate assistance to the Middle Eastern peoples and leaders who must bear the actual responsibility for peacemaking.[77]

Mr. Johnson's five principles were promptly translated into the form of a draft U.N. resolution and laid before the General Assembly by Ambassador Goldberg.[78] Without being entirely pro-Israel, the American proposal quite obviously aimed at the kind of peace settlement that would safeguard Israel's essential rights—the only kind of peace settlement, in the American view, that would have a chance of enduring. Yet for that very reason the plan was bound to be unacceptable to the Arabs, to Soviet bloc states, to India, and to many others whose sympathies currently inclined much more strongly toward the Arabs than toward Israel.

The very idea of "negotiated arrangements with appropriate third-party assistance," to quote the language of the U.S. draft, struck many observers as unrealistic at a time when the daily exchanges between Arab and Israeli spokesmen in the U.N. Assembly hall were setting new records in vituperativeness. "Never has any dialogue been harder to imagine," commented Maurice Couve de Murville, the French Foreign Minister.[79] Rumania was one of the few U.N. members that openly came out in favor of negotiations and agreements leading to a lasting settlement. Albania, in contrast, introduced a truculent resolution that went even beyond the Soviet draft and condemned not only Israel but the United States and Britain as well.[80]

The chances of any favorable action on the U.S. draft were further undermined by Israel's own actions. Not only had Foreign Minister Eban been heard to declare that Israel would not return to the armistice lines even if the General Assembly demanded it by a vote of 121 to 1.[81] Israel was also incurring a vast amount of criticism by its alleged harshness to refugees and others in the newly occupied territories. On June 28, moreover, it took the legally questionable step of integrating the municipal administrations of Israeli and Jordanian Jerusalem, thus in effect incorporating the former Jordanian sector into its own territory. Even the White House and State Department were quick to disavow this action, which was difficult to reconcile with U.S. declarations concerning the need for adequate recognition of Jerusalem's special status as a city sacred to Christians, Jews, and Muslims.[82] Its effect on governments less indulgent toward Israel may be imagined.

Since neither the Soviet nor the American plan seemed likely to win a two-thirds majority in the Assembly, other delegations had meanwhile been actively seeking a middle ground. India and other "nonaligned" powers threw their support to a compromise draft, elaborated by Yugoslavia, which insisted on full withdrawal by Israel but refrained from condemning the latter as an aggressor.[83] An alternative offered by the Latin American countries (and ultimately supported by the United States) likewise called for Israeli withdrawal but included various political provisions relating to freedom of international waterways, solution of refugee problems, and the internationalization of Jerusalem,[84] an objective particularly sought by the Vatican. In all, five separate proposals were tabled for the Assembly's consideration.

As had so often happened in matters of major importance, none of the five received the needed two-thirds majority when the votes were taken on July 4. The Latin American draft came closest to success, with 57 favorable votes to 43 opposed and 20 abstentions. The resolution of the nonaligned countries, supported by the U.S.S.R. and France but opposed by the United States, Great Britain, and Israel, won 53 votes to 46 opposed and 20 abstentions. The Soviet Union's draft was rejected paragraph by paragraph, and the United States declined to press its own resolution to a vote in view of the fact that it had already thrown its support to the Latin American alternative. The Albanian draft condemning Israel, the United States, and Britain won only 22 votes to 71 opposed and 27 abstentions, again including that of France.

The Assembly did manage at its July 4 meeting to adopt two incidental resolutions, one of them appealing for assistance to refugees[85] and the other declaring the measures Israel had taken in Jerusalem to be invalid and calling on Israel to rescind them and desist from any action that would alter Jerusalem's status.[86] The United States, while agreeing that there should be no unilateral action that might prejudice the future of Jerusalem, abstained on this second resolution. Ten days later, as Israel showed no sign of compliance, the Assembly adopted a second resolution reiterating its demands in stronger terms.[87] Again the United States abstained. While deeply regretting the Israeli actions, Secretary Rusk explained, the United States simply did not feel that the resolution as framed was the way to deal with the Jerusalem situation.[88]

Having failed of its major purpose in convening the Assembly, the U.S.S.R. still showed interest in securing the adoption of some kind of face-saving resolution that would at least make the whole procedure appear less futile and afford some sop to Arab opinion. Consultations continued for another week, and there are indications that the chief Soviet and American representatives—Foreign Minister Gromyko and Ambassador Goldberg—came remarkably close to agreement on a new draft resolution which would have satisfied at least some of the basic requirements of both powers. In this joint draft, withdrawal of Israeli forces behind the armistice lines would apparently have been linked with recognition of such essential Israeli interests as the acknowledgment of Israel's right to national existence, a termination of the state of belligerency, and, in consequence, freedom of navigation through the Suez Canal and the Strait of Tiran.[89]

Acceptance of such principles as an inducement to Israeli withdrawal would clearly have represented a notable change in the Soviet position—so notable, in fact, that some observers could ascribe it only to a fear that Communist China would be the beneficiary if the U.S.S.R. came away from New York without a resolution. It was the Arab delegations—some said specifically the Algerians—who apparently vetoed the plan at the last moment, thus impelling Gromyko to renew his denunciation of the United States and eventually leading the Soviet Union to deny the whole story.[90] In any event, the failure of this last try for agreement on the night of July 20-21 left the Assembly with no practical alternative to adjourning its labors and referring the whole Middle Eastern situation back to the Security Council.[91]

General international tension had by this time subsided markedly as a result of the Glassboro meetings and other factors, and Soviet behavior appeared definitely more conciliatory than had been true a few weeks earlier. Some of the naval vessels sent into the Mediterranean had by now returned to the Black Sea, and Chairman Brezhnev, in a speech of July 5, had seemingly gone out of his way to emphasize the "political" (as distinguished from military) character of the struggle in the Middle East. At the same time, Brezhnev had insisted, that struggle was at bottom a "confrontation between the forces of imperialism . . . and the forces of national independence, democracy and social progress"—and in such a confrontation it was the Soviet Union's duty "to frustrate the plans of imperialism . . . and to help the Arab states uphold their freedom and independence."[92] That this duty was considered to extend to the entire Soviet bloc was confirmed once again at a meeting of Communist leaders in Budapest on July 11-12, with President Tito again participating but, this time, without a Rumanian representative.[93]

Moscow's evident disinclination to see the war renewed was reflected in its reaction to new outbreaks of fighting in the war zone. Israel, throughout these weeks, had remained in military occupation of huge tracts of conquered territory extending to the Suez Canal in the west, the Jordan River in the east, and the Golan Heights in the north. Exchanges of machine gun and mortar fire with the Egyptians on the other side of the Suez Canal had begun as early as July 1, with each side characteristically accusing the other of responsibility, and within a few days the conflict had again shown signs of escalating out of control as artillery and jet planes joined the fray.

Yet a renewal of large-scale hostilities could be in no one's interest, and Moscow now appeared to recognize the fact. From July 8 onward, there were fresh consultations in the Security Council which revealed general agreement on the desirability of stationing observers from the U.N. Truce Supervision Organization along the Suez Canal. After further heavy fighting, this step was carried out with the consent of the two belligerents on July 17.[94] Clashes thereafter became less frequent and more restricted in scope, although the commencement of exchanges of gunfire between Israeli and Jordanian forces on opposite banks of the river offered a fresh reminder that the whole cease-fire situation remained extremely precarious.

More serious, perhaps, than the threat of an immediate renewal of hostilities was the possibility of a new arms race, spurred by Soviet shipments to the Arabs, which might lead to a new explosion of hostilities at some later date. In pursuance of its broad commitment to help the Arabs administer a "resolute rebuff" to any aggressor, the U.S.S.R. was plainly losing no time in trying to rebuild at least a semblance of Arab defense capability. By mid-July, Israeli sources asserted that about 100 MIG's and over 100 tanks had reached Egypt either directly or via Algeria. Other arms shipments were known to have gone to Syria and Algeria itself. Even Jordan, which had never accepted Soviet arms in the past, was being encouraged to look to Moscow for the rebuilding of its shattered military establishment. Meanwhile the U.S.S.R. offered no response to a suggestion in President Johnson's June 19 speech to the effect that any new arms shipments to the Middle East might at least be registered with the United Nations as a first step toward controlling the arms race in that area.[95]

In face of these manifestations, the United States was already considering the possibility of a resumption of its own more limited arms aid to Israel, Jordan, and Saudi Arabia. The most desirable objective, Secretary Rusk emphasized at his July 19 news conference, would be "some understanding among the arms recipients and the arms suppliers to put some sort of ceiling on the arms race in the Middle East. . . . We will continue to work at this in the United Nations and in capitals. I would not be able to say today that I am encouraged about the prospects, because the resupply of certain of the countries by the Soviet Union has been going on apace, and this will raise security questions for not only Israel but also certain of the Arab countries."[96]

Behind such statements lay the realization that the Arab countries, for all their shared hostility to Israel, were as torn by mutual rivalries, jealousies, and conflicts of interest as had been true before the war. Even amid the shock of defeat there still persisted a basic division between Egypt, Syria, Iraq, and Algeria, the "revolutionary" countries which remained the special objects of Soviet attention, and Jordan, Saudi Arabia, and other countries like Libya and Kuwait whose attitudes and international attachments remained more flexible.

Jordan, whose King now warned that he would have no alternative to accepting Soviet arms unless his country's needs could be met from other sources,[97] had been pursuing a particularly independent line and was even suspected of being not totally averse to a political settlement with Israel. But the Israeli occupation of Old Jerusalem and the West bank territories, plus the flight of refugees across the Jordan and the attempts at passive or even active resistance by those who remained in occupied territory, had produced all kinds of frictions with the neighboring country and maintained a state of tension that was not greatly alleviated by Israel's reluctant readmission of about 14,000 refugees in the course of the summer.[98]

Some other Arab governments showed intermittent gleams of realism. In spite of all the talk of a new "war of liberation," few Arab regimes—except perhaps those of Syria and Algeria—showed any eagerness to pass from declamation to action. By July 23, even Abdel Nasser was intimating that while he fully intended to continue the fight, he was not slamming the door on a "political" settlement or even refusing to talk with the United States.[99] Indeed, the U.A.R. President had many reasons for espousing a policy of greater sobriety than he had thought appropriate in May and June. Economic troubles, aggravated by the closure of the Suez Canal, and conspiratorial activities in his own Army might well have counseled a degree of caution even without the accompanying deterioration of U.A.R. prospects in Yemen and South Arabia.

U.A.R. representatives thus espoused a noticeably moderate line when the Foreign Ministers of the thirteen Arab countries assembled in Khartoum, the Sudan, at the beginning of August to prepare the way for a new "summit conference" of Arab leaders. In addition to making a dramatic offer to resolve its quarrel with Saudi Arabia, Abdel Nasser's government was now described as favoring some kind of collective, though indirect, guarantee of Israel's existence along the lines of the abortive U.S.-Soviet plan at the United Nations. But neither on these nor on other current questions of Arab policy were the governments represented at Khartoum able to reach full accord, and major political issues were put off to the summit conference which, it was agreed, should meet at the end of August. One particularly touchy question, the future of the oil embargo against Western "aggressor" countries, was referred for further study to a special meeting of the competent ministers in Baghdad.[100]

Agreement on the oil embargo still eluded the Arab regimes when the Baghdad meeting convened at mid-August. Most Arab countries clearly wanted the embargo maintained, even if it appeared to be doing little harm to the countries affected. The main dissenters were Saudi Arabia, Kuwait, and Libya, important oil-producing countries that had played little part in the recent war but obviously had a great deal to lose if they were to continue denying oil to their most important customers. In the absence of a unanimous recommendation, this issue too was reserved for final settlement at the "summit."

Equally without immediate result was a Middle Eastern peace mission undertaken by President Tito in mid-August. The Yugoslav leader's apparent aim was to give new impetus to the idea of a political settlement which would secure Israeli withdrawal from the occupied territories and provide indirect guarantees to Israel, though without requiring outright Arab recognition of that country. Though sympathetically noted in the U.A.R. and Iraq, this Titoist approach was too conciliatory for the Syrians and, at the same time, too devious for the Israelis, who had little use for the Yugoslav President's views and continued to insist that the only peace settlement they would consider was one openly negotiated with the Arab states.

Differences among the Arab countries tended to grow wider as the war receded, and it was considered something of a diplomatic triumph for the Sudan, as the host government, that the Khartoum summit was able to convene at all. Even so, the leaders of the four North African governments failed to attend in person, and Syria, which had vainly urged a postponement, was unrepresented when the conference met on August 29. To add to the sense of disarray, the U.A.R. was by this time going through what appeared to be the most serious internal crisis it had yet experienced. Abdel Nasser, before leaving for Khartoum, had reluctantly taken action against a group of disgruntled officers who had been dismissed in the wake of the war and had since been plotting to bring about either their own rein-

"NO SIT, NO SPLIT."

© 1967, *Chicago-Sun Times.* (Reproduced by courtesy of
Wil-Jo Associates, Inc. and Bill Mauldin)

statement or, in the extreme case, a *coup d'état.* Among the 50 officers and civilians arrested on August 25 was Field Marshal Abdel
Hakim Amer, one of Nasser's oldest collaborators, who was subsequently to commit suicide while under house arrest and awaiting
interrogation.

The treachery of old friends seems not to have shaken Abdel Nasser's determination to persevere in the more conciliatory political line that recent adversities had forced upon him. Repeating his reference to a "political solution" with Israel, the Egyptian leader seems to have frankly conceded at Khartoum that the U.A.R. was in no position to undertake a new military offensive. He also admitted, though not for publication, that he had been mistaken about the supposed participation of U.S. and British aircraft in the events of June 5. As the Khartoum conference ended on September 1, the participants still professed to agree on the harsh principle of "No peace with Israel, no negotiation with Israel, no recognition of Israel and maintenance of the rights of Palestinian people in their nation."[101] The significant feature of their deliberations, however, was not so much the repetition of old phrases as the common understanding that the elimination of "the consequences of aggression" and the withdrawal of Israeli forces must be sought by diplomatic rather than military means. That this represented a marked retreat from earlier positions was evidenced by the refusal of the Algerian and Syrian governments (and of Ahmed Shukairy of the Palestine Liberation Organization) to go along with it.

Equally unpalatable to Arab militants were some of the other decisions of the Khartoum conference—especially the decision to abandon the oil embargo forthwith and authorize the immediate resumption of oil shipments by any Arab government that so chose. As already noted, the governments most eager for this decision were Kuwait, Saudi Arabia, and Libya; and it was scarcely a coincidence that these three countries also undertook at Khartoum to provide the greater part of an annual subsidy of $392 million to the U.A.R., Jordan, and Syria as the countries that had suffered most from the war. Although the prompt resumption of oil shipments would afford definite relief to Western countries, the more important benefit of passage through the Suez Canal was still to be denied them. In view of Israel's occupation of the east bank of the Canal, Abdel Nasser declared, he was prepared to keep the waterway closed as long as the other Arab states were willing to share the financial burden.

The prospect of Saudi financial assistance must also have played a compelling part in Abdel Nasser's decision to persevere in his resolve to liquidate his unsuccessful venture in Yemen, bring home the 25,000 or so Egyptian troops still in that country, and make a new attempt to coexist with King Faisal of Saudi Arabia. Possibly the most important achievement at Khartoum was a new agreement between President Nasser and King Faisal, effected with the aid of Sudanese President Ismail al-Azhari, whereby the U.A.R. would withdraw its troops from Yemen, Saudi Arabia would discontinue its aid to the Yemeni royalists, and a tripartite commission consisting of Morocco, Iraq, and the Sudan would oversee the execution of the bargain and try to restore harmony in Yemen itself.[102] All that seemed lacking to the success of this agreement—assuming that Abdel Nasser carried out his share of the bargain—was the concurrence of the Yemeni republican government headed by President Abdallah al-Salal. But the nerves of this ex-Nasser puppet had become increasingly frayed in recent weeks as Egyptian support had dwindled and the prospect of his own dethronement had become more imminent; and the Yemeni President now gave notice that his government considered the new agreement an encroachment on Yemen's sovereign rights and would refuse to be bound by it.

Agreement on Yemen was nevertheless of special importance at this period because affairs in the adjacent South Arabian Federation were also approaching a climax and Great Britain was preparing to abandon the territory to its warring factions even before its scheduled independence date, now set for January 9, 1968. British troops had already been pulled out of the South Arabian hinterland and concentrated in Aden town in preparation for evacuation, and much of the territory was given over to civil war between the two nationalist factions that were struggling to take their place. Here, too, Abdel Nasser's interests no longer seemed to be in the ascendant. A radical, Marxist, but non-Nasserist group known as the National Liberation Front was increasingly asserting its predominance over the pro-Nasser Front for the Liberation of Occupied South Yemen (FLOSY), which had earlier claimed most of the headlines but whose real strength now appeared to be largely confined to the trade-union movement within Aden itself. More trouble plainly lay ahead in this unquiet part of the world, but it would be a different kind of trouble from what had seemed likely a few months earlier.

With British and American influence in the Arab countries at an all-time low, the United States and Britain were experiencing a further impairment of their Middle Eastern position through the sapping of the CENTO alliance which still retained nominal responsibility for defense of the "northern tier." For the first time in its twelve-year history, the CENTO Council failed to hold its regular annual meeting in 1967 owing to Pakistan's request for an indefinite postponement. The Muslim members of CENTO had not been unaffected by the religious and anti-imperialist overtones of the Middle Eastern conflict, and in varying degrees had shown that their sympathies, too, lay rather with the Arab states than with Israel. At the end of July, the chiefs of state of Turkey, Iran, and Pakistan had held their own meeting in Tehran to record the fact that they also regarded a withdrawal of Israeli forces as essential to Middle Eastern peace and, to that extent at least, were unprepared to follow the more deliberate lead of the United States.[103]

The Shah of Iran, who was looking forward to a gala coronation ceremony in October in celebration of the achievements of his 26-year reign, visited Washington in August amid the customary blaze of Iranian-American cordiality.[104] Thanks largely to its oil resources, Iran had made notable economic progress of late years and was now nearing the point where it would no longer require U.S. economic aid.[105] But such positive developments, while by no means to be undervalued, could not disguise the fact that the structure of international relationships in the Middle East was undergoing profound changes. A meeting of CENTO representatives which Secretary Rusk was able to arrange in New York in the early days of the General Assembly's regular session was accompanied by widespread speculation that CENTO might soon be dissolved altogether in recognition of its diminishing usefulness.[106]

16 : Where There Is No Peace

Although the events of the summer had modified the Middle Eastern setting in innumerable ways, they had signally failed to affect its central reality. That reality still lay in the fact that Israel had won its war with the Arabs, seized territory from three of its Arab neighbors, and given notice that it would not relax its hold—if ever—until the Arab governments swallowed their pride and agreed to hold direct peace negotiations. Backed by the Soviet Union, the Arab states continued to insist with equal firmness that they would not discuss a settlement with Israel—if ever—until Israeli forces withdrew from the conquered territories and returned to the positions they had occupied before June 5. Even the impasse over negotiations in Vietnam was not more complete. As in Vietnam, moreover, the deadlock appeared to hinge on technicalities but actually reflected diametrically opposed objectives which none of the contending parties was yet prepared to relinquish.

As the Middle Eastern cease-fire entered its fourth month, the situation nevertheless appeared in some respects to be settling into a kind of "normality" in which there was no longer much danger of a clash among major powers. Although its diplomatic relations with several of the Arab states were still in abeyance, the United States had by this time relaxed its ban on travel to all but Syria and the U.A.R.,[107] and private contacts were beginning to be reestablished. In Cairo, a small group of U.S. diplomatic officers was once again transacting business under the auspices of the Spanish Embassy. Even now, however, the situation remained explosive and the danger of a new flare-up was never remote. Heavy fighting between Israel and Egypt broke out at the Suez Canal on September 4, and an even more serious pair of clashes occurred on September 20-21 at the very time when the U.N. Assembly, now convened in its 22nd Regular Session, was preparing to refocus its attention on the quest for permanent peace. New terrorist incidents were also beginning to occur in Israeli-occupied Jordan and even within Israel proper; and Israel itself caused intermittent consternation in Washington and elsewhere by actions that seemed to reflect an intention of remaining indefinitely in the conquered territories.

Such manifestations were all the more embarrassing to the United States because Washington had by this time reached a definite decision to resume its arms shipments to the area in an endeavor to offset the Soviet shipments to Moscow's client states. The rebuilding of Egypt's military power was now far advanced; yet Israel was still cut off from its former sources of supply in France, and King Hussein of Jordan was still hesitant to accept the Soviet arms that were being pressed upon him. In mid-September it became known that the United States would no longer delay the shipment of 48 A-4 Skyhawk fighter-bombers it had promised Israel in 1966. Not many weeks later, Washington further confirmed that it had authorized shipments of spare parts and other military equipment to Lebanon, Saudi Arabia, and Tunisia as well as a number of jet fighters previously ordered by Morocco and Libya. If arms for Jordan were still in abeyance, it was mainly because the Jordanian Air Force was now believed incapable of operating the 36 F-104 Starfighters promised to King Hussein's government at an earlier period. The Pentagon did announce, however, that training of officers from Saudi Arabia, Lebanon, Jordan, and certain other states would be expanded while the training of officers from Iraq and the Sudan would be discontinued.[108]

It was amid such familiar portents that the General Assembly had reconvened on September 19 to assess the peace prospects that had proved so elusive during the recent emergency session. As always, Ambassador Goldberg in his opening address to the Assembly laid heavy stress on the element of conciliation;[109] but to judge from the subsequent statements of Foreign Minister Gromyko, Foreign Minister Eban, and a succession of Arab Foreign Ministers, the positions of the contending parties still remained too firmly frozen to allow of any room for compromise. No one, however, was willing to dismiss outright the possibility, so frequently mooted on earlier occasions, of general agreement on some kind of "package" which would combine the elements of Israeli withdrawal, Arab recognition, and an end of the state of war. Backstage consultation was now beginning to focus on the idea of sending a personal representative of the Secretary-General to the Middle East with a mandate from the Security Council to see what kind of arrangements might be negotiated on the spot. Agreement on even this minimum plan would be difficult to achieve, however, unless there was first an agreement concerning the broad political principles on which any negotiations would have to be based.

This slight movement toward peace was rudely if temporarily interrupted on October 21 when Egyptian patrol boats in the harbor of Port Said loosed three of their Soviet-supplied "Styx" missiles to sink the Israeli destroyer *Elath* some distance off the coast, inflicting a toll of 19 dead, 91 wounded, and 28 missing.[110] As usual, there were sharply conflicting claims as to whether the *Elath* had been on peaceful patrol or on an aggressive mission, and whether or not it had violated Egyptian territorial waters. What was not open to question was the anger of the Israelis and the vigor with which they conducted themselves in a new outbreak of fighting at the Suez Canal three days later. Before the shooting ended at Suez City on October 24, two oil refineries representing a substantial part of the U.A.R.'s refining capacity had been set afire and were blazing beyond hope of salvage.

"Those who light a fire cannot ask for protection from the flames," said Israeli delegate Gideon Rafael as the Security Council assembled in New York to try to head off this new threat of large-scale war. Rejecting the customary Soviet bid for a condemnation of Israeli "aggression," the Council unanimously agreed on October 25 to adopt another cease-fire resolution which named no culprits but condemned the recent "violations" of the cease-fire and demanded the immediate cessation of all prohibited military activities.[111]

This crisis past, the ten nonpermanent members of the Security Council could resume their search for a peace formula acceptable both to the big powers and to their Middle Eastern friends. The idea of naming a U.N. mediator had by this time gained wide acceptance, but no such figure would have a chance of success until the U.N. had pronounced itself on the critical issue of Israeli withdrawal from the occupied territories and the conditions under which it might be accomplished. A draft resolution elaborated by Denmark was rather vague on this crucial point, while an Indian draft was more precise; but neither one was vague enough to satisfy the Israelis, who still had no intention of withdrawing in the absence of far-reaching guarantees. Though Mr. Eban had intimated that Israel would not necessarily refuse to talk with a U.N. envoy if his mission were properly defined in advance, Premier Eshkol in Jerusalem was talking as if Israel intended to hold the occupied territories indefinitely.[112] By the beginning of November it was apparent that the ten nonpermanent members would not be able to bridge the withdrawal gap and that the quest for peace must pass to other hands.

It was Hussein of Jordan who now picked up the sputtering peace torch. On a visit to the United States in the first week of November, the Jordanian ruler made a series of remarkable statements in which he stressed the urgency of reaching a political settlement before the "moderate" mood engendered at Khartoum was dissipated by the agitation of Arab militants in his own and other countries. To achieve such a settlement, Hussein acknowledged, the Arab countries would have to be prepared for far-reaching concessions, especially in regard to the recognition of Israel's right to exist in peace and security. Asserting that he reflected Abdel Nasser's views as well as his own, Hussein urged Israel to make concrete proposals for the Arabs to consider. Such proposals, he cautioned in an obvious deviation from Israeli views, would naturally have to provide for the return of Old

Jerusalem and the other occupied territories as well as a solution of the refugee problem.[113]

Although the U.A.R. refrained from endorsing Hussein's statements, its own publicity continued to sound a relatively moderate note that contrasted sharply with the intransigence of the Syrians and Algerians. Cairo's only positive action at this stage, however, was a demand that the Security Council meet again to consider the dangerous situation created by Israel's refusal to withdraw from the conquered territories. Meeting in response to this request on November 9, the Council found itself still facing the familiar choice between two opposite approaches, each apparently incapable of winning majority approval. India, Mali, and Nigeria proposed a resolution calling unequivocally for Israeli withdrawal from all occupied territories and, in a halfhearted attempt to sweeten the pill, expressing general support for principles of legality and the right of national existence.[114] This text was supported, with reservations, by the U.S.S.R. The United States, in an alternative resolution presented by Ambassador Goldberg, likewise proposed that Israel should withdraw. Once again, however, withdrawal was treated in the American draft as part of a larger complex of issues, based on President Johnson's "five points," which it was now proposed to adjust with the aid of a representative of the Secretary-General.[115]

The familiar argument that now resumed was varied only by the introduction of a constructive Soviet proposal to increase the number of U.N. observers in the Suez Canal area and provide them with improved facilities. This plan was to be separately approved by the Council, without a formal vote, on December 8.[116] Meanwhile, in an attempt to break the deadlock on the issue of Israeli withdrawal, the Latin American countries made plans to revive their earlier proposals to the Emergency Session of the General Assembly. This time, however, it was Great Britain that stepped forward with what turned out to be a successful compromise—one that offered enough satisfaction to the various interests at stake to escape Israeli condemnation, divide the Arab states, and overcome a last-minute Soviet blocking effort. Spurred by new military clashes between Israel and Jordan, the Council on November 22 unanimously approved the British draft resolution and thus, in effect, made the first concrete move toward a settlement in nearly six months of U.N. effort.[117]

The Security Council resolution of November 22, which was henceforth to represent the basic charter of U.N. peacemaking efforts, was fully satisfactory to no one but gained at least preliminary acceptance by everyone concerned except the Syrians, who contended with typical exaggeration that it merely called for an Arab surrender. The U.S.S.R., and other Arab and pro-Arab states, went along with the resolution because it did at least call plainly for Israel's withdrawal. The United States and most other members of the Council accepted it because it linked withdrawal to an enumeration of principles for a lasting peace as well as providing for the designation of a Special Representative of the Secretary-General to assist the parties' efforts to this end.

Admittedly the resolution was less comprehensive than the United States would have wished. Of President Johnson's original five points —"recognized rights of national life, progress in solving the refugee problem, freedom of innocent maritime passage, limitation of the arms race, and respect for political independence and territorial integrity"— several were rather weakly stated, though only the point about the arms race was entirely left out. Although events were to show that this was an omission of some seriousness, Ambassador Goldberg could at least point out that the resolution was entirely consistent with U.S. policy as the President had defined it.

U Thant lost no time in naming Ambassador Gunnar V. Jarring of Sweden as Special Representative and in instructing him to proceed to the Middle East as promptly as possible to assist in peacemaking efforts under the terms of the November 22 resolution. Whether the Jarring mission succeeded or failed, it would at least oblige the belligerents to formulate their aims more precisely and decide just which of their demands they would insist upon. Israel, though it expressed willingness to talk to Mr. Jarring, would obviously be in no hurry to begin its withdrawal, would continue to insist on direct negotiations with the Arabs, and would be inclined to "sit tight," proceed with its gradual absorption of the conquered territories, and await an adjustment of the Arab stance. Those Arabs who were realistic enough to see the need for some retreat from the official Arab position as formulated at Khartoum would face the more difficult problem of trying to formulate a line of action that would safeguard at least the essence of Arab interests.

An awareness of these difficulties undoubtedly prompted Abdel Nasser's declaration that the U.N. resolution was "insufficient" and "unclear" and should be examined by the Arab leaders at another summit conference. With the consent of all but Syria, which refused to have anything to do with the resolution, it was accordingly decided to convene a top-level meeting at Rabat, Morocco, on December 9. This date, however, was presently found impracticable for a number of reasons, among them a new crisis in Yemen and the news that Chairman Brezhnev would be visiting Cairo in early January, conceivably with tidings that would influence the political outlook. Though Jordan urged that the search for a political settlement be pressed without further delay, the Arab Foreign Ministers at a Cairo meeting on December 9-11 agreed that the Rabat "summit" should be postponed to January 17, 1968. Overt references to the U.N. resolution and the Jarring mission were deleted from the summit agenda in an apparent attempt to placate that section of Arab opinion, led by Syria, which continued to reject the whole procedure as a "sellout."[118]

While these discussions were going on in Cairo, the General Assembly in New York had been discussing the problems of the U.N. Relief and Works Agency for Palestine Refugees (UNRWA) in its endeavor to provide for both the "old" refugees from the war of 1948-49 and the "new" refugees from the recent fighting. About the urgency of UNRWA's need for support there was no room for doubt; but there was as usual considerable doubt about where the necessary funds were to come from. Of the $47.5 million sought by UNRWA Commissioner General Laurence Michelmore for the coming year, only $26,270,340 (including up to $22.2 million to be provided on a matching basis by the United States) was subscribed at the regular U.N. pledging conference held December 6.[119] Many of the states that pledged no financial contribution did subsequently cast their votes in the General Assembly in favor of an American resolution calling for more adequate aid to refugees, together with a second resolution asking emergency aid for all persons displaced by the June war.[120]

Ambassador Jarring had by this time set up a headquarters in Cyprus and was commencing a preliminary round of visits to the capitals of those belligerent countries—all but Syria—that were willing to receive him. In the meantime, the interested governments were beginning to ventilate their own ideas on some of the points involved in a peace settlement. Israel, for example, had announced at the United Nations that it was ready to cooperate with its Arab neighbors in a five-year plan to rehabilitate the Arab refugees and integrate them permanently into the economic life of the region—though only as part of a general peace settlement.[121] This plan, it is true, seemed to stand little chance of acceptance by the Arab governments, which were fundamentally opposed to any arrangement for the refugees that failed to provide for their reabsorption into Israel.

Jordan and the U.A.R., however, were also sending up trial balloons that seemed to suggest a readiness for at least limited concessions. Alternately bellicose and pacific, Cairo had noticeably moderated its language about the Gulf of Aqaba and now suggested that if Israel would evacuate the Sinai region and thus make possible the reopening of the Suez Canal, it might agree to the establishment of a demilitarized frontier zone and even to the recognition of Israel's right to national existence. Hussein of Jordan, meanwhile, was credited with a scheme (which he later disavowed) whereby if Israel relinquished its conquests on the West Bank, Jordan would accept a partial demilitarization of that area.[122] Still another sign of fluidity in Arab attitudes was the discontent expressed by several Arab governments with the bumbling performance of Ahmed Shukairy, whose resignation as chairman of the Palestine Liberation Organization was announced later in December.[123]

Such developments were obviously not to be read as harbingers of an early peace. Shukairy's ouster, for example, was ostensibly intended to clear the way for more effective coordination of underground activity in Israeli-occupied territories. Some Arab countries, like Syria, remained totally opposed to a political settlement; and all of them were affected in some degree by unofficial but powerful agitation for renewal of the war. The idea of a "fourth round" against Israel had natural attractions for any Arab who felt himself involved in the disgrace of the recent "setback." The practicability of such an exercise might depend primarily on the attitudes of the outside powers on which the Arab countries still relied for the means of warmaking— particularly on the way in which the U.S.S.R. decided to pursue the rebuilding of its Middle Eastern fortunes.

17 : Arms and the Great Powers

For some observers of international affairs, the enlargement of the
Soviet role in the Middle East and the Mediterranean was to stand
out as the most significant world development of 1967.[124] Far from
sharing in the defeat of its Arab protégés, it was by this time clear
that the U.S.S.R. had profited by their discomfiture to extend its own
influence and achieve a more powerful position in the region than it
had ever previously occupied. From Algeria to Yemen and from
Syria to the Sudan, the Soviet Union had seized new footholds or
developed old ones at a moment when the slump in British and American influence had given it practically a clear field. The very ease of
these successes might raise some doubt about their solidity and permanence; but there could be little doubt that the over-all trend in the
closing months of 1967 had been heavily in Moscow's favor.

The formula by which these successes had been attained had two
simple ingredients: support of the Arab cause at the United Nations
and, more potent still, military support in the form of arms shipments
ostensibly designed to retrieve the local balance of power. In the
U.A.R., such shipments were estimated by the end of 1967 to have
restored from 80 to 90 per cent of the June losses, in part with tanks
and aircraft of more modern design which were accompanied by
improved antiaircraft equipment a well as hundreds of Soviet advisers
and technicians. A good-will visit by ten Soviet twin-jet bombers at
the beginning of December gave ostentatious expression to the much
closer military relationship that had developed in recent months.

Yet to a man of Abdel Nasser's independent temperament this
heavy reliance on a single foreign government was bound to be irk-
some. Already there had been signs that the U.A.R. President was
hoping to dilute his Soviet dependence by lowering the pitch of his
quarrels with Great Britain and even the United States. Some such
calculation may well have underlain his comparative moderation on
the question of peace with Israel. In addition, there had been conversations early in November with an unofficial American emissary,
Robert B. Anderson, which led to no immediate result but may have
helped pave the way for a lifting of the U.S. restriction on travel to the
U.A.R. in mid-November.[125] With Great Britain, the U.A.R. went

so far as to renew the diplomatic relations it had broken off in 1964. In what seemed a further effort to reassure the West, Abdel Nasser's official spokesman stated that the U.S.S.R. would not be given military "bases" in the U.A.R., although the word "base" was not precisely defined.[126]

There were, however, other possible *points d'appui* for the Soviet fleet in the Mediterranean, which was now being maintained at considerably greater strength than before the June war—35 to 46 vessels was the usual enumeration—and at times approached numerical parity with the U.S. Sixth Fleet of 50 or 60 ships. France was preparing to evacuate its great base at Mers-el-Kebir in Algeria, which it was legally entitled to retain until 1975; and there were unconfirmable rumors that the Russians might soon be moving in with the consent of Colonel Boumedienne's government. Algeria had been second only to the U.A.R. as a recent recipient of Soviet MIG's, tanks, and experts, although its government, too, was described as restive about its dependence on the U.S.S.R. and anxious to open up new sources of arms supply.[127]

The extent of Soviet arms aid to Syria was more difficult to establish, and the intransigence of the Syrian leadership, which openly disagreed with the Soviet Union over the Security Council resolution of November 22, seemed hardly to recommend it for unqualified Soviet support. Nevertheless, Prime Minister al-Zayen paid another visit to Moscow at the beginning of December in the course of which he not only expressed gratitude for the U.S.S.R.'s "all-round assistance" but was promised further support for Syria's "just struggle."[128] Jordan still hesitated to accept the Soviet offer to reequip its forces, nothwithstanding the United States' reluctance to go forward with its own arms deliveries. Iraq, on the other hand, had not only received consignments of Soviet aircraft—its Air Force was by now reported to exceed its prewar size—but, as will be seen, was preparing to grant its benefactor important economic advantages as well.

The Soviet Union was not entirely alone in its efforts to improve its position among the Arab states. France, too, had gained a political advantage in the area through its prewar disavowal of Israel and subsequent insistence on Israeli withdrawal from the conquered territories—a position strongly reaffirmed by President de Gaulle in a celebrated press conference on November 27.[129] Like the Soviet Union, France had been working to convert this psychological advan-

tage into solid material benefits. On the one hand, it had sternly maintained its ban on arms sales to Israel, at least in regard to aircraft
and other major items. On the other, it had apparently been holding
out the prospect of arms shipments to Arab countries as a bait in the
pursuit of other gains. In the most notable use of this technique, it
became known early in December that the French government-
controlled oil company had been granted exploration and production
rights in a huge tract of territory in southern Iraq. French interests
were also known to be bidding for other mineral concessions in that
country, and an Iraqi military mission visited Paris in late autumn
with what appeared at the time to be an excellent prospect of obtaining Mirage V fighter-bombers and other military equipment. Apart
from an agreement on the sale of some armored gun carriers, however,
no military deals were actually consummated during 1967.[130]

A good deal of mystery surrounded France's intentions in the
Middle East, and even its policy concerning arms for Israel was the
subject of contradictory reports.[131] But the mere possibility of obtaining French arms was sufficient to whet the appetite of other countries.
Syrian Premier al-Zayen, just back from Moscow, set out again on a
mission to Paris with the reported aim of obtaining arms in exchange
for marketing rights in Syria's newly developed oil production. The
Franco-Syrian agreement announced December 15 did not, indeed,
make any reference to military aid, but stressed the hopes of both
governments for expanded economic, technical, and cultural cooperation. Particularly extolled by President de Gaulle was the prospect
that Syria, in exchange for such assistance, would "open her doors
wide to French language and culture."[132]

In Iraq, France's oil coup had affected only a part of the country's
rich petroleum resources. The U.S.S.R itself, it now appeared, was
also to profit by Iraq's assistance in making an entry on the Middle
Eastern oil scene. On December 17, Iraq and the U.S.S.R. concluded
an agreement designed to expedite the completion of five Soviet-
financed industrial projects. A week later, a second agreement—
explicitly described as a payoff for Soviet support in the Mid-East
crisis—opened the way to Soviet participation in oil exploration,
production, and marketing in an undefined area that was generally
assumed to lie in northern Iraq, separate from the recent French
concession. Not only did the Soviet move appear to presage intensified
Iraqi hostility toward the Western-owned Iraq Petroleum Company,

which had at one time held a monopoly position in the country. It was also interpreted as a new strategic setback for the West and quite possibly the forerunner of additional Soviet moves aimed at gaining control of the Middle East's oil wealth.[133]

For Israel, the reconstruction of Arab military establishments, the continuance of frequent frontier clashes and acts of sabotage, and the Arab talk of a "fourth round" of fighting offered little inducement to relinquish the strategic advantages gained in the June war. Nor could Israel be expected to rest indefinitely on its current military superiority while its neighbors were acquiring MIG-21's and other advanced products of Soviet military technology. An order for 50 of France's Mirage V fighter-bombers, placed as much as two years earlier, was still being held up; and the United States was only now beginning delivery of the 48 A-4 Skyhawk attack bombers that had also been ordered long before the war.

Thus it was only to be expected that Israel should explore the possibility of obtaining further military aid from the United States, in spite of Washington's well-known antipathy to becoming a "major arms supplier" in the Middle East. Israeli military men were described as particularly anxious to acquire 50 F-4 Phantom fighter-bombers, the most advanced in the U.S. inventory, plus an assurance of continuing arms availability over the next several years. Although the initial State Department response to these Israeli soundings was described as almost wholly negative,[134] the approach of a presidential election in the United States seemed likely to create a climate more favorable to Israeli desires, and Premier Eshkol was thought certain to pursue the issue when he visited the United States early in 1968.

Developments in the Red Sea and the Arabian peninsula seemed likely to exert their own influence on the Middle Eastern balance of power. Here, too, Soviet influence seemed to be on the rise as other influences waned. In Yemen, Abdel Nasser had by this time scrupulously carried out the Khartoum agreement to remove his forces; the last Egyptian units, apart from a few stragglers, were out of the country by the end of November. Instead of the reconciliation of Yemeni political factions envisaged at Khartoum, however, the civil war between royalists and republicans had once more broken out—and this time it was not the Egyptians but the Russians who were speeding to the republicans' assistance.

The turning point in Yemen's muddled affairs occurred on November 5 when President al-Salal, a consistent foe of the Khartoum agreement, was ousted by a military coup and supplanted by a three-man Presidential Council of moderate political complexion led by the scholarly Abdul Rahman al-Iryani. The new regime would seem to have tried and failed to strike a bargain with the royalists and their Saudi Arabian backers which would have made possible an internal compromise but still preserved the republican form of government. These overtures having been rejected and with the royalists again taking the offensive, the republican leaders apparently saw no alternative to seeking assistance from the U.S.S.R. and adopting a more radical political line such as would qualify them for Soviet aid. By November 22, royalist units were beginning to menace the capital, and it was reported that four MIG's and 40 Soviet technicians had arrived on the scene and that twenty additional Soviet planes were on the way. Later reports were to speak of 75 to 100 Soviet supply flights and the shipment of 10,000 tons of equipment.[135]

Even this demonstration of Soviet support was insufficient to quell the ardor of the royalists, who rapidly closed a ring around Sana and by December 26 had caused Soviet and other diplomats to flee the capital. Each side, meanwhile, charged massive foreign intervention on the side of its enemies. With the royalists asserting that Soviet pilots were fighting on the republican side, the republicans countered by charging Saudi and even American intervention on the side of the royalists. (The latter report, at least, was clearly untrue.) Meanwhile attempts at mediation through the tripartite committee set up at Khartoum proved ineffective, although the opposing sides did agree on the last day of the year to meet at a preliminary "reconciliation" conference to be held in Beirut on January 12, 1968. Only time would tell how seriously the U.S.S.R. regarded its new commitment to the republicans, how hard it would try to maintain its foothold in Yemen, and how far it might seek to develop a springboard for wider ventures in the Persian Gulf and East Africa.

These same weeks also witnessed the final throes of the British-ruled South Arabian Federation and its replacement by the new, independent People's Republic of Southern Yemen, the only new nation to come to birth in 1967. Soviet influence played no direct role in this development, and the U.S.S.R. appeared to hold no special advantages in the new state apart from the general sympathy it enjoyed in "revolutionary" Arab nationalist circles. The final arrangements for Southern Yemen's independence, which formally took effect on November 30, were hastily concocted at Geneva in meetings between the British and representatives of the National Liberation Front, which had by this time won out in the internal power struggle and was to provide the nucleus of the new national administration headed by President Qahtan Muhammad al-Shaabi.

Like other new states, Southern Yemen was promptly recognized by the United States[136] and admitted to the United Nations "by acclamation"[137] in spite of its feeble economic base and less than reassuring political attitude. Fiercely nationalistic and anti-Western by definition, the new government seemed to see its main task as that of bringing about an eventual union with Yemen; but some of its members also voiced disconcerting expansionist ambitions with respect to neighboring Muscat and Oman and other Persian Gulf territories. The suspicion was even voiced that Southern Yemen's new leaders might offer the Russians a naval foothold at the abandoned British base in Aden. One thing seemed sure: the decline of Nasserist influence in the peninsula, even if permanent, had been accompanied by a total evaporation of the Western position in this strategic area.

Western interests suffered still another blow during this period in the crisis over Cyprus which brought Greece and Turkey to the brink of war in late November and tore a gaping hole in allied solidarity in the Eastern Mediterranean. This crisis, which is described in a later chapter, [138] was prevented by adroit diplomacy from developing into a conflict that might have proved as dangerous and destructive as the Arab-Israeli encounter. The avoidance of war was greatly assisted by the fact that the Soviet Union did not, in this instance, encourage the bellicose proclivities of either contestant and refrained from interfering with efforts by the United States and others to ensure a peaceful outcome. The net result of the crisis, however, was to leave the Soviets' Mediterranean position unimpaired while subjecting that of the West to still further uncertainties. It thus offered no significant departure from the general pattern of Middle Eastern affairs in a year that had brought much misery to the peoples involved, a series of reverses for the West, and a corresponding increase in the influence of the Soviet Union.

4 : East-West Pause

To most Americans, the events in Vietnam and the Middle East posed issues of absorbing interest that urgently demanded resolution on their visible, intrinsic merits. The heat and dust arising from these local conflicts quite often obscured the fact that their real significance transcended geographic limitations and thus defied assessment in purely regional terms. Supremely passionate in themselves, both the anti-Communist struggle in Vietnam and the conflict between Israel and the Arab states had a recognizable place in the pattern of global East-West rivalry that had so strongly imprinted itself on the world's history ever since 1945. Neither of these localized conflicts could realistically be isolated from the larger confrontation between the Communist and Western powers. Those powers, despite some changes of emphasis and limited progress toward mutual understanding, were still animated at bottom by opposite political and social philosophies, committed to sharply incompatible foreign policies, deeply mistrustful of each other's intentions, and determined so far as possible to deny each other the benefits of even localized political success.

There had been a time when these broader ramifications of the East-West impasse had been more readily acknowledged than was true in 1967. Yet even the lessening intensity of the "cold war" during the 1960's had clearly not eliminated the radical opposition between the great powers of East and West or, more especially, between the United States and the Soviet Union, the holders of

138

the major share of power and responsibility within the two groups. That outright war among nuclear powers would be catastrophic for all concerned had, of course, been repeatedly acknowledged by leaders of both camps. Only Communist China rejected this seemingly self-evident proposition. But while the Soviet Union appeared by this time to have abandoned any idea of promoting world revolution by international conflict, it had by no means renounced all use of force in the service of revolutionary aims. It had, in fact, repeatedly expressed its enthusiastic support for so-called "wars of national liberation" such as the one that was currently being conducted under Communist leadership in Vietnam. The United States, with equal decisiveness, had reserved its right to oppose such ventures, both in its own interest and in the interest of people who, like the South Vietnamese, apparently preferred a non-Communist existence.

The United States, in other words, was fighting in Vietnam because its leaders believed a Communist conquest of South Vietnam would represent not only a tragedy for the South Vietnamese but a threat to non-Communist (including American) interests over a much wider area. Similarly, the United States' support of CENTO and its limited assistance to Israel and certain moderate Arab governments were rooted not merely in local interests and sympathies but in a basic unwillingness to allow the Middle East to fall under Soviet domination, either directly or through governments subservient to Moscow. Whether well or badly conceived, such policies transcended mere local considerations and were shaped by a broad, general conception of the political forces in the world at large.

Recognition of the continuing opposition between Soviet and American aims had not, however, prevented the United States from working to eliminate sources of friction, promote mutual understanding, limit the competition in armaments, and generally encourage the Soviet Union and its allies in Eastern Europe to adopt a live-and-let-live attitude in relation to non-Communist countries. For a time, at least, these endeavors had appeared to be having some success. The Soviet Government, since the advent of Brezhnev and Kosygin, had shown a certain reluctance to involve itself in foreign adventures, a readiness to adjust at least some issues by negotiation, and a disposition to turn inward and devote itself more vigorously to the improvement of Soviet society and to trying to reinforce its challenged position within the Communist world itself.

This favorable trend had, however, been seriously slowed if not completely interrupted by the progressive "escalation" of the Vietnam conflict from 1965 onward. Although the United States insisted that the war in Vietnam presented no obstacle to further improvement in U.S.-Soviet relations, the U.S.S.R. had increased its verbal and material support of North Vietnam and, at the same time, declared it futile to think about improved relations as long as the U.S. "aggression" in Vietnam continued. As the international atmosphere darkened, progress toward the solution of outstanding East-West issues had ground practically to a halt. Successive intensifications of the American military pressure on North Vietnam had even raised a possibility that the Soviet Union might at some point consider itself forced to respond with military action of its own. Coming on top of these already threatening conditions, the major crisis which developed in the Middle East in June 1967 afforded the world its most anxious moments since the Cuban missile confrontation of 1962.

More than one theory was advanced in the West in an attempt to account for Soviet conduct during these years. Some observers maintained that the Soviet leadership—or at least its dominant members, since it was reasonable to believe they sometimes differed among themselves—had genuinely sought *détente* with the United States and had only reluctantly shelved this objective when American actions in Vietnam made it impracticable. With its leadership of world Communism under sharp challenge by the Chinese, it was suggested, the U.S.S.R. could not do less than it was doing for the Communist regime in North Vietnam, and, above all, could not possibly let itself be caught in any "deals" with the Americans. Liquidation of the American venture in Vietnam, according to this view, was the *sine qua non* of any basic improvement in East-West relations. This in fact was a view that Moscow itself had frequently expounded.

While such a theory did not lack verisimilitude, some evidence could also be adduced in support of an alternative, in many ways more sinister interpretation. Conceivably Moscow had never intended to settle its major differences with the United States and the West on any basis the Western governments could accept. Conceivably it had merely been playing for time and using the idea of "peaceful coexistence" and "relaxation of tensions" as a tactical device in the way that Soviet leaders of an earlier generation had habitually done.

Since the Cuban missile crisis, it had been generally understood that the U.S.S.R. was heavily outclassed by the United States in terms of nuclear striking power, supposedly the decisive element in modern warfare. In this position of at least momentary military inferiority, saddled in addition with the Sino-Soviet dispute as well as a wide variety of internal problems, the Soviet leaders might merely have granted themselves and the Soviet people a breathing spell until such time as the external struggle could be resumed with greater confidence.

Even such a tactical maneuver would not have been without value from the standpoint of longer-range Soviet aims. Tentative indications of a milder temper in the Kremlin had already dissipated what remained of the "cold war" spirit in the West and produced a far-reaching relaxation of its political and military vigilance. Americans, when they thought of the Soviet Union, no longer thought primarily in terms of hostility. In Western Europe, the idea of war with the U.S.S.R. had virtually lapsed from consciousness, and American resistance to Communism in such remote places as Vietnam was regarded with incomprehension and distaste. NATO, with General de Gaulle's assistance, appeared to be losing both its organizational coherence and its sense of mission. Even the collective attempt to promote the economic development of the resurgent countries was being pursued with rather less conviction than in the years when economic development had been widely seen as a phase of the East-West competition.

Even while the Western countries were responding to its smiles, however, indications had begun to appear that the Soviet Union was preparing to redress the military balance and try to make up its deficiencies in nuclear-tipped long-range missiles. Though Secretary McNamara insisted late in 1966 that the United States retained a superiority of three or four to one in intercontinental ballistic missiles and would maintain its capacity to inflict unacceptable damage on any assailants even after a surprise attack, he also noted that the U.S.S.R. appeared to have been stepping up the pace of its own I.C.B.M. deployment over the past year and, unlike the United States, was apparently initiating the deployment of an antiballistic missile system as well.[1] These disclosures sufficed in themselves to suggest that the Soviet Union would not content itself with a position of permanent strategic inferiority to its principal rival. Further revelations in the course of 1967 were to suggest that it was actually forging ahead of the United States in some branches of military technology and, moreover, was much more resolute than the latter in its willingness to face the costs and hazards of an accelerated arms race. In conjunction with what seemed the new boldness of Soviet foreign policy in the Middle East and elsewhere, such evidence made it impossible not to wonder whether the period of relative *détente* was about to be superseded by a chapter of sharpened danger and antagonism.

18 : Détente *in the Balance*

A deliberate sharpening of East-West antagonism seemed far from the intentions of any major government (except, possibly, the Chinese) as 1967 began. "Our objective," President Johnson declared in his January 10 State of the Union message, "is not to continue the cold war, but to end it."[2] The Soviet leaders, presumably, had special reasons for hoping that the coming months would be free from serious international disturbances. In November, the Soviet Union planned to commemorate an event of momentous importance in its own history and, as everyone agreed, the history of the world. November 7, 1967 would mark the 50th anniversary of the "Great October Socialist Revolution" which had brought the Bolsheviks to power in Russia and served to establish the Soviet Union as a factor of great and steadily increasing influence in international affairs. No avoidable unpleasantness was to mar the festival of self-congratulation which Moscow planned for that occasion.

Even its bitterest critics conceded that the Soviet Union had cause for pride in difficulties overcome and new possibilities opened up during this turbulent half-century. Yet with all its undeniable accomplishments, it was equally clear that this rapidly maturing nation of 234 million people remained far short of the universal abundance its prophets had foretold. The U.S.S.R. still wrestled with vast internal problems whose full solution could only lie in the distant future. The far-reaching reforms in industrial management and agricultural policy initiated under Brezhnev's and Kosygin's leadership were still in their initial stages, while popular demand for a larger share of material goods had already reached peak intensity. An irrepressible ferment among those dedicated to the intellectual life presented a continuing, sometimes frightening challenge to the guardians of ideological purity. The failure thus far to issue a final version of the Eighth Five-Year Plan, for 1966-70, suggested that arguments might still be going forward in the Soviet leadership about the long-term allocation of resources as between military needs, industry, agriculture, consumer goods, and such costly ventures as the exploration of outer space and aid to developing countries.

The Soviet military position, though extremely powerful in continental terms, still lacked the flexibility and global reach ascribed to the American defense establishment. Admittedly capable of raining sudden atomic destruction on American cities, the Soviet Union could do so only at the risk of almost certain destruction by surviving American missiles and bombers. Attempts to mitigate these handicaps by constructing an aircraft carrier or two and the deploying of an anti-missile network might perhaps add to the U.S.S.R.'s freedom of international action, but only at the cost of an additional strain on its material resources which would not, perhaps, yield any increase in essential security in the long run.

Many of these problems were of a sort that was normal in the life of any great power; and the significant point about the Soviet Union in the mid-1960's was that it tended to act like a normal great power rather than an uninhibited instigator of world revolution. This change in the Soviet style, together with the increasing assertion of normal human attitudes on the part of the Soviet population, might in some ways constitute an offense against the Leninist revolutionary tradition so fulsomely praised in Soviet propaganda. Such, in fact, was clearly the opinion of those implacable "Marxist-Leninists" who spoke for Communist China. Yet nothing could have been more encouraging to the rest of the world than the apparent dwindling of Soviet revolutionary fervor and the reemergence of a mentality more akin to that of non-Communist countries. If Moscow and the West could once begin to look at their relationship in an objective spirit, it seemed that solutions to their actual problems ought not to be too difficult to find.

A similar sense of relaxation, moderation, and diminished revolutionary fervor was apparent in most of the Communist countries of Eastern Europe. No longer classifiable as Soviet "satellites" and no longer dominated by Moscow to anything like the extent that had

been true at an earlier period, most of the latter still found it preferable to follow the Soviet lead in international questions while seeking
their own "road to socialism" in internal and economic matters. Such
tendencies had been carried even further by Yugoslavia, which had
revolted against Soviet domination as far back as 1948, considered
itself as much "nonaligned" as Communist, and agreed with Moscow
only when it chose to do so. Rumania, of late, had begun to act on
rather similar principles and had openly differed with the Soviet Union
on basic questions of Communist and international policy. At the
opposite extreme, Albania had completely cut its ties with the "Soviet
bloc" and become a small but obstreperous follower of Communist
China.

China's own emergence into a position of total independence and
of absolute hostility to the U.S.S.R. and its policies was presumably
the most dismaying of all contemporary world developments from the
standpoint of the Soviet leadership. This rift in the "camp of socialism" was undeniably a major blot on the 50-year record of triumphant
Marxism-Leninism. After several years of doctrinal polemics and
mutual vilification, the relations between the two leading Communist
powers had by 1967 deteriorated to a point at which even the validity
of the basic Sino-Soviet mutual defense pact of 1950 was freely called
in question. Russians, by this time, were beginning to speak openly
about the possibility of war with China and to give the impression
that they regarded that country as an even more dangerous foe than
the "imperialist" United States.[3]

The Sino-Soviet conflict and the accompanying disarray in the Communist world had clearly exercised a decisive influence in the shaping
of Soviet policy on other issues. Normal international relations were
out of the question while this scandalous condition persisted, and the
Soviet leadership had endeavored for several years to organize a
world-wide meeting of Communist parties for the express purpose of
castigating the Chinese party for its doctrinal errors and restoring
"unity" in the world Communist movement. Failure to implement this
plan had been mainly due to the stubborn opposition of Yugoslavia,
Rumania, and some of the other Communist governments and parties
which, though critical of Chinese actions, were almost equally mistrustful of any plan for reimposing Communist "unity" on the Soviet
model.

A series of meetings among Communist leaders in the early weeks of 1967 indicated that this resistance had not diminished in spite of the increasingly unedifying course of recent events in China, whose "Great Proletarian Cultural Revolution" had by this time degenerated into a condition bordering on outright civil war. Relations between the Soviet and Chinese governments were meanwhile plummeting toward a new low as the result of contumacious behavior by Chinese students on their way home through Moscow, informal reprisals by Soviet citizens, and a violent Chinese reaction which included prolonged mob harassment of the U.S.S.R.'s Peking embassy and its personnel. By mid-February, the Soviet Communist party newspaper *Pravda* was openly recommending to the Chinese that they get rid of Chairman Mao Tse-tung as a first step toward rejoining the "socialist" community.[4] Though Moscow was popularly assumed to be in contact with some of the Chinese opponents of Mao Tse-tung's leadership, it seemed at the moment to lack sufficient leverage in China to protect even its own dignity.

With such unruly neighbors to the East, it must at times have been difficult for the Soviet leaders to give attention to the pressing business confronting their country in the West. There were, however, a variety of issues in the field of East-West relations, some of them of long standing and others of more recent date, which were reaching a decisive stage in the winter of 1966-67 and could make 1967 a critical turning point in the whole relationship between the Communist and Western worlds. Among them were questions relating to the arms race, the future of Germany and Europe, and the policy of creating mutual understanding and tempering the "cold war" through increased trade, cultural and technical exchanges, and other exercises in good neighborly relations.

In all these areas, two contradictory tendencies appeared at work in both the Eastern and the Western camps. On one hand was the impulse toward *détente,* the building of "bridges," the settlement of outstanding problems, and the alleviation of past antagonisms; on the other, the persistence of long-held enmities, ingrained suspicions, and mistrust for the future which tended to counteract and neutralize the more constructive trend. On the side of the United States and the other Western powers, there was an unmistakable desire to improve relations with the Communist camp so far as this could be done without jeopardizing their own essential interests and security. To Western minds, it seemed that the Soviet Union should have a parallel interest in improving the East-West relationship, and should be even more strongly impelled in that direction by its troubles with China. At the same time, it was apparent that U.S.-Soviet differences over Vietnam presented a difficulty of some magnitude which might, from the Soviet viewpoint, even be felt to overshadow any advantages to be gained from further *détente*. The relative influence of these different factors could only be assayed as the governments of East and West got down to practical discussion of the issues confronting them.

In the all-important field of arms control, the world community already had two important if limited achievements to its credit, both of them made possible mainly by agreement between the United States and the U.S.S.R. One of these was the Treaty Banning Nuclear Weapon Tests in the Atmosphere, in Outer Space, and Under Water, concluded in Moscow in 1963;[5] the other, the Treaty on Principles Governing the Activities of States in the Exploration and Use of Outer Space, Including the Moon and Other Celestial Bodies, which had been approved by the United Nations in December 1966 and was to be signed by over 60 governments on January 27, 1967.[6] In addition to providing for freedom of scientific investigation and barring claims of sovereignty in outer space, this second treaty had some importance from the disarmament standpoint in that it prohibited military activities on the moon and other celestial bodies and forbade the placement of nuclear weapons or other weapons of mass destruction on celestial bodies, in outer space, or in orbit around the earth. So far as was known, neither the Soviet Union nor the United States had any plans for doing any of these things. Still, their formal prohibition by an international treaty was looked upon as an additional safeguard of some significance.

With agreement on these two matters pinned down, the governments of the United States, the U.S.S.R., and other countries participating in the search for "general and complete disarmament" would confront three further tasks of comparable urgency. One of these would be the attempt to extend the 1963 test-ban treaty in such a way as to cover underground as well as above-surface and underwater tests—an endeavor frustrated thus far by Soviet refusal to accept the limited measure of international, on-site inspection the United States deemed necessary to ensure that the agreed prohibitions would be faithfully observed. A second project was an attempt to bar the further spread or "proliferation" of nuclear weapons by means of a treaty pledging both nuclear and nonnuclear powers to cooperate in limiting such weapons to the five powers that already possessed them—the United States, the U.S.S.R., Great Britain, France, and Communist China. A third and more novel undertaking, announced by the United States in January 1967, was the plan to engage the Soviet Union in bilateral discussions looking toward a mutual agreement to refrain from deploying antiballistic missile systems. As already explained,[7] it was the view of Secretary McNamara and the President that such an agreement would spare both powers important financial outlays while leaving intact the existing arrangement under which their security against one another was based essentially on the mutually deterrent effect of their offensive weapons.

Matters relating to the future of Germany and Europe were also reaching a stage at which important new decisions would be required. Developments in both the Communist and non-Communist parts of Europe had by this time largely broken down the old, rigid division at the "Iron Curtain" and created a highly fluid situation affecting the interests and policies of the European nations and of their outside friends. Historically, the actions of the U.S.S.R. in Germany and Europe had appeared to be governed by two main aims. Its primary effort, in which it had been largely successful, had been directed to strengthening the position of the Communist-ruled "German Democratic Republic," which exercised the functions of government in the Soviet-occupied Eastern zone of Germany and, under the presidency of Walter Ulbricht, had become one of the strongest though not the best-loved member of the East European Communist bloc. The other, and hitherto less successful, Soviet effort had been aimed at weakening the position of the Western-allied German Federal Republic, disrupting and weakening NATO and the other collective military, economic, and political arrangements in which West Germany participated along with other Western governments, and agitating for the withdrawal of the United States and its military forces from Europe.

One of the principal tools of this long-term Soviet campaign, most recently applied on several occasions during 1966, was a recurrent proposal that existing defense systems in Western and Eastern Europe be scrapped and replaced by an all-European security system without the Americans.[8] To most of the Western governments, it had seemed that the most likely effect of such an arrangement would be to deprive the Western European countries of the American protection they had hitherto enjoyed and place them instead under the somewhat doubtful protection of the U.S.S.R.—a change that would naturally have much to recommend it from a Soviet though hardly from a Western point of view. But similar ideas were not without attraction even in Western Europe, especially at times when Soviet policy looked comparatively benign and American policy was unpopular. French President de Gaulle was himself an advocate of restricting the American influence in Europe and forming closer ties with the U.S.S.R.; and his removal of France from NATO's military organization during 1966 had at least temporarily impaired the effectiveness of Western defense arrangements in much the way the Russians themselves had apparently sought.

More recent developments in Western Europe, however, had taken a turn that was much more problematical from the standpoint of Soviet aims. A new government had come to power in Western Germany in late 1966, headed by Chancellor Kurt Georg Kiesinger of the Christian Democratic Union and Vice-Chancellor and Foreign Minister Willy Brandt of the Social Democratic party. Professing unaltered loyalty to the West and NATO, the Kiesinger-Brandt regime had set in motion a determined effort to ameliorate the Federal Republic's hitherto icy relations with the Communist East. The primary aim of the new government was not to disrupt the Soviet bloc but simply to overcome the paralysis to which the Federal Republic had been condemned by its past refusal to recognize the East German regime or to have anything to do with those governments that did (other than the U.S.S.R. itself). West Germans had not ceased to hope that the Eastern and Western sections of their country would ultimately be reunited under a regime accepted by the German people as a whole. But since Moscow clearly did not intend to let this happen in the foreseeable future, the new government in Bonn had decided to make the best of a bad situation and try to alleviate the existing split in Germany and Europe by reaching out for economic, cultural, and even political ties with governments beyond the "Iron Curtain."

In pressing for closer ties with the East, the Bonn government did not plan to go so far as to accord legal recognition to the East German regime, which Bonn had always regarded as an artificial and illegal construction with no valid authority even in East Germany. As a practical matter, however, Kiesinger and Brandt showed much greater readiness than their predecessors to meet the East Germans halfway in dealing with questions of common interest. Equally important, they made known their eagerness to "build bridges" to the other Communist countries of Eastern Europe in much the way the United States had been trying to do. German trade with Eastern Europe was already considerable, but there was room for further expansion as well as the creation of many new ties in noneconomic fields.

This in itself would be a difficult undertaking in view of the detestation in which West Germany had been held in Eastern Europe ever since World War II. To the men in Bonn, however, it seemed that the dispelling of such antagonisms and the gradual relaxation of tension in Europe was the best and probably the only way to create a situation in which the reunification of Germany itself might eventually be brought about. The overriding aim, Chancellor Kiesinger explained, was "to relax and remove tensions from our relations with the Eastern European countries and with the Soviet Union. . . . We see such a challenge, the task of our generation, in the peaceful rebuilding of our relations with the East, including an end to the German problem."[9]

Traditionally mistrustful of everything that happened in Western Germany, the Communist governments reacted to these overtures with very diverse feelings. The most favorable responses came from the more distant members of the Communist bloc. Rumania, which had began to make a fetish of its independence in foreign policy, went so far as to sign an agreement with West Germany at the end of January which looked to the establishment of full diplomatic relations; and West German spokesmen expressed the hope that similar action would be taken by Hungary, Czechoslovakia, Bulgaria, and Yugoslavia. Poland, on the other hand, had suffered heavily at German hands, feared a German attempt to recover some of the former German territories it had annexed at the end of the war, and was much more hostile to the whole idea. But the most vehement opponent of West Germany's "new course" was the Ulbricht regime in East Germany. In obvious fear of being outflanked by their Western rivals, the East German authorities exerted heavy pressure on the other Eastern governments to reject Bonn's overtures. At the very least, the East Germans contended, Bonn ought to be made to pay a price for any advantages it might gain in Eastern Europe—and that price should certainly include formal recognition of the "German Democratic Republic."

Such differences within the "camp of socialism" could not be welcome in Moscow, and there are indications that the Soviet regime was itself in doubt about how to handle the matter. After a period of hesitancy, it offered the G.D.R. a measure of preliminary support by issuing on January 28 an official statement denouncing alleged "Nazism and militarism" in the Federal Republic and calling renewed attention to its own quite different program for European security.[10] This, however, was no more than a holding action until the position of the Communist governments could be worked out in common.

In the meantime there was other pending business that would help to test the intentions of governments in both East and West. Quite apart from the Vietnam situation, the East-West atmosphere had been impaired of late by a variety of minor frictions. Two of these, both reflecting the differences between Communist and Western concepts of legality, involved the fate of Americans caught in the toils of Communist police and judicial systems: Buel Ray Wortham, sentenced to imprisonment in the U.S.S.R. for currency violations and other minor offenses, and Vladimir Kazan-Komarek, a former Czechoslovak citizen convicted of subversive activities by the authorities of his former homeland. After a period of public anxiety and active diplomatic effort, both Americans were freed by the respective governments before their detention could cause more serious complications.[11] Less readily assuaged was Yugoslavia's anger over the bombing on January 29 of Yugoslav diplomatic establishments in three American and two Canadian cities, presumably by exiled opponents of the Tito regime. Recurrent manifestations of anti-Tito feeling in the United States did nothing to predispose the Yugoslav President in favor of American policy in Vietnam, the Middle East, or elsewhere.

There were various influences within the United States that did not greatly favor President Johnson's policy of trying to promote relations with Communist countries at a time when the latter were doing all they could to aid America's adversaries in Vietnam. The persistence of long-established anti-Communist attitudes, especially among Americans of more conservative bent, was largely responsible for the fact that more progress had not been made in past years on such favorite administration projects as the enactment of a bill to encourage trade with the Eastern countries and the ratification of a consular convention with the U.S.S.R., negotiated as far back as 1964. These two issues would again be coming up for congressional consideration in 1967, together with the new treaty on outer space. The action of Congress was expected to provide an indication as to how

seriously the United States itself was interested in reducing the scope
and intensity of the East-West conflict.

19 : Ups and Downs

The strands of the East-West fabric—disarmament, German affairs,
trade and treaty relations, and the like—were too closely interwoven
to be readily separable for purposes of historical scrutiny. What happened to one set of threads affected all the others, and the entire
fabric was pulled now one way, now another by world developments
involving the interests of the leading powers. The new American
proposal to discuss a "freeze" on the deployment of antiballistic
missiles, for example, had scarcely been presented in Moscow[12]
before the issue became entangled with the discussions about a bombing halt and peace negotiations in Vietnam—discussions which, as
already noted, reached a critical stage at the time of Premier Kosygin's
visit to London on February 6-13. As was pointed out in an earlier
chapter, the Soviet Premier's only public contribution to a Vietnam
solution during his London visit was his hint that peace talks "could"
occur if the United States would stop bombing North Vietnam—an
assurance much too vague for the United States in view of what it
was learning about the North Vietnamese attitude from other sources.[13]
Yet the way in which the hope for a cessation of Vietnam hostilities
was raised and then deflated on this occasion was bound to affect the
discussion of other East-West questions as well. All such discussions
would now take place against a backdrop of continued and intensifying war in Southeast Asia instead of the peace negotiations which for
a few days had appeared within reach.

In the course of his London visit, Kosygin agreed to a number of
arrangements for closer British-Soviet relations[14] but threw a preliminary dash of cold water on the American plan for a mutual
renunciation of defensive missiles. It seemed to him, the Soviet
Premier suggested at a news conference on February 9, that defensive
missiles were much to be preferred to offensive ones, and that instead
of quibbling about the relative costs of different weapons systems it
would be best to work for the renunciation of *all* nuclear armaments
and the destruction of nuclear weapons.[15] Instead of responding to

the U.S. initiative, in other words, the Soviet Premier reiterated a long-standing Soviet proposal which was already known to be unacceptable to the United States because, in the American view, the principal effect of a ban on nuclear weapons would be to eliminate the U.S. nuclear superiority and tip the strategic balance in favor of the U.S.S.R. with its powerful ground forces.

Kosygin's official response to President Johnson's letter, as revealed by the President on March 2, was slightly more encouraging. The Soviet Government, Mr. Johnson indicated, was still opposed to a discussion limited to the nondeployment of defensive missiles. It would, however, be willing "to discuss means of limiting the arms race in offensive and defensive nuclear missiles." By broadening the discussion in this way, the U.S.S.R. would presumably put itself in a position to demand a curb on American offensive missiles as the price of any limitation on Soviet defensive missiles—hardly a disadvantageous bargain from the Soviet point of view. Nevertheless, President Johnson indicated that the proposed conditions were acceptable to the United States and that he looked forward to discussions of the subject in Moscow.[16] Soviet representatives, however, still showed little interest in getting down to concrete discussions, and up to the middle of June even the time and place of such talks had not been agreed upon.[17] Since the United States was meanwhile holding off decisions on its own antimissile defenses until the Soviet attitude was clarified, the U.S.S.R. would seem to have found it convenient to delay matters as long as possible even while going forward with the construction of its antimissile network.

Soviet policy wore a more cooperative face in the discussions of the Eighteen-Nation Disarmament Committee (E.N.D.C.). That body, the main forum for multilateral disarmament efforts, opened its sixth year of deliberations in Geneva on February 21 with all its members present except for France, whose government disagreed with the basic approach of the other participants and had consistently declined to occupy the seat assigned to it. With no immediate prospect for solution of the impasse over inspection of underground nuclear tests, the 1967 sessions of the E.N.D.C. were expected to concentrate primarily on the issue of a nuclear nonproliferation treaty; and hope had been widely expressed that a detailed text could actually be agreed upon in time for submission to the U.N. General Assembly at its autumn session. "Agreement on a treaty to stop the spread of nuclear weapons will be an historic turning point in the long effort to bring the atom to heel," said President Johnson in a message to the conference. "It will, I am confident, permit further cooperative steps to reduce nuclear armaments. Plain sanity calls for a halt to the competition in nuclear arms."[18]

Contrary to most past experience, the immediate obstacle to conclusion of a nuclear nonproliferation treaty did not arise from any major differences between the United States and the Soviet Union. Treaty or no treaty, neither of those powers appeared to have any intention of handing out nuclear weapons to nations that did not already possess them. Both governments seemed to think, however, that a treaty formally barring nuclear proliferation would be a good idea, and there had even been hopes that they could agree on the terms of a draft treaty for joint presentation to the other members of the E.N.D.C. Although these hopes were still some distance from realization, it was already evident that the principal obstacle to agreement on nonproliferation would be presented not by the nuclear powers themselves but by the attitudes of nonnuclear powers both in and outside the E.N.D.C.

Favorable as most of them were to the principle of nonproliferation, many of the nonnuclear countries resented the discrimination inherent in any permanent division of the world into nuclear and nonnuclear powers. A number of nonnuclear governments, moreover, showed acute anxiety lest their own national interests be adversely affected by a nonproliferation agreement. India, for example, felt that if it was to renounce the possession of nuclear weapons for itself, it should be given a guarantee of protection in case of trouble developing with a hostile nuclear power like Communist China. Brazil insisted on a right to carry out peaceful atomic explosions for economic development purposes, notwithstanding the fact that the technology involved was largely identical with that for nuclear weapons. Still greater difficulties were presented by the attitude of some of the Western European countries—particularly Italy and Western Germany, which was not a member of the E.N.D.C. but made its opinion strongly felt. These governments particularly feared that nonproliferation arrangements might get in the way of their peaceful nuclear power programs and, in addition, that international inspection of their atomic activities might result in the loss of precious industrial secrets.

As a result of these and similar anxieties, the question of just who was to carry out the inspections needed to ensure compliance with a nonproliferation treaty was destined to hold up progress in the E.N.D.C. for many months and to cause a serious crisis in relations between the United States and several of its European partners. The American Government had long maintained that inspection responsibility should be entrusted to the International Atomic Energy Agency, one of the United Nations family of agencies which had its headquarters in Vienna. The U.S.S.R., after initial resistance, had come around to the same opinion. But Western Germany, Italy, and the other members of the six-nation communities in Western Europe were already being inspected by their own atomic organization, the European Atomic Energy Community or Euratom; and they insisted that no other inspection was called for. This was a contention that the Soviet Union, with its ingrained distrust of Western Germany and of West European cooperative arrangements, professed itself unable to accept. It must be I.A.E.A. inspection or nothing, Moscow insisted. The United States, while doing what it could to pacify its own allies, exerted all its ingenuity in trying to find a compromise solution that would give a voice to both Euratom and I.A.E.A., either concurrently or successively. Up to the beginning of June, however, it had quite failed to find a formula that would satisfy its own friends on the one hand and the U.S.S.R. on the other. Progress on this issue seemed even more effectually blocked than the still unscheduled discussions on a defensive missile ban.

Likewise at a standstill, though not without hope of fresh advances in the future, was Western Germany's effort to promote *détente* and expand its own relationships in Eastern Europe. Although the Soviet bloc countries were still divided on this issue, East Germany had seized the opportunity to fortify the *status quo* by concluding new defense treaties with Poland and Czechoslovakia, both of which then concluded a new friendship treaty of their own. In apparent support of these endeavors, Party Secretary Brezhnev came forward on March 10 with a strong statement attributing Bonn's maneuvers to the most sinister motives and citing its resistance to the nonproliferation treaty as further evidence of its unregenerate ways.[19]

Continuing the anti-Bonn campaign, a conference of representatives of 25 Communist parties (not including Rumania or Yugoslavia) assembled at Karlovy Vary, Czechoslovakia, in April to denounce West Germany's alleged aggressive designs, reaffirm the orthodox Communist view on security in Europe, and put forward a European "action program" aimed at blocking the renewal of the NATO treaty when it came up for reconsideration in 1969.[20] While the U.S.S.R. thus gained a fresh endorsement of its European program, the Kremlin had cause for disappointment in the continued failure of other Communist parties to support its hopes for a multiparty conference on the China problem. Nor could the German issue be considered in any way settled, since the attitude of Hungary and some of the other participants left open the clear possibility that they might still come to terms with Western Germany as soon as circumstances permitted. For the time being, however, Bonn's diplomatic offensive appeared stalled, and subsequent exchanges of letters between Chancellor Kiesinger and Premier Willi Stoph of East Germany served only to highlight the impasse that had developed over the question of recognizing the East German regime.[21]

More significant progress was achieved on the American end of the East-West relationship, where President Johnson and his aides had been pressing for Senate approval of the U.S.-Soviet consular pact and the new U.N. space treaty. Together, these two instruments had come to be regarded as a kind of acid test of American intentions in East-West affairs. Each had aroused significant domestic opposition; yet the weight of national feeling seemed clearly to incline toward the cautiously optimistic view of East-West relations espoused by such authorities as former Ambassador George F. Kennan. Testifying in Senator Fulbright's general review of American foreign policy, that veteran interpreter of Soviet conduct had recently assured the Senate Foreign Relations Committee that "the changes that have come over Soviet Communism and the mental world of its leaders, particularly in the years since Stalin's death, have been hopeful rather than alarming ones" and, "if properly understood and met from the non-Communist side, hold encouraging rather than menacing connotations for the prospects for world stability."[22]

The more problematical of the two treaties now before the Senate was the Consular Convention between the United States and the U.S.S.R., signed in Moscow in 1964[23] but never previously submitted to the Senate because of administration fears that it would fail to win the two-thirds majority required for formal approval. The purpose of this instrument was to establish a legal framework which would permit each country to open consular offices and would guarantee the basic rights of its nationals in the territory of the other party. But certain unusual provisions in the treaty, among them one that granted diplomatic immunity to consular employees, had aroused fears that it might also create new opportunities for Soviet espionage in the United States. J. Edgar Hoover, Director of the Federal Bureau of Investigation, had strongly opposed the treaty on these grounds, and his views had been widely echoed by those who either shared his apprehensions or opposed agreements with the Soviet Union on principle.

To overcome this deep-seated resistance required extraordinary efforts by the administration over a period of weeks. Mr. Hoover was eventually persuaded to state that the F.B.I. would be able to handle any increased security problems resulting from the treaty, and the State Department let it be known—a trifle anticlimactically—that there were no plans for actually opening any consulates even after the treaty went into effect.[24] Various amendments, reservations, and understandings proposed by members of the Senate, many of them designed to make the application of the treaty dependent on a reformation in the Soviet attitude concerning Vietnam, were ultimately defeated after the administration had warned that they would be certain to antagonize the Soviet Union and would probably cause it to lose all interest in the pact. With the active support of some Republican legislators, the treaty was eventually accorded Senate endorsement on March 16 by a vote of 66 to 28, three more than a two-thirds majority. Formal ratification by President Johnson took place on March 31 amid expressions of hope that the Soviet Government would also ratify promptly. Moscow, however, took no action on the matter during 1967.

The Treaty on the Peaceful Uses of Outer Space, as signed on January 27 and officially communicated to the Senate on February 7,[25] raised fewer security problems. This multilateral pact did not require the admission of Soviet personnel to the United States, but did provide some rights of inspection over activities that might be undertaken by the U.S.S.R. or other signatories on celestial bodies. The Joint Chiefs of Staff seemed willing to support the treaty, provided that the United States took steps to enhance its own "verification capability" in space; and complaints about "vague and fuzzy language" were dealt with in clarifying "understandings" worked out in the Senate Foreign Relations Committee.[26] On April 25, the Senate gave its advice and consent to ratification by an unequivocal vote of 88 to 0.

Ratification by the President followed on May 24. Moscow, too, acted promptly in this instance, as did Britain and other signatories. By the time the treaty went into effect on October 10, some 84 states, including France, had decided to accept its provisions.[27]

The Johnson administration was less successful in obtaining congressional backing for its third main venture in East-West bridge-building. This was the so-called East-West Trade Relations Act, a bill to promote peaceful American trade with the U.S.S.R. and Eastern European countries which had been developed after prolonged studies within the administration and had first been submitted to Congress early in 1966.[28] In the administration view, both political and economic considerations spoke in favor of a measure whose principal purpose was to free the United States of various restrictions on the conduct of its own foreign trade that had been imposed in the heyday of postwar anti-Communism. In particular, the administration sought the right to grant most-favored-nation treatment to Eastern countries, where appropriate, on the same basis as it was traditionally accorded to non-Communist nations. As with the consular convention, official pleas to Congress for greater flexibility in dealing with the Communist countries were mingled with assurances that the administration planned nothing detrimental to U.S. interests.[29] But while the issue was heatedly discussed in Congressional circles, no move was made to bring it up for formal consideration.

Doubly embarrassing to the administration in these circumstances was its inability to act favorably on two proposals in the East-West trade field that originated with the U.S.S.R. itself. A request from Moscow to purchase a small, two-man submarine for research in oceanography was turned down, after much delay, on security grounds.[30] Likewise rejected for security reasons, although a formal decision was deferred until July, was Moscow's unprecedented proposal to submit a bid for the construction of turbines and generators for the Grand Coulee Dam in the American Northwest.[31] A third project, involving a proposed Export-Import Bank loan of up to $50 million to finance the construction of an Italian automobile factory in the U.S.S.R., had meanwhile run into a degree of congressional opposition that likewise foreshadowed ultimate disapproval[32] and suggested the depth of adverse sentiment prevailing in congressional quarters on the whole issue of economic relations with the Communist countries in time of war in Southeast Asia.

Some minor East-West matters were successfully adjusted during

"THEY'RE NOT HELPING THINGS ANY"

Flannery in *The Baltimore Evening Sun*

these months. Controversies relating to Soviet fishing activities in Pacific coastal waters were resolved by intergovernmental agreement;[33] a cultural pact with Rumania was renewed;[34] Poland agreed to use a portion of the money it owed the United States to promote the study of the English language.[35] Only technical details appeared to stand in the way of inaugurating the long-planned New York-Moscow commercial air service,[36] though these were not overcome in time for the 1967 tourist season and in fact were destined to persist beyond the end of the year.

Meanwhile new frictions were developing, made all the sharper in some instances by the edginess of Communist officials as they confronted the rising spirit of independence among their own writers and intellectuals. One of the most sensational occurrences of 1967 was the defection from the Soviet Union of Svetlana Alliluyeva, daughter of the late dictator J. V. Stalin, who turned up at the U.S. Embassy in India in March, entered the United States in April with comments somewhat unflattering to the existing Soviet leadership, and made known her intention of seeking fuller self-expression[37] and publishing her life story.[38] In spite of every effort to avoid offense to Moscow in so delicate a matter,[39] the United States could not prevent a storm of outrage in Soviet publicity media. For *Pravda,* Svetlana's defection was nothing less than a "deliberate American provocation" aimed at discrediting the Soviet Union in its 50th anniversary year.[40] The defection of two Hungarian diplomats to the United States in the course of the spring caused comparable reactions in Budapest.[41]

These incidents had their part in a wider growth of international tension whose origins may have extended as far back as February, when the U.S.S.R. and Communist China are supposed to have reached an agreement about the transit of Soviet aid shipments across China to North Vietnam.[42] By May, in any case, Soviet official behavior was beginning to take on some of the aspects of "deliberate provocation" that Moscow saw fit to attribute to the American Government. It was on May 10 that the United States first had occasion to protest the "bumping" by a Soviet warship of an American destroyer engaged in a training exercise in the Sea of Japan. A second incident of the kind occurred next day. Although the United States preferred to regard these occurrrences as accidental, similar incidents were shortly being reported by the Sixth Fleet in the Mediterranean,[43] where tension between the Arab states and Israel was rapidly increasing and Moscow was loudly supporting the more militant Arab governments. Concurrent disturbances in Yemen and Hong Kong[44] were not, perhaps, directly attributable to Soviet machinations; but they too played a part in creating a sense of alarm that was further heightened by Moscow's May 30 decision to augment its naval forces in the

Mediterranean and its complaint of June 2 about the American bombing of one of its ships in a North Vietnamese port.[45] By the time hostilities between Israel and the United Arab Republic broke out on the morning of June 5, the world seemed poised for as grave a crisis as any in recent experience.

20 : Impact of the Middle East Crisis

Although the Israeli-Arab war of June 5-10 did not in the end produce as serious an international crisis as the Cuban missile confrontation of 1962, it did form a minor watershed in the history of East-West relations and, in addition, cast doubt on some of the optimistic assumptions about Soviet policy so prevalent in recent years.[46] Moscow's open encouragement of Arab bellicosity before and during the crisis seemed singularly wanting in the sense of responsibility apparent in its earlier attempts to moderate the quarrel between India and Pakistan. Its readiness to challenge and harass the United States bespoke a degree of recklessness astonishing in a power that had seemed of late to shun the dangers of collision with its mightiest antagonist. The strong reaffirmation of its commitment to the Arab governments after their defeat bore all the earmarks of a daring bid to entrench itself even more strongly in the Middle East and to found its own preeminence on the discomfiture of Arab hopes.

Yet it is important to note that Soviet policy observed a significant measure of restraint throughout the Mid-East crisis. Soviet authorities not only disclaimed responsibility for Abdel Nasser's original action in closing the Gulf of Aqaba, but seem to have made at least intermittent attempts to curb the Egyptian leader's impetuosity. Once fighting had broken out, Premier Kosygin lost no time in advising President Johnson of his government's desire to avoid involvement; and Soviet delegates cooperated as fully as could be expected in the Security Council's reiterated demands for a cease-fire. Subsequent pledges of support for the Arabs, while verbally generous and even incendiary, carefully avoided commitments to specific action. The new arms consignments dispatched to the U.A.R. on the morrow of its defeat were apparently accompanied by words of caution against any attempt to reopen hostilities.

As has already been pointed out, this seeming ambivalence in Soviet policy may well have been connected with differences of opinion within the Soviet leadership of a kind not wholly unlike the differences between "hawks" and "doves" in the United States.[47] Secretary Brezhnev, Premier Kosygin, and President Podgorny have been plausibly identified with a "dove" faction which is supposed to have been primarily concerned with internal problems and anxious to avoid "rocking the boat" during the Soviet anniversary year. But other Soviet leaders of more mistrustful bent, it has been suggested, may have gained an impression that the U.S.S.R. was being deliberately challenged by the United States through such developments as the escalation in Vietnam, the defection of Mrs. Alliluyeva, a military coup in Greece (for which the United States had been widely held responsible),[48] and the subsequent use of Israeli air power against the Arabs. The feeling that Moscow was bound to respond to such a "pattern" of U.S.-inspired disruptive activity might well account for some of the more bellicose manifestations of Soviet policy during the spring. Those who held such views may even have argued for some kind of military move against U.S. interests in the wake of the Arab defeat by Israel.

Though unsuccessful in committing the Soviet Government to active intervention on behalf of the Arabs, these "hawkish" elements would seem to have retained some influence even after Kosygin had gone to New York in mid-June to press the pro-Arab, anti-Israeli case before the United Nations. Their final bid to divert Soviet policy into a more bellicose channel appears to have been made at the June 20-21 meeting of the Central Committee of the Soviet Communist party in Moscow. Evidence of their defeat could be seen in two separate developments: in President Podgorny's visits to the Middle East to urge moderation on Abdel Nasser and other Arab leaders; and, within the U.S.S.R., in the continuation of a purge of the Soviet upper bureaucracy which had begun with a shake-up in the security services in the wake of the Alliluyeva defection. Nikolai G. Yegorychev, First Secretary of the Moscow party organization and apparently a leading "hawk," was dismissed from his party post a few days after the Central Committee meeting. Aleksandr N. Shelepin, another "hawkish" figure who had at one time seemed destined for the highest Soviet honors, was soon afterward relegated to the second-rank position of Chairman of the All-Union Council of Trade Unions.

It was only after the "hawks" in Moscow had been silenced that Kosygin apparently felt able to respond to the intimations from Washing that President Johnson would be glad to talk with him during his visit to the United Nations. The meetings of the two leaders at Glassboro on June 23 and 25 undoubtedly constitute one of the more picturesque interludes in East-West history, but produced no softening of the opposed positions on either Vietnam or the Middle East. While there was also some discussion of bilateral problems at Glassboro, the only point on which specific agreement appears to have been reached was the importance of coming to an understanding on a nuclear non-proliferation treaty.[49] Yet the mere fact that the American and Soviet leaders had met and intended to keep in touch provided a measure of reassurance that the East-West antagonism would not be allowed to get out of hand.

The moderate note in Soviet policy seemed generally to be in the ascendent throughout the next few weeks. Podgorny, as already noted, was touring the Arab lands and cautioning against renewal of the war. Kosygin, rather startlingly, paid a visit to Cuba on his way back to Moscow from New York; but it later turned out that his main object in Havana had been to try to exercise a similar restraining influence on Premier Castro and discourage the latter's idea of trying to foment guerrilla revolutions throughout Latin American.[50] At the United Nations, the defeat of the Soviet plan for condemnation of Israel was followed later in July by an abortive attempt to work out a joint American-Soviet resolution for presentation to the General Assembly.[51] Yet despite these indications of a more moderate spirit, Soviet actions in relations to the Arab states—particularly in the supply of arms to the U.A.R. and others—gave evidence that Moscow fully intended to maintain its position in the Arab world and, if possible, extend it. Further proof of the Soviet determination to play a more active role in this part of the world could be found in the indications that Soviet naval strength in the Mediterranean would henceforth be maintained at a considerably higher level than before the crisis.

Among the explanations advanced for this Soviet thrust in the Middle East was Moscow's supposed concern to forestall an increase in the Middle Eastern influence of Communist China. That power, characteristically enough, had associated itself with the most rabid Arab viewpoints, had accused the U.S.S.R. of conniving with the United States to betray the Arabs, and had vehemently denounced the

Glassboro meetings as another step toward "a global American-Soviet deal intended to enhance the anti-China, anti-Communist, antipeople and counterrevolutionary Washington-Moscow alliance and intensify the suppression of the surging revolutionary struggle of the peoples of the world."[52] Sino-Soviet relations, as the result of this and other factors, were now again reverting to the extreme antagonism that had prevailed earlier in the year.[53]

The European Communist bloc had also sustained a certain amount of damage in the course of the Middle East crisis, which had opened new fissures among the Eastern governments and, in some cases, between the party leaders and the rank and file of party members and citizens. The official pro-Arab line adopted by most of the Communist governments proved widely unpopular. In Poland, the issue became involved in a continuing struggle between Communist "hard-liners" and "moderates," with overtones of anti-Semitism in the official denunciation of "Zionists" and Israeli sympathizers. In Czechoslovakia, sympathy for Israel lent new impetus to a continuing struggle within the intellectual community for a freedom of expression that Communist authorities were still doing their best to limit. Yugoslavia's President Tito maintained a surprisingly pro-Arab and therefore pro-Soviet stance throughout the crisis; but this windfall for Soviet policy was offset by the contrary stand of Rumania, which took the opportunity to intensify its independent attitude, boycotted successive meetings called to coordinate Communist aid to the Arab states, and quite refused to follow the Soviet lead in the United Nations.

As the summer advanced, Rumania offered further demonstrations of its independent attitude. At meetings of the Grand National Assembly, party Secretary Ceausescu and others stressed Rumania's adherence to the Warsaw Pact and its support of North Vietnam but made equally clear its refusal to bow to Soviet pressure, its insistence on the necessity for Arab-Israeli negotiations, its disagreement with some aspects of Soviet disarmament policy, and even its satisfaction over improved relations with the United States,[54] where Premier Ion Gheorghe Maurer had recently been received by President Johnson in the course of a world tour. Rumanians seemed unimpressed by *Pravda*'s warning that "Washington's notorious bridge-building policy" was merely "a flagrant . . . manifestation of the jesuitical policy to undermine the unity of socialist countries."[55] Foreign Minister Corneliu Manescu was already counting on U.S. support in his bid to become the first Communist President of the U.N. General Assembly when that body reconvened in September.

Rumania also remained in the forefront of the movement for closer ties with Western Germany. A Rumanian Embassy had recently been opened in Bonn, and Vice-Chancellor Brandt was warmly welcomed when he came to Rumania at the beginning of August to sign an economic collaboration treaty. Czechoslovakia, too, had by this time agreed with Bonn to exchange trade missions with limited consular functions, and Hungary showed signs of moving in the same direction. East Germany, however, still insisted that any normalization of relations with Bonn must depend on political recognition of the German Democratic Republic; and Poland under party Secretary Wladyslaw Gomulka maintained an equally obdurate stand. Even President de Gaulle, who visited Poland early in September and repeatedly urged the Poles to display more diplomatic flexibility, made no visible impression on his official hosts despite his warm reception by the Polish public.

The Soviet Union itself took no important initiative in European questions during the summer, apart from the naming of a new Soviet Marshal, Ivan I. Yakubovsky, to head the forces of the Warsaw Pact as successor to Marshal Andrei A. Grechko. (The latter had been shifted to the Soviet Defense Ministry to fill a vacancy left by the death of Marshal Rodion Y. Malinovsky.) While they showed continuing interest in cementing relations with France, the Russians on the whole gave evidence of a certain hesitancy in the conduct of foreign policy, as though still feeling the shock waves of the "hawk-dove" controversy and still assessing the implications of their Middle East setback. Relations with the United States in these post-Glassboro months remained distinctly chilly, and there was some slowdown in the tempo of U.S.-Soviet cultural exchanges—scarcely a surprising phenomenon in view of the concurrent intensification of the war in Vietnam. Yet Moscow's rather phlegmatic reaction to the stepped-up bombing of North Vietnam that began in August[56] suggested a continuing reluctance to deepen its commitment to Hanoi at the risk of new complications with the United States.

21 : New Round in the Arms Race?

The most positive outgrowth of the Glassboro conversations was a joint decision by the Soviet and American governments to pool their efforts to secure the completion of a nuclear nonproliferation treaty. Agreement on the control provisions of such a treaty still eluded the governments assembled at Geneva; but it might still be possible to secure agreement on the rest of the treaty while leaving the control article to be worked out later. A draft treaty without the control article was accordingly worked out during the summer by chief negotiators William C. Foster and Aleksei A. Roshchin and, after approval by their own and allied governments, was formally laid before the Eighteen-Nation Disarmament Committee on August 24. Submitted in the form of identical American and Soviet drafts rather than a joint draft, the treaty spelled out both the commitment by the nuclear states to refrain from disseminating nuclear weapons and the corresponding commitment by nonnuclear states to refrain from acquiring such weapons.[57]

This was constructive as far as it went. President Johnson was entitled to comment that the submission of an agreed text "brings us to the final and most critical stage of this effort."[58] In addition to leaving open the question of international control, however, the new drafts also bypassed the nonnuclear countries' demand for guarantees of protection by the nuclear powers. This matter, the two sponsors had agreed, was too complicated for inclusion in the treaty and should be dealt with separately, perhaps through a U.N. resolution. But since these reserved issues were the very ones that had been holding up agreement, the reception of the Soviet-American initiative by other interested governments could not be very enthusiastic. Though Moscow hinted that it might eventually compromise on the issue of I.A.E.A. versus Euratom inspection,[59] the attitudes of India, Nigeria, Brazil, Italy, and others indicated that full agreement on a nonproliferation treaty was still some way off.

In the meantime there were indications that the whole issue of nuclear nonproliferation might be thrust into the background by an intensifying arms race among the nuclear powers themselves. Communist China, which had boycotted all international disarmament efforts but had been making rapid progress in nuclear and missile technology, shocked the world by exploding its first hydrogen or thermonuclear bomb on June 17. This feat appeared to strengthen the probability that Mao Tse-tung's regime might be able to develop a practicable nuclear warhead as early as 1970 and an intercontinental ballistic missile within an additional year or two. Even France had not yet exploded a hydrogen bomb, although it expected to do so in 1969 and carried out three preliminary atmospheric nuclear tests at its Pacific proving ground in June and July. Although the United States and the U.S.S.R. were still confining themselves to underground testing as required by the 1963 test-ban treaty, they too appeared increasingly preoccupied both by the possibility of changes in the existing nuclear balance and by the prospective impact of new weapons on their respective security positions.

Thus far, the United States appeared to retain its decisive edge so far as strategic nuclear weapons were concerned. By this time, however, it was generally recognized that the U.S.S.R. was in the process of closing the gap, both by deploying additional missiles and by equipping them with more powerful warheads which, some said, already gave it an advantage in "deliverable megatonnage."[60] A further potential threat to the strategic balance was the U.S.S.R.'s apparent determination to continue with the deployment of its antiballistic missile net. No one appeared to know exactly what the Russians were doing in this field, nor just how effective defensive missiles would be in destroying incoming offensive missiles before their arrival on target. But if the U.S.S.R. were to succeed in setting up a workable A.B.M. (antiballistic missile) system while the United States had none, it was difficult to see how the effectiveness of U.S. missiles in deterring a Soviet attack could fail to be impaired. Moscow, moreover, had continued to evade the U.S. proposal to discuss a mutual limitation of such weapons. Secretary Rusk indicated on September 8 that there was "some urgency" about setting a date for these talks.[61] The inference left by his remarks was that the United States would otherwise feel it had no choice but to start deploying an A.B.M. system of its own.

Some authorities were by this time beginning to maintain that the A.B.M. itself was becoming obsolete as the result of progress toward a new weapon, the so-called multiple-warhead missile or MIRV (multiple independent reentry vehicle), which would be equipped with a sufficient number of separate warheads to saturate any fore-seeable defensive system. The United States, it was understood, was well along in the development of such a weapon—its Poseidon missiles were already slated to have multiple warheads—and the U.S.S.R. was also said to be working on it. But no proposals for dealing with this development at the international level had yet been formulated.[62]

The result of such speculation had been an intensification of the demands in Congress and elsewhere for the prompt deployment of defensive A.B.M.'s by the United States. Interested opinion remained somewhat divided as to whether production and deployment of the still untried Nike-X missile would really be an effective answer to the perils the United States appeared to face. Secretary McNamara, for one, still maintained that a full-scale antimissile defense would cost far more than it was worth, and that the best way to counterbalance a Soviet defensive system was to build more and better offensive missiles. But the Joint Chiefs of Staff and members of the interested congressional committees seemed disinclined to stake the national security on this reasoning. In their opinion, the Russians' acquisition of an antimissile system made it all the more necessary for the United States to have one too. By September, some action along these lines was beginning to appear a political if not a military necessity.

As this domestic debate approached its boiling point, a character-istic compromise was worked out within the administration and an-nounced by Secretary McNamara in a speech at San Francisco on September 18.[68] There was, the Secretary of Defense reiterated, no point at all in spending $40 billion to deploy a "heavy" missile defense to protect American cities against a possible Soviet attack. Such a move, he said, would merely prompt the Soviets to increase their offensive capability, just as the United States had lately been increasing its own offensive capability in response to Soviet moves. The real answer to the Soviet problem, Mr. McNamara asserted, would be "a properly safeguarded agreement first to limit, and later to reduce, both our offensive and defensive strategic nuclear forces." If such an agreement proved unattainable and a nuclear arms race became unavoidable, he added, "the United States possesses in ample abundance the resources, the technology, and the will to run faster in that race for whatever distance is required."

China, however, was described by Mr. McNamara as presenting a different kind of problem. On the one hand, it might be more prone to miscalculation or "irrational behavior"; on the other, its actions would be easier to defend against. What the United States therefore proposed to do, Mr. McNamara said, was to invest the relatively modest sum of $5 billion in a "light" deployment of A.B.M.'s which would take about five years to construct and would be specifically directed against possible Chinese missile attack. Such an arrangement, Mr. McNamara added, would have two subsidiary benefits: increased security for American missile sites in case of a Soviet attack, and some protection for the public in case an I.C.B.M. was accidentally launched by any of the nuclear powers. Production of this "light" A.B.M. system, which would be known as Sentinel, was to begin at the end of 1967.

As with other administration compromises in other fields, this plan gave little comfort to those Americans who opposed the arms race in principle, and equally little to those who felt that stronger protection against Soviet missiles was needed. Abroad, the response was almost uniformly unfavorable. NATO governments were upset because they had not been consulted and because the new policy looked in some respects like a retreat to the "Fortress America" concept. Feeling at the United Nations was well summed up by Secretary-General Thant, who expressed concern "that the nuclear arms race may be pushed to unimaginable levels by a new race for anti-missile missiles, anti-anti-missile missiles and the whole new armory of weapons and counter-weapons associated with the concept of ballistic missile defenses and the means to overcome such defenses." "A new round in an unending nuclear arms race," U Thant declared in the introduction to his annual report, released September 19, "could upset the delicate balance of stability that exists at the present time between the nuclear superpowers, and could give rise to new fears and tensions which would offset the small but hopeful progress that has been made towards a *détente* and disarmament."[64]

In anticipation of such reactions, Mr. McNamara had gone out of his way at San Francisco to emphasize that the American decision in no way lessened the urgency or desirability of a U.S.-Soviet agreement on "the limitation of strategic nuclear offensive and defensive forces." At Geneva, Adrian S. Fisher of the U.S. Arms Control and Disarmament Agency assured the E.N.D.C. that the new move would further, not hamper, that body's work and would strengthen the case for a nonproliferation treaty.[65] Yet the atmosphere of the Geneva discussions could not be unaffected by such a development. Even if a nonproliferation treaty was eventually concluded, many observers reasoned, it might have only marginal significance if the nuclear powers were meanwhile restarting their own arms race.

The Soviet Union did not immediately comment on the issues raised by Mr. McNamara's speech. While it may have shared the suspicion of some American observers that the new A.B.M. system would be more concerned with meeting a possible Soviet attack than Mr. McNamara had admitted, Moscow did not withdraw its support of the nonproliferation project and presumably reserved the larger issue for consideration after the November anniversary celebrations. The general trend of Soviet thinking on international questions at the moment could be gauged from Gromyko's annual presentation before the new session of the General Assembly on September 22. Harsh though basically noncommittal on Vietnam, bitingly denunciatory on Western Germany, the Soviet Foreign Minister seemed equally unyielding in his insistence on Israel's withdrawal from the conquered territories. His principal contribution to the disarmament discussion was a revival of the old Soviet plan for a convention that would ban the use of nuclear weapons outright but would be unaccompanied by any provision for international control or enforcement.[66]

That the U.S.S.R. was already engaged in a broad expansion of its armaments and military posture was to become increasingly evident while the General Assembly awaited an opportune moment to take up the disarmament question. The Soviet state budget, announced October 10, officially projected an increase in defense expenditure from 14.5 billion rubles in 1967 to 16.7 billion, or $18.5 billion at the official exchange rate, in 1968. (Such figures, in the opinion of U.S. experts, represented roughly one-half the U.S.S.R.'s real military outlay.)[67] Although the new budget also provided that consumer goods output would for the first time expand more rapidly than the output of heavy industry, close analysis revealed that the main effect of the cutbacks in heavy industrial goals would be to permit increased output of arms and munitions in the years immediately ahead.[68] Similarly, the enactment of a new Soviet draft law which reduced the term of compulsory military service by one year—to two years in the Army and Air Force, and three in the Navy—could be attributed to changes in the Soviet population structure rather than to any intention of reducing the U.S.S.R.'s over-all armed strength of 3,220,000.[69]

The disclosure during these weeks that the U.S.S.R. was building its first aircraft carrier—actually a helicopter carrier—offered a further indication that Soviet military men were becoming less defense-minded and more interested in the projection of Soviet military power beyond their country's territorial limits, a trend already evidenced by the expanded Soviet naval presence in the Mediterranean.[70] Even more startling was Secretary McNamara's revelation that the Russians appeared to be extending their military power into outer space in a way that, while it might be technically permissible under the new outer space treaty, seemed hardly consistent with the spirit of that instrument.

Analysis of recent Soviet space shots, the Secretary of Defense explained on November 3, gave indications that the Russians were developing a special type of nuclear bomb that could be placed in orbit above the earth and, at a given point—usually before completing a full orbit—could be dropped directly on its target, allowing a maximum of three minutes' warning time instead of the fifteen-minute warning available in the case of conventional intercontinental missiles. Should American surmises about this "fractional orbital bombardment system" or FOBS be correct, Mr. McNamara said, the Russians could conceivably achieve an "initial operational capability" with the new weapon as early as 1968.[71] Technically, it appeared, they would not be violating the space treaty unless one of their weapons was to make one or more complete orbits of the earth.

Characteristically, Mr. McNamara professed himself unworried by this new development. The weapon in question, he said, was so unwieldy and inaccurate that the United States had decided years earlier that there was no need to develop one. (It was, however, authoritatively reported some weeks later that the United States was developing a somewhat comparable weapon, a missile or "space bus" carrying a number of thermonuclear warheads which could be dropped sequentially as it passed over enemy cities.)[72] The three-minute warning available to the United States, Mr. McNamara further stated, was already being extended by the use of new over-the-horizon radars which would detect such weapons more readily than the existing Ballistic Missile Early Warning System. Furthermore, the Secretary of Defense recalled, the United States would still retain the ultimate protection afforded by its capacity to "absorb a surprise attack and strike back with sufficient power to destroy the attacker."[73]

Not all interested Americans appeared convinced of the adequacy of such safeguards, and it was not immediately clear that Mr. Mc-Namara's reasoning would carry more national conviction than appeared to be true in the case of the antiballistic missile. What did seem reasonably certain was that any new American move to offset the growth and diversification of Soviet military capabilities would in fact spur the Soviet Union to still further efforts and thus tend to unravel what remained of the limited arms control arrangements so laboriously put together in the past half-dozen years.

Some signs of unraveling, or at least of lessened momentum, could already be detected at Geneva, where the E.N.D.C. had been kept in session in the vain hope that a nonproliferation treaty might somehow be drafted in time for submission to the General Assembly before the end of the year. This prospect, however, waned rapidly during the autumn weeks. International inspection and control was still the major sticking point; and the only important advance during this period was an agreement among the five members of Euratom (other than France) concerning the sort of control provisions they could accept. This in turn was used by the United States as a basis for further efforts at compromise, with its allies in NATO and with the Soviet Union.[74] In trying to dispel the nonnuclear countries' resistance to I.A.E.A. safeguards, President Johnson went so far as to announce that the United States itself was willing to submit to I.A.E.A. supervision even though entitled to claim exemption under the terms of the proposed treaty. "When such safeguards are applied under the treaty," the President said on December 2, "the United States will permit the I.A.E.A. to apply its safeguards to all nuclear activities in the United States—excluding only those with direct national security significance. Under this offer, the agency will then be able to inspect a broad range of United States nuclear activities, both governmental and private, including the fuel in nuclear-powered reactors owned by utilities for generating electricity, and the fabrication and the chemical reprocessing of such fuel."[75] The United Kingdom made a parallel announcement.

By this time, however, the E.N.D.C. at Geneva had given up hope of reaching agreement in 1967 and was preparing an interim report to the General Assembly in which it simply noted that work on the nonproliferation treaty was continuing.[76] The Assembly, in turn, decided before adjourning on December 19 that the issue was important enough to justify a resumption of its session in the spring. Accordingly, it asked the E.N.D.C. to provide it with a further report of progress by March 15, 1968.[77]

Among its other actions in the disarmament field, the Assembly reaffirmed its desire for general disarmament[78] and a suspension of all nuclear weapon tests[79] and warmly endorsed a Treaty for the Prohibition of Nuclear Weapons in Latin America,[80] concluded months earlier on Latin American initiative, that purported to establish that area as the world's first nuclear-free zone. The whole discussion on disarmament, however, revealed an undercurrent of dissatisfaction on the part of the nonnuclear countries with what they plainly felt to be the irresponsible attitude of the nuclear states, particularly the United States and the U.S.S.R. The clearest reflection of this discontent was the reaffirmation of an earlier Assembly decision to convoke a special conference of nonnuclear-weapon states, to be held in Geneva in the summer of 1968.[81] As for Gromyko's draft convention barring the use of nuclear weapons, it provoked the usual sharp debate between those who favored the idea and those who, like the United States and even France, considered that such a paper prohibition would be delusive and even dangerous. Like similar Soviet offerings in the past, the plan fell short of formal adoption by the Assembly but was officially commended in a resolution—adopted by 77 to 0 with 29 abstentions, including that of the United States— that urged negotiations to conclude an "appropriate" convention.[82]

A really effective ban on the use of nuclear weapons would undoubtedly have afforded widespread satisfaction at a moment when the great powers appeared to be embarking on still another round in the nuclear spiral. To contribute to the real security of nations, however, such a pact would not only have had to be genuinely enforceable on all the nuclear powers, including France and China, but would have needed to be buttressed with provisions to avoid a major imbalance in nonnuclear types of armament. Given the unlikelihood of any plan that would satisfy all the varied interests at stake, the world appeared to face another of those breathless periods in which the nuclear contestants would seek security in keeping ahead of, or not too far behind, each other. No reasonable person could fail to hope that political differences among the nuclear powers could be kept within such bounds as to make a resort to the new weapons as unlikely as it promised to be unprofitable.

22 : Moscow Jubilee

Even in 1967, it was the evident desire of Party Secretary Brezhnev that an attack against the Soviet world should appear wholly un-profitable to anyone who might be rash enough to consider it. A warning against such folly provided the climax of the four-hour speech with which the Soviet party chief, in the presence of many though not all of the leaders of world Communism, inaugurated the 50th anniversary celebration of the Bolshevik Revolution on November 3. ". . . The Soviet people will not flinch," Brezhnev declared, "if some-one is mad enough to make an attempt upon the security of the Soviet Union and of our allies. Such an attempt, wherever it might come from—the north or the south, the west or the east—would encounter the all-conquering might of our armed forces. No shields and no dis-tances are too great for that might."[83] Such choice of phraseology suggested that Brezhnev's warning might be intended for the Com-munist Chinese no less than for possible Western adversaries.

The Soviet party leader seemed vexed by Chinese and Cuban charges that the Soviet approach to world affairs lacked revolutionary zeal. "Our foreign policy is socialist and consistently revolutionary in its entire content," he insisted. "But Marxist-Leninists have always realized that socialism cannot be implanted by one country in another by military force . . . and they are convinced that there is no need to resort to wars between states for it to be victorious. . . . The Soviet Union . . . continues to advocate renunciation of attempts to settle issues in relations between the two social systems by means of war." To his denunciations of U.S. policy and promises of aid to North Vietnam, Brezhnev appended a sharp reproof for "the stand of Mao Tse-tung's group, which is hampering coordinated assistance to Vietnam from all the socialist countries, including China."[84]

These forthright comments did little to advance the Soviet hope of summoning a world conference of Communist parties to deal with the China question. The very attendance list at the anniversary cele-brations reflected the extent to which Soviet control of world Com-munism had loosened. The Chinese, the Albanians, and the leaders of most of the Asian parties stayed away entirely. North Korea, hitherto believed to be on Moscow's side in the Sino-Soviet controversy, took minimal notice of the occasion, while North Vietnam's delegate performed a typical balancing act in which he paid open tribute to China as well as the Soviet Union. President Tito, for all his recent complaisance in Middle Eastern affairs, determinedly resisted the proposed world conference, as did the Rumanians and many others. The Cuban delegation not only withheld its support but repeatedly snubbed its Soviet hosts, apparently to dramatize Castro's resentment over Soviet opposition to his revolutionary tactics in Latin America. At no time in the past half-century had the country of the "victorious revolution" appeared to wield so little influence over the Communist movement as a whole.

The anniversary period was equally barren of constructive innovation in Soviet internal affairs. A promised constitution that was to have crowned the edifice of "socialist democracy" failed to materialize, while an amnesty affecting thousands of persons in prisons and labor camps was mainly notable for its omission of Andrei D. Sinyavsky and Yuli M. Daniel, two writers whose conviction on charges of having circulated anti-Soviet propaganda abroad had attracted world-wide attention. In economic affairs, the apparent abandonment of the Five-Year Plan for 1966-70 and the publication of one-year plans for 1968, 1969, and 1970 suggested that long-range planning guidelines were still undetermined. Even in outer space, the Soviet Union produced no spectacular manned flight of the kind that had sometimes cast luster on earlier political gatherings.

The disappointing character of the Moscow celebrations, in which Brezhnev held the limelight from start to finish, seems not to have dampened the Kremlin's feeling that it was essential to proceed with steps to meet the Chinese challenge. If it was impossible to hold a full meeting of the world's 88 Communist and Workers' parties, the Soviet leaders apparently reasoned, they would have to make do with a partial one. On November 24, a fortnight after the close of the Moscow celebrations, it was announced that eighteen parties had agreed to the scheduling of a preliminary, consultative meeting which would be held in Budapest in February 1968. No one was thinking in terms of "excommunication" or interference in other parties' affairs, *Pravda* explained; on the contrary, the meeting would concentrate on positive tasks and the promotion of cohesion and unity in the struggle against imperialism.[85] But such assurances were less than satisfactory to the Rumanian, the Yugoslav, and various other parties.

By the year's end, only 70 of the 88 had manifested their intention of being present at the Budapest meeting.

Rumania's independent stand was further underlined at the beginning of December by a governmental change that elevated Party Secretary Ceausescu, the symbol of nationalist defiance, to the position of Chief of State in succession to Chivu Stoica. Unlike its Eastern European neighbors, Rumania had neglected thus far to renegotiate its mutual assistance treaty with the U.S.S.R.; and the differences over this and other issues were not resolved when Ceausescu visited Moscow in mid-December for two days of talks with the Soviet leaders. Although Rumania did attend a subsequent meeting of Communist governments on the Middle East,[86] its presence served mainly to soften the expressions of antipathy toward Israel, with whose government Rumania had maintained diplomatic relations and now planned a series of joint industrial ventures.

The attitudes of more orthodox Communist governments were also a source of concern in Moscow. President Ulbricht of East Germany was again complaining about the maneuvers of the rival German government in Bonn, which had not only evaded his bids for political recognition but was still pursuing its campaign for closer ties with other Communist governments. Even the U.S.S.R. had lately appeared to view the Bonn government with less disfavor. There had been desultory conversations between Bonn and Moscow about the possibility of a new, indirect attack on the problem of Germany's division through an exchange of "renunciation of force" declarations between the Federal Republic and the Warsaw Pact members, collectively or individually. Admittedly, Bonn's refusal to recognize East Germany would constitute an obstacle to this procedure. Meanwhile, it was continuing its efforts in Eastern European capitals and preparing to propose to Yugoslavia a resumption of diplomatic relations after a lapse of years.

Sensing its growing isolation even within the Communist world, the East German regime would seem to have turned to the Kremlin with a renewed and urgent demand for support. According to some accounts, it even proposed a resumption of the campaign of harassment against West Berlin, virtually shelved since Khrushchev's day. The Soviet leadership itself may still have held conflicting views on the German question. Some said that Brezhnev favored a very "tough" line, Kosygin a milder one. In any event, the Kremlin responded to

Ulbricht's appeals on December 8 with a shattering denunciation of the Federal Republic's internal politics and foreign policy, accompanied by the demand that Bonn explicitly renounce its claims to West Berlin as well as the former German territories annexed by Poland.[87] Soviet diplomatic notes of similar tenor were conveyed to the United States,[88] Great Britain, and France.

This abrupt proceeding bade fair to undo a whole year's painstaking diplomatic effort on Bonn's part. For West Berliners, the realignment of Soviet and East German views would obviously cancel any hope for Christmas passes to visit their relations in the East. The exaggerated assertion that West Germany was being taken over by neo-Nazis and militarists was once again refuted by the allied governments in diplomatic notes delivered in Moscow at the year's end;[89] but such corrections of the record seemed hardly likely to mitigate the new harshness of Soviet policy. West Germany, which was more immediately affected, found it advisable to frame a soft answer in which it mildly rejected the Soviet charges and reaffirmed its desire for improved relations.[90]

Ulbricht's struggle to hold back the clock had its counterpart in other Communist-ruled countries. Czechoslovakia, after years of relative immobility, had also become the scene of an extraordinary political and intellectual ferment which was causing increasing difficulties for the regime of President and Party Secretary Antonín Novotný. Disagreements over the scope and tempo of economic reform had been accentuated by a conflict between younger, technically minded Communists and dyed-in-the-wool ideologists of the Novotný stamp; and to this had been added the congenital discontent of Slovak elements who resented the preponderant position of the more numerous Czechs. By December, revolt was brewing in the Czechoslovak party apparatus and Novotný's days as leader appeared to be numbered. But if Novotný fell, how long would Ulbricht last? Again the East German President apparently appealed to Moscow, this time for support of his Czechoslovak colleague. Secretary Brezhnev made a special trip to Prague on December 8 in order to attend a meeting of Czechoslovakia's ten-member party presidium, which is said to have been equally divided for and against the tottering Novotný but to have been dissuaded by Brezhnev's intervention from giving him the final push.[91] So much influence the Soviet Union still possessed; but the reprieve was only temporary, as would be revealed on January 5, 1968 when Novotný was ousted as party leader and limited to an increasingly shaky presidency.

The U.S.S.R. had a few problems of its own as it began the 51st year of Bolshevik rule. The economy, at least, seemed reasonably well in hand at the moment. The grain harvest had been adequate; industrial production, by Soviet figures, had increased by 10 per cent during 1967; Soviet publicists could not forgo a little gloating over the difficulties being experienced by the pound and dollar. But the political cross currents within the Soviet leadership had not yet been stilled, and adherents of the Shelepin or "Komsomol" group (the "hawks" of the June crisis) were still being weeded out. Among them, apparently, was the head of the state committee in charge of exchange programs with foreign countries, which was officially abolished December 23.[92] Young Soviet intellectuals, meanwhile, still showed a remarkable readiness to take personal risks in pressing for broader freedom of expression.

If Communist affairs were under less than perfect control, the same was undoubtedly true of relations with that part of the world that had remained non-Communist in spite of Lenin's sweeping predictions to the contrary. Unlike their Chinese compeers, the Soviet leaders by this time appeared to have largely given up the expectation that the capitalist world would soon succumb to its own contradictions or crumble before the onslaught of the world's revolutionary forces. Yet they could not as yet be said to have fully adjusted their own political attitudes or rid themselves of the ingrained fears and prejudices that still prevented a reasonable settlement of East-West problems. It was easy to suggest, in 1967, that only the war in Vietnam still barred the way to far-reaching East-West accommodation. Undoubtedly, Vietnam made matters immensely more difficult, not only by inflaming traditional animosities on both sides but by keeping alive the possibility of actual armed confrontation. But even without Vietnam, it may be questioned whether the evolution of Soviet thinking had progressed to a point where the Soviet leaders could have responded affirmatively to American offers of friendship. As things stood, their hostile behavior could only accentuate official caution in Washington, invigorate the persistent anti-Soviet trends in American opinion, and thus create new barriers to accommodation on both sides.

The most serious manifestation of this process was, of course, the revival of the competition in ballistic missile and antimissile systems. But a similar trend could also be observed in other connections. One case in point was the persistent congressional refusal to endorse the President's proposals looking toward an increase in East-West trade. Another was the renewed preoccupation with matters of espionage and political warfare that became apparent on both the Soviet and American sides following the defection to the United States of Mrs. Alliluyeva and, more recently, of Lieutenant Colonel Yevgeny Runge, a key Soviet intelligence agent.[93] There were other frictions over fishing practices and similar matters.[94] Even the long-promised New York-Moscow air service failed to get started during 1967, though here red tape rather than political prejudice appeared to be responsible.[95]

On the credit side, it would have been unwise to overlook the importance of the successful Johnson-Kosygin effort to avoid a direct confrontation at the time of the Middle East war. Later in the year, the Soviet Government earned some supplementary thanks for refraining from any step to aggravate the Greek-Turkish crisis over Cyprus. Yet its attitude on Vietnam could hardly fail to raise a doubt about its supposed desire for peace in that country;[96] while its Middle Eastern policy after the six-day war seemed redolent of selfish ambition. By its exploitation of the Arab defeat to advance its own position, the Soviet Union undoubtedly contributed to an important change in the balance of power in the Mediterranean and the Middle East. Limited Soviet involvement in such countries as Yemen and Nigeria offered a further indication that the sense of opportunism had not gone out of Soviet policy and that the caution of the early Brezhnev-Kosygin years might be increasingly discarded as Soviet armed power increased.[97]

5 : Will Success Spoil the West?

A recurring obligation of American leaders in the 1960's was the issuance of public assurances that the United States, despite its global commitments and deepening involvement in the Far East, maintained an undiminished concern for the strength and welfare of the Atlantic "community" and the solidarity of its partners in North America and Western Europe. That such assurances should occasionally have been found necessary was not surprising. The prospect of a gradual diminution in America's extraordinary postwar involvement with its Atlantic neighbors had been implicit in the whole development of world affairs since the end of the postwar period and the achievement of European recovery. As its European partners regained the capacity and the desire to shift for themselves, it was natural for the United States to limit its exertions in their behalf as well as its attempts to guide their common evolution. What was most remarkable in the world of 1967 was not the fact that the relationship of twenty years earlier had weakened in some respects, but rather that so much of it still persisted.

A striking measure of this persistence was the fact that the United States, more than two decades after World War II, was still maintaining 255,000 troops in Western Germany, plus another 75,000 elsewhere in Europe, and supplying the top commander and much of the subordinate military talent committed to the defense of Western Europe under the North Atlantic Treaty. Even those Americans who favored a substantial reduction in the military forces deployed beyond the Atlantic recognized the common interest of the United States and its allies in ensuring that the countries of Western Europe were protected against Soviet aggression. But the possibility of such aggression was by this time generally thought to be much less acute than in the past; and many Americans considered that the European members of the alliance were doing less than their "fair share" toward the defense of their area at a time when the United States was having increasing difficulty in meeting its non-European military commitments, particularly in Vietnam. France, in 1966, had virtually dissociated itself from the common defense by withdrawing the last of its forces from NATO command and forbidding the peacetime use of its territory by the forces of its allies. Provisionally, France still remained a party to the North Atlantic Treaty; yet the arbitrary procedure it had followed in disengaging itself from the NATO military structure could hardly strengthen the desire of the United States to maintain its own commitment at full strength. Additional arguments in favor of reducing the number of American troops in Europe could be found in the progress of military technology, especially the development of long-range airlift capabilities and the increasing tendency to base the deterrence of aggression on the threat of retaliation by international ballistic missiles rather than on local forces.

To the somewhat problematical condition of Western defense in the mid-1960's was added a growing political and psychological rift between the United States and most of its Western partners. In part, this feeling of mutual disenchantment was the natural result of a perhaps overly close association during a long period of years. In part it also reflected basic differences in the evaluation of world political trends, particularly with respect to the alleged threat presented by the policies of the Communist countries. Europeans and Canadians, by and large, had never taken the supposed Communist threat with quite the same seriousness as the United States. During the "cold war" years, they had often been antagonized by Washington's vigorously anti-Communist policies in Europe and, to an even greater degree, in Asia. Since 1965, the progressive intensification of the war in Vietnam had crystallized this feeling and, in many Western quarters, created an outright abhorrence for U.S. actions not only in Southeast Asia but in other parts of the world as well. Such feelings seldom rested on any profound analysis of American policies or the reasons for them. They had, however, done much to damage the close and confident relationships of earlier years.

This negative trend was all the more remarkable because it occurred at a period when the economic interdependence between the United States and its Atlantic partners had become more marked than ever before, and when American business investment in the other industrially developed countries of Europe and North America was breaking all records. Yet this very omnipresence of U.S. business enterprise in some ways deepened the sense of alienation from and hostility toward the United States. On the one hand, it aroused fears of U.S. economic domination and strengthened the anti-American feelings for which President de Gaulle had become so persuasive a spokesman. It also fomented jealousy of the U.S. technical-industrial preeminence and resentment of the so-called "technological gap" and the "brain drain" that was depriving Great Britain and other allied countries of some of their best professional talent. Such factors tended to accentuate the anti-American revulsion occasioned by Vietnam.

Though there was no parallel revulsion against Europe on the part of the United States, there were abundant signs that the United States had less attention to spare for Europe at a time when national concern was so heavily concentrated on the Far East and, in a slightly lesser degree, on the direct relationship with the U.S.S.R. To say that Europe was being "downgraded" by the United States would clearly have been an overstatement; yet it seemed equally clear that it no longer held its former preeminence in American thinking, private or official.

Such psychological dislocations were not confined to those relationships that directly involved the United States. A similar feeling of disenchantment could be perceived in the relations among the Western European countries and, in some instances, in their internal politics as well. With economic recovery complete and the Soviet threat apparently waning, there had seemed no vital reason for the Western countries to continue holding together and repressing their centrifugal tendencies as they had generally managed to do in the 1940's and 1950's. Viewed as a collective entity, the West of the mid-1960's appeared to have lost its sense of direction. Its peoples, by and large, were given over to the enjoyment of their new-found affluence and only casually concerned with the important public problems that still loomed on the horizon.

Yet the Western situation would have been fraught with great uncertainties even had a sense of civic responsibility been more in evidence. With the gradual change in world conditions, the dogmas and institutions of past years had lost much of their relevance; yet the new guidelines that would ultimately determine the future of Europe, of the Atlantic community, and of relations with the Communist East were not yet visible. Those Western governments that were parties to the North Atlantic Treaty, for example, were approaching the date when the original twenty-year commitment undertaken on April 4, 1949 would come up for reexamination. France's attitude with respect to remaining a party to the treaty beyond 1969 appeared highly problematical, and some of the other member governments appeared uncertain whether the alliance should be continued in its original form. There was much talk of a need to reverse the emphasis in NATO by converting it from an instrument for the common defense to a device for reaching accommodation with the Eastern countries. Some individuals even seemed to favor Moscow's idea of letting NATO lapse completely and replacing it by a European security pact without the United States.

Still another dimension of uncertainty arose from the unpredictable quirks of individual personality, particularly in the case of the 76-year-old soldier who had lately begun a new seven-year term as President of the Fifth French Republic. President de Gaulle's imperious nature, political prejudices, unshakable will, and gift for Delphic utterance had propelled him into so marked a position of ascendancy that the whole destiny of the West appeared at times to hinge upon the whims of this single individual. In face of French obstruction, attempts at common action by other Western nations—including the United States—tended at times to appear as ineffectual as the pranks of mischievous schoolboys. Determined as he was to promote the dignity and interests of France, General de Gaulle had not shrunk from subverting the dignity and interests of France's allies. This tension between the narrow interests of France and the wider interests of the community of which France formed a part had by 1967 become the central theme of Western affairs, one that largely overshadowed the older, still critical issue of the relationship between the United States and Europe.

23 : The West at Play

In this situation of general unease and drift, a handful of specific problems claimed the attention of Western governments as they prepared for the next phase of their continuing adjustment to changing world conditions. Widely different in kind, these problems were of comparable weight in terms of their importance to the Western future.

First among them was the situation created by Great Britain's bid to become a member of the six-nation European Economic Community or Common Market, a proposal first advanced in 1962, vetoed by President de Gaulle in 1963, but renewed by Prime Minister Wilson in late 1966.

Second was the fate of a common effort to promote the expansion of trade within and beyond the Western community through the multilateral tariff negotiations known as the "Kennedy Round," initiated in 1964 and soon to be reaching their climax at Geneva.

Third was the endeavor to devise additional means of financing future world trade by creating a new mechanism for international payments, a project whose leadership had fallen to the major financial nations composing the "Group of Ten."

Fourth was the need to complete the readjustments in the common defense necessitated by changing military and political conditions, the French withdrawal from NATO defense arrangements, and the growing difficulty of financing the deployment of British and American forces in the territory of the Federal Republic of Germany.

A fifth problem, not much noticed thus far but soon to rank with the other four, had to do with the conditions governing international inspection of peaceful nuclear activities under the nuclear nonproliferation treaty being negotiated at Geneva.

Most of the Western governments had their individual ideas on most if not all of these issues; but it was France, as the most nationalistically minded and deeply opinionated among the Western nations, that had done most to define the limits within which their solution could be sought. This was almost as true of the efforts in which France was not participating—such as the "integrated" defense of the West and the search for a nonproliferation treaty—as of those in which it continued to lend a hand. Throughout the whole range of

Western endeavor, French insistence on the primacy of national interest and on the rejection of "supranational" arrangements was the
rock around which each project had to be steered if it was not to
founder altogether.

What no one could be entirely sure about was the degree to which
these negative attitudes reflected the desires of the French nation, as
distinguished from the lonely individual who actually decided French
policy. Broadly speaking, it seemed to most observers that the French
public took de Gaulle's anti-Americanism in stride, was somewhat
uneasy about his European policy, but was moved to overt dissatisfaction only by his austere approach to France's internal economic
and social affairs. These impressions were largely borne out by the
elections to the French National Assembly which were held on
March 5 and 12, 1967 and, to the general astonishment, came close
to depriving the Gaullist party of its majority as well as elevating the
French Left—including the Communists—to its most influential position in years. That this outcome amounted to a rebuke to de Gaulle
seemed undeniable, at least so far as domestic matters were concerned.
His characteristic response, however, was to accentuate the very
policies his critics appeared to find most objectionable. Increased
resistance to Britain's Common Market bid was matched, in domestic
policy, by a controversial but ultimately successful demand for special
decree powers to deal with economic and social questions.

Western Germany's new government, in office since December 1,
1966, presented a much less inflexible appearance as Chancellor
Kiesinger and Vice-Chancellor Brandt set out to mend the various
fences that had been damaged in the process of supplanting former
Chancellor Ludwig Erhard. Domestically, the Federal Republic was
experiencing its first postwar economic recession and entering on a
period of government-imposed austerity marked by sharply reduced
budgetary allocations for defense and other purposes. There was also
some uneasiness about the activities of a small, ultraconservative or
neo-Nazi group known as the National Democratic party, which was
in the process of gaining minority representation in a number of
German state parliaments. Opinions differed about the seriousness of
this phenomenon, but most Germans appeared more troubled by the
adverse publicity it aroused abroad than about any inherent threat to
democratic practices within the Federal Republic.

In foreign policy, three major aims appeared to animate the new

West German leadership: (1) restoration of friendship with France, which had cooled perceptibly during the Erhard period, in part at least because of the former Chancellor's pro-American leanings; (2) retention of friendship with the United States; and (3) establishment of closer contact with Communist-ruled Eastern Europe. Of the three, improvement of relations with France appeared to present the fewest problems, despite the Germans' apparent disagreement with French views on the question of British entry into the Common Market. West German relations with the United States were already good, although important differences were soon to arise in connection with an inherited dispute about the financing of U.S. troops in Germany as well as the more novel issues presented by the nuclear nonproliferation treaty. The greatest uncertainties surrounded the new attempt at building bridges to the Communist world, a venture that faced powerful opposition from East German and other sources and, as noted in the preceding chapter, was destined to achieve only moderate success during 1967.

The government of the United Kingdom was immersed in more serious difficulties in the winter of 1966-67, largely because of persistent inability to pay its way in the world while sustaining the burdens of a welfare state and clinging to the vestiges of a global political and military position. In trying to maintain high standards of consumption at the expense of industrial modernization and production for export, Great Britain had for years been spending more abroad than it was able to take in through trade and "invisible" transactions. Thus far, its economy had been kept afloat primarily by the willingness of its Western partners, acting directly or through the International Monetary Fund, to come to the rescue with periodic credits designed to help meet past indebtedness and gain time to put the national finances in order. In the summer of 1966, however, Prime Minister Wilson's government had put into effect a rigorous deflationary program aimed at reducing consumption and imports, achieving a "healthy" balance-of-payments surplus in 1967, and maintaining the pound at its established exchange value of $2.80.

In conformity with these broad objectives, the drive to bring the national payments into balance had become the principal determinant of British policy abroad as well as at home. Overseas defense expenditure was being drastically curtailed, partly in response to what was described as an improving international climate but also, and more fundamentally, because the government had concluded that the economy would no longer sustain a global military role. Similiar considerations had prompted the decision to renew Britain's once-vetoed application for entry into the European Economic Community. The competition afforded by membership in the Common Market, it was believed, would be the best means of stimulating long-needed reforms in the structure of British industry. The E.E.C. members, apart from France, seemed generally sympathetic to this objective. Everything would therefore depend on whether or not General de Gaulle had modified his earlier view that the United Kingdom was not sufficiently "European" to qualify.

While waiting for the French President to pass judgment, the British continued to feel the pinch of overseas commitments inherited from an earlier age. The acceptance of continuing responsibility for the colony of Southern Rhodesia, whose white minority government had flaunted British policy and international opinion by declaring independence in November 1965, had exposed the United Kingdom to economic sacrifice, international opprobrium, and sharp domestic controversy. Its plans for military disengagement from other colonial or former colonial possessions had involved it in bitter disputes with the local authorities in independent Malta and in the soon-to-be-independent South Arabian Federation (Aden). Its position in Gibraltar was being made increasingly uncomfortable by Spanish pressures aimed at a transfer of sovereignty. Communist China could at any time create acute difficulties for its administration of Hong Kong—and would do so later in 1967. Small wonder that many Britons longed to exchange their global commitments for a firm association with their Western European neighbors.

The fate of Britain's application to the E.E.C. would also affect the fortunes of its partners in the seven-nation European Free Trade Association (EFTA), set up in 1960 as a stopgap until relations with the E.E.C. were straightened out. Few of the other Western European countries, however, faced acute domestic or international problems as 1967 began. There was some intermittent tension between Italy and Austria about the situation in the Italian-ruled South Tyrol (Alto Adige). Spain was racked by labor and student unrest which had caused the government of General Francisco Franco to cut short a promising experiment in political liberalization. Portugal represented something of a political liability to its Western associates because of its nondemocratic internal regime and the vociferous international criticism of its policies in Africa. At the other end of Europe, Greece and Turkey were perennially at loggerheads over their conflicting interests in Cyprus, and Greece was also a prey to growing internal instability which was to lead in April to a military coup with highly unsatisfactory implications for its own future and for NATO's position in the Eastern Mediterranean.[1]

Canada offered its own variations on the typical worries of the Western countries. Two trends were becoming especially evident in this 100th anniversary year of the Canadian Confederation, an occasion that was to be celebrated with characteristic éclat at Expo 67, the Montreal World's Fair. A powerful upsurge of economic nationalism, under way for several years and directed especially against economic penetration by the United States, gave rise early in 1967 to a sharp controversy with Washington over the status of U.S.-owned banks in Canada. The specific issue was ultimately compromised,[2] but the basic problem remained. Rather more sensational were the evidences of growing discontent and self-assertiveness on the part of Canada's 6 million French-speaking citizens, whose demands for a more equal position in Canadian society were beginning to challenge the bases of the confederation and were soon to be taken up by President de Gaulle in connection with his continuing agitation against the supposed "hegemony" of the United States.[3]

Aggravated by a slackening of economic activity in many Western countries, such difficulties contributed to a widespread sense of malaise that tempered to some extent the exuberant Western mood of the 1960's. The exuberance was tempered rather than extinguished, however. By and large, the peoples of the West continued to enjoy an unprecedented material well-being and were content to leave the vexing problems of international policy to the responsible officials.

American authorities, despite their preoccupation with Vietnam, were well aware of these underlying problems of the Western relationship and were far from making the error of attributing them exclusively to the malign influence of the French President. Particularly disconcerting from Washington's point of view was the dawning recognition that the new West German government, despite its professed desire for American friendship, was going to have its own views on common problems and would be rather less hesitant than its predecessor about differing with American policy. U.S.-West German relations deteriorated markedly in the early weeks of 1967, in part as a result of personal factors—President Johnson and Chancellor Kiesinger appeared to have gotten off to a bad start—and in part because of sharp differences of opinion about troop costs and nuclear nonproliferation. Irritation was running high when former High Commissioner John J. McCloy visited Western Germany in March to offer a new formula on the troop cost issue which did much to relieve the immediate friction.[4] Alerted to the deteriorating mood not only in Germany but in Western Europe as a whole, Vice-President Humphrey shortly afterward undertook a "working visit" to Western capitals for the purpose of reaffirming American interest in Western affairs and urging prompt agreement on outstanding problems.[5]

A more dramatic manifestation of American concern was President Johnson's decision to fly to Germany for the funeral of former Chancellor Konrad Adenauer, whose death on April 19 was a fresh reminder of how rapidly the European scene was changing. With discussions on troop costs, nonproliferation, tariff reduction, and international monetary reform all approaching a climax, the President could not have been expected to produce ready-made solutions on this solemn occasion. He did, however, exchange courtesies with President de Gaulle and other Western leaders and publicly agreed with Chancellor Kiesinger that the historic German-American friendship must be maintained in a spirit of "constant, complete, and full consultation."[6] Restoration of the close and confident relationship that had prevailed in Adenauer's and Erhard's time—should it prove possible—would surely be of assistance in coping with the upcoming Western problems of trade, finance, defense, and policy toward the non-Western world.

24 : Trade and Financial Arrangements

It was a characteristic of the Western situation in the mid-1960's that so many of the immediate problems requiring governmental decision were concerned with economic and financial issues rather than with the overriding question of security against armed attack that had been so dominant a preoccupation in earlier years. Not less characteristic was the fact that these financial and economic discussions, though mainly concerned with devising improved arrangements for the future, were strongly and sometimes critically influenced by the current difficulties of individual Western governments. The balance-of-payments problems of Great Britain and the United States, together with the budgetary difficulties of the German Federal Republic, repeatedly obtruded themselves upon the discussion of longer-range issues and helped to shape the decisions reached—or, as in the case of Britain's Common Market application, to prevent the reaching of any decision at all.

That the United Kingdom and most other Western European nations would eventually find their places in an expanded European Economic Community had been one of the underlying assumptions of Western policy through most of the 1960's. The obstacle to this consummation, as General de Gaulle had made clear, had little to do with the complicated technical adjustments involved in widening the E.E.C. framework to accommodate Britain and other new members. The essential obstacle was de Gaulle's belief that Great Britain was too close to the United States, and too little "European" in spirit, to be an acceptable partner for the continental nations. The most immediate task for British policy, accordingly, was to dispel these reservations and convince the General that Britain was in fact a European power that could add strength to a united Europe and, in Prime Minister Wilson's phrase, help ward off the danger of "industrial helotry" to an outside power.

In a series of exploratory visits to Common Market capitals during the early weeks of 1967, Mr. Wilson and Foreign Secretary George Brown were able to confirm the impression that the other Common Market members were generally favorable to British membership. True, there was some question about the attitude of Western Germany, which seemed basically favorable to British aspirations but very anxious not to offend the French and, moreover, irritated by some phases of British policy on other questions. On the whole, however, the auguries seemed favorable enough to justify a firm commitment on Britain's part. Backed by an overwhelming vote of the House of Commons, the government on May 11 made formal application to join the E.E.C. as well as its two sister institutions, the European Coal and Steel Community and the European Atomic Energy Community (Euratom). Ireland and Denmark also applied for admission to the E.E.C., while Norway, Sweden, and other EFTA members prepared to follow suit.

Not until this formal step had been taken did President de Gaulle make clear, in a press conference held on May 16,[7] that his own views remained completely unaltered. While he did not again intend to "veto" negotiations, the General intimated, he still considered Great Britain basically unqualified for membership—and hence, presumably, inadmissible. The reaction to this statement served at least to indicate that most other E.E.C. governments were by this time as determined to bring Britain in as the French were to keep it out. De Gaulle's presence failed to dampen the display of pro-British feelings at a ceremonial meeting held in Rome on May 29-30 to celebrate the tenth anniversary of the Treaty Establishing the European Economic Community. The E.E.C. Commission, the executive organ headed by Walter Hallstein of West Germany, had long favored British membership; and the continuance of a "European" and pro-British stand seemed assured by the designation of Jean Rey of Belgium as President of the new, unified Commission which, by previous agreement, was to serve all three European communities from July 1 onward.

De Gaulle had not forbidden the E.E.C. to talk about the British application, which was accordingly taken up by the E.E.C. Council of Ministers in July. The arguments with which Foreign Minister Couve de Murville attempted to rationalize France's opposition were more varied than convincing. On the one hand, he contended, British accession would dangerously weaken the existing six-nation association; on the other, it would also make Western Europe look so strong that the Russians would take fright and the chances of East-West *détente* would be endangered. In any case, M. Couve de Murville intimated, Great Britain would clearly have to resolve its current financial problems before it could qualify for Common Market membership. Strung out by various stalling tactics, discussions about the date when formal negotiations with Britain and other new applicants might begin continued well into the autumn.

In the meantime the Western governments, including France and the United States, were able to reach a significant measure of agreement on much broader measures of tariff reduction and international monetary reform. The multilateral tariff negotiations known as the Kennedy Round, initiated in 1964 under the auspices of the General Agreement on Tariffs and Trade (GATT), had also had as their point of departure the expectation that Britain would soon be joining the Common Market and that there would presently emerge in Western Europe a powerful economic union with which, in President Kennedy's phrase, the United States would have to "strike a bargain" if its own and the world's trade were to meet the resultant challenge and derive the appropriate benefits. The late President had accordingly sought and obtained congressional authority to negotiate reciprocal tariff reductions with other nations and economic groupings over a five-year period ending June 30, 1967. With this authority, it was hoped, the United States would be able to negotiate reductions of up to 50 per cent in the prevailing tariffs on industrial goods, together with suitable arrangements to promote trade in agricultural commodities and advance the trading interests of the developing countries.

Conditions had vastly altered since these goals were formulated. President Kennedy himself was dead. Great Britain had failed to enter the E.E.C. on the expected timetable. That organization, in turn, had shown less than the expected interest in "striking a bargain" on American terms. The United States itself, as the Kennedy Round got under way, had shown marked unwillingness to reduce the tariffs that protected some important segments of its trade against the blasts of foreign competition. As 1967 opened, most of the big issues remained unresolved and no one was sure that the United States and the E.E.C., as the principal contestants among the 50 or more participating nations, would be able to reach a useful agreement in the six months remaining before the authority voted by Congress expired. The death of Christian A. Herter, the President's Special Representative for Trade Negotiations, at the end of 1966 had introduced new complications by creating a vacancy at the head of the American negotiating team which was not formally filled until late in January with the appointment of former Deputy Special Representative William M. Roth.

Three main tendencies defined American strategy in the incredibly complicated negotiations of the next few months.[8] The first was a steady emphasis on the urgency of reaching agreement, buttressed by warnings that failure to do so would in all probability inaugurate a new era of cutthroat rivalries between competing trade blocs. Second, an attempt was made to demonstrate the United States' sincerity of purpose by certain unilateral gestures of a liberal character, among them the discontinuance, partial or total, of earlier tariff increases on watch movements and sheet glass[9] and a relaxation of safety standards affecting imported automobiles.[10] Third, and ultimately most critical, was the U.S. insistence that the prospective reductions in industrial tariffs be matched by corresponding measures in the agricultural field. More specifically, it was revealed at the beginning of 1967 that the United States was demanding the conclusion of an international grains agreement which, in addition to ensuring a continuing outlet for American grain exports in the E.E.C. area, would set minimum prices for the wheat exports of all countries and would assist in meeting world food deficiencies by making grain and other agricultural supplies available to developing nations.

Resistance to this last project, primarily by Great Britain rather than the Common Market, soon emerged as one of the two chief obstacles to over-all agreement. The other seemingly insurmountable difficulty arose from European and Japanese insistence on a reduction in the American tariff on certain chemical products which, in conformity with U.S. legislation, were valued for tariff purposes on the basis of their "American selling price" rather than the lower prices prevailing in their countries of origin. Given the manifest reluctance of Congress to accommodate this demand, the "A.S.P." issue appeared quite capable of wrecking the entire negotiation as week succeeded week, deadline followed deadline, and the "war of nerves" among the leading contenders intensified.

That the negotiations did not collapse but ultimately turned out better than anyone had ventured to predict was largely due to the skill and dedication of three men, Mr. Roth of the United States, Jean Rey as chief negotiator for the Common Market, and Eric Wyndham White, Director-General of GATT and the author of a series of ingenious compromises that served to resolve one deadlock after another. Their collective masterpiece was an agreement to meet the issue of chemical tariffs by breaking it into two separate "packages," one containing reciprocal concessions which would be granted under all circumstances, the other containing additional concessions which would be available to the United States on condition that Congress took action to eliminate the "American selling price" system.

It was midnight on May 15 when Mr. Wyndham White announced that "the essential elements in the Kennedy Round have . . . been successfully negotiated." "The most ambitious attempt ever made to achieve the liberalization of international trade," he declared, had been crowned by results "of a far greater magnitude than those obtained in any previous trade negotiation." Although most of the original goals had obviously not been fully realized, the United States and its trading partners would still be cutting tariffs on roughly one-third of their industrial and agricultural imports. These reductions, in most cases phased over a period of years, were estimated to average 33-35 per cent on industrial products and somewhat less for agricultural products. Among the supplementary features of the agreement were a new International Grains Arrangement that would, among other things, finance the shipment of 4.5 million tons of grain to hungry nations in each of the next three years; an extension, also for three years, of the Long-Term Cotton Textile Arrangement negotiated in 1962; and agreement on an international antidumping code.[11]

While much too far-reaching for protectionist interests in the United States,[12] disinterested observers acknowledged that the Kennedy Round agreements had left much unfinished business for the future. In concentrating on the reduction of tariffs, they had largely neglected the problem of nontariff barriers, which sometimes limited trade more severely. Particularly disappointing to the United States and others was the failure to make more adequate provision for the needs of the developing countries, whose inability to compete on equal terms with the advanced industrialized nations had in the end been very imperfectly allowed for. The United States had also failed to achieve an assured outlet for its agricultural production within the area of the Common Market. Considering the possibilities of total failure that had persisted up to the last minute, however, President Johnson could hail the final agreements, as signed by 46 nations in Geneva on June 30, as a "historic landmark in cooperation among nations."[13]

A second, perhaps equally historic landmark was established two months later when the principal Western nations agreed upon the minimum essentials of a plan for controlled expansion of world monetary reserves. The need for this undertaking, which had been under study for a number of years and had been vigorously promoted by the United States since mid-1965, arose from the fact that while the volume of world trade was already increasing at a rapid rate, the supply of gold, which, with pounds and dollars, formed the basis of the international monetary system, had remained practically stationary. Unless steps were taken to supplement the existing means of exchange through the creation of a new international monetary unit or some other form of internationally sanctioned credit arrangement, it was possible to foresee a situation in which the growth of world trade would be inhibited by lack of monetary "lubricant" and might even go into reverse.

Like other plans requiring close cooperation among Western nations, this seemingly reasonable proposal had found its sternest opponent in the government of France. President de Gaulle's financial ideas were less concerned with meeting emerging needs as others saw them than with ending the "privileged" position of the pound and the dollar and restoring gold to its original status as the sole basis of the world financial system. There was no present need for any expansion of "international liquidity," French spokesmen insisted. On the contrary, they argued, its most likely effect would be to prolong the instability in world finance by taking the pressure off Great Britain and the United States to exercise the financial discipline required to eliminate their balance-of-payments deficits.[14]

Although such reasoning was a logical outgrowth of de Gaulle's nationalist views, it was a fact that the failure of Britain and the United States to balance their international accounts had had an unsettling effect on the international financial picture and, in the British case at least, had repeatedly diverted attention from long-range planning to the meeting of immediate financial crises. The United States, with a substantial export surplus and a gold reserve that still exceeded $13 billion, was in a much less vulnerable position than the United Kingdom. But the United States was also suffering from a chronic deficit in the balance of payments as usually defined, had felt compelled to limit the flow of investment capital to other developed nations, had utilized its right to draw on the assistance of the International Monetary Fund, and had seen its hopes of early equilibrium repeatedly frustrated by the effects of the Vietnam war. Not a few financial observers had asked how long it would be able to maintain the long-established policy of buying and selling gold at the fixed price of $35 an ounce.[14a]

The international inconveniences attendant on this state of affairs had been mitigated by various forms of cooperation among Western governments and financial institutions, notably by so-called "swap" arrangements among central banks and by an eight-nation "gold pool" organized to steady the price of gold on the London market. France, despite frequent manifestations of a "go-it-alone" spirit, continued to participate in some of these arrangements. In January,

Finance Minister Michel Debré annoyed the United States and others by renewing his government's agitation in favor of a revaluation of gold in relation to the dollar; but he also took part in an informal agreement with his British, American, German, and Italian opposites to try to stem a trend toward higher interest rates which had been especially inconvenient to the two English-speaking countries.[15] In March, France acted concurrently with other creditors in the renewal of $1 billion in stand-by credits extended to the United Kingdom.[16] The general tone of international financial discussion in early 1967 was less than bland, however. Secretary of the Treasury Henry H. Fowler, in a speech of March 17, complained that the United States' financial partners were not cooperating sufficiently in helping it to meet its balance-of-payments problems and implied that the United States itself might soon be forced to adopt a less cooperative line.[17] The meaning of this veiled hint was made more explicit by a subsequent argument among American bankers about the possibility of a change in current gold-buying policies.[18]

A further disappointment for the United States was a broadening of the opposition to its ideas on international monetary reform and an increase in "international liquidity." This issue technically lay within the province of the so-called Group of Ten, an *ad hoc* assemblage of major financial powers that included Great Britain, France, West Germany, and other Common Market nations. In earlier discussions within this group, France had appeared to stand more or less alone in its resistance to any increase in world momentary reserves; but at an April meeting of E.E.C. Finance Ministers, M. Debré succeeded in winning West Germany and other Common Market partners to at least qualified support of the French position. In return for this concession, France did agree for the first time that a plan for the deliberate creation of new international reserves might properly be considered. But where the United States had advocated the creation of a wholly new reserve currency or international monetary unit, the French insisted that any new reserves should take the more restrictive form of additional rights to borrow from the International Monetary Fund—and that they must be subject to that organization's strict controls and repayment requirements. In addition, France and the other Common Market countries gave indications that they would insist upon an increase in their collective voting power within the Fund, thus in effect obtaining a veto over such borrowing.[19]

These differences were clarified, though not resolved, at a joint meeting of the Group of Ten and the executive directors of the I.M.F., held in Washington on April 24-26.[20] Concurrently, the United States gained some relief from current financial pressures when the West German Bundesbank agreed, as part of a new arrangement on the troop-finance issue, to maintain its practice of holding dollars rather than converting them into gold[21] as France had been doing. Further international meetings held in Paris in June and in London in July produced some narrowing of the differences on the liquidity problem, and it was eventually agreed that an outline plan for the establishment of "automatic drawing rights" in the International Monetary Fund should be drawn up in time for that institution's annual meeting in September.[22]

The real break in the situation did not, however, occur until late August, at a moment when General de Gaulle had aroused widespread hostility by his obstreperous behavior on a visit to Canada[23] and when U.S.-German relations had once again been patched together by a Kiesinger visit to the United States.[24] Still another meeting of the Group of Ten was held in London on August 26, with Secretary of the Treasury Fowler and William McChesney Martin, Jr., Chairman of the Board of Governors of the Federal Reserve System, representing the United States. Here agreement was finally reached on what President Johnson termed "the greatest forward step in world financial cooperation in the twenty years since the creation of the International Monetary Fund itself."[25]

Technically, the London agreement consisted in the acceptance of an "Outline of a Contingency Plan" for the creation of special I.M.F. drawing rights, to be laid before the I.M.F. at its September meeting. These special drawing rights, it was now agreed, would be available to all members of the Fund in proportion to their basic quotas in that institution, although the actual use of such rights should not, on the average, exceed 70 per cent of a member's total allocation during the initial five-year period. The amount of drawing rights to be created was not specified, and was generally expected to be modest—perhaps on the order of $1 billion a year during the first five years. Activation of the plan, moreover, would require an 85 per cent affirmative vote of the I.M.F. membership, which would be unobtainable without the concurrence of the Common Market countries.[26] But since M. Debré professed to see the London plan as a

French success,[27] it seemed unlikely that France would try to sabotage it or that resistance would be encountered from other Fund members.

The French Finance Minister did occasion fresh anxiety when he appeared at Rio de Janeiro to address the governors of the International Bank and Fund at their September meeting. Implementation of the new plan, M. Debré now seemed to imply, must still depend on elimination of the American balance-of-payments deficit as well as a review of voting procedures and other provisions in the I.M.F.'s articles of agreement. Germany and other E.E.C. members appeared to support at least the second of these demands, in which the United States itself expressed concurrence. Some uncertainty thus persisted even after September 29, when it was agreed without a formal vote to have the drawing rights plans put into final form by March 31, 1968 as a preliminary to ratification by member governments of the I.M.F. Three-fifths of the latter, controlling four-fifths of the weighted votes, would have to ratify before the plan could actually go into effect. Yet the chances seemed good that within another two years the world would possess a system for the controlled growth of monetary reserves that could be further improved and expanded as conditions might warrant.[28]

25 : NATO and Western Defense

These seemingly constructive trends in trade and monetary affairs were matched by what most interested observers regarded as a further deterioration in arrangements for the common defense, particularly in Western Europe. The military defense of that key area had never been fully assured by NATO dispositions within Europe itself. Ultimately, it had always depended on the deterrent power of the American strategic force of bombers and, more recently, missiles. Yet the international "shield" force of 29 divisions or so which was charged with repelling an assault on Western Europe and was commanded from SHAPE, the NATO headquarters outside Paris, had none the less been regarded as an essential element in the Western security system. At a minimum, it had served to warn a potential aggressor that he could not take over Western Europe without a fight. And now the shield appeared to be in some danger of disintegrating under the combined influence of nationalism, political complacency, and mounting financial pressure.

By far the heaviest single blow to NATO's defense capabilities had been France's action of 1966 in withdrawing from NATO command the 70,000 troops it was maintaining in Western Germany, dissociating itself from common military planning, and denying its allies the peacetime use of French territory for military purposes. Although Secretary McNamara seemed disinclined to take these moves too tragically,[29] other authorities in NATO were frank to admit their concern. At the very least, the impediment to conventional military operations presented by France's attitude seemed likely to force a resort to nuclear weapons at an earlier stage of hostilities than would otherwise have been the case.[30] In addition, France's decision had put its allies to tremendous inconvenience and expense in relocating their forces, installations, supply lines, and military headquarters before the French-imposed deadline of April 1, 1967. The Supreme Headquarters of the Allied Powers in Europe (SHAPE), under the American General Lyman L. Lemnitzer, was obliged to remove from Rocquencourt to Casteau (near Mons), Belgium. NATO's Central European Headquarters was transferred from Fontainebleau to Brunssum in the Netherlands. The U.S. military headquarters in Europe, in turn, was compelled to leave Saint-Germain and reestablish itself in Stuttgart, Germany.

Among the indirect consequences of France's withdrawal from the common defense was an intensification of the long-standing tendency of other member countries to reduce their own NATO commitments. In varying degrees and for different reasons, this tendency was now affecting not only the smaller NATO members but also the United States, Great Britain, and Western Germany, the three powers which, with some French support, had thus far provided the backbone of Western Europe's defense.

The long-standing American misgivings about the presence of 330,000 American troops in Europe at a time of war in Vietnam and serious balance-of-payments problems at home had found their clearest expression in the resolution submitted by Mr. Mansfield to the Senate in August 1966, which called for a "substantial reduction of U.S. forces permanently stationed in Europe."[31] Opposed by the administration primarily on the grounds of its unilateral character, the Mansfield resolution was resubmitted at the beginning of 1967 with the support of as many as 43 Senators as well as such outside authorities as Lieutenant General James M. Gavin, a former Ambassador to France, who told the Senate Foreign Relations Committee in February that in his opinion a corps of two divisions would suffice to demonstrate the American commitment. Together with a more broadly drafted resolution submitted by Republican Senator Jacob K. Javits, the Mansfield text was referred to a specially constituted Senate committee which took testimony during the spring and heard the expected warnings from Secretaries Rusk and McNamara, among others, that any "substantial reduction" of U.S. forces in Europe would be both politically and militarily inadvisable. But though they strongly opposed any permanent reduction of U.S. strength in Europe, administration spokesmen did not at all exclude the possibility of some "redeployment" of American forces assigned to NATO. Secretary McNamara and others had suggested that selected units could even be brought back to the United States but kept available for a quick return to Europe in case of trouble. There was also talk of withdrawing at least one of the six divisions currently stationed in Western Germany unless a more acceptable financial arrangement could be arrived at with the Bonn government.[33]

The United Kingdom's defense policies had been much more sharply affected by financial limitations. Early in 1966, the British had determined on a drastic cutback in their military forces overseas which would, among other things, entail the virtual abandonment of their Middle Eastern footholds and a somewhat more gradual reduction of their "military presence" at Singapore and elsewhere in the Far East. A new Defense White Paper issued on February 16, 1967 envisaged an acceleration of this process and, in addition, cast fresh doubt on the future of the 51,000-man British force which had thus far been maintained in Western Germany. Since the danger of Communist aggression in Europe had virtually disappeared, according to the British argument, the best procedure would be to try to extend the existing East-West *détente* through a mutual reduction in the forces of both NATO and the Warsaw Pact.[34] With or without such an East-West understanding, British authorities further intimated, they themselves would have no alternative to making massive withdrawals from their forces in Germany unless the Bonn government could provide more adequate financial assistance in keeping them there.

To the West German Government, the presence of American and British forces on German soil was important not only for military reasons but because it provided a psychological assurance that the Federal Republic would not be left to fight alone in case it was attacked. Largely for this reason, Bonn had gone so far as to shoulder a substantial part of the financial burden the presence of these foreign forces entailed. Under a system of "offset payments" in existence for a number of years, the Germans had committed themselves to purchase British and American goods and services, primarily military in character, in amounts sufficient to offset a specified proportion of the foreign exchange costs incurred by the two governments in keeping their forces in Germany. Great Britain, however, had lately begun to demand substantially increased assistance of this kind, and the United States had insisted on strict implementation of certain conditions that the West Germans had begun to find onerous. With financial difficulties of their own to face, the Germans had protested that they could no longer accommodate their allies to the desired extent. This stand had caused a great deal of recrimination and, in conjunction with the differences over the nuclear nonproliferation treaty, was probably the most substantial factor in the deterioration of American-West German relations in the early months of the Kiesinger administration.

Since late 1966, the issue of force levels and support costs had been under discussion in a special tripartite committee set up by the three governments, Mr. McCloy being the American representative. After devising a stopgap arrangement for the period up to mid-1967, this group turned its attention to longer-range problems and, in the course of the spring, came up with an outline plan for the period July 1967–June 1968. At the basis of the new arrangement, as formally disclosed on May 2[35] after piecemeal revelation of its principal elements, was an American proposal to get away from past controversies over the direct offsetting of military costs and shift the emphasis to the exercise of financial cooperation over a wider area. In addition to procuring American military goods and services on a reduced scale, the Germans undertook to aid the U.S. balance of payments more directly by investing $500 million in U.S. Government securities and continuing to refrain from converting their accumulated dollar balances into gold. Great Britain, on its side, was to have the benefit of nearly $150 million in German purchases as well as an additional $19.6 million in military purchases by the United States.

As part of this same arrangement, the three allies acknowledged the inevitability of some reduction—although that word was avoided —in the level of the British and American forces to be maintained in Germany after January 1, 1968. Subject to NATO concurrence, Great Britain planned to "redeploy" to its own territory a brigade of 6,500 men and a fighter-bomber squadron. The United States, in turn, proposed to "redeploy" back across the Atlantic as many as 35,000 men, including two infantry brigades and support units and four squadrons of tactical fighter aircraft. These American forces, like those of the British, were to remain fully committed to NATO. They would, it was stated, go to Germany once a year for exercises, and would be kept in "a high degree of readiness" to return to Europe whenever circumstances might require. The saving to the United States in foreign exchange, it was estimated, would amount to around $100 million a year.[36] Although the Joint Chiefs of Staff were described as quite unhappy about the new arrangement, for which they found no "military" justification, Secretary Rusk seemed confident that it would not significantly affect NATO's military capability.[37]

The Secretary of State did not pretend that this was a "mutual" reduction of forces of the kind envisaged in the recent British White Paper. There had, he conceded, been no indication that the countries of the Warsaw Pact would respond with a parallel reduction in their own forces.[38] Indeed, the Communist countries no longer showed much interest in a mutual "thinning out" of forces in Central Europe such as had been discussed in earlier years. Instead of half measures, present Communist policy appeared to aim at doing away with NATO altogether as suggested in the recent declaration at Karlovy Vary.[39]

A good deal of thinking had meanwhile been going on in NATO quarters about the role of the alliance in the changing context of East-West relations and the possibility of shifting its emphasis from military defense to political conciliation. At the suggestion of Foreign Minister Pierre Harmel of Belgium, the NATO Council had decided in December 1966 to undertake a study in depth of the changes that had occurred in international relations since the alliance was founded, and of ways to strengthen it "as a factor for durable peace."[40] While awaiting the results of this study—informally known as the "Harmel Exercise"—NATO's various organs had been engaged on a variety of pending projects. Members of the civilian headquarters in Paris were preparing to transfer their offices to Brussels in accordance with another decision of the North Atlantic Council. The permanent

Council of Deputies had been much concerned with trying to adjust the differences on the nuclear nonproliferation treaty.[41] A new seven-nation NATO Nuclear Planning Group, formally established in December 1966, had held its inaugural meeting in Washington and engaged in a general discussion of antiballistic missile defenses, tactical nuclear forces, and a Turkish plan for the use of atomic mines or "demolition munitions" in frontier areas.[42] The NATO Defense Ministers, in turn, had seized the opportunity afforded by France's withdrawal from strategic discussions to bury the obsolete doctrine of "massive retaliation" and endorse the strategy of "flexible response" which NATO had in practice been following for the past half-dozen years.[43]

Despite a perennial emphasis on the need for improved political consultation among the NATO allies, the association continued to be weakened by the pursuit of divergent and even conflicting foreign policies. To the standing inter-allied disagreements over Vietnam, nuclear nonproliferation, and the Portuguese territories in Africa—to say nothing of the Greek-Turkish quarrel over Cyprus—was added, in the spring of 1967, the sensational difference between France and most other NATO members with respect to the war in the Middle East. Once again, the French President imposed upon his country a policy much closer to that of the Soviet Union than to that of any allied government. This latest demonstration of allied disunity provided a particularly incongruous background to the regular spring session of the North Atlantic Council, which took place in Luxembourg on June 13-14 with Secretary Rusk as the American representative.

The danger of a Soviet-American clash over the Middle East appears if anything to have heightened the interest of the NATO leaders in seeking a broad improvement in East-West relations, a subject that occupied the Council more fully than at any previous meeting. Past efforts in this direction, the Council conceded, had "not always met with success."[44] All the more reason, the Foreign Ministers seemed to feel, to intensify the pursuit of a general East-West *détente*. "The political phase of NATO has . . . begun," commented Ambassador Harlan Cleveland, the U.S. Permanent Representative. ". . . NATO is not only moving, bag and baggage, from the Porte Dauphine in Paris to the old Evere airfield in Brussels; NATO is also moving from peacekeeping to peacemaking, from the management of a cold war to the management of *détente*."[45] Ambassador Cleveland did not maintain that the *détente* could be considered permanent at this moment when even the "summit" meetings at Glassboro still lay in the future. Still less did he suggest that the time had come for NATO to disarm. The first requirement of "*détente* management," he affirmed, was to maintain the "credible military deterrent" which, he felt, had been instrumental in persuading the U.S.S.R. to "maintain a policy of prudent restraint" toward Europe.

Yet the task of maintaining a "credible military deterrent," in Europe and elsewhere, continued to be fraught with major difficulties. While the Western allies were bending their hopes on accommodation with the East, the erosion of their over-all military position was proceeding at an accelerated pace. Libya, for example, had given notice in the wake of the Middle East war that the U.S. air base and the three British military posts in its territory must be promptly withdrawn. The future of the U.S. bases in Spain was also subject to growing doubt as the existing accords neared their 1968 expiration date. Possibly more serious, it was becoming evident that the recent triangular understandings between the United States, Great Britain, and Western Germany had not sufficed to ensure a solid defensive structure even in the heart of the Continent.

Adverse fortune continued to buffet the British defense establishment, already stretched thin by the Wilson government's economy policies and increasingly dependent on the United States for its essential tools. Although the British were still hoping to maintain some semblance of a "world role" with the aid of 50 of the expensive American F-111 swing-wing attack planes which would soon be coming off the assembly lines, Mr. Wilson announced in June that Britain would refrain from buying America's Poseidon missiles for the four Polaris submarines it was building. Early in July, the United Kingdom's long-range air defense planning suffered a heavy blow when France withdrew, ostensibly for financial reasons, from plans for joint development of the advanced fighter plane that was to have followed the F-111 and become the "core" of the Royal Air Force after 1975. Two weeks later, a new Defense White Paper announced that there would be still further reductions in defense expenditure and manpower and that Britain would withdraw completely from the Far East by the mid-1970's—a decision the United States had for years been seeking to avert.[46]

These changes would not directly affect the level of allied forces in Germany. But the Germans themselves, it now appeared, were also planning a sharp reduction in the armed forces they had been providing for their own and the common defense. As part of Chancellor Kiesinger's program of drastic budget cuts, it was reported early in July that West German defense spending in the next few years would be trimmed by $500 million a year and that the 461,000 uniformed personnel in the German Armed Forces, supposedly being built up to a NATO target of 508,000, would actually be reduced to around 400,000. As a further economy measure, it was reported, the West German Air Force would abandon its dual capability for delivering conventional or nuclear weapons—the latter supplied by the United States—and restrict itself in future to a conventional role.[47]

Despite the promises of consultation so recently exchanged by Messrs. Johnson and Kiesinger, these announcements appear to have caught the United States by surprise. Conflicting statements and news leaks from rival West German ministries made it extremely difficult to know exactly what was planned; but Washington lost no time in manifesting the sharpest disapproval. Detailed consultation in NATO should precede any decision on force levels, the State Department admonished. Secretary McNamara abruptly canceled a projected visit to Bonn. Chancellor Kiesinger, already planning a visit to Washington, advanced the date after explaining to a baffled television audience that, thanks to the anticipated decrease in "support payments," the Armed Forces would really be getting more money than before.[48]

Before Mr. Kiesinger took off across the Atlantic, his government acted to defuse the crisis by adopting a "defense guideline" that purported to bar any really substantial reduction in uniformed personnel before 1971.[49] Meeting in Washington on August 15-16, the President and the Chancellor agreed that there should be consultation and agreement in NATO before *either* country again proposed to reduce the forces committed to the alliance. Although Germany was definitely following a more independent course than in the past, Mr. Kiesinger emphasized, it was none the less fully committed to cooperation with the United States and to the strengthening of NATO's integrated defense system.[50] Later disclosures concerning German budgetary and defense planning sustained the impression that the prospect of any drastic cuts had been at least temporarily warded off.[51]

But no ally could long avoid treading on another's toes in an association where critical decisions at the national level affected the interests of all members. In September, the United States itself added to Britain's difficulties by reneging on an agreement designed to help finance the projected purchase of F-111 aircraft and other military equipment. As a partial offset to the $2.5 billion or more the British proposed to spend in the United States for these purposes, Washington had agreed to let them compete for the manufacture of some $325 million worth of U.S. military items, including seven wooden-hulled minesweepers valued at $60.7 million. To the extreme annoyance of the British and the embarrassment of the administration, this last item was killed in mid-September when Congress inserted in the Defense Department appropriation bill an amendment specifically providing that U.S. naval vessels could be built only in American shipyards. Noting that this action jeopardized much larger deals important to both countries—for the irate British talked openly of canceling the whole F-111 arrangement—the President could only instruct the Secretary of Defense to look for other ways of meeting the American commitment.[52]

Additional problems were created by a long-standing congressional urge to punish countries that carried on even the most limited trade with North Vietnam. A House amendment to the foreign aid bill, designed to prohibit cash sales of military equipment to any country trading with North Vietnam, was denounced by the administration as offering no military advantage in the Far East but threatening to undermine NATO, kill the F-111 deal, and call in question even the maintenance of U.S. troops in Great Britain. Although this particular prohibition was deleted by a Senate-House conference committee,[53] the issue was fated to remain a recurrent source of irritation in interallied relations.

Potentially more serious were the effects of Secretary McNamara's September 18 disclosure that the United States had decided to deploy a "light"antiballistic missile defense system, ostensibly directed against the potential threat of a Chinese missile attack.[54] Not only did this unexpected announcement cause consternation in the NATO Nuclear Planning Group, which was about to hold its second meeting in Ankara and had expected to be consulted in advance of any such far-reaching decision.[55] To European and some American minds it also suggested that the United States was becoming more inclined to seek security within its own territorial limits and, in consequence, less prone to concern itself about the security of Europe.[56] Such, of course, was the trend that General de Gaulle had long predicted and the Russians had been doing their best to encourage. Further evidence of a tendency to limit American overseas commitments was seen by some in a report—promptly denied in Washington—that the United States was already planning a temporary reduction in the six home-based divisions it was committed to send to Europe in case of war.[57]

The unsettling effect of such developments was very evident during the mid-autumn period when the NATO civilian staff and the accompanying diplomatic missions were removing from Paris and occupying the temporary headquarters constructed outside of Brussels. General Lemnitzer was frank to concede the military difficulties created by France's withdrawal and the reduction in military forces planned by several other governments.[58] Yet even problems of this magnitude seemed almost trivial in comparison with the political and financial troubles that were now beginning to crowd upon the Western association.

26 : Nationalism and the British Devaluation

A surprising number of the West's most nerve-racking difficulties were traceable in one way or another to the nationalistic forces that boiled with scarcely diminished fury beneath the thin crust of Western solidarity. In France, the crust had already broken through and hot lava was welling out in still indeterminate volume. But there were other sections of the Western community where nationalist feeling asserted itself in much more primitive forms. The quarrel between Greece and Turkey over Cyprus, which had more than once come close to producing outright military conflict within the NATO membership, assumed such dimensions in the course of the autumn as almost to rival the Arab-Israel crisis.[59] Cyprus, it could be argued, was a Middle Eastern rather than a "Western" problem; but similar collisions of national, ethnic, or cultural allegiances also affected several of the most "Western" members of the alliance.

The perennial tension between Belgium's French- and Flemish-speaking inhabitants need not detain us, since it gave rise to no international issue during 1967 and did not prevent the Brussels government from fulfilling its obligations as a member of NATO and other

Western organizations. Still less is it necessary to speak of the rising force of Scottish and Welsh nationalism in the United Kingdom, or of Ireland's historic claim to the British-ruled Northern Irish counties. A more immediate cause of alarm was the terrorist agitation against Italian rule in the Southern Tyrol, an agitation supported by private groups in Austria and apparently in Western Germany. Serious tension between Italy and Austria developed over this issue in the course of the summer, although it fell short of precipitating an actual break in diplomatic relations.

Spain's long-standing campaign to oust the British from Gibraltar threatened on at least one occasion to bring on a dangerous international incident. Early in the year, the Franco regime attempted to supplement its quasi-blockade of the land approach to Gibraltar by promulgating new air navigation rules which, if literally followed, would have gravely endangered the colony's air communications. Fortunately, the Madrid authorities refrained from pressing matters to the crisis point; but new difficulties developed a few months later in connection with a British plan to hold a referendum in Gibraltar in order to determine the true preferences of the inhabitants and thus provide an answer to Spanish agitation for a transfer of sovereignty.

The British were well aware that Gibraltar's 25,000 inhabitants had no desire to exchange British for Spanish rule. This fact, of late years, had been at least as influential as strategic or prestige considerations in determining the British to continue their resistance to Spanish pressure. Spain, apparently foreseeing that the referendum would do nothing to strengthen its claims, made every effort to prevent its being held or, at least, to discredit it in advance. In this endeavor it was supported by a number of anticolonial governments which, as members of the U.N. Special Committee of 24 on Colonialism, were opposed in principle to all forms of colonial rule no matter how the people concerned might feel. Over the opposition of the United Kingdom and the abstention of the United States, this U.N. group declared on September 1 that the holding of the proposed referendum would be in conflict with past U.N. resolutions and that Great Britain and Spain should promptly negotiate "an end to the colonial situation in Gibraltar."[60]

Despite this admonition, the referendum took place as scheduled on September 10 and, as foreseen, resulted in a practically unanimous vote in favor of continued British rule. This formality being out of

the way and the issue of self-determination resolved to its own satisfaction, Great Britain expressed willingness to resume discussion of
the problem with Spain. That country, however, responded that
Britain must first bow to the opinion of the United Nations.[61] At a
later stage, it secured an endorsement of its position by the U.N.
General Assembly[62]—whose exhortations, however, were seldom
heeded by the British when they concerned the exercise of colonial
responsibilities.

Most Americans tended to regard such disputes as typically "Old
World" phenomena. It required a transatlantic visit by General de
Gaulle to remind them that a potentially more explosive situation
was developing on their own doorstep as a result of the discontent of
the French-speaking Canadians residing in the Province of Quebec and
elsewhere in Canada. Unhappy as they undoubtedly were about their
disabilities in a predominantly English-speaking country, most French
Canadians had thus far seemed content to seek salvation in a reform
of Canada's existing federal structure rather than in the separatist
program put forward by a few extremists under the slogan of "Free
Quebec." Nor had their general sense of linguistic and cultural affinity
with France impelled them to ask French support in their political
struggles.

President de Gaulle, however, began in the summer of 1967 to
manifest so lively and possessive an interest in the French Canadians
that it was difficult not to wonder why it had taken him three-quarters
of a century to discover them. Like many other heads of state, de
Gaulle had accepted an invitation to visit Expo 67 and go on to
Ottawa for meetings with Canadian Government leaders. In preparing himself for this visit, he apparently reached the conclusion that
the people of French Canada, in addition to being a worthy expression
of the French genius, represented a potential front-line force in his
continuing battle against American "hegemony." The fact that they
were also citizens of an allied state appears to have had little significance in the French leader's mind. Canada's role was merely incidental; what counted, apparently, were France on one side, the
United States on the other, and, between them, the French Canadians
—whose allegiance and destiny, in de Gaulle's eyes, must obviously
be determined by their French inheritance.

Arriving in the Saint Lawrence on July 23 aboard the French
cruiser *Colbert,* the French President prefaced his official engage-

ments with a rapid tour of Quebec Province. The ecstatic greeting of the populace in one town after another inspired increasingly explicit statements of his new theme. The climax was reached in a supposedly impromptu speech in Montreal on July 24 in which he not only spoke openly of "liberation" but gave voice to the extreme separatist slogan, *"Vive Québec Libre!"* In the context of Canadian politics, this was much more than a gross discourtesy to the government whose guest de Gaulle was. Even French Canadians agreed that it constituted an unheard-of interference in Canadian internal affairs. Great was the turmoil in Canada, in France, and elsewhere in the world. Such statements, said Prime Minister Lester B. Pearson next day, were "unacceptable" to the Canadian people and government. De Gaulle, in prompt response to this rebuke, canceled his visit to Ottawa and boarded an American-built Air France jetliner for his return to Paris.

His foray into Canadian politics did not, on the whole, produce the kind of effects the French leader had presumably intended. The performance confirmed the dour judgment of de Gaulle's critics and shook the confidence of many of his French supporters. In Canada itself, the immediate effect was a reaffirmation of the Canadian allegiance of French-speaking as well as English-speaking citizens. Some Canadians were heard to remark that even the United States, for all its undeniable influence on Canada's destiny, was unaccustomed to meddle directly in its neighbor's political concerns.

But what to other statesmen would have been a humiliating setback seemed only to stir the French President to more uncompromising self-assertion. At home, the special powers he had extorted from the National Assembly were now employed in pushing through an unpopular profit-sharing plan, an increase in social security contributions, and a reduction in benefits. Abroad, the watered-down project for international monetary reform was permitted to receive the sanction of the Group of Ten and the International Monetary Fund; but the resistance to British membership in the E.E.C. was intensified and, with it, the more or less subterranean campaign that France had been waging against the position of the pound and dollar in international finance.

The United Kingdom was by this time feeling the harsh financial effects of the closure of the Suez Canal and the resultant increase in shipping costs which, in conjunction with a wildcat strike of Liver-

"GENERAL DE GAULLE'S GOOD WILL TRIP TO CANADA"

Gib Crockett in *The Washington Star*

pool dockworkers, was undermining its hopes for a 1967 balance-of-payments surplus and giving rise to fresh rumors about an impending devaluation of the pound. Prime Minister Wilson's assumption of direct responsibility for economic affairs at the end of August did little to stem these apprehensions. British reserves declined in September for the fifth successive month. Interest rates were rising sharply, particularly in the United States, where Congress was hesitating to enact the tax increase proposed by President Johnson. In an attempt to stem the resultant outflow of funds from the United Kingdom, Great Britain on October 19 raised its own bank rate to 6 per cent. France, meanwhile, was beginning to lend more explicit statement to its views about the need for an alternation in the status of the pound. Admission to the Common Market, M. Couve de Murville told his E.E.C. colleagues on October 23, was not to be thought of until Great Britain corrected its balance of payments and redefined the role of the pound in such a way as to convert it from a world reserve currency into a national currency.[63]

A series of public relations mishaps accentuated the feeling of disarray in London as successive by-elections registered the government's loss of public support. Lord Chalfont, the minister in charge of negotiations with the E.E.C., was accused of threatening to withdraw troops from Germany unless the latter used its influence to get Britain into the Common Market. Foreign Secretary Brown denounced Britain's most prominent newspaper magnate at a public dinner attended by U.S. businessmen. Amid demands for the Foreign Secretary's resignation, the pound dropped early in November to its lowest level in a decade. Another half-point increase in the bank rate and a new international credit of $250 million, arranged with France's participation to permit repayment of an earlier British debt to the I.M.F., failed to improve the situation. Britain's October trade gap, at almost $300 million, was the largest since January 1964.

By November 10, the Wilson government had apparently reached the conclusion that devaluation was inevitable and that it only remained to work out the least damaging way of carrying out the operation. While the government consulted its financial partners about the possibility of another loan to ease the transition, reserves began pouring out of London by the millions. Only the United States and Britain itself attempted to stem the tide by purchasing the sterling that others were so eager to unload.

It fell to Chancellor of the Exchequer James Callaghan to make the crushing announcement that the Wilson government had been fighting for three years to avoid. The pound, he confirmed on November 18, was being devalued immediately by 14.3 per cent, from the $2.80 value it had nominally possessed since 1949 to $2.40. Concurrently, the Chancellor announced an even more rigorous austerity program aimed at restricting consumer demand and promoting exports. The bank rate was raised to 8 per cent, and defense expenditure was to be reduced by a further £100 million a year—though this, it was said, would not affect current troop dispositions.

To tide Britain over the emergency, Mr. Callaghan further reported, the government was arranging for $3 billion in new international credits, of which $1.4 billion would be provided by the I.M.F. and some $1.6 billion by foreign central banks. Arrangements for "over $1.5 billion" in central bank credits were in fact completed, without French participation, on November 23. The $1.4 billion "standby credit" from the I.M.F. took longer to arrange, since it required approval by France and other Group of Ten members who would be putting up a part of the money in case the credit was actually drawn upon. Largely on French insistence, Great Britain was obliged to formulate a detailed program of budget cuts, balance-of-payments targets, and periodic consultations which added up to the most rigorous international financial surveillance imposed on a Western country since France's own devaluation of 1958.[64]

Some two dozen other countries—none of them major financial powers—devalued their currencies in the wake of the British action. Though handled with all the decorum that circumstances permitted, the whole transaction caused vast uncertainty in international financial affairs, cast doubt on the new plan for I.M.F. special drawing rights, and gave rise to heightened uneasiness about the position of the dollar, the chief remaining bulwark of international financial stability now that the pound had succumbed.

In a prompt endorsement of Britain's "healthy and constructive" action, President Johnson insisted that the United States remained as determined as ever "to meet its international monetary responsibilities" and maintain the value of the dollar by continuing to buy and sell gold at $35 an ounce.[65] Yet it was obvious that the U.S. balance of payments and, consequently, the dollar itself would now come under even heavier pressure unless Washington took strong preventive action, presumably beginning with a tax increase. Adding to the uneasiness of large dollar holders was the disclosure on Tuesday, November 21, that France had ceased contributing to the London gold pool five months earlier and that the United States, which had taken over France's share, was now providing 59 per cent of all the gold sold through the London facility.

The consequence of these disclosures and the rumors that accompanied them was an unrestrained rush to buy gold for dollars which was estimated to have reduced the U.S. gold stock by at least $200 million before the weekend. No amount of determination in Washington could long hold out against such an onslaught, which France was clearly doing nothing to dampen even if it was not, as many suspected, actively fomenting it. Other Western governments, however, were less prepared to see the existing monetary system destroyed. On Sunday, November 26, the governors of the seven central banks which had continued to participate in the gold pool met in Frankfurt and acted to dampen the speculative fever by pointing out that their reserves were more than sufficient to maintain the existing gold price and exchange-rate pattern.[66] This action, subsequently buttressed by an agreement increasing by $1.75 billion the lines of credit available to the United States in the form of currency "swap" facilities,[67] sufficed for the moment to stem the hemorrhage and restore a measure of stability in the world's financial markets.

Though impossible to trace with precision, France's role in these transactions was almost everywhere considered to have been the reverse of constructive. But President de Gaulle seemed wholly unrepentant as he prepared to deliver his semiannual lecture at a press conference scheduled for November 27, five days after his 77th birthday.[68] France, the General said, was not responsible for "the squalls that brought down the rate of the pound and threaten that of the dollar"—although, he added, such disturbances might have the good effect of leading toward the ultimate restoration of an international monetary system based on gold. More important, the French President was at pains to dispel any idea that the devaluation had improved Great Britain's chances of admission to the Common Market. On the contrary, he averred, the "permanent disequilibrium" in the British economy had made that country's "incompatibility" with the Common Market even more obvious than before. Even to begin negotiations about British membership, de Gaulle declared, would amount to "sounding the knell" of the European community— whereas a strengthening of the community, rather than its destruction, was required if Europe was to "balance the immense power of the United States." If not an outright "veto" on British membership, this was clearly the French President's strongest statement on the matter to date.

In the course of his press conference, General de Gaulle also delivered himself of some unflattering comments on the U.S. "appropriation" of certain French business enterprises—achieved in large part, he said, not so much by the organic superiority of the United States as by "the dollar inflation they export to others under cover of the gold-exchange standard." He also commented adversely on the behavioral tendencies of Israel and of the Jews, whom he described as "always an élite people, sure of itself and used to dominating." About the "French nation" in Canada, on the other hand, the General was nothing less than lyrical. What was needed, he said, was "a complete change in the present structure of Canada" which would elevate Quebec "to the rank of a sovereign state" and thus enable it to play its part in developing the country and standing up to "the invasion of the United States." Again it was the United States that stood forth as the ultimate menace. Almost the only aspect of America's world role that de Gaulle had not yet found reason to criticize was the difficult mediatory effort Washington had just undertaken in the attempt to head off a new war in the Eastern Mediterranean.

27 : Trouble in Hellas

The Western governments had had their moments of uneasiness about conditions on NATO's Eastern flank even before the Middle East crisis and the enlargement of the Soviet fleet in the Mediterranean. The Turkish Government, as already noted, had for years been showing diminished enthusiasm for NATO and the United States, in part at least because of Washington's past refusals to sanction Turkish intervention on behalf of the beleaguered Turkish-speaking minority in Cyprus. Greece, as self-appointed watchman over the interests of the dominant Greek-speaking element in Cyprus, had also been less than satisfied with the attitude of the United States and its other Western allies. Quite aside from the Cyprus issue, moreover, Greece had experienced increasing difficulty in managing its affairs according to the rules of parliamentary democracy. In April 1967, it had brought disgrace upon itself and the "Atlantic community" by succumbing to a military coup and the imposition of a particularly unappealing type of military dictatorship.

Though obscured at times by the bewildering interplay of Greek parties and factions, the origins of this tragic mishap were rooted in a continuing Left-Right struggle that went all the way back to the end of the Greek civil war in 1949. The forces of the Right, by 1967, had come to be primarily identified with the Greek Army and, to a somewhat less marked degree, with the entourage of the young King Constantine II. The leftist forces included both the Communist-front party known as the United Democratic Left and, more prominently, the Center Union led by ex-Premier George Papandreou in concert with his son, Andreas. A former California economics professor, Andreas Papandreou had returned to Greece to implicate himself in various left-wing causes and had lately been accused of direct involvement in a serious leftist conspiracy—the so-called ASPIDA affair—within the Armed Forces. The trial of the officers involved in this affair, in conjunction with the government's evident intention to try Andreas Papandreou himself, had by early 1967 become the most sensational issue in Greek politics. Increasing the gravity of the situation was an apparent determination on the part of the Papandreous' leftist supporters to bring about the fall of the existing, moderate government and remodel the Greek political system according to their own preferences.

But any such ambition was rudely deflated on the night of April 20-21 when a group of Army officers, acting on a NATO plan drawn up for use in the event of civil disturbances, seized the government in a bloodless coup and installed a three-man military dictatorship consisting of Lieutenant General Gregory E. Spandidakis, Colonel George Papadopoulos, and Brigadier General Stylianos Patakos. The naming of a civilian, Constantine V. Kollias, to the Premiership did not disguise the essentially military character of the new regime, whose initial political ineptitude was exceeded only by its extremely conservative, nationalist, and anti-Communist outlook. More serious than its temporary ban on beards and miniskirts were its actions in dissolving Parliament, abolishing hundreds of labor and youth organizations, imposing rigid censorship of the press, and rounding up over 6,000 alleged leftists, including the Papandreous, who were confined for varying periods in conditions of more or less extreme discomfort.

While the world at large voiced shocked dismay at these proceedings in the cradle of Western democracy, the majority of the Greek public accepted the new order with resignation if without enthusiasm.

This passivity was not exclusively attributable to fear or to the strongly anti-Communist feelings that were prevalent outside the major cities. In part, at least, it also reflected the somewhat ambiguous position in which the coup had placed not only King Constantine but also the United States, Greece's most powerful and influential friend. The King, who had himself been widely expected to lead a royalist coup against the Papandreous, was plainly unhappy at the way things had turned out, but seemed unable to offer effective resistance to the military men whose virtual prisoner he had become. American authorities seemed equally unhappy, yet equally hesitant to come out with a firm denunciation of the new junta. Most Greeks, indeed, appeared convinced that the United States was the real author of the coup and that the generals had merely acted at its bidding.[69] No convincing evidence has been produced in support of this theory; in fact, Ambassador Phillips Talbot appears to have made every effort to counsel moderation on both sides in the interests of heading off a showdown. Once the coup had taken place, however, the United States was understandably hesitant to take action which, if it did succeed in bringing down the junta, might easily precipitate renewed civil war between Greek Communists and anti-Communists.

In this uncomfortable situation the United States resorted to the familiar if unpromising tactic of trying to encourage the junta to behave in a democratic manner. Some leverage was afforded by Greece's dependence on U.S. military aid, and Washington promptly announced that it was "reviewing" its Greek aid programs and awaiting evidence of an intention to reestablish democratic institutions.[70] Secretary McNamara, at the May meeting of the NATO Defense Ministers, went so far as to intimate directly to General Spandidakis that the junta's attitude was endangering the continuance of U.S. military aid; and shortly afterward it was revealed that Washington had in fact been holding up "major items" of military equipment in the hope of furthering a return to constitutional government.[71] This form of pressure proved wholly insufficient to attain the desired ends, however, and junta statements foreshadowing an eventual return to constitutionalism remained exceedingly nebulous. By late summer, when King Constantine paid a prolonged visit to the United States, it seemed that both the monarch and the American Government were becoming resigned to an indefinite continuance of junta rule despite the arbitrary manner in which Greece's new masters were exercising their usurped authority.

If the situation in Greece had any redeeming feature from an American viewpoint, it lay not so much in the junta's ruthless suppression of Communist tendencies as in the comparatively enlightened character of its foreign policy. Democratic Greek governments had generally felt obliged to cater to the explosive forces of nationalist sentiment. The junta, in contrast, was able to base its foreign policy decisions on a more or less realistic appraisal of the forces and interests involved. This relative freedom of maneuver was to prove particularly valuable in the dangerous confrontation between Greece and Turkey that was now impending.

Such confrontations were a familiar element in the recent history of these two allies, each of which had long claimed a proprietary interest in the related nationality group in Cyprus. Both Greece and Turkey had remained fundamentally dissatisfied with the 1960 settlement under which Cyprus had become an independent republic with a Greek-speaking, Turkophobe President, Archbishop Makarios III, and a government in which the Greek element had come to exercise *de facto* control while the Turkish minority—some 120,000 people in a total population of 600,000—were relegated to the position of virtual outcasts. Practically all Greeks, in Cyprus and in Greece itself, professed to aim at an eventual political union (*Enosis*) of the two countries, though there were differences as to when and how such a union might be brought about. Turkey, on the other hand, was not only violently opposed to *Enosis* but deeply concerned for the safety of the Turkish minority in Cyprus. Both Greece and Turkey maintained contingents of troops in Cyprus under the 1960 treaty, and Turkey claimed the right to intervene militarily if such action should be necessary to protect the members of the Turkish community.

Since the last major crisis over Cyprus in 1964, Turkish Cypriotes had had the additional protection of an international peace-keeping force, comprising some 4,500 men from eight nations and organized and commanded by the United Nations under a mandate from the Security Council. Although it had played a vital role in dampening the warlike ardor of the rival Cypriote communities, this costly expedient had never been intended as more than a stopgap until a permanent solution of the Cyprus issue could be arranged by negotiation among the parties concerned. With NATO encouragement, the Greek and Turkish Foreign Ministers had met repeatedly to discuss the bases of a possible settlement; but little progress had been achieved in view of the radically divergent aims of the two governments and the further complications arising from the independent attitude adopted by President Makarios.

The military coup in Athens interrupted these Greek-Turkish exchanges and caused considerable uneasiness among the Greek community in Cyprus, where *Enosis* with a military-dominated Greece was felt to have few attractions and it was feared for a time that a parallel coup might be brought off against President Makarios. Tension on the island was running high, and the desirability of maintaining a U.N. presence was recognized even by the U.S.S.R., which, in contrast to its attitude in the Arab-Israeli conflict, had avoided all-out commitment to either the Greek or the Turkish interest and seemed genuinely interested in the avoidance of major disturbances. With Soviet support, the Security Council unanimously voted on June 19 to extend the mandate of the U.N. Force for a further period of six months.[72]

By September, the new junta in Athens was becoming sufficiently well established to take the initiative in seeking a new diplomatic encounter with the Turks. Apparently underestimating the difficulties, it even announced that a definitive solution of the Cyprus problem was in the offing. But a meeting between Greek Premier Kollias and Turkish Premier Suleyman Demirel, held on the Greek-Turkish frontier on September 9-10, produced no agreement beyond a vague reference to cooperation and future *rapprochement*.[73] Even had an agreement unexpectedly been achieved, it would have had limited value unless it could also have been made acceptable to President Makarios and the other interests in Cyprus itself.

Conditions on the island were by this time moving toward a dangerous climax, made more threatening by the presence of numerous armed groups over and above the U.N. Force and the small contingents of 950 Greeks and 650 Turks permitted by the treaty. The authorized Greek force had been augmented by the clandestine infiltration of an estimated 8,000 to 11,000 members of the Greek Army. A much smaller number of Turkish troops had also been infiltrated. There were also local forces: a Greek Cypriote National Guard of 10,000 (plus 10,000 reservists) and a Turkish Cypriote militia of 5,000 backed by an estimated 17,000 irregulars.[74] The commander of the Greek Cypriote National Guard was also a Greek Army officer, General George Grivas, a nationalist firebrand who had led the Greek Cypriote resistance to Great Britain in earlier years and had been deputed to his current post by the Athens government. It was General Grivas' force that ignited the powder barrel on November 15 with a large-scale raid on two Turkish villages that touched off the worst communal fighting since the 1964 crisis. Halted by U.N. intervention some eight hours later, the clashes caused 28 Turkish deaths.

While Greek and Turkish Cypriotes sprang to arms, the United States and Secretary-General Thant issued their customary appeals for restraint. In Ankara, however, the Turkish cabinet took the position that Turkey could be restrained no longer but must exercise its right of military intervention unless conditions in Cyprus were adjusted to its satisfaction. A set of far-reaching demands was drawn up for submission to the Greek Government. As public excitement mounted, Turkish jets began to fly over Cyprus—not for the first time—and the elements of an invasion force assembled in Turkey's southern ports. The Turkish press was soon clamoring for an invasion and denouncing in advance the hostile attitude imputed to Greece and the United States.

If Turkey invaded Cyprus, Greece would undoubtedly feel compelled to intervene on behalf of the Cypriote Government. Yet its ability to intervene effectively would be limited both by distance and by the disorganized state of the Greek Armed Forces, repeatedly purged as a result of the ASPIDA affair and the April coup. On the other hand, the demands submitted by the Turkish Government were seen in Athens as aiming less at protecting the Turkish Cypriotes than at humiliating Greece and scoring a resounding diplomatic victory. Turkey's first demand—that General Grivas be recalled to Greece—was promptly complied with under the guise of a return for "consultations." The further demand that Greek forces in Cyprus be reduced to the treaty level caused greater difficulties, however, and was not accepted in Greece's preliminary reply to the Turkish note on November 22. Popular frenzy in Turkey had by this time reached the boiling point. Dismissing the Greek communication as inadequate, Ankara let it be known that an invasion of Cyprus would begin the following day.

In face of so urgent a threat to the peace, an immediate meeting of the Security Council might have seemed the obvious course. The main deterrent was the uncertainty of the Western powers about the attitude of the U.S.S.R., which had so often used its veto to frustrate effective, U.N. action in the past. Prompt action, however, was clearly essential, and Washington lost no time in offering its good offices to Greece and Turkey and naming a high-level envoy for this purpose. On the evening of November 22, the President announced that former Deputy Secretary of Defense Cyrus R. Vance was already en route to Ankara and Athens in furtherance of U.S. efforts to assist the two governments in finding a peaceful way out of the situation and averting the danger of war.[75] Two other peace emissaries—José Rolz-Bennett of the U.N. Secretariat and NATO Secretary-General Manlio Brosio—were also hastening to the scene and were to lend the fullest cooperation to Mr. Vance's efforts in the critical days ahead.

While the most immediate problem was obviously that of persuading the Turks to cancel their invasion preparations, it was already apparent that the invasion would be canceled only as part of a larger arrangement which would have to include a reduction or withdrawal of the "external" forces in Cyprus and also, presumably, a strengthening of the U.N. Force itself. Such a program, at bottom, was not unacceptable to either of the rival governments. To Turkey, it offered the prospect of a Greek retreat, a favorable change in the local situation in Cyprus, and a more secure position for the Turkish minority. To Greece it would afford an opportunity to withdraw with dignity from a clearly untenable position. The vital necessity was to forestall the invasion and thus gain time to draw up an agreement which the Turks could claim as a victory but the Greeks need not regard as a defeat. This, in essence, is what Mr. Vance was able to accomplish over the next few days as he shuttled back and forth between the Turkish and Greek capitals, patiently extracting agreement on one point after another.

This diplomatic effort was facilitated by the gradual emergence of an international consensus which, in this instance, found even the U.S.S.R. on the side of the peacemakers. Moscow, which had never shown any love for Greece's military regime, had actually come forward as early as November 22 with an official statement urging "restraint and . . . common sense" by all concerned and warning against the dangers of a military clash.[76] In line with this position, the Security Council, which had meanwhile been convoked at Cyprus' request, agreed early on November 25 (without a formal vote) to endorse U Thant's appeal for calm as well as his subsequent recommendation that all external forces be withdrawn from Cyprus except for those of the U.N. itself.[77]

By December 3, matters had progressed so far that U Thant was able to issue a formal peace appeal with the assurance that its terms would be accepted by both Greece and Turkey. Briefly, it contemplated the reduction of Greek and Turkish forces in Cyprus to treaty levels; the dismantling of military preparations on both sides; the demilitarization and disarmament of the Greek Cypriote National Guard and other local military forces (except police); and a commensurate increase in the responsibilities and personnel of the U.N. Force.[78] Such a program might not do much to solve the basic problem of coexistence between Greek and Turkish Cypriotes, but it would at least reduce the danger of new outbreaks and, by restricting Greece to the narrow role envisaged in the 1960 treaty, would presumably postpone any idea of *Enosis* to the indefinite future.

There still remained a potentially serious obstacle in the attitude of President Makarios, who had been virtually ignored in the earlier phase of the negotiations yet obviously had an interest in arrangements that so vitally affected his country. Two visits from Mr. Vance had reconciled the Archbishop to the departure of the Greek Army contingents, which he himself had often found troublesome. Concerning the proposed disarmament of the Cypriote National Guard, however, the Archbishop appeared much more dubious; nor did he take very kindly to the idea of an expanded U.N. Force to maintain internal peace in what was, after all, a sovereign country. Makarios' position did not, however, impress observers as altogether negative. With Greece substantially out of the picture, the Archbishop seemed not unwilling to make a fresh attempt at conciliating the Turkish Cypriotes. The reestablishment of harmony and concord between the Greek majority and the frightened, resentful Turkish minority would clearly be no easy task; yet it was equally plain that it represented the only way—short of a massive exchange of populations— in which the problem of Cyprus could ever be brought to a genuine and lasting solution.

In the meantime the temporary mandate of the U.N. Force was again about to expire. With the withdrawal of Greek troops already under way, U Thant proposed in a report to the Security Council that the force be extended for another three or six months, at the same time noting that his own good offices were still available in the search for a peaceful settlement. Since even the Cypriote Government admitted the necessity of continuing the U.N. Force beyond its scheduled expiration date, the Security Council unanimously decided on December 22 to authorize a further three-month extension expiring March 26, 1968. In doing so, the Council also invited the parties to take advantage of the Secretary-General's proffered good offices and "undertake a new determined effort" toward keeping the peace and arriving at a permanent settlement.[79]

While these arrangements were being worked out, Greece had gone through still another internal crisis and seen the virtual evaporation of any remaining hope for an early return to constitutional government. In an attempt to capitalize on the junta's growing unpopularity, King Constantine had seized the initiative with a bold but ineffectual attempt at a countercoup designed to oust the junta and restore civilian authority. His proclamation, issued on December 13 from the northern military base of Larissa, failed to elicit the hoped-for military support, and the royal family precipitately fled to Italy with Premier Kollias. The junta, naming a compliant general as Regent and designating Colonel Papadopoulos as Premier, moved rapidly to consolidate its authority and initiate a purge of royalist supporters in the Government and Armed Forces.

As at earlier stages, the United States disclaimed responsibility for what had happened, expressed stern disapproval of the junta's attitude, yet did little that could have weakened its hold. The junta, it was asserted, had lost its claim to "legitimacy," and diplomatic recognition of the new setup would be delayed in the hope of a quick return to constitutional government. Ambassador Talbot was not recalled from Athens, however, nor was there any interruption in the shipments of small arms, ammunition, and replacement parts that were ostensibly necessary to permit Greece to fulfill its role as a member of NATO. The failure to take a more vigorous stand in favor of constitutionalism and democracy undoubtedly was motivated by well-grounded fears that the political situation in Greece might deteriorate still further if the junta were to be overthrown in the aftermath of the King's flight. At the same time, U.S. inaction tended to undercut the King's position in bargaining with the junta about the conditions under which he might still return from his voluntary exile.

For King Constantine had not abandoned hope of snatching victory from defeat by getting the junta to pledge an early return to constitutional democracy as the price of his own return to Greece. Lengthy exchanges took place, and the junta leaders made a number of minor concessions, announcing their retirement from the Army, declaring an amnesty for an indeterminate number of political prisoners, and promising that a new constitution would be submitted to popular referendum in April—or, at latest, in September—of 1968. They did not, however, make any commitment about the holding of popular elections, and all the indications suggested that Papadopoulos and his associates were settling in for a long term of office. As with the leadership of Franco Spain at the other end of the Mediterranean, Greece's new masters seemed to feel that the West was bound to tolerate them for strategic reasons and that there was no pressing reason for them to conform to a democratic ideology in which they did not believe.

28 : The Game Continues

As luck would have it, King Constantine's abortive coup took place at the very moment when representatives of the principal Western governments were convening in Brussels for the semiannual ministerial session of the NATO Council, the first to be held in NATO's new civilian headquarters. The news from the Eastern Mediterranean might have occasioned greater dismay had not the Western statesmen already been plagued by numberless uncertainties growing out of the British financial crisis, the persistence of speculative attacks on the dollar, and the attitude of General de Gaulle as expounded at his recent press conference.[80]

Reactions to the French President's November 27 statement had been nothing if not irate. De Gaulle's arguments "simply will not hold water," Prime Minister Wilson had declared in stressing Great Britain's determination to press for Common Market membership. "Intolerable," was Prime Minister Pearson's word for the General's remarks on Canada, which had been read in Ottawa as a prescription for destroying Canadian unity. Israel expressed "deep regret" at what it termed "a grave affront to the Jewish people and the state of Israel."[81] Although the American Government made no official comment, de Gaulle's apparent venture into anti-Semitism—which he later disclaimed in the most categorical terms—plus his supposed campaign against the dollar evoked wide public condemnation and even precipitated the beginnings of an informal boycott movement.

Secretary Rusk seemed unshaken by de Gaulle's attitude in a December 2 address on the theme of "Atlantic partnership" and U.S.-European relations. Great Britain, Mr. Rusk insisted, had an essential role to play in Europe, and the United States had every intention of persevering in its own European policy. In an apparent reversion to President Kennedy's "twin pillar" theory, which had envisioned the construction of a united Europe to balance the strength of the United States,[82] the Secretary of State disclaimed any American ambition to dominate its Atlantic associates. "We would welcome now, as before," Mr. Rusk said, "a European caucus, if they want to call it that, in NATO, something like a European defense community, as a full partner in a reconstituted alliance. . . . There is nothing in our economic, military, and political relationship that we're not willing to discuss and share in order to accommodate the growing strength and confidence of a uniting Europe."[83]

Such disclaimers of selfish ambition might have had a more resounding impact if the United States had still been speaking from the position of strength it had seemed to occupy a few years earlier when the "twin pillar" theory was first put forward. To a casual view, however, the U.S. position of late 1967 seemed one of almost unprecedented weakness in some of the essential elements of national power. Beset by deep anxieties at home, unable to terminate the war in Vietnam, immersed in what seemed a highly uncertain battle to maintain the value of the dollar, the United States could not expect its gestures of partnership to be as enthusiastically hailed across the Atlantic as might have been true in former years. Indeed, it was reduced on occasion to urging—almost begging—its Western associates to display a little more partnership of their own.

This shift in the relative position of the United States and its European friends had just been strikingly demonstrated at the annual ministerial session of the Organization for Economic Cooperation and Development (O.E.C.D.), held in Paris on November 30-December 1. Under-Secretary of State Eugene V. Rostow, the principal American spokesman, had made an eloquent plea for more cooperation from European surplus countries in reestablishing world balance-of-payments equilibrium. As the United States reduced its deficit, Mr.

Rostow argued, European countries must be prepared to reduce their own surpluses through increased capital exports, increased purchases of U.S. goods, and more sharing of military burdens. Not uncharacteristically, this concept of mutual responsibility had been vigorously challenged by French Finance Minister Debré. The reestablishment of equilibrium, Debré maintained, was a task for the deficit countries alone, and it was up to the United States and Britain to exercise the financial discipline that represented the only lasting solution. "Opinions diverged," the final communiqué discreetly reported, "on the share of responsibility of different countries in the search for equilibrium."[84]

Without disputing the importance of financial discipline, the United States was more preoccupied at the moment with the short-range problem of keeping the dollar afloat amid the backwash of the British devaluation. Though President Johnson reported on December 6 that the speculative attack on the dollar had been "decisively repelled,"[85] the depletion of the United States gold stock was already causing alarm and American authorities were known to be dissatisfied with the state of international defenses against a further gold-buying spree. According to French reports, Washington was even going so far as to ask the other participants in the London gold pool to impose some form of mandatory restraints on gold trading. Certain unspecified measures aimed at dampening gold speculation were in fact agreed upon at a Basel meeting of central bankers on December 11-12; but the unmistakable concern displayed by U.S. representatives on this occasion precipitated a further gold-buying wave and did nothing to enhance long-term confidence in American currency or financial policies.[86]

In trying to improve the balance of their international accounts, both the United States and Britain would presumably feel compelled to take another look at their military programs and particularly the deployment of their forces overseas. To what extent these reappraisals might affect the military position in Central and Southern Europe could not immediately be foreseen; but it was not without irony that the need for such a review should present itself at a moment when the state of East-West political and military relations was also giving rise to renewed anxiety. The cause of East-West *détente* had not been flourishing as vigorously as had been hoped at the time of NATO's Luxembourg meeting. The war in Vietnam had continued to intensify. The Soviet military presence in the Mediterranean had been maintained on a scale that was beginning to cause serious concern in NATO quarters. The United States and the U.S.S.R. appeared to stand on the verge of a new round in the nuclear missile race. Hopes for an easement of tensions in Central Europe had been set back by Moscow's December 8 blast against the Bonn government.[87] And now the financial plight of Great Britain and the United States appeared to threaten a further impairment of the Western defense structure on the Continent and, perhaps, to heighten the possibility that nuclear weapons would have to be used from the outset of any conflict in that theater.

This hazardous situation did not deter the NATO Defense Ministers, meeting without France on December 12, from formally approving the new strategy of flexible (i.e., nonnuclear) response, together with an unpublished five-year plan for NATO force levels and a proposal to establish a multinational destroyer fleet (the Standing Naval Force Atlantic) to deal with sudden emergencies. Defense Secretary McNamara, whose impending retirement had recently been announced in Washington, was not present at this meeting, at which the United States was represented by Deputy Secretary of Defense Paul H. Nitze.[88]

Apart from formal approval of these military decisions, the NATO Foreign Ministers were free to concentrate on political problems when the full North Atlantic Council held its ministerial session at the new Brussels headquarters on December 13-14. The Council's major task at this session, at which Secretary Rusk was the American spokesman, was to approve a set of guidelines for the future activity of the alliance that would carry forward the shift to a more overtly political emphasis envisaged at Luxembourg.

A philosophical basis for the proposed shift was now at hand with the completion of the special study resulting from the so-called Harmel Exercise. In contrast to some earlier expressions, this document did not at all contend that defense had become obsolete. On the contrary, it ascribed to the Atlantic alliance two equally vital functions: (1) the maintenance of an adequate military defense, and (2) the promotion of East-West *détente* with a view to bringing about "a just and lasting peaceful order in Europe accompanied by appropriate security guarantees." In the form in which it reached the Council, the Harmel document also stopped short of proposing that NATO itself should engage in East-West negotiations. The role of the alliance, it suggested, would be to act as "an effective forum and clearing house for the exchange of information and views" so that each of the allies would known what the others were doing and could adjust its own actions accordingly. "As sovereign states," the report said in an obvious bow to France, "the allies are not obliged to subordinate their policies to collective decision," but "the chances of success will clearly be greatest if the allies remain on parallel courses." It therefore urged that "the practice of frank and timely consultation . . . be deepened and improved" and that each of the allies bear in mind "that the pursuit of *détente* must not be allowed to split the alliance." Even France could find no serious objection to so bland a statement, which stopped well short of proposing any new mechanism or procedure for consultation on East-West matters. France at the moment was maintaining a rather conciliatory line on Atlantic Treaty matters and gave the impression that it would remain in the alliance at least until 1970.

A more immediate issue discussed on the fringes of the Brussels meeting was France's opposition to the opening of negotiations on Great Britain's application to join the Common Market. Despite de Gaulle's discouraging comments, the British application was still officially before the E.E.C., and still strongly favored by the Community's other five members as well as by Commission President Jean Rey. De Gaulle himself, in his November 27 statement, had seemed to see a possibility of including Britain "in some kind of arrangement on commercial exchanges with the Continent"—in other words, a form of "association" that would also be open to other applicants. But this halfway solution had been flatly rejected by Prime Minister Wilson, who had hinted to M. Rey that if Britain were in fact excluded it would have to reconsider its plans for increased technological cooperation with Community members.[90]

The showdown within the Community occurred at a two-day meeting of the Foreign Ministers, held in Brussels on December 18-19. Five of the six participants, as foreseen, expressed themselves in favor of immediately opening negotiations with the British. But M. Couve de Murville, as French representative, once again stopped the enterprise in its tracks by insisting that the British economy must recover before negotiations would be possible. The British application was not actually thrown out, but was permitted to remain on the table together with those of other current applicants. Even Couve de Murville admitted that the question remained open, would undoubtedly be further discussed in the course of 1968, and could be expected to move toward a positive solution as and when the United Kingdom began to bring its finances under control.[91]

The year was thus to end with France still in the Atlantic alliance and with Britain still outside the Common Market, but with neither arrangement bearing any aspect of permanence and with the future of the Western association still further obscured by uncertainties growing out of the financial plight of Britain and the United States and the revival of Soviet pressure in the Mediterranean and in Germany. Under such circumstances, the achievements of the earlier part of the year—the successful conclusion of the Kennedy Round and the provisional agreement on special drawing rights—appeared to have at best a conditional value.

In addition, the peoples on both sides of the Atlantic exhibited growing signs of disenchantment and spiritual malaise as old convictions weakened and the aims and ideals of the past two decades became corroded. The drive toward European unity no longer seemed to hold quite the same attraction for European young people, whose sense of disaffection now tended to find expression either in social withdrawal or, in some cases, in active rebellion of the "Provo" or "Red Guard" type. The prevalence of such attitudes did not necessarily mean that the West was hastening toward its decline and fall. It did suggest that the combination of material well-being and apparent physical security that had prevailed in the West in recent years raised problems no less perplexing than those associated with the privations and physical dangers of an earlier time.

6 : Africa Struggles On

The extraordinary exertions of American policy in Asia and the Far East had their counterpart in a somewhat more relaxed approach to the problems of other parts of the "third world." Particularly was this true in the Africa of the mid-1960's. Africa, to be sure, was a continent of unquestioned and rapidly growing importance; but it was one in which the United States had no long-established tradition of active involvement, and in which the vast political changes of the postwar decades had inspired Americans with a friendly but on the whole a rather casual interest. The threat of Communist takeovers in Africa had not, by and large, appeared sufficiently acute to warrant sustained American preventive efforts of the sort that had been undertaken in Europe and Asia and, more recently, in Latin America. The American economic stake in Africa had increased rapidly during the postwar years, but by the mid-1960's it still did not exceed some $2 billion in private investment, $1.3 billion in annual exports, and under $200 million a year in economic aid programs.[1] In cultivating friendly relations with both new and older African governments, the United States had not on the whole attempted to compete for influence with such experienced African powers as Great Britain, France, Belgium, Portugal, and Spain.

It was only when its European friends appeared unwilling or unable to deal effectively with some critical African situation that the United

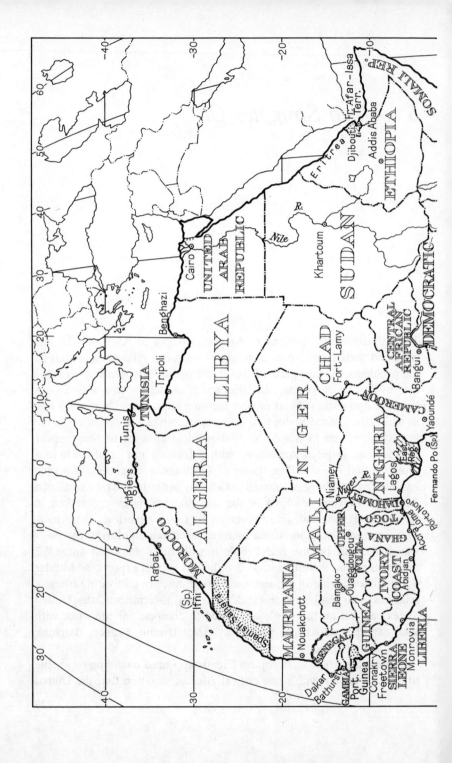

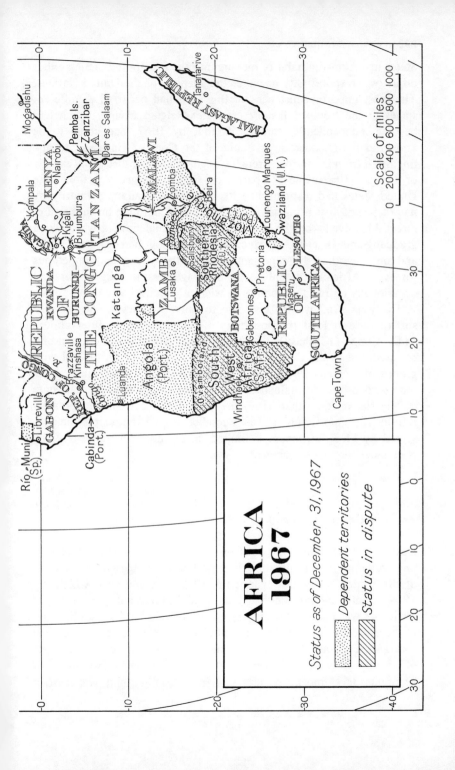

AFRICA 1967

Status as of December 31, 1967

Dependent territories

Status in dispute

Scale of miles
0 200 400 600 800 1000

Mogadishu

KENYA
Nairobi

Pemba Is.
Zanzibar
Dar es Salaam

TANZANIA

MALACASY REPUBLIC

Tananarive

Kampala

UGANDA

RWANDA
Kigali

BURUNDI
Bujumbura

THE CONGO

MALAWI
Zomba

Beira

Lourenço Marques

Mozambique (Port.)

REPUBLIC OF CONGO

Brazzaville
Kinshasa

Katanga

ZAMBIA
Lusaka

Salisbury

Southern Rhodesia (U.K.)

Swaziland

LESOTHO
Maseru

Pretoria

BOTSWANA
Gaberones

REPUBLIC OF SOUTH AFRICA

GABON
Libreville

Río Muni (Sp.)

Congo

Cabinda (Port.)

Luanda

Angola (Port.)

Ovamboland

South West Africa (S.Afr.)

Windhoek

Cape Town

States had formed a habit of moving into the foreground, acting either on its own responsibility or under the auspices of the United Nations. The most important instances of this kind had occurred at different stages in the troubled history of the ex-Belgian Congo, which had become independent in mid-1960 and, by 1967, had come to be known as the Democratic Republic of the Congo (Kinshasa) to distinguish it from the former French Congo, officially called the Republic of Congo (Brazzaville). Apart from such emergency actions, the United States had distinguished itself in African affairs primarily by its practice of dispensing advice and urging moderation on those more directly involved—on the one hand, the colonial powers which were gradually and sometimes grudgingly surrendering their responsibilities, and on the other the representatives of the young and impetuous forces of African nationalism, whose eagerness to take power had occasionally outrun their ability to wield it effectively.

The year 1967 was to give rise to only two new situations of a sort to raise at least the possibility of direct American intervention. In the Congo (Kinshasa), the United States would provide a measure of assistance to the Central Government in its attempts to deal with groups of mercenaries who were identified with "neocolonial" rather than with pro-Soviet influences. In the important West African state of Nigeria, on the other hand, the United States would deliberately refrain from interfering in a civil conflict despite the temptation presented by Moscow's open, if limited, intervention in support of the Nigerian Federal Government.

29 : The United States and Africa

Despite the inherent limitations on its African role, four aspects of the evolving African situation had particularly engaged the interest of the United States throughout the 1960's. A continent which, by 1967, counted 39 independent states as well as half a dozen dependent territories was naturally being shaped not by one but by a multiplicity of historical trends. Amid a baffling diversity of peoples and political forms, Africa could be viewed at one and the same time as the scene of an unprecedented experiment in decolonization, a laboratory of economic development, an arena of racial conflict, and, not least, a remote but none the less potentially critical battlefield of the "cold war."

Different elements in the African medley stood out more or less prominently as attention shifted from one section of the continent to another. Decolonization, in terms of the abrogation of external political rule, had by 1967 been largely completed except in those areas in the southern third of the continent that bore the imprint of Portuguese, British, or South African administration; and the status of these remaining "colonial" areas was among the most burning questions of international politics. But decolonization, in its wider sense, involved not merely the winning of formal independence but also the achievement of real, substantial independence, economic as well as political, and the exercise of this independence in accordance with the standards of performance expected of modern states. From this point of view, almost the whole of Africa was still immersed in the decolonization process, and opinions differed as to how effectively the new governments were using their authority. Many of them had experienced great difficulty in finding a form of political organization suited to the new conditions. A wave of military coups which had gathered momentum through the mid-1960's and continued into 1967 suggested that neither democracy on the Western model nor the one-party democracy espoused by certain African leaders provided a fully satisfactory answer.

In addition, a number of the new African governments had been greatly, perhaps excessively, concerned with combating the residual, "neocolonial" influence still exercised by or on behalf of the former colonial powers in the administrative and economic fields. The Congo (Kinshasa) was a striking case in point. Other newly independent countries, like Nigeria, were in danger of being torn apart by tribal conflicts. Tribal affinities and antipathies, which often extended across the arbitrary political frontiers inherited from the colonial period, were sometimes productive of sharp international antagonisms of the kind that had developed between Rwanda and Burundi and between Somalia and its East African neighbors. Other African countries, like Algeria and Morocco, had quarreled over material interests; still others, over conflicting personal ambitions and political viewpoints, as had been true between Ghana and most of its East African neighbors before the overthrow of President Kwame Nkrumah by a military coup in 1966.

A partial counterweight to these divisive tendencies was provided by newly established organs of political and economic cooperation, among which the Organization of African Unity (O.A.U.), the U.N. Economic Commission for Africa, and the African Development Bank were broadest in scope. There was also a separate organization linking the French-speaking African countries, as well as an embryonic regional organization centering on the East African states of Kenya, Tanzania, and Uganda. The trend toward regional cooperation was one that the United States had particularly sought to encourage, in Africa as in other parts of the world. President Johnson had praised the movement in glowing terms ·in a major address on African policy in May, 1966,[2] and the small U.S. economic aid program in Africa was currently being reoriented in such a way as to place maximum emphasis on multilateral and regional as opposed to purely national development projects.[3]

A further bond of union among the states of Africa south of the Sahara was the powerful racial feeling that had grown up in the decades of colonial subjection and now found its most vehement expression in the condemnation of racial discrimination as practiced in certain white-ruled African territories. On the emotional plane, this movement was scarcely distinguishable from the drive against "colonialism" in Southern Africa. To the African mind, colonialism and racial discrimination were twin evils, practiced by the same people and equally destined to be brought to an end through the replacement of minority (white) by majority (black) rule. For historical reasons, however, the elements of racial discrimination and colonialism were combined in different ways in different territories. South Africa, whose policy of racial segregation or *apartheid* stood out as the prototype of all that was offensive to African racial feeling, was emphatically not a "colonial" territory but an independent state— and one that itself exercised a form of colonial domination by holding in subjection the former mandated territory of South West Africa. Portugal, though plainly a colonial power in any but a technical sense, claimed to practice no racial discrimination in its African territories, though this point too was vehemently disputed by its critics. In the case of Great Brtain's self-governing colony of Southern Rhodesia, whose white government had declared independence in 1965 and had since been veering toward a discriminatory racial policy of the South African type, the African countries and the United Kingdom itself had been *opposed* to the termination of colonial authority until racial discrimination was ended and black majority rule was assured.

Despite these differences, there could be no mistaking the strength of feeling these racial issues had stirred in Africa as a whole; nor was there much doubt that pressures were building up within the white-ruled sections of Africa that could some day cause an explosion of undetermined proportions. The apprehension of racial conflict in Southern Africa provided a somber undertone in all discussion of African matters in the United Nations and elsewhere.

Should such a racial conflict occur, there seemed little doubt the U.S.S.R. and China, already active in various phases of African affairs, would seize the opportunities for advancing their respective interests. There were frequent reminders that both Communist governments—and Cuba, too—intended to play a continuing role in African affairs despite past rebuffs at the hands of some of the African countries. Chinese and Cuban agents were periodically reported to be training guerrilla fighters and spreading subversion from bases in the Congo (Brazzaville) and in Tanzania. The U.S.S.R., though apparently less involved in clandestine operations in recent years, had long been active in seeking clients among the African governments, and at one time had seemed likely to gain an ascendancy in Guinea and perhaps in other newly independent states.

Aside from its continuing influence in the United Arab Republic, shipments of Soviet military equipment in recent years had earned the U.S.S.R. positions of some strength in Somalia and particularly in Algeria, which had received important consignments of Soviet jets and tanks within the past year or so. Underlining the militant posture of the Algerian Government headed by Colonel Boumedienne, these shipments had caused considerable anxiety in neighboring Morocco, Libya, and Tunisia and had touched off something of a minor North African arms race. Morocco's King Hassan II had arranged in 1966 to buy twelve U.S. jets, and was understood to be hoping for more in the course of 1967. In some respects, North Africa was beginning to resemble the Arab East in its division between Soviet-supported "revolutionary" countries—mainly Algeria—and more conservative governments like Morocco, Tunisia, and Libya that looked primarily to the United States to maintain the local balance.

These varied trends had helped to keep American attention focused on the African continent in recent years, but had not been judged in

Washington to call for any major policy innovations apart from the growing stress on regional cooperation and the accompanying reorientation of the economic aid program. In his 1967 State of the Union message,[4] President Johnson voiced familiar views about regionalism, self-help, and interracial cooperation in Africa but did not attempt to penetrate beneath the surface of current affairs. In particular, he refrained from commenting on the two chief African issues that currently confronted the international community and would soon demand important policy decisions. One of these was the poor success of the economic sanctions ordered by the U.N. Security Council since 1965 with the object of bringing down Southern Rhodesia's rebellious white government. The other concerned the ways and means of implementing a recent decision by the General Assembly to the effect that South Africa had forfeited its right to administer South West Africa and that the United Nations must assume direct responsibility for bringing the people of that territory to independence.

Some indication of the U.S. approach to these questions was offered by Ambassador Goldberg in a January 27 address to the American Negro Leadership Conference on Africa, a group set up to stimulate and channel the interest of American Negroes in African affairs.[5] While emphasizing the need to eliminate the vestiges of colonialism and racial discrimination in Africa, the U.S. Representative's statement stopped well short of endorsing the impetuous attitudes that had become current in African nationalist circles. Indeed, his remarks were keyed to a distinctly cautionary pitch. Reproving the disregard for procedural rules and the rights of others which he said had been displayed by some African delegates to the United Nations,[6] Mr. Goldberg warned sharply against being in too much of a hurry. The United States, he said, was committed to "orderly and realistic progress" in Africa; but it was also convinced that "the best way to solve difficult problems is not by dramatic confrontations but by patient dialogue."

Illustrating this principle by reference to the Rhodesian problem, Ambassador Goldberg explained that the United States' "moderating and responsible" participation in an international approach to this issue had been designed to further "orderly progress toward self-determination and equality" in Southern Rhodesia while, at the same time, avoiding the danger of "violence, extremism, racism, and instability in the heart of Africa." Similarly, he said, in South West

Africa the United States advocated a "peaceful and practical solution . . . consistent with the General Assembly's resolution." In dealing with the South African Government itself, Mr. Goldberg added, the United States would not cease "its search for peaceful and practical means" of inculcating "the need for a policy of justice and equity for all its peoples." In the same spirit, finally, the United States considered that the initial step in dealing with the Portuguese territories in Southern Africa must be "for the parties to commence a genuine dialogue on the basis of recognition of the principle of self-determination."

This characteristic stress on patience, moderation, and "dialogue" in dealing with Africa's most intractable problems appeared to spring directly from a time-honored national belief in the essential reasonableness of human beings and their ability to reach agreement based on respect for one another's point of view. Critics of the U.S. position were quite unfair when they imputed such sentiments merely to economic self-interest and concern for the safety of American investments in Africa. It may be true that there were contradictions between a political policy of furthering racial and political justice for black Africans and an economic practice that tended to concentrate U.S. investment in white-ruled African territories. Yet the bias in favor of conciliation and the avoidance of unnecessary confrontations was too deeply rooted in the American outlook to be ascribed merely to economic motives.

A more basic weakness in the American approach, some critics argued, was a lack of realism in assuming that the problems of colonialism and racial discrimination in Africa could ever be adjusted by conciliation and mutual agreement. "Dialogue" with Portugal, South Africa, or the illegal regime in Southern Rhodesia, most African governments felt, would be a sheer waste of breath. The white regimes in Southern Africa, in their view, had already made it sufficiently clear that they would never willingly concede the rights that were being demanded on behalf of their black populations. The time for dialogue was past, most African governments reasoned, and the time for action was at hand. If action through the United Nations could be made effective, that course was naturally to be preferred. If not, there would remain the possibility of direct and violent action such as was already being initiated in some sectors under the auspices of the Liberation Committee of the Organization of African Unity. Should the United

States refuse to sanction a resort to forceful measures, there were other powers like China, Cuba, and the Soviet Union that presumably would not be so squeamish.

This basic difference on the liberation question had not prevented the maintenance of friendly and fruitful relations between the United States and a multitude of individual African governments. Among the distinguished African visitors to Washington during the winter of 1966-67 were King Hassan of Morocco, who was promised additional military equipment as well as quantities of American wheat,[7] and the Emperor Haile Selassie of Ethiopia, who made a point of *not* requesting American aid (other than private investment) but presumably acquainted the President with his country's development plans as well as his anxieties about the nationalist ferment on Ethiopia's borders with Somalia and French Somaliland.[8]

A further mark of American interest in African affairs was the seventeen-day tour of twelve African countries that was undertaken in May by Under-Secretary of State Nicholas deB. Katzenbach, the highest U.S. official to visit Africa in a number of years. In the course of his itinerary, which included countries like Guinea and Tanzania that had not always been lenient judges of American policy, Mr. Katzenbach listened to a variety of criticisms on current American attitudes toward Africa. The culmination of his trip, however, was highly positive in tone. In an address of May 26 at the Haile Selassie I University in Addis Ababa, Mr. Katzenbach explained the new co-operative principle—"cooperation among donors and cooperation among recipients"—that, he said, was already making itself felt in U.S. assistance programs in Africa. That continent, the Under-Secretary emphasized, had little time in which to accomplish its transition into the twentieth century, in education, in transportation, in agriculture and natural resources; but already it had made startling progress. "Africa is on the move," Mr. Katzenbach said. "I knew that before I came. Now I believe it."[9]

30 : The Congo and Nigeria

A few years earlier, most observers would have agreed that the pace of African progress would be largely determined by the success of the ex-Belgian Congo and Nigeria, two countries particularly rich in population and resources that had come to independence almost simultaneously in 1960. Although the Congo's first years had been darkened by strife and disorder, its basic prospects had not ceased to appear favorable; whereas Nigeria had for several years stood out as the very model of an African country engaged in the orderly realization of its great potentialities. Both countries, however, had been vexed by serious internal conflicts which, by the beginning of 1967, were threatening to make a mockery of earlier hopes.

Most of the recent problems of the Democratic Republic of the Congo (Kinshasa) were involved in one way or another with what was known both there and elsewhere as the struggle against "neo-colonialism." Soviet and Communist influence had been curbed in the early years of Congolese independence, and the U.N. military units which had been stationed in the country at the beginning of its independent life had been withdrawn in 1964. Thereafter, the Congolese Central Government, headed by Premier Moïse Tshombe and later by President Joseph D. Mobutu, had been left to face an enormous task of reconstruction in which it clearly needed all the disinterested external assistance it could obtain. Its difficulty lay in the fact that the best available source of financial aid and specialized skills was Belgium, the former colonial power, whose aid was suspect by definition. "Belgium," to the Congolese mind, denoted not merely the government in Brussels but a sinister complex of interests that included businessmen, administrators, engineers, teachers, military men, and, above all, an international mining company, the Union Minière du Haut-Katanga, which possessed vast holdings in Katanga Province and had been repeatedly charged with nefarious moves directed against the Congo's independence and unity.

The Congolese experience of 1967 can best be understood as a series of collisions between the Congolese Central Government and the elements of this mysterious "neocolonial" complex, whose activities, though perhaps less coordinated and less villainous than the Congolese imagined, were difficult to trace in detail and widely suspect both in Africa and elsewhere. The initial confrontation, which interrupted the Congo's vital copper exports for several weeks in early 1967 and nearly precipitated a diplomatic break with Belgium, was relatively simple in character. In a display of economic nationalism of the sort familiar in most new countries, Mobutu had undertaken to gain control of his country's most important national resource by

AFRICAN PROBLEM AREAS

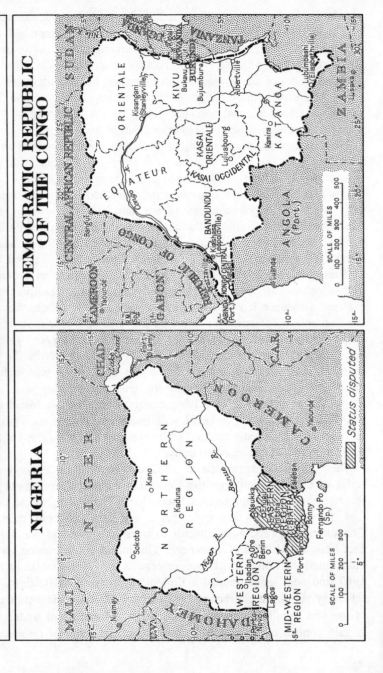

NIGERIA

MALI

NIGER

CHAD

Lake Chad

Niamey

Sokoto

Kano

Kaduna

NORTHERN REGION

Benue R.

Benue R.

WESTERN REGION

Ibadan

Ife

Benin

Lagos

MID-WESTERN REGION

Niger R.

Nsukka

Enugu

Onitsha

EASTERN REGION

BIAFRA

Calabar

Port Harcourt

Bonny

Fernando Po (Sp.)

DAHOMEY

Porto Novo

(U.V.)

Fort Lamy

CAMEROON

Yaoundé

C.A.R.

Status disputed

SCALE OF MILES
0   100   200   300

DEMOCRATIC REPUBLIC OF THE CONGO

CENTRAL AFRICAN REPUBLIC

SUDAN

CAMEROON

Yaoundé

GABON

R.M. (Sp.)

Bangui

Congo

REPUBLIC OF CONGO

EQUATEUR

ORIENTALE

Kisangani (Stanleyville)

KIVU

Bukavu

Bujumbura

UGANDA

RWANDA

BURUNDI

TANZANIA

Albertville

KASAI ORIENTALE

Luluabourg

KASAI OCCIDENTAL

BANDUNDU

Kinshasa (Léopoldville)

KONGO CENTRAL

CABINDA (Port.)

Matadi

Luanda

ANGOLA (Port.)

KATANGA

Kamina

Lubumbashi (Elisabethville)

Lusaka

ZAMBIA

SCALE OF MILES
0   100   200   300   400   500

expropriating the Union Minière and establishing a state-owned Congolese company to exploint Katanga's mineral wealth. A threatened resort to commercial reprisals by Union Minière was eventually averted with the assistance of the Belgian Government, which helped to devise a compromise under which the new Congolese company would hold supreme control but Union Minière would remain to carry on the actual operations through an associated company.[10]

This matter being settled and a degree of stability established in Congolese affairs for practically the first time since independence, Mobutu was able to turn his attention to longer-range matters such as monetary reform and the introduction of a new, "revolutionary" constitution that would provide for strong presidential government, a one-chamber parliament, and a maximum of two political parties. As part of this effort toward normalization, Mobutu also undertook to disband the various groups of white mercenary soldiers that had been more or less identified with the cause of ex-Premier Tshombe, Mobutu's predecessor in the control of Congolese affairs. Tshombe, who had been dislodged from power in 1964 and had gone into exile in Spain, had been widely regarded in the past as a "front man" for Union Minière and other "neocolonialist" influences and had earned the execration of African nationalists by his attempt to operate Katanga Province as an independent state in 1960-63.

Some accounts of the strange events of the summer of 1967 allege that such mercenary leaders as Colonel Robert Denard and Major Jean Schramme, the one a Frenchman and the other a Belgian, were involved in a far-reaching plot to bring about an uprising in the Congo and thus engineer Tshombe's return to power. They themselves insisted, however, that while they thought highly of Tshombe and his methods, their only immediate concern was to protect themselves and their followers against possible reprisals following Mobutu's demobilization order. Events, in any case, began going out of control on July 1 as the result of a serious mishap to Tshombe himself. Apparently betrayed by someone in his personal entourage, the exiled leader was kidnaped in flight over the Balearic Islands and conveyed to Algeria as an involuntary guest of Colonel Boumedienne's government. Following intensive interrogation by Algerian security authorities, the Congolese ex-Premier was declared liable to extradition to the Congo, where he had already been sentenced to death on a charge of high treason. Boumedienne's failure to sign the extradition order was attributed not to sympathy for Tshombe but to dissatisfaction over the Congolese Government's rather lukewarm stand in the Middle East war.

Four days after Tshombe's seizure, on July 5, revolt broke out in the Congo itself. Mercenaries and Katangese troops under Major Schramme's command opened operations at two widely separated points, the frontier town of Bukavu and the airport at Kisangani (formerly Stanleyville). Foreseeing that they would be blamed for this development, France and Belgium promptly disavowed the mercenaries and expressed their support for the Central Government. The State Department, after arranging for the evacuation of U.S. dependents from Bukavu, vigorously echoed these sentiments. Washington place little credence in Mobutu's assertion that the disturbances were being fomented by Belgium, Spain, France, and Portugal. Nevertheless the United States supported a resolution, unanimously adopted by the U.N. Security Council on July 10, which condemned "any state" assisting or providing facilities to anti-government mercenaries and called on governments to deny such assistance.[11]

Responding to a direct appeal from President Mobutu, the United States also undertook to furnish practical assistance to the Central Government in its efforts to put down the rebellion. On July 9 it was disclosed that three C-130 military transport aircraft were being sent to the Congo, with their crews, to provide the Central Government with "long-range logistical support." The planes would have a "noncombatant" status, it was explained, and would stay clear of actual fighting. Aside from helping the Central Government to restore order, Secretary Rusk stated, the U.S. gesture was designed to head off a dangerous wave of anti-white feeling in the wake of the revolt.[12]

This explanation failed to allay the uneasiness of Senators Fulbright, Mansfield, and other legislators who were already upset about the use of presidential authority in Vietnam and feared the development of a similar involvement in Congolese affairs. In a few individual cases, these congressional misgivings may have been motivated in part by a lingering regard for Tshombe and dislike of the Kinshasa regime. More fundamentally, however, they reflected a growing resistance to the whole idea of foreign commitments assumed without congressional approval. While these objections had no perceptible effect in the Congo situation, they were undoubtedly remembered by the administration when the possibility of similar intervention in Nigeria arose soon afterward.

The prompt arrival of the three American planes—one of which remained in the Congo until December—was helpful in reestablishing the situation at Kisangani and was credited by the Congolese Government with a decisive influence in bringing about the collapse of the revolt. It did not, however, prevent the death of some hundreds of Congolese in the ensuing disorders; nor did it prevent a group of about 150 mercenaries and 1,200 Katangese under Major Schramme's command from fighting their way across the eastern Congo to join their fellows in Bukavu, where they were to defy the Central Government for several months. Nor did American support of the Kinshasa government prevent a series of hostle manifestations, directed against both Belgium and the United States, which nearly led to the discontinuance of Belgian civilian assistance to the Congo.

So precarious did the situation of the Mobutu government appear that for a time there was doubt that the Organization of African Unity would be able to hold its annual "summit" conference, which had been scheduled to meet in Kinshasa on September 11-14. Although the conference ultimately was held on schedule, only about half the eligible heads of state and government were present to hear the keynote address that U Thant came from New York to deliver.[13] In a manifestation of suport for President Mobutu, the conference issued a declaration insisting that white mercenaries leave the Congo under pain of concerted military action by the rest of Africa. More practically, it also decided to enlist the aid of the International Committee of the Red Cross in getting the mercenaries and Katangese out of Bukavu while protecting them against possible massacre by the Congolese forces who had surrounded them there.[14] The evacuation plan developed in the following weeks envisaged flying the mercenaries out to Malta en route to their home countries, while the Katangese would either go to Zambia or be resettled in the Congo under an amnesty.

Negotiations on the evacuation plan were still going forward when it was reported on November 1 that the Congo had been invaded by a second, somewhat smaller mercenary force, this one allegedly coming from Portuguese Angola and apparently led by Colonel Denard. In the confusion created by this second mercenary thrust, which seemed to be directed against the heart of Katanga Province, the original force of mercenaries under Major Schramme was able to slip across the international frontier into Rwanda, there to await evacuation which would still be pending at the end of the year. The second mercenary force, meanwhile, disappeared as suddenly and mysteriously as it had come. Most observers concluded that its purpose had been purely diversionary, although President Mobutu insisted that the real object had been to overthrow his government as part of a new plot hatched by Union Minière. Despite these grave suspicions, the Congolese President is said to have declined a Soviet offer of emergency aid with MIG jets flown by Soviet-trained Congolese pilots.[15]

This was not the first time that Portugal had been accused of permitting its territory of Angola to be used for the assembly of mercenaries and similar anti-Congolese activities. Though itself contending with an Angolan revolutionary movement that was openly supported from the Congo, Portugal had always denied such charges and now continued to do so in face of renewed expressions of outrage by African governments and of concern by the United States. Ignoring Portugal's pleas of innocence and its demands for an impartial investigation, the Security Council on November 15 approved a special resolution— adopted by consensus rather than by formal vote—that condemned the alleged failure to prevent the use of Angola as a base for armed attacks against the Congo and called for immediate cessation of any form of assistance to the mercenaries.[16] Thus another black mark was added to Portugal's official record, which was meanwhile suffering further damage as a result of its alleged involvement in the civil war in Nigeria.

Nigeria's melancholy experiences in 1967 can be summarized more rapidly because, though possibly of darker omen for the future of Africa, they did not involve the United States or the United Nations in any comparable degree. Since the overthrow of its first independent government by a military coup in January 1966, the dominant issues in this most populous of African countries had hinged on internal tribal relations rather than the international question of "neocolonialism." Aggravated by large-scale massacres, a deadly enmity had come to prevail between the Ibo inhabitants of Nigeria's semi-autonomous Eastern Region and the backers of the military-dominated Federal Government at Lagos, largely run by northern Nigerians identified with the Hausa tribe. The government of the Eastern Region, led by Lieutenant Colonel Odumegwu Ojukwu, had for months been threatening to leave the federation and declare its independence unless the Federal Government under Lieutenant Colonel (later Major General) Yakubu Gowon conceded it full rights to manage its own affairs.

All attempts at conciliation by other African governments having failed, the Eastern Region carried out its threat on May 30, 1967 by declaring itself an independent republic and taking the name of "Biafra" from the bight of the Gulf of Guinea on which it fronted. Although no established government recognized the self-proclaimed republic, the strict "hands-off" policy adopted by London and Washington proved less than satisfactory to the Federal Government at Lagos, which particularly resented its inability to purchase arms in any quantity from either Britain or the United States. A further source of annoyance was London's failure to back up more vigorously the Federal Government's insistence that the Shell-BP petroleum concern, whose principal facilities were located in the East, continue to pay royalties into the Federal treasury rather than making payments to the rebellious Eastern authorities as the latter demanded.

Rather tardily, the Federal Government opened military operations against the East in July and managed to capture the university town of Nsukka and the port of Bonny. Thereafter the campaign proceeded at a snail's pace, and all attempts to push on to the Biafran capital at Enugu were foiled. In August, Biafra turned the tables by invading the Midwestern Region, capturing the regional capital of Benin with the aid of local Ibos, and pressing as far as Ore in the Western Region. This thrust, apparently aimed at Lagos itself, was to prove the high point of Biafra's campaign. Federal troops reentered Ore at the beginning of September, recaptured Benin on September 20—severe reprisals against the Ibo townspeople followed—and reinvigorated the drive against Enugu, which was finally taken in the early days of October. Biafran resistance nevertheless continued even after the fall of the capital.

Meanwhile the conflict was threatening to assume the aspect of a confrontation between "Communist" and "neocolonialist" influences, with the United States enjoying the good will of neither side. The Federal Government, frustrated by British and American neutrality, had eventually succeeded in obtaining a few war planes from Czechoslovakia and Poland, and on August 19 it was revealed that the Soviet Union itself had also entered the picture. Fifteen Soviet transport planes, it was said, had arrived in Lagos and were unloading disassembled jet fighter planes of Czechoslovak or Soviet manufacture. Training crews had accompanied or followed the aircraft, and by the beginning of September Lagos claimed to have a force of twenty planes completely ready for action. Though air operations remained very limited, the arrival of the planes at this critical juncture was to appear in retrospect as one of the war's decisive turning points.

The United States had seldom stood idle when the U.S.S.R. provided planes to African or Asian countries. Its usual practice had been to provide a counterweight by furnishing American planes to one or more neighbor countries. Yet such a procedure seemed clearly unsuited to the special cirucumstances prevailing in Nigeria, where assistance to Biafra would have meant direct support of a rebellion against a government recognized by the United States. Though apparently under some pressure to reconsider its policy of neutrality in the wake of the Soviet move, the administration remembered its recent difficulties over the Congo and determined to maintain its policy of noninvolvement. It merely issued a statement regretting the Soviet action and reaffirming its belief that "all nations have a responsibility to avoid any exploitation of this situation for ideological or other political purposes."[17]

To the Lagos government, this stand seemed almost as reprehensible as direct American support for Biafra. Nigerians had never shown any leaning toward Communism, yet could not help contrasting the attitude of the Soviet Union with that of their supposed friends in the West. Even the British were now relenting and preparing to furnish arms on a substantial scale. American professions of neutrality were seen in Lagos as nothing but "thinly disguised support" of the Eastern Ibos—motivated, it was suggested, by a concern for "cheap oil supplies."[18] Asserting that the Biafrans had made extensive arms purchases from private dealers in the West, Federal spokesmen increasingly began to depict the secession as a "neocolonialist" maneuver comparable to the earlier secession of Katanga from the Congo. Portugal, in particular, was repeatedly accused of aiding the Biafrans with clandestine shipments of arms and men. Some reports implicated Spain and France as well.[19]

In addition to the misery it was causing in Nigeria itself, the continuance of civil war in one of Africa's "showcase" countries was clearly damaging to wider African interests. As early as their Kinshasa meeting in mid-September, the African heads of state and government had deputed six of their number (later reduced to four) to consult with the Nigerian chief of state on means of bringing the conflict to an end.[20] General Gowon, who was mistrustful of outside mediation and preferred to insist on Biafra's unconditional submission, had at first been unenthusiastic about this procedure. But it was late November before an O.A.U. delegation led by the Emperor Haile Selassie arrived in Lagos, and by that time the growing military stalemate and seeming impossibility of striking a decisive blow had weakened the Nigerian leader's resistance. With General Gowon's agreement, it was decided to entrust another African chief of state, Lieutenant General J. A. Ankrah of Ghana, with the delicate task of contacting the rebels and finding out on what terms they would be prepared to reenter the fold. The Biafrans, however, showed no intention of surrendering their hard-won independence,[21] and nothing ultimately came of the O.A.U. initiative. With the Federal military advance at a standstill, the end of the year found General Gowon calling for a determined effort to finish the war within another three months.

31 : Rhodesia and the Portuguese Territories

In terms of history, constitutional status, and contemporary policy, Southern Rhodesia and the Portuguese African territories of Angola, Mozambique, and Portuguese Guinea had little in common with one another. Southern Rhodesia was a self-governing British colony whose white rulers had unilaterally declared independence of the United Kingdom, defied the authority of both the mother country and the United Nations, and set out to intensify an already discriminatory racial policy with the aim of withholding political power from the territory's black majority. Angola and Mozambique, the Portuguese territories on which international attention had thus far focused most sharply, were technically classified not as colonies at all but as overseas provinces of Portugal. Nominally administered on nonracial and nondiscriminatory lines, both territories had none the less become the scene of armed revolts that showed the discontent of at least a section of their black populations.

Despite their obvious differences, Rhodesia and the Portuguese territories held a similar place in the Africa of 1967. In both, the essential feature was the subjection of a black majority to economic, social, and political domination by an alien white minority. Angola, Rhodesia, and Mozambique, moreover, shared a common position as white-ruled territories on the frontiers of the independent, black-governed section of Africa. As the North-South antagonism in Africa intensified, white-ruled Southern Africa was increasingly coming to resemble a besieged fortress of which Angola, Southern Rhodesia, and Mozambique were primary defensive bastions while industrialized and racially segregated South Africa could be said to represent the inner citadel.

Within the past few years, African nationalist pressure against these northern outposts of "colonialism and racial discrimination" had increasingly tended to shift from the purely political to the politico-military plane. Resolutions condemning the policies of the responsible governmental authorities were still adopted each year in the United Nations; but they were now being supplemented to an increasing degree by what looked like the beginnings of an "African liberation struggle." Armed revolt had broken out in northern Angola as early as 1961, and that territory had since been increasingly subjected to incursions by armed raiders based in the Congo. On a smaller scale, Mozambique was subject to similar harassment based in Tanzania; and there had also been nationalist disturbances in Portuguese Guinea. Southern Rhodesia, since its seizure of independence on November 11, 1965, had also been threatened with guerrilla and terrorist action, although this threat had not yet materialized in any serious way.

In response to these activities and threats, cooperation within Southern Africa was also being strengthened. South Africa had been giving important assistance to Southern Rhodesia in overcoming the effects of U.N. economic sanctions, and was soon to provide it with military assistance as well. Portugal, which had likewise refused to invoke U.N. sanctions against Southern Rhodesia, was also beginning to move in the direction of defense cooperation and already acknowledged a common defensive interest with South Africa. South African Defense Minister P. W. Botha, in turn, paid tribute to the "strength and resolution of our Portuguese neighbors" in facilitating South Africa's own defensive task.

An incidental effect of this North-South division was the ambiguous position in which it placed a number of black African countries that happened to lie to the south of the dividing line. However powerful their racial feelings, such countries as Zambia and Malawi (the former Northern Rhodesia and Nyasaland) were compelled to cooperate to some extent with their Portuguese and Rhodesian neighbors as a matter of sheer economic survival. Full participation in U.N. sanctions against Rhodesia, for example, would have spelled economic suicide for Zambia, though President Kenneth Kaunda had been among the sharpest critics of the Rhodesian regime and was spurring a strenuous effort to reduce his country's dependence. The new states of Botswana and Lesotho, as virtual enclaves in South African or South African-controlled territory, were in an even more difficult position in which they had virtually no choice but to cooperate with their powerful neighbor.

A situation in which some African governments were unable to participate fully in policies inspired by African nationalism was bound to lead to occasional friction among the African states themselves. Yet it also kept open at least the theoretical possibility that there might eventually develop a more cooperative pattern of relationships among a considerable number of white- and black-ruled African countries. The policy of South African Prime Minister Balthazar J. Vorster, who professed to see no inconsistency between *apartheid* at home and cooperation abroad, seemed explicitly directed to this end. At least one black African leader, President H. Kamuzu Banda of Malawi, had adopted a line of policy that seemed to reflect the influence of similiar ideas. Yet it remained a question whether any kind of permanent cooperation would be conceivable in view of the exacerbated state of racial feeling that now prevailed in both the black and the white communities of Southern Africa. The gradual intensification of this racial hostility was perhaps the most significant development in a year when actual political events remained essentially inconclusive.

In Southern Rhodesia, the mandatory but "selective" economic sanctions invoked by the U.N. Security Council in December 1966[22] and applied by the United States, among others, from the beginning of 1967[23] appeared initially to be having little or no impact on the position of the rebel regime headed by Prime Minister Ian D. Smith. Portugal and South Africa, which controlled Rhodesia's trade routes, had refused to apply the sanctions—South Africa, in particular, had seen to it that the Rhodesians received ample supplies of petroleum products—and a number of other governments had less ostentatiously continued normal trade with the rebellious colony. By September, U Thant would note in the introduction to his annual report that while there had been "a significant decline in trade between Southern Rhodesia and many of its trading partners in most of the commodities listed in the resolution of the Security Council," the sanctions did not appear to have "caused the illegal authorities insuperable difficutlies." On the contrary, U Thant said, the policies of South Africa and Portugal had actually "strengthened the economic position of the illegal regime and fortified it in its defiance of the international community."[24]

These findings were not surprising to those African nationalists who had decried the loopholes in the 1966 sanctions resolution and insisted that the use of force—preferably by Great Britain, as the responsible sovereign in the territory—was the only way of ousting Rhodesia's illegal regime. It was because Great Britain had refused to contemplate the use of force—or even to agree to an economic blockade that could involve it in a "confrontation" with South Africa, its second most important trading partner—that the resort to partial U.N. sanctions had been adopted in the first place. The United States, in line with its preference for "patient dialogue" rather than "dramatic confrontations," had gone along with this temperate British approach even though it would clearly have preferred a somewhat more energetic policy.

Even after the imposition of U.N. sanctions, London had not given up hope that the Rhodesian problem could be resolved by negotiating with the Rhodesian authorities an agreement looking toward majority (i.e., African) rule within a reasonably brief period. Despite the poor results of past contacts with Prime Minister Smith, another special British envoy—Lord Alport, a former High Commissioner in the Rhodesian territories—was sent out to Salisbury in June 1967 and subsequently reported that the majority of Rhodesian whites would also favor a negotiated settlement. The difficulty, as always, was that most Rhodesian whites quite obviously wanted to retain control and therefore favored a very different kind of negotiated settlement from the one the British were prepared to accept. The prospect of bridging the differences seemed hardly to be enhanced by Prime Minister Smith's subsequent espousal of a racial policy explicitly based on the "separate development" principle already established in South Africa.[25]

A wholly different approach to the problems of Southern Africa was meanwhile being instituted in the name of the so-called African liberation movement, a loosely organized network of cooperating or competing nationalist groups which was patronized by the Liberation Committee of the Organization of African Unity and supported in varying degree by a variety of African and non-African governments.

Tanzania, the U.A.R., Algeria, Communist China, the U.S.S.R., and Cuba were all believed to be involved in this activity, particularly in the training of exiled African nationalists for guerrilla operations in their homelands. Southern Rhodesia was now to have its first direct experience of the guerrilla-type activity that had hitherto been largely confined to the Portuguese territories but now seemed to be spreading all along the rough demarcation line between white- and black-ruled Africa.[26]

During the last ten days of August, Rhodesian authorities reported a series of clashes with infiltrating "terrorists" in a remote Western region which allegedly resulted in the wiping out of a Communist-armed band of over 100. A majority of this group, it appeared, were South Africans rather than Rhodesians and had been proceeding by way of Zambia, Rhodesia, and Botswana with a view to undertaking guerrilla operations against South Africa.[27] That such a movement should even have been attempted suggested the scope of the problem that now faced not only the white-ruled countries but also those African states which, like Zambia, sympathized with the objectives of the liberation movement but were also concerned for their own security if violence broke out in neighboring countries. Among the immediate consequences of the affair was the arrival in Rhodesia, presumably with Mr. Smith's approval, of an undisclosed number of uniformed South Africans, equipped with helicopters, armored cars, and trucks, who gave every indication of having come to stay. Their presence, South African Foreign Minister Hilgard Müller later explained, was covered by a regional mutual security arrangement that included Malawi, Botswana, and Lesotho as well as the white-ruled countries of the area.[28]

As the North-South opposition hardened and Prime Minister Smith fought off "extremist" white attacks against his self-styled "moderate" policy, the anticolonial governments continued to insist that the basic responsibility for driving his regime from office remained with the United Kingdom. The alleged failure of economic sanctions and the need for stronger measures, including the use of force, were dominant themes as the debate on Southern Rhodesia resumed at the United Nations with the convening of the 22nd General Assembly in September. Forty-nine governments, mainly African, Asian, and Communist, presently joined in sponsoring a lengthy resolution that again declared the use of force to be the only effective and speedy way for the United

Kingdom to bring down Rhodesia's "illegal racist minority regime."

Anticipating such demands, Foreign Secretary Brown had just renewed his warning that Great Britain remained immovably opposed either to the use of force against Southern Rhodesia or to the tightening of economic sanctions in a way that would invite economic war with South Africa. It was really too early to say that sanctions had failed, British spokesmen argued; more time was needed for their effects to become apparent. Once again, the British position was supported by the United States, which likewise expressed its abhorrence of forcible, violent solutions as well as its determination to persevere in helping to seek a just and peaceful settlement. Such words of caution did not, however, dissuade the Assembly from approving the proposed resolution on November 3 by the substantial vote of 92 to 2 (Portugal and South Africa), with Britain, the United States, and other Western countries abstaining.[29]

Still another attempt to resolve the issue by direct negotiations was doomed to collapse within a few days of the Assembly's vote. George Thomson, British Secretary of State for Commonwealth Relations, was in Salisbury early in November but found Mr. Smith more unyielding than ever and returned to tell the House of Commons that the differences between the two governments were even greater than earlier discussions had indicated.[30] Rhodesia's self-proclaimed independence was by this time two years old and, to all appearances, in no danger of early evaporation. Its government's pressure for the enactment of a rigid racial segregation law offered renewed proof, if any was needed, of its rejection of multiracial solutions and its decision to build the country's future on the shaky foundations of white supremacy.

There was less activity in Portugal's African territories during 1967. Six years after the initial outbreak in Angola, any immediate threat to Portuguese rule had been stamped out and the independence movement had been restricted to guerrilla nuisance raids of greater variety than effectiveness. C. L. Sulzberger of *The New York Times* reported in November that such raids were currently being pressed by "three Angolan, two Mozambican and one [Portuguese] Guinean group . . . from the two Congos, Senegal, Guinea, Zambia and Tanzania." Admittedly, Sulzberger added, this widely diffused guerrilla menace was being contained at heavy cost. The bulk of the Portuguese Army—over 100,000 troops—was now stationed in Africa, and the bill for African military defense was estimated at $175 million a year.[31] Yet Portuguese spokesmen appeared sublimely confident that the situation in the "overseas provinces" was under control and that time would vindicate their policy. Glittering economic prospects— the discovery of important oil deposits off the coast of Cabinda, plans for a huge hydroelectric development on the Zambezi River in Mozambique—could be trusted, they felt, to blunt the nationalist appetite and float Portugal's African empire and its inhabitants on a rising tide of material abundance.[32]

It need hardly be added that the disappearance of Portuguese rule in Africa was predicted with equal certitude by such nationalist leaders as Eduardo Mondlane, the American-trained chairman of the Front for the Liberation of Mozambique. Deriding American pleas for a "dialogue" with Portugal, Mr. Mondlane admitted that his group had received training and arms from the U.S.S.R. and other Communist nations but insisted that there had been no Communist interference in the actual management of the liberation movement. From an initial group of 150 Algerian-trained guerrillas in 1964, Dr. Mondlane and his American wife asserted, the armed forces of their movement had grown to a strength of some 5,000 to 7,000 uniformed fighters now operating in the northern provinces of Mozambique.[33]

While the movements for the liberation of Portuguese Africa were clearly less than united among themselves, innumerable U.N. resolutions had shown that their aims enjoyed the fullest sympathy of the independent African states as well as the entire "anticolonial bloc" of Asian, African, and Communist nations. Not content with demanding freedom and independence for the peoples of Portuguese-dominated territories, the anticolonial nations had of late years become intensely critical of the economic and military support provided Portugal by its Western allies. Not only did Portugal benefit from Western investment in its African territories, the anticolonialists reasoned, but its commercial ties and membership in NATO undoubtedly gave it the opportunity to purchase arms in the West and to divert men and equipment to its African possessions. However vigorously they denied the charge, the United States and other Western powers were widely regarded as partners in Portugal's repression of African nationalist aspirations.[34]

Portugal, of course, was also in trouble with the United Nations over its alleged intrusions into the affairs of such countries as the Congo and Nigeria. The Security Council resolution of November 15, denouncing its failure to prevent a group of white mercenaries from using Angola as a base for armed attacks against the Congo,[35] reflected what seemed a growing if understandable tendency to condemn Portuguese actions by a far more rigorous standard than was applied in judging the external interference to which Portugal itself was subject.

A comparable state of mind inspired the annual, blanket condemnation of Portuguese policies in Africa that was adopted by the General Assembly on November 17. Denouncing Portugal's "colonial war" as "a crime against humanity and a grave threat to international peace and security," this resolution once again affirmed the right of the peoples under Portuguese rule to freedom and independence; appealed to all states to help them gain it; called for an end of foreign investment and of financial support for Portugal; and particularly called on Portugal's NATO allies to deny that country all forms of military aid, including sales of weapons or equipment and the training of personnel either in or outside of NATO.[36]

The feeling behind such declarations was far removed from the spirit of "dialogue" that Mr. Goldberg had sought to encourage. The United States, as everyone had anticipated, found itself quite unable to support so far-reaching a resolution, although it categorically rejected "the sweeping and unsubstantiated accusations purporting to show [U.S.] complicity . . . with Portuguese policies in Africa."[37] But if the United States was not an accomplice of Portuguese policy, it was certainly one of the victims in the sense that its association with Portugal—together with its distaste for extremist courses in Africa—inevitably tarred it with the brush of colonialism in the eyes of a majority of the world's governments. It was of more than symbolic significance that the anti-Portuguese resolution, which received 82 affirmative votes, was opposed by only seven governments and that these included South Africa and Portugal itself as well as the United States, Britain, Spain, Australia, and the Netherlands.

32 : South West Africa and Apartheid

African debates in the United Nations too often evoked the image of an angry man determinedly battering his head against a stone wall. Violent as the impact undoubtedly was, the wall did not come down but appeared to grow more solid from year to year. Almost the only African question that had seemed at times to hold out at least a possibility of constructive movement was the long-standing issue of the status of South West Africa, the one-time German territory that South Africa had been ruling since World War I, first as a League of Nations mandate and more recently through a widely questioned exercise of its own authority. The refusal of the South African Government to render an accounting of its stewardship to the United Nations, in conjunction with its gradual introduction into South West Africa of its own hated policies of *apartheid,* had by the mid-1960's convinced a growing majority of U.N. members that steps must be taken to relieve South Africa of any further responsibility in the territory and reassert the overriding authority of the international community.

An attempt at action through the International Court of Justice having proved inconclusive, the General Assembly on October 27, 1966 had adopted a far-reaching resolution in which it declared the mandate over South West Africa at an end, asserted that the territory henceforth came under the direct responsibility of the United Nations, and established a fourteen-nation Ad Hoc Committee "to recommend practical means by which South West Africa should be administered, so as to enable the people of the territory to exercise the right of self-determination and to achieve independence."[38] Not without misgivings, the United States had supported this resolution and later accepted membership on the Ad Hoc Committee, as did the U.S.S.R., Czechoslovakia, and other countries. The British and French governments, which would also have a vital role to play in the enforcement of any further decisions respecting South West Africa, had been even more doubtful about the wisdom and practicability of the proposed action and had refused to become involved.

Some of the doubts about the Assembly's decision had to do with legal questions and with the state of advancement of South West Africa's half-million or more inhabitants, whose experience under South African tutelage had offered little if any preparation for modern nationhood. A more immediate problem was presented by the attitude of South Africa itself, which was still in physical control of South West Africa and had given no indication that it would submit to dispossession at the hands of the U.N. Indeed, it seemed perfectly conceivable that South Africa would be willing to defend its position by force, should anyone be prepared to use force against it. The new U.N. committee would therefore face a particularly delicate task in trying to devise "practical means" of bringing South West Africa to independence in accordance with the Assembly's wishes.

An awareness of the difficulties of this assignment had been clearly evident in the January speech in which Ambassador Goldberg had dwelt so strongly on the need for "patient dialogue" with the South African Government and the finding of a "peaceful and practical solution . . . consistent with the General Assembly's resolution."[39] A comparable stress on "careful exploration and evaluation of all avenues to peaceful change" distinguished the remarks of U.S. Representative William P. Rogers at one of the early meetings of the Ad Hoc Committee, which also began its deliberations in the course of January.[40] Consistent with this cautious approach, the United States presently joined forces with Canada and Italy, two other committee members, in submitting a formal proposal that seemed to envisage a considerable lapse of time before South West Africa would actually become independent. For the moment, the three powers recommended merely the appointment of a special U.N. Representative, assisted by a Council, to gather information, establish contacts, and make recommendations to the General Assembly.

But there were other members of the committee who favored not only a more rapid emancipation of South West Africa but also a more forthright approach to the problem of possible South African resistance. The committee's four African members advocated that South West Africa be made fully independent, after a transitional period of U.N. administration, as early as mid-1968. South Africa, they further proposed, should simply be asked to withdraw from the territory and threatened with enforcement action through the Security Council if it refused. The idea of Security Council enforcement was also warmly supported by the U.S.S.R. and Czechoslovakia, although those governments went even beyond the African states and urged that South West Africa be made independent forthwith. Still another plan, supported by Mexico, Chile, and Japan, envisaged a temporary U.N. administration while an attempt was made to come to agreement with South Africa on the actual transfer.

None of these plans seemed very likely to fulfill the Assembly's declared purpose. South Africa still appeared quite unwilling to leave voluntarily, and would presumably have to be driven out by force if at all. Yet it was equally apparent that the United States and the other Western powers would be unwilling to sanction a resort to forceful measures and would find ways of defeating any proposal to this effect that might later be submitted to the Security Council. While the Ad Hoc Committee tiptoed around this central dilemma, South Africa complicated the situation still further by announcing plans to set up a self-governing, semiautonomous regime in Ovamboland, the extreme northern section of South West Africa encompassing nearly half the territory's overwhelmingly black population. No member of the committee regarded this extension of the *apartheid* principle as a satisfactory alternative to South West African independence. But since the committee could not agree on any positive proposal, there was nothing to do but acknowledge its failure and turn the issue back to the General Assembly, which was already scheduled to convene in special session to consider the Committee's recommendations.

As was to be foreseen, the problem which the Ad Hoc Committee had failed to resolve proved equally resistant to solution in the General Assembly itself. In an eight-week session that began on April 21—technically, the Assembly's Fifth Special Session—that body achieved a measure of agreement on the less controversial aspects of the problem but was once again obliged to sidestep the critical issue of how South African rule should be terminated. As in the Ad Hoc Committee, proposals looking to the use of force through the Security Council commanded solid backing from the African, Asian, and Communist countries; and, as in the committee, their adoption was prevented by the unwillingness of the Western governments, now joined by most Latin American states, to approve such extreme measures. In what was widely if erroneously viewed as a retreat from the comparatively "hard" position the United States had adopted the year before, Ambassador Goldberg continued to stress the importance of opening a "dialogue" with South Africa.[41] The anticolonial countries, although they had no confidence in this approach, could not fail to perceive that no resolution embodying their own views would pass the Assembly by the necessary two-thirds majority. In the end, all references to enforcement action were simply laid aside in the interests of passing at least the truncated resolution that was approved on May 19 by a vote of 85 to 2 (South Africa and Portugal), with the United States and 29 other countries abstaining in token of their continued misgivings.

By the terms of the May 19 resolution,[42] the Assembly established an eleven-nation U.N. Council for South West Africa which was to have the assistance of a Commissioner nominated by the Secretary-General. To this Council was assigned the not inconsiderable task of proceeding to South West Africa with a view to taking over the administration of the territory, ensuring the withdrawal of South African police and military forces and civilian personnel, and administering the territory until independence—which was, if possible, to be achieved by June 1968, a date some thirteen months off. Subsequently, on June 13, 1967, the Assembly elected the members of the new Council —most of them anticolonial nations, although none of the great powers was included—and accepted the nomination of Constantin A. Stavropoulos of the U.N. Secretariat as acting Commissioner.[43]

It was August before the new Council got around to holding its inaugural meeting. In accordance with the Assembly's instructions, its first move was to query the South African Government about its intentions and ask it to "kindly indicate the measures that the Government of South Africa proposes to facilitate the transfer of the administration of the Territory to [the Council]."[44] South Africa, however, had no intention whatever of turning over the territory to such a group. In a letter addressed to the Secretary-General on September 26, the South African Foreign Minister pointed out that his government regarded both of the Assembly's recent resolutions— that of October as well as that of May—as illegal and invalid.[45] So far from preparing to abandon the territory, South African authorities were going ahead with a variety of measures looking toward increased racial segregation. To the horror of much of the civilized world, they were also bringing to trial within South Africa a group of 37 (later 35) alleged South West African terrorists under a new law imposing a retroactive death penalty.

The efforts of the past year, it seemed, had been largely wasted, and the impasse between South Africa and the U.N. majority was firmer than ever. U Thant, for one, maintained in the introduction to his annual report that past measures had been insufficient and that "meaningful progress in decolonization in South West Africa can take place only if effective pressure is brought to bear by the Security Council."[46] Although the Secretary-General did not say whether he was thinking in terms of economic or military pressure, the demand for some form of effective action by the Security Council was plainly growing as the General Assembly convened for its regular autumn session.

Effective action through the Security Council, however, would still require the concurrence of the United States, Great Britain, and other permanent members whose unwillingness to support such action was already known. Undeterred by this negative outlook, the Assembly nevertheless adopted on December 16—by a vote of 93 to 2 (South Africa and Portugal), with many Western abstentions—a resolution calling on South Africa to withdraw from South West Africa without delay and requesting the Security Council to take unspecified but "effective" steps to enable the U.N. to fulfill its responsibilities.[47] With U.S. support, the Assembly also adopted a resolution denouncing the illegal arrest, deportation, and trial of the 37 alleged terrorists and appealing to all states and international organizations to assist in halting it.[48]

While waiting to take action on South West Africa, the Assembly had also voiced its usual condemnation of *apartheid* in South Africa itself. Prime Minister Vorster's campaign for peaceful coexistence and economic and technical cooperation with neighboring black-ruled countries had failed to mitigate the detestation in which South African internal policies were held, not only in black Africa but in most of the outside world. The United States, a long-time critic of South African racial policies, had been made even more sensitive to the unwholesome consequences of *apartheid* by a diplomatic contretemps earlier in the year when a fear of unpleasant incidents had denied the integrated crew of the aircraft carrier *Franklin D. Roosevelt* the opportunity to enjoy the hospitality of Capetown, thus causing needless offense to South Africans as well as much controversy at home.[49]

Most critics of *apartheid* agreed that the systematic denial of equality to South Africa's nonwhite inhabitants was creating a situation that contained the seeds of violent conflict in the future. Yet there still remained the familiar division of opinion as to what could or should be done about the situation. An arms embargo urged by the Security Council in 1964 had clearly failed to sway South Africa from its course, and a majority of the United Nations had gone on record in a General Assembly resolution of 1966 as declaring that "universally applied mandatory economic sanctions" now offered the only road to a peaceful solution of the problem.[50] The Western powers, however, had thus far declined to associate themselves with this view. The United States, as Mr. Goldberg had said in January, was still engaged on a search for "peaceful and practical means" of impressing upon the South African Government "the need for a policy of justice and equality for all its peoples."[51]

Under these circumstances, the course of the annual debate in the 1967 General Assembly could have been predicted in advance. The majority view was embodied in a resolution, approved December 13, which reiterated the conviction that the situation in South Africa constituted a threat to international peace and security and that "universally applied mandatory economic sanctions" were the only means of achieving a peaceful solution. Accordingly, the Security Council was asked to resume consideration of the question of *apartheid* "with a view to . . . the adoption of more effective measures" to end the practice.[52] Great Britain and the United States, whose economic ties with South Africa came in for the usual intensive criticism during the debate, reaffirmed their own abhorrence of racism but abstained from voting, as did a number of other Western states that had legal or political reservations concerning the majority draft. South Africa and Portugal, isolated but seemingly unshaken by the predictions of catastrophe to which their policies continued to give rise, once again voted "No" as they had habitually done at this and earlier Assembly sessions.

Unwilling as it was to risk an economic "confrontation" with South Africa, Great Britain had strictly maintained its embargo on arms sales to that country in conformity with the Security Council resolution of 1964. The financial difficulties which had just caused the devaluation of the pound had, however, given rise to considerable pressure for a relaxation of the arms ban, which had also been scrupulously maintained by the United States but was reportedly being breached by France. Putting principle ahead of interest, Prime Minister Wilson nevertheless announced shortly after the new U.N. resolution that the embargo would be maintained. In doing so, he ran an obvious risk of retaliation by the South African Government, which had provided the United Kingdom with certain naval facilities whose usefulness had if anything increased with the closure of the Suez Canal and the evaporation of Britain's Middle Eastern position. This risk, however, Britain's Labor government was still prepared to face.

33 : African Political Trends

The events of 1967 in other parts of Africa raised fewer issues of a sort to demand immediate American decision, although they obviously contributed to shaping the conditions in which American policy would operate in future years. For the United Arab Republic and the other Muslim countries of Northern Africa, the great event of the year was the six-day war between the Arab states and Israel, which excited Algeria to a frenzy of anti-Israeli and anti-Western feeling and occasioned scarcely less explosive reactions in the Sudan, Libya, Tunisia, and Morocco. While the Sudan considerably enhanced its diplomatic prestige through its sponsorship of the subsequent Khartoum conference of Arab leaders, Algeria's support of the "Palestinian" cause and its resistance to any compromise with Israel propelled it into an even more notable ascendency among the "revolutionary" Arab states. Undoubtedly inspired in part by the poor domestic record of the Boumedienne government, this militancy also helped to strengthen Algeria's already close association with the U.S.S.R. New shipments of Soviet arms were reported in the wake of the six-day war, and, as already noted, the subsequent disclosure that France was preparing to quit its Algerian naval and air base at Mers-el-Kebir raised some apprehension lest this facility be made available in support of Soviet Mediterranean ambitions. Algeria was also credited with putting pressure on Libya to oust the British and Americans from their military positions and adopt a more "revolutionary" line, although these efforts would seem to have had at best a rather moderate success.

Less directly involved in the Middle Eastern ferment were Tunisia, where President Habib Bourguiba remained a vigorous critic of Abdel Nasser's policies, and Morocco, whose disapproval of Washington's attitude toward Israel did not prevent it from signing a new $34 million U.S. food aid agreement in October. Increasingly dissatisfied with the scale of American military assistance, Morocco was now investigating other sources of supply and was reported to have obtained a few Soviet-designed tanks from Czechoslovakia, whose arms sales policies appeared poorly coordinated with those of the larger Communist power.[53]

In addition to its rivalry with Algeria, Morocco had long been embroiled with Spain over territorial questions, especially its claims to Spanish-ruled Ifni and Spanish Sahara. Reports of intermittent discussions with Madrid strengthened the impression that Spain was prepared to surrender the valueless Ifni but remained determined to keep the Spanish Sahara, whose rich phosphate deposits it hoped to develop with private American assistance. Generally, however, Spain's policy in Africa had taken the opposite course to that of Portugal and had emphasized the avoidance of trouble with the African anti-colonial movement. Partly as a result of U.N. pressure, Madrid had already agreed in principle to grant independence to the West African territory of Spanish Guinea (Río Muni and Fernando Po), although the date and modalities of the transfer were still being discussed with representatives from those territories.[54] In resolutions adopted at its autumn session, the General Assembly showed a certain impatience about delays in the decolonization of the Spanish territories but appeared disposed for the moment to give Spain the benefit of the doubt.[55]

Anticolonial pressures faced a stronger obstacle in French Somaliland, where nationalist disturbances in 1966 had determined General de Gaulle to hold a referendum in which the colony's 125,000 inhabitants would be asked to choose between remaining with France and becoming independent but sacrificing French aid. The town-dwelling Somalis, who represented about a third of the population and looked on the neighboring Somali Republic as their natural homeland, were strongly opposed to French rule and did their best to obstruct the referendum held on March 29, 1967. Nevertheless, French strong-arm tactics and the pro-French sentiments of the Afar nomads in the back country sufficed to produce a two-to-one majority favoring continued French administration. France thereafter moved to consolidate its position by expelling nonresident Somalis, setting up an all-Afar government council, and rechristening the colony "French Territory of the Afar and Issa." Though these proceedings aroused comparatively little protest at the time, the General Assembly later expressed regret at France's disregard for its opinions and repeated earlier admonitions to speed decolonization and grant Somali independence.[56]

The irredentist movement that centered in the Somali Republic had also been a source of major concern to Kenya and to Ethiopia, whose domestic tranquility was further disturbed in 1967 by nationalist agitation among the Muslims of Eritrea. In May, 1967, Kenya formally complained to the U.N. and the O.A.U. about Somali frontier harassment, which was estimated to have cost as many as 3,000 lives within the past four years. The situation was, however, alleviated soon afterward by a peaceful change of government in Somalia that deserves to rank among the most constructive African developments of the year. A new, moderate-minded administration headed by Prime Minister Muhammad Ibrahim Egal moved promptly to improve relations with Kenya and Ethiopia and also to lessen Somalia's one-sided dependence on Soviet economic and military aid. President Kaunda of Zambia was persuaded to mediate between Kenya and Somalia on behalf of the O.A.U., and, in one of that organization's outstanding political achievements, both countries agreed in October on a resumption of diplomatic relations and a renewed attempt to alleviate conditions on their common frontier.[57] Conversations were also initiated with Ethiopia in the hope of finding a solution consistent with the interests of both parties.

Another triumph for the regional principle as applied to East Africa was the decision of Kenya, Tanzania, and Uganda to try to rebuild and expand the regional economic system that had existed under the British but had largely broken down since independence. Such an effort would necessarily require a measure of economic sacrifice by Kenya, the most highly developed of the three; but in June the Presidents of the three countries signed a Treaty for East African Cooperation providing for the establishment of an East African Community and common market. By the time the new organization formally came into being on December 1, Somalia, Zambia, and Ethiopia had applied for membership and expressions of interest were being received from the Congo (Kinshasa), Burundi, and others.[58]

The new East African Community was the most advanced product of the regional movement so frequently stressed by the United States and also by the U.N. Economic Commission for Africa, which had blueprinted a series of four such groupings in East, West, North, and Central Africa. In West Africa, the regional principle had not so far been highly developed, but work on a draft agreement to set up a West African Economic Community was started following a fourteen-nation meeting in Dakar, Senegal, in November.

Political instability and local quarrels remained a serious impediment to consolidation in West Africa. Military coups in Togo, Sierra Leone, and Dahomey during 1967 eliminated all pretense of democratic government in three more African countries, while the threatened regime of President Jean-Bedel Bokassa in the Central African Republic was kept in power only by the intervention of French mobile units which had been specially groomed for such eventualities. In Ghana, on the other hand, conditions appeared to be moving back toward normalcy following the overthrow of the Nkrumah dictatorship in 1966. Guinean President Sékou Touré, aware of the shortcomings of the Soviet assistance on which he had largely relied in the past, seemed also to be seeking a more constructive path and belatedly attempting to mend his government's relations with France and with neighboring West African states.

While offering no major pronouncement on African policy during 1967, President Johnson continued to see as many African leaders as possible and to assure them of the unflagging American interest in their concerns. The Moroccan and Ethiopian rulers who had visited Washington early in 1967 were followed during the year by a succession of chief executives that included President Banda of Malawi, President Gregoire Kayibanda of Rwanda, President Felix Houphouet-Boigny of the Ivory Coast, Prime Minister Leabua Jonathan of Lesotho, President Hamani Diori of Niger, General Ankrah of Ghana, and President Ahmadou Ahidjo of Cameroon. In November it was announced that Vice-President Humphrey would be leaving at the end of 1967 to attend the sixth inaugural of Liberia's durable chief executive, President William V. S. Tubman, and would go on to visit seven other countries in West, East, and North Africa.[59]

Perhaps the most thoughtful comment on African trends in 1967 was that of Pope Paul VI, who departed from Vatican precedent by releasing on October 31 a special "Message to Africa" purporting to be addressed to Africans of all faiths and at all levels of society. Commending the predominantly "orderly and peaceful" emergence of 36 new African states since World War II, the Sovereign Pontiff at the same time expressed "great grief and concern over the disorders and the violence which have continued to trouble various African countries, causing sufferings and miseries, especially to unarmed peoples" and at times—as, presumably, in Nigeria—assuming "almost the proportions of genocide." Leaders and peoples alike, said Paul VI, must "resist the temptation to violence and . . . avoid and check the abuse of power"; and racism, both white and black, must also be condemned.[60] These, naturally, were counsels of perfection as applied to the Africa of 1967, or, for that matter, to other parts of the world. Yet surely they indicated the only way in which this youngest of the continents could begin to overcome its present turmoil and play the fruitful role of which it had once seemed capable.

7 : Around China's Rim

Critics of American policy in Vietnam were much addicted to complaining that President Johnson and his administration gave no consistent explanation for the increasingly costly and burdensome American effort there. At one moment, it was said, American soldiers were alleged to be fighting in Vietnam to demonstrate the sanctity of America's word and redeem the pledges of past administrations; at another, to safeguard the right of the South Vietnamese to choose their own form of government; or to prove that aggression and "might makes right" had no place in the modern world; or to refute the Communist assertion that "wars of national liberation" would bring about the downfall of the "imperialist system" and ensure the world-wide victory of Communism; or simply to defend American interests in a distant continent where countries whose security was important to the United States were threatened by the ambitions of predatory neighbors.

While there was certainly an air of prestidigitation about the way in which these varied formulas were manipulated by official spokesmen, there would have been less confusion had it been realized that they amounted not to a grab bag of alternative explanations but to different facets of a single explanation. Any intelligent observer could see that Southern and Eastern Asia were torn by sharply opposed political tendencies: on one hand, the dynamic and revolu-

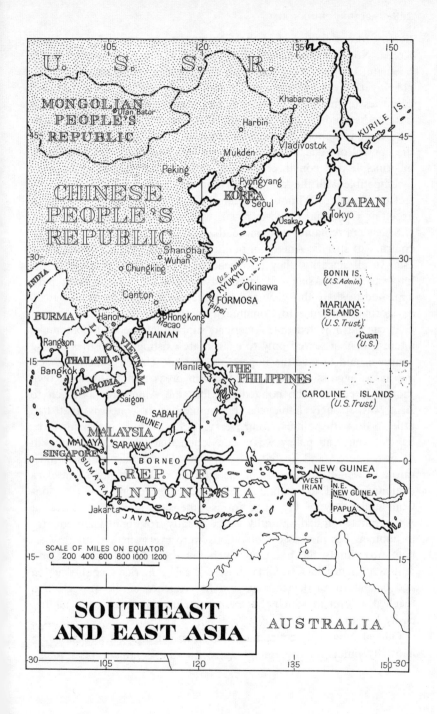

SOUTHEAST AND EAST ASIA

tionary forces embodied in the Communist regimes of China, North Korea, North Vietnam, and the National Liberation Front of South Vietnam; on the other, the more conservative, non-Communist, but not invariably unprogressive outlook that predominated in other countries of the area. In Washington, successive American administrations had judged it to be in the U.S. interest to oppose the Communist and support the non-Communist forces that were disputing the control of Asia. Most Americans were opposed to Communism in principle and convinced that its methods and ethical values were incompatible with the kind of world in which the United States could feel comfortable. Without deluding themselves about the chances of upsetting Communist rule in places where it was already established, U.S. leaders remained convinced that its further extension would be contrary to specific American political, strategic, and economic interests. In all sincerity, they also believed it would be contrary to the interests of the Asian peoples themselves—who, for the most part, appeared to share this view and in some cases had themselves put up a vigorous resistance to Communist encroachments.

It can be objected that American support of the non-Communist interest in Asia served only to exacerbate existing animosities in that continent and to give the impression that the United States was acting as an aggressively intrusive force in areas remote from its own shores. It can also be pointed out that the American approach to Asia was strongly influenced by humanitarian concerns that had little to do with political controversy. Yet, clearly, the driving force behind American policy was a conviction that the United States, in its own interest and in that of Asia's non-Communist peoples, must throw its weight on the side of the latter in so far as they themselves exhibited a will to maintain their independence and build a non-Communist way of life. The forms, intensity, and effectiveness of American action had naturally varied greatly from one Asian country to another, but the basic motivations were everywhere similar. Vietnam was simply the point at which, by the mid-1960's, the Communist pressure had become most critical, American counteraction had become most determined, and the violence of the struggle had reached a level at which the basic principles at stake were all too easily lost to view.

Official judgments concerning the American interest in Asia were naturally influenced by the presence on that continent of a major

Communist power whose animosity toward the United States and its Asian friends ("running dogs of imperialism," as it customarily called them) exceeded by far the antipathy to Communist China occasionally voiced within the United States. Whatever the United States attempted in Asia and the Western Pacific—in India or Pakistan, Indonesia or Malaysia, Vietnam, Taiwan, Japan, Korea, or, even further afield, in Australia or New Zealand—was influenced by a consciousness of China's actual and potential power, its radical hostility, and its increasing capacity for mischief. Countries like North Vietnam or North Korea would not in themselves have weighed so heavily in the American scale, whatever the respect their military performance might inspire in periods of open conflict. What really counted, even when the local Communist rulers appeared to differ with the men in Peking, was the Chinese power behind them.

Secretary Rusk put the matter with great succinctness in what, rather paradoxically, turned out to be one of 1967's most controversial foreign policy statements. "Within the next decade or two," Mr. Rusk observed at his October 12 news conference in answering a question about Vietnam and its bearing on American security, "there will be a billion Chinese on the mainland, armed with nuclear weapons, with no certainty about what their attitude toward the rest of Asia will be.

"Now, the free nations of Asia will make up at least a billion people. They don't want China to overrun them on the basis of a doctrine of world revolution. The militancy of China has isolated China, even within the Communist world, but they have not drawn back from it. They have reaffirmed it [in welcoming an Albanian delegation] as recently as . . . two days ago.

"Now, we believe that the free nations of Asia must brace themselves, get themselves set, with secure, progressive, stable institutions of their own, with cooperation among the free nations of Asia stretching from Korea and Japan right around to the subcontinent, if there is to be peace in Asia over the next ten or twenty years. We would hope that in China there would emerge a generation of leadership that would think seriously about what is called 'peaceful coexistence,' that would recognize the pragmatic necessity for human beings to live together in peace rather than on a basis of continuing warfare.

"Now, from a strategic point of view, it is not very attractive to think of the world cut in two by Asian Communism reaching out through Southeast Asia and Indonesia, which we know has been their objective, and that these hundreds of millions of people in the free nations of Asia should be under the deadly and constant pressure of the authorities in Peking, so that their future is circumscribed by fear.

"Now, these are vitally important matters to us, who are both a Pacific and an Atlantic power. After all, World War II hit us from the Pacific, and Asia is where two-thirds of the world's people live. So we have a tremendous stake in the ability of the free nations of Asia to live in peace; and to turn the interests of people in mainland China to the pragmatic requirements of their own people and away from a doctrinaire and ideological adventurism abroad. . . .

"That does not mean that we ourselves have nominated ourselves to be the policemen for all of Asia. . . . But we have our part; we have accepted a share, and we have accepted that share as part of the vital national interest of the United States. . . ."[1]

It is indicative of the way in which the Vietnam war had disoriented the normal processes of American political thought that so lucid an exposé could be denounced as an appeal to racist emotions reminiscent of the long discredited "Yellow Peril" doctrine. Not only was Mr. Rusk's statement free from racist overtones; it was noticeably open-minded in its insistence on the hope of an eventual modification of Chinese political attitudes. Though his insistence on the necessity of resisting Chinese external ambitions elicited scant applause in the American atmosphere of October 1967, it was difficult for cooler observers to discount entirely his assertion that a nuclear-armed China would represent a prima facie threat to the security of neighboring countries. Right or wrong, his statement is likely to stand out as one of the more successful attempts to articulate the underlying assumptions of American policy in Vietnam and throughout Asia.

The actions prompted by these assumptions in Vietnam itself, where the United States had spared neither life, wealth, nor reputation in its determination to prevent a Communist conquest, have been examined at some length in an earlier chapter. This chapter will review more briefly the salient aspects of American policy "from Korea and Japan . . . around to the subcontinent," attempting at the same time to convey some notion of the internal confusion that tempered Communist China's impact on the life of neighboring countries in 1967. The discussion will focus primarily on the development among the non-Communist Asian nations of a sense of common interest inspired, in considerable measure, by the example of anti-Communist resistance in Vietnam and the perception of comparable dangers affecting other Asian countries.

34 : Stagnation in the Subcontinent

The ambitions imputed to Asia's Communist governments had not, on the whole, aroused great or sustained interest in India or Pakistan. More concerned with their own religious, territorial, and political antagonisms than with the larger dangers allegedly threatening from beyond the Himalayas, both of those large and populous nations had tended in the main to stand aside from regional efforts with an anti-Communist political tendency. Pakistan, it is true, had been a founding member of the Southeast Asian and Central Treaty Organizations (SEATO and CENTO), established in 1954 and 1955 respectively; but though it still retained nominal membership in both alliances, it no longer showed much interest in Western-sponsored collective defense schemes and on the whole displayed a rather warmer feeling toward Communist China than toward its British and American allies. India, as befitted the originator of the doctrine of nonalignment, had held aloof from "military blocs" on principle and persisted in this attitude despite the cooling of its friendship with Communist China and the Chinese invasion of a part of its territory in 1962. In view of these attitudes, it was not to be expected that either India or Pakistan should show much eagerness to join in any of the rudimentary regional organizations which, with American encouragement, had recently begun to emerge among the nations of Southeast Asia and the Pacific.

Of more immediate concern to the two subcontinental powers were the problems left over from their bitter but inconclusive war over Kashmir in the summer of 1965. At a Soviet-sponsored conference in Tashkent in January 1966, both governments had agreed to withdraw their forces from each other's territory and make a new attempt at peaceful coexistence. Since that time there had been no further clashes of importance, but equally little progress toward solution of the major problems that divided the two countries. Pakistan's sense of alienation from the West, fed since 1962 by the American and British policy of furnishing arms to India to aid its defense against China, had been further aggravated by a cutoff of major arms shipments to both countries at the time of the war of 1965. India, since the death of Prime Minister Lal Bahadur Shastri and his replacement by Mrs. Indira Gandhi at the beginning of 1966, had been a prey to growing domestic turbulence and to near-famine conditions resulting from unfavorable weather and other factors. Despite substantial grain shipments from the United States and a few other countries, another bad harvest in 1966 had raised the specter of widespread hunger in 1967 unless ways could be found of meeting a new grain deficit estimated at 10 million tons.

The renewed threat of famine in India presented one of the more urgent challenges to American policy at the outset of 1967. Thus far, the United States had experienced little difficulty in providing both the grain and the ships to meet the greater part of India's emergency needs. There had, however, been much delay and uncertainty because of Washington's reluctance to grant assistance without conditions, its desire to secure the participation of other grain-exporting nations in a genuinely multilateral food aid program for India's benefit, and, above all, its insistence that India itself take steps to increase the productivity of its agricultural economy in order to avoid the recurrence of such emergencies. Reasonable as they appeared in Washington, such stipulations and the manner in which they were implemented had already bred considerable resentment in New Delhi and gone far to cancel out the beneficial political effects of the U.S. assistance.

Just what solution the United States envisaged for the new food crisis facing India in 1967 was not revealed until as late as February 2, when President Johnson at length presented to Congress a series of recommendations designed to provide 6.6 million of the needed 10 million tons of grains. With 1.6 million tons already "in the pipeline" under earlier authorizations, the President explained, he was allocating another 2 million tons immediately and asking Congress to approve the shipment of a further 3 million tons, valued at $190 million, during the balance of the year. These shipments, he added, would be made available only on the condition that they were "appropriately matched" by other countries. Furthermore, they would be counted as part of the U.S. contribution to Indian economic development through the aid consortium organized by the World Bank.[2] Congress having signified its assent,[3] the President allocated a further 1.5 million tons in May and still another 1 million in September, in spite of evidence that the performance of other countries was not coming up to expectations.[4] Although the shipments failed to avert considerable suffering in parts of India, the gathering of a bumper harvest in 1967 held out the hope that the need for American assistance would be substantially reduced in 1968. A new agreement concluded at the end of the year did, however, provide for the shipment of a further 3.5 million tons of American food grains through June 1968.[5] Pakistan, meanwhile, had benefited by two successive agreements with the United States covering the shipment of 1.5 million tons to help meet its less critical situation.[6]

Political conditions in India had meanwhile deteriorated alarmingly. The general elections held on February 15-21, the fifth since India's independence, resulted in a shattering rebuff for the governing Congress party, which suffered a sharp reduction in its parliamentary majority and at least temporarily lost political control in eight of India's seventeen states. Mrs. Gandhi somehow clung to the Premiership, but her influence within her own party was seriously shaken and it was all she could do to secure the later election of Zakir Hussain, a Muslim, to succeed the retiring Sarvepalli Radhakrishnan as President of the Indian Republic. One of the few redeeming features in an otherwise thoroughly unhappy situation was the inability of Indian Communists to capitalize on the prevalent disorder in view of their own division into stridently pro-Chinese and pro-Soviet factions.

Other developments in the subcontinent did little to alleviate the gloom in which Washington perused the election results. Temporarily halted in 1965, the arms race south of the Himalayas was clearly reviving again. Pakistan had for some time been getting tanks and planes from China to replace the American equipment lost in the recent war. India, in turn, had obtained some new military equipment from the U.S.S.R.; and the United States had been greatly perplexed as to when and on what terms it should resume its own arms aid in the subcontinent. Not wishing to see the two rivals come to blows again or to favor one of them above the other, Washington was equally reluctant to see either of them moving toward dependence on a Communist power. Torn by these conflicting apprehensions, it announced in April a decision that infuriated both India and Pakistan. The United States, the State Department disclosed, had simply decided to provide no more grant military aid to either country and would limit itself in future to supplying spare parts for the equipment they already had.[7]

India was particularly irritated by this decision because its own need for American spare parts was not great and it consequently felt that the new policy would work to the advantage of Pakistan. But Pakistan, already disillusioned with its Western ties, found no reason to applaud a decision that barred the acquisition of heavy U.S. military equipment and would tend to increase its dependence on Communist sources. Indicative of Pakistan's growing coolness toward the United States was its later request for the withdrawal of Peace Corps volunteers on the ground that it required more "sophisticated" assistance. No comparable shadows marked the subsequent visit of President Muhammad Ayub Khan to the Soviet Union, where it was agreed to draw up a plan for increased economic cooperation and trade during the period ending in 1975.[8]

As a Muslim country, Pakistan naturally supported the Arab side in the Middle East war and found considerable fault with American attempts to maintain an "evenhanded" policy as between Israel and the Arab states. More surprising, and even more prejudicial to relations with Washington, was India's equally strong support of the U.A.R. and opposition to Israel both during the war and afterward. Mrs. Gandhi's reference to the embattled Abdel Nasser as a "force for progress"[9] earned scant approval in the United States; nor did it prevent the Egyptian leader himself from subsequently delaying the arrival of much-needed grain shipments in India through his insistence on maintaining the closure of the Suez Canal. Though obviously not prompted by an expectation of material reward, Mrs. Gandhi's adherence to the Arab-Soviet line in the Middle East presumably made a favorable impression on the Soviet Government, which later promised a contribution of 500 million rubles ($550 million) in support of India's Fourth Five-Year Plan covering the period 1966-70.[10]

Trouble between India and China was also building up again as the xenophobe trend in China's "Cultural Revolution" became more marked. In June, Peking's expulsion and harassment of two Indian diplomats accused of spying was followed by several days of mob attacks and unofficial sieges directed against the Indian Embassy in Peking and the Chinese Embassy in New Delhi. By September, shooting incidents along China's border with the Indian protectorate of Sikkim were raising fears of a new Chinese invasion. Although this threat evaporated with the advent of cold weather, there seemed no end to India's internal troubles. Food riots, language riots, religious riots trod on each other's heels. In November, Calcutta and the state of West Bengal, where neither the Congress party nor the leftist United Front had been able to govern effectively, were gripped by a sharp political crisis and general strike whose outcome was undecided at the year's end.

There were undoubtedly positive elements in the Indian situation —sporadic industrial growth, a slow improvement in agriculture, the gradual acceptance of "family planning" as a means of coping with India's gigantic population problem. Yet for every hopeful sign there seemed a dozen motives for discouragement in the writhings of this vast and turbulent land. Its growing political disarray could only sharpen the contrast with Pakistan's apparent political stability and impressive economic growth. American assistance to India over the twenty years since independence had, no doubt, helped it gain time for further struggle with an almost superhuman array of problems. But it began to seem as if the first twenty years of India's independent history had been essentially inconclusive. The really decisive years might still lie ahead.

35 : The Zone of Consolidation

That a more hopeful trend could be discerned among the non-Communist nations of the Far East and the Pacific was one of the few points on which the American administration and its critics appeared in general agreement during 1967. Ever since the autumn of 1965, when the failure of an attempted Communist coup in Indonesia had paved the way for the establishment of a progressive-minded military government marked by strongly anti-Communist and even pro-Western leanings, there had been indications that a majority of the countries in this part of the world were recovering from past uneasiness about advancing Communism, becoming less inclined to impute sinister motives to the United States, and gaining in strength, determination, and readiness to cooperate with one another.

President Johnson, whose visit to seven Pacific nations in the fall of 1966 had done much to publicize the new trend, returned to what had become a favorite theme in his 1967 State of the Union message. "One result of our stand in Vietnam is already clear," the President declared. ". . . The peoples of Asia now know that the door to independence is not going to be slammed shut. . . . The performance of our men in Vietnam—backed by the American people—has created a feeling of confidence and unity among the independent nations of Asia and the Pacific. . . . For the first time in history, a common outlook and common institutions are already emerging. . . . Asians are engaged tonight in regional efforts in a dozen new directions. Their hopes are high. Their faith is strong. Their confidence is deep."[11]

While it was natural for the administration to make the most of any favorable trend at a time of widespread discouragement concerning Vietnam,[12] the generally positive character of developments in Eastern Asia was acknowledged even by those who differed with important aspects of American policy. Professor Edwin O. Reischauer, a former Ambassador to Japan who testified in January before the Senate Foreign Relations Committee, echoed at least some of Mr. Johnson's optimistic language. "However slow the progress in most of Asia," he said, "the general movement, I feel, is upward economically and toward more viable political and social systems. The threat of unitary world Communism sweeping Asia has largely faded, and the menace of Chinese domination—if ever it was a real menace in the military sense—is growing weaker. Almost all of the countries of Asia are gaining in national cohesiveness and in confidence. In some areas there has been encouraging progress toward the development of a healthy sense of regional cooperation. Some of these things may be happening because of our Vietnam stance, but fundamentally they are happening for other more basic reasons and in some cases despite our stand in Vietnam. If the present Vietnam crisis can be resolved without either great escalation or a headlong retreat by the United States, I believe that we can count on the situation in Asia continuing slowly to improve, rather than to deteriorate."[13]

The war in Vietnam had undeniably complicated the destinies of all the countries in this extensive region. The idea of actually fighting Communism alongside South Vietnam and the United States had offered scant attraction even to those few countries whose governments had found it to be necessary in their own national interest. Australia and New Zealand, it is true, could claim that their participation in the conflict had the broad backing of national opinion as registered in their general elections of late 1966. For Thailand, the Philippines, and South Korea, the extent of public backing was more doubtful and the risks of participation had in some ways been greater. By the winter of 1966-67, all three of these Asian countries were being subjected to Communist pressures at home which could be viewed at least in part as a form of retaliation for their association with the anti-Communist effort in Vietnam.

Thailand, whose military-dominated government had seldom wavered from its stanchly anti-Communist and pro-American stand, had been providing bases for American air operations in Laos and Vietnam ever since 1964. By the beginning of 1967, it was playing host to over 35,000 U.S. troops and was represented in Vietnam itself by a 300-man support unit, to be followed later in the year by a battalion of combat troops and eventually by a full division. As already noted, the Bangkok government further agreed in April to the stationing of a number of B-52 bombers on its territory for more effective operation against nearby Vietnamese targets. The importance of these contributions was profusely acknowledged by Secretary Rusk and by the President himself, who entertained King Bhumibol Adulyadej on an official visit to Washington in June.[14] Less gratifying, though not as yet considered a cause for serious alarm, was the fact that Thailand itself was contending with a low-grade, Chinese-backed insurgency, mainly in the northeastern provinces bordering on Laos, which had tended to increase in scale as the Thai involvement in Vietnam deepened.

The Philippines, which had sent a 2,200-man military engineering unit to Vietnam, faced a comparable distraction in a revival of the Communist-led Hukbalahap insurgency which had been active in Central Luzon in the early postwar years. Supposedly quelled by the late President Ramón Magsaysay in the mid-1950's, the Huks were once again on the warpath and causing evident concern to President Marcos and his administration. As in Thailand, there were sociological explanations for what was, at bottom, a movement of land-hungry peasants; yet it seemed not to be entirely a coincidence that it should flare up at just the moment when the Philippine Government had become engaged in combating Communism overseas.

The Republic of Korea, whose 45,000 combat troops represented a much larger contribution to the Vietnam enterprise, was also contending with intensified Communist pressure along the heavily guarded military demarcation line that separated it from Communist North Korea. Since the fall of 1966 there had been repeated incursions by North Korean troops and infiltrators within and south of the Demilitarized Zone, and a number of casualties had been sustained among the South Korean forces and among the 50,000 U.S. troops who still manned a part of the line under the United Nations flag. No serious threat to South Korean survival had yet been seen in these attacks, however, and in other respects the United States could take considerable pride in the achievements of the small American-backed republic.[15] South Korea's economic resurgence in the past few years had been truly impressive, and the orderly reelection of President Chung Hee Park on May 3 could be viewed as a mark of equal maturity in political affairs, though this impression was somewhat clouded a month later by the disorder that accompanied and followed elections to the South Korean National Assembly.

More varied conditions prevailed among the nations that had avoided—or at least tried to avoid—direct involvement in the Vietnam conflict. In Laos and Cambodia, Vietnam's closest neighbors, these efforts at noninvolvement had been fundamentally unsuccessful. Laos, contrary to the clear intent of the Geneva agreements of 1962,[16] had itself remained a theater of civil war in which the U.S.-supported government of Prince Souvanna Phouma was under attack not only by insurgents of the Communist-led Pathet Lao but also by North Vietnamese regular troops, whose main mission appeared to be the protection of the infiltration routes running from North to South Vietnam. Unpublicized Laotian cooperation with the United States in bombing the infiltration routes had served to attract the anger of the Communists without, apparently, substantially reducing this illicit traffic.

Cambodia was also heavily involved in the Vietnamese hostilities in virtue of its position next to the battle zone and the freedom with which, in spite of official denials, its territory appeared to be used as a sanctuary by Vietcong and North Vietnamese forces. The attitude of Prince Norodom Sihanouk, Cambodia's chief of state, was just the opposite of Souvanna Phouma's. Instead of cooperating with the Americans in trying to keep his territory free of intruders, he stoutly maintained that the only intruders were the Americans themselves and their South Vietnamese confederates. Prince Sihanouk obviously did not desire a Communist future for his country, and carried out elaborate political maneuvers designed to prove his independence of all the great powers, including China. But though his basic aspirations seemed not to differ from those the United States professed to be fighting for, his deep suspicion of American motives aggravated every friction and in recent years had precluded even the most rudimentary cooperation.

Direct preoccupation with the Vietnam situation tended to diminish with the distance from the theater of operations. Burma, under General Ne Win's military government, was still maintaining its policy of self-insulation from every form of regional concern. Indonesia, for its part, was still immersed in the agonizing problem of what to do with President Sukarno, the flamboyant, Communist-influenced chief of state who had led it into such deep water before the 1965 coup and still remained as a distracting center of controversy and an impediment to reconstruction. In March, 1967, Indonesia's military rulers finally responded to massive popular pressure by stripping Sukarno of his remaining powers and vesting all executive authority in General Suharto, the head of the military government, who assumed the title of Acting President. Concurrently, provisional arrangements for managing the country's towering external indebtedness were worked out with its principal Western creditors, and the effort to reestablish cooperative relations with neighboring Malaysia and Singapore, the objects of Sukarno's ill-fated "confrontation" policy, was given new impetus.[17]

Singapore and Malaysia, which had only recently split after an unsuccessful attempt at political union, were preoccupied not only with the reconstruction of their own relationship but with Great Britain's impending reduction of its defense forces in the Far East, which centered on the great base at Singapore. Like Australia, New Zealand, and the United States, these two Southeast Asian governments would have greatly preferred the retention of a permanent British "military presence" in the area; but they were already aware that some reductions were in the offing and that their security would in future have to be based on broader arrangements. One result of this prospect had been the emergence of more tolerant views about the Far Eastern role of the United States. Prime Minister Lee Kuan Yew of Singapore, a vigorous critic of U.S. attitudes and actions in the past, appeared to have tempered his suspicions and now admitted the need for American power to balance the power of Communist China. On several occasions the leftist but anti-Communist Mr. Lee indicated that he personally would welcome a permanent American military presence in the area and quite realized the importance of preventing a Communist victory in Vietnam.[18] Some well-placed American observers inferred that such sentiments were more widely prevalent than other non-Communist statesmen thought fit to acknowledge in public.[19]

Japan and the Republic of China on Formosa (Taiwan) had, in different ways, relied on U.S. military protection over a much longer period. Both governments had had their differences with Washington, but both seemed basically favorable to a continuance of their American ties. Formosa, at this time of upheaval on the Chinese mainland, had little attention to spare for other matters, although its leaders showed no intention of violating their promises to the United States by attempting a reinvasion of continental China. In May, Nationalist Vice-President and Prime Minister C. K. Yen visited Washington, heard a lecture on Asian cooperation, and was assured by the President that the United States remained firmly committed to the defense of Taiwan as well as the upholding of the Republic of China's rights in the United Nations.[20]

The Japanese-American relationship was more complex, as befitted the status of the two most populous and highly developed among the non-Communist Pacific nations. Though largely dependent on the United States for the assurance of its external security, Japan had preferred a more neutral course in foreign affairs and had held aloof from Vietnamese commitments even while stressing its eagerness to help in arranging a peace. In other respects, Japan showed growing interest in playing a responsible, independent role in world affairs, particularly through economic and technical cooperation with other Asian and Pacific nations. This trend, indeed, could be ranked with the recent political overturn in Indonesia as one of the main impulses behind the spirit of Asian regionalism that was now so much in evidence.

The basic stability of Japanese foreign policy seemed further assured by the outcome of the parliamentary elections held on January 29, in which the ruling Liberal Democratic party of Premier Eisaku Sato retained its absolute majority in the Lower House although, as always, it fell far short of the two-thirds majority that would be needed to modify Japan's pacifist constitution and prepare the country for wider defense responsibilities. The continuing strength of the Liberal Democrats and the poor showing of the neutralist-minded Socialists were thought to augur well for the continuance of the basic U.S.-Japan Security Treaty even beyond 1970, the date when it would be open to denunciation by either party. There were, however, a number of bilateral questions—notably the continuing U.S. occupation of Okinawa and the other Ryukyu Islands—on which the Japanese felt strongly and which would presumably have to be adjusted in the meantime if a healthy relationship was to be preserved. (See further Section 37.)

Cooperative endeavors that involved a shifting cast of Asian and Pacific nations went forward unspectacularly throughout the early months of 1967. There were occasional snags, among them a reduction in projected U.S. support for the U.N.'s Mekong River development scheme because of Washington's reluctance to finance projects in Cambodia.[21] But promising new enterprises were also getting under way, particularly the $1.1-billion Asian Development Bank which the United States had done much to bring into being and which was now beginning operations in Manila.[22] In April, there was a general discussion of Asia's economic outlook at the Tokyo meeting of the U.N. Economic Commission for Asia and the Far East (ECAFE), at which equal stress was laid on the need to accelerate economic growth and the importance of working in common toward that end.[23] Also in April, there took place in Washington three successive meetings of countries actively concerned with Pacific and Southeast Asian security: the annual session of the SEATO Council, meeting for the first time without France; a similar meeting of the tripartite ANZUS Council; and a special meeting of representatives of the "Manila powers," the seven countries that were actually fighting the Communists in Vietnam and whose leaders had held a "summit" meeting in Manila in October 1966. Inevitably, it was the Vietnam situation that occupied the foreground in all of these meetings, the results of which have been noted in an earlier chapter.[24]

More novel interest surrounded a meeting held in Manila at the end of May between representatives of the Philippines, Malaysia, and Thailand, the governments that had joined in 1961 to form the economic and cultural grouping known as the Association of Southeast Asia (ASA). This small organization had all but gone under during the time when Indonesia was quarrelling with its neighbors, and its member governments were quite aware of its limitations now that Indonesia was again eager to become a participant in regional schemes. The principal result of the Manila discussions was a recognition of the desirability of a wider Southeast Asian association in which Indonesia and Singapore could also be included.[25] Action along these lines would not be long delayed.

Still other Asian meetings were in prospect; but meanwhile the Pacific skies were darkening ominously. On April 27, after a rapid visit to the Far East, Defense Minister Denis Healey confirmed Great Britain's determination to reduce its forces in Singapore and Malaysia from 50,000 to 30,000 in the next year and to make further withdrawals thereafter. However necessary from a British financial standpoint, such a prospect was deeply disturbing to Britain's friends in the Far East and could only accelerate the trend toward greater dependence on the United States, the one remaining non-Communist great power in the Pacific. Australia's new Prime Minister, Harold Holt, had already read the signs of the times and beaten a well-worn path to Washington as well as moving to consolidate Australia's relations with its Pacific neighbors. On a further visit to the President in June, Mr. Holt offered fresh evidence that his government had become the most understanding and determined supporter of U.S. policy in the Pacific.[26]

Another cloud in the Far Eastern heavens was the increasingly menacing behavior of Communist China in these weeks of growing tension that was soon to explode in the war in the Middle East. To the continuing Communist harassment of Thailand, the Philippines, and Korea were being added an increasing number of instances of direct and violent Chinese pressure on neighboring countries. Chinese mob attacks and harassment of foreign embassies and diplomatic personnel, initially employed against the Soviet Union in January and February, were extended in April to Indonesia and in June to India. British authorities in Hong Kong were plagued from early May onward by an interminable series of violent, Communist-fomented demonstrations. As the temperature mounted, Peking produced a further sensation by announcing on June 17 the explosion of its first hydrogen bomb, an achievement full of sinister meaning for any country within range of China's still rudimentary air and missile force. There could have been no stronger reminder that Chinese developments would continue to influence the Asian future at least as profoundly as the constructive efforts from which the United States now drew such encouragement.

36 : Disturber of the Peace

Future historians will face no more difficult task than the determination of what exactly was going on in China during these months—or, for that matter, throughout the period of the "Great Proletarian Cultural Revolution" that seems to have begun as early as the autumn of 1965. Such knowledge as seeped to the outside world, though abundant in some respects, was too fragmentary and too fraught with contradictions to permit more than tentative inferences. What seemed at the time of greatest importance to outsiders was the fact that China's internal convulsion was not only limiting its role in current world affairs but greatly damaging its public "image" and international reputation through the peculiarly offensive kinds of behavior to which it gave rise.

This did not mean that China had wholly ceased to count as a factor on the international scene, still less that the outcome of its internal struggles could be of anything but decisive importance for the future of Asia and the world. It did mean that international events in 1967 were only marginally influenced by Chinese developments, and that the attitude of the Peking regime could to some extent be discounted as a factor in immediate policy decisions. It was largely for this reason that the United States felt able to step up its air war against North Vietnam and bomb closer and closer to the Chinese frontier with relatively little fear of Chinese retaliation.

At least some aspects of the Chinese internal struggle were clearer in 1967 than they had been in 1966, when the Cultural Revolution first forced itself on world attention. What Mao Tse-tung and his adherents were obviously engaged upon was an all-out struggle to defend the purity of "Marxist-Leninist" revolutionary traditions against the "revisionist" tendencies—i.e., the pragmatic trend toward moderation and compromise—that had taken command in the U.S.S.R. and Eastern Europe and, apparently, made large inroads in China's own Communist apparatus. Associated with Chairman Mao in his attack on ideological backsliding were such leading figures as

Vice-Chairman and Defense Minister Lin Piao, the presumed heir to Mao's authority, and Chen Po-ta, the official leader of the Cultural Revolution. The chief offenders among the opposite faction—those accused of "taking the capitalist road" and pursuing a "bourgeois-reactionary line"—were repeatedly identified as President Liu Shao-chi and Party Secretary Teng Hsiao-ping. For months on end these leaders and their associates were denounced and vilified with all the resources of official publicity. Instead of being arrested, tried, or liquidated, however, they apparently still clung to their official position and spun their "counterrevolutionary intrigues" while waiting for the pendulum to swing in their direction.

Up to the end of 1966, the Maoist assault on "revisionism" had been mainly confined to verbal propaganda, with little violence apart from the roughhousing of the teenage "Red Guards" whose help the Maoists had ill-advisedly invoked in the endeavor to cow their opponents and discredit traditional Chinese loyalties. In 1967, the struggle was to assume more violent forms. By the turn of the year, reports from Nanking, Shanghai, and other centers were beginning to tell of bloody clashes between Red Guard detachments and industrial workers and similar "counterrevolutionary" elements. Some of these encounters would seem to have gone badly from a Maoist standpoint. Although the Chinese Army had thus far stood aloof from the struggle, it was instructed late in January to abandon its neutrality and pitch in on the side of the "revolutionary masses"—i.e., the Maoists. From that point onward the situation dissolved into virtual chaos. In some areas, the Army supported the Maoists, as instructed; in others, it appeared to be making common cause with the opposition. The Red Guard movement itself began to splinter as different Red Guard factions clashed with each other in many districts.

As the disorder spread and the Maoists cast about for more effective means of asserting their authority, it became increasingly evident that their only chance of regaining control was to compromise with at least the more moderate opposition elements. Thanks largely to the cool-headed maneuvers of Premier Chou En-lai, a lonely pragmatist among the ideologues, by March the Maoists appeared to have ridden out the worst of the storm and gained an opportunity to set about the reestablishment of order. The lull, however, was short-lived. Chairman Mao himself still seemed to repudiate any notion of compromise, and attacks on his political opponents were soon resuming with redoubled fury. Almost every day a new revolt was reported from Inner Mongolia, Szechwan, or some other outlying region. A major crisis occurred in July when three Maoist emissaries were briefly detained by oppositionists in the industrial city of Wuhan, where government control was very imperfectly reestablished in the following weeks. In August, even worse trouble was reported from Canton and elsewhere in southern China. Opposing military units fought with tanks in the streets of Canton, and loyal troops sent in from the north were only partially effective in reimposing order.

By early September, Chairman Mao and his adherents appeared to have realized the imperative need to put a stop to factional fighting, curb the Red Guards and other "ultra-left" extremists, take steps to reopen the schools and universities, and try to revive economic activity and recoup the production losses of recent months. With Army assistance, a determined drive was now launched to reestablish order and discipline and stabilize the country. Disorder was still rife as the regime marked its eighteenth anniversary on October 1, but in the following weeks it gradually became apparent that the Cultural Revolution was moving into a more moderate phase even though its basic goals appeared unchanged and its opponents persisted in their defiance.

Of China's foreign relations during this period it can only be said that they provided a cacophanous accompaniment to the internal struggle but gave little evidence of any broad political design. In its essentials, Chinese foreign policy remained extremely cautious and carefully shunned the risks of outright conflict. At the same time, it displayed an unbridled aggressiveness and a total lack of inhibition in violating the ordinary decencies of international behavior.

Perhaps the nearest approach to a coherent foreign policy move was the campaign of mob violence and external pressure against the Portuguese territory of Macao that had begun in late 1966 and culminated on January 29, 1967 in the imposition of a series of humiliating conditions that virtually established the local Communist Chinese as the supreme authority on this isolated bit of Portuguese soil. Here, at least, the Chinese gained some sort of tangible advantages; whereas the repeated mob attacks on foreign diplomatic establishments and the continuing unruliness of Chinese personnel abroad appeared to serve no useful purpose except to feed the appetite for violence that was sustaining the Maoist offensive within China. As already noted, resort to such tactics began in January with anti-Soviet manifestations by Chinese students who were returning home via Moscow to take part in the Cultural Revolution. The mob harassment of the Soviet Embassy in Peking that followed these disturbances was repeated in April against the Indonesian Embassy and its personnel, this time in retaliation against anti-Chinese rioting in Indonesia. In June it was India's turn, with a Chinese siege of the Indian Embassy in Peking matched by an unofficial Indian siege of the Chinese Embassy in New Delhi. Burma, where there had also been rioting against local Chinese, escaped attacks on its embassy but none the less incurred the wrath of the Chinese leaders, who seemed to feel no hesitation in breaking with one of China's few remaining friends in Asia. The Chinese economic aid program in Burma was discontinued early in July, and by August the Chinese party Central Committee was openly calling for the overthrow of the Ne Win regime.

The intensity of these manifestations varied with the ups and downs of the Chinese internal struggle, reaching a peak in July and August when the turmoil in China was at its height. The terrorist offensive in Hong Kong, initiated in May but met with firm police action by the British authorities, was officially taken up by the Peking regime at the end of June. A series of official protests to the British Government was climaxed by an "ultimatum" and, on August 22, the invasion and destruction of the British Chancery in Peking by Red Guards and other disorderly elements. Conditions during the next few days were extremely tense as the British stood by for a possible Chinese move to take over Hong Kong. No such move occurred, however, and the situation gradually eased as the pace of the Cultural Revolution slackened from September onward.

In the meantime, however, there had been a new attack on the Soviet Embassy in Peking on August 17, ostensibly in protest against the anti-Chinese behavior of Soviet seamen whose vessel was being detained at a Manchurian port. With Italy, there was a diplomatic crisis over propagandist displays by visiting Chinese vessels; and lesser frictions occurred with the Mongolian People's Republic, Kenya, and others. In September, military clashes along the Sikkim border revived the fear of open hostilities with India. Even Cambodia, normally one of China's most tractable neighbors, complained of Chinese interference in its internal affairs and, in mid-September, was on the point of recalling its diplomatic mission when Prince Sihanouk was dissuaded by a soothing message from Chou En-lai.

The United States, which had never established diplomatic relations with China's Communist regime, was spared direct involvement in such incidents. The long-established, intermittent contacts between the U.S. and Chinese Ambassadors in Warsaw continued normally during 1967 and, presumably, were especially useful in alerting the Chinese to the limited significance of U.S. military moves in Vietnam. Without such a channel of communication, President Johnson could hardly have extended the bombing of North Vietnam with such confidence "that Peking knows the United States does not seek to widen the war."[27] In addition, the readiness of the United States to maintain these contacts presumably served as an indirect assurance to the Chinese that Washington had no intension of trying to profit by China's internal turmoil by launching hostile actions against it.

Yet the atmosphere in China was obviously far from conducive to the establishment of unofficial Sino-American ties in cultural and other fields, such as the United States had unsuccessfully sought to encourage during 1966. The only new U.S. initiative along these lines —an offer to permit the shipment of American drugs to combat epidemics reported raging in China—was contemptuously rejected in Peking.[28] Professor Reischauer and other Far Eastern experts continued to warn against alarmist views concerning China and to insist that a basis for coexistence must eventually be found. Members of the Johnson administration also continued to express the hope for an eventual improvement in Sino-American relations. China, however, seemed more than ever averse to any accommodation with "imperialism," especially in its American form. As the year went on, its expressions of ideological antipathy began to find an echo in the tendency of Washington spokesmen to justify the U.S. presence in Vietnam by reference to the alleged danger of a "militant Asian Communism" centering in Peking.[29]

A further impediment to Sino-American *détente* could be seen in the rapid progress of China's nuclear and missile program, the explosion of its first hydrogen bomb on June 17, and the subsequent American decision to deploy a limited antimissile network ostensibly directed against possible Chinese missile attack. Although Peking continued to insist that it would never be the first to use nuclear weapons and would never abandon the struggle for their prohibition and destruction,[30] its refusal to participate in arms limitation discussions under the United Nations could scarcely fail to cast some doubt on the innocence of its intentions. Its whole political attitude, in fact, was almost everywhere regarded as the reverse of reassuring. Later in the year, when the U.N. General Assembly undertook its annual debate on the representation of China in the world organization, Peking would find few apologists even among those delegations that favored its admission to U.N. representation on grounds of principle. The usual motion to expel the Republic of China from its U.N. seat and substitute a delegation from the Communist "People's Republic" would thus be defeated in November by a slightly heavier majority than in 1966.[31]

37 : Asian Cooperation and Pacific Security

American spokesmen who related the U.S. effort in Vietnam to the general theme of security in the Pacific were not quite such rootless improvisers as some of their critics appeared to imagine. Military security, for the United States and its friends, had been the primary concern of U.S. policy in the Pacific through all the years since World War II. It was almost entirely for defensive military reasons that the United States had retained control of Okinawa and the Trust Territory of the Pacific Islands, concluded mutual security treaties with Japan, South Korea, Formosa, the Philippines, Australia, and New Zealand, and, from 1950 onward, urged Japan to rise above the narrow concept of insular "self-defense" and assume its share of responsibility for the defense of free world interests in the Pacific.

This overriding concern with military security had, of course, been tempered by an awareness of the importance of economic and social progress in the Pacific area, both as a means of blunting the Communist challenge and as an objective worth pursuing for its own sake. Yet even the new American enthusiasm for cooperation among the Asian and Pacific nations was not uninfluenced by a concern for security factors. Cooperation for peaceful ends, Washington authorities reasoned, could do much to strengthen the defensive capabilities of individual Far Eastern countries and might even provide a basis for defense cooperation on a regional scale. Richard M. Nixon was not straying far from administration concepts when he wrote in *Foreign Affairs* of the need for a regional security system in the Pacific that would be based on existing cooperative structures, backed by the power of the United States, and capable of focusing its own resources on the deterrence of aggression.[32]

But however conscious of the dangers to security in the Pacific, few if any of the countries affected showed genuine interest in adding a military dimension to their cooperative endeavors. The reluctance to contemplate any move in this direction or, for that matter, even to take a clear-cut anti-Communist political stand was very evident at the second ministerial meeting of the nine-nation Asian and Pacific Council (ASPAC), held in Bangkok on July 5-7 a few weeks after the Chinese thermonuclear explosion. Japan, which had actively promoted the formation of ASPAC in 1966, had stressed the organization's nonmilitary character from the first and took the lead at Bangkok in discouraging any talk of defensive cooperation and keeping the emphasis strictly focused on economic and social development.[33]

A similar emphasis characterized the latest addition to the array of Asian regional organizations. This was a five-nation grouping known as the Association of Southeast Asian Nations (ASEAN) which sprang full-blown from a meeting of Foreign Ministers held at Bangkok on August 8. Essentially the outgrowth of an Indonesian initiative, the purpose of this new unit would be to join the efforts of Indonesia and Singapore with those already undertaken by Malaya, Thailand, and the Philippines in economic, cultural, technical, scientific, and social collaboration and mutual assistance.[34] Such a mission would presumably go far to supersede the work of the existing, tripartite Association of Southeast Asia (ASA), whose Foreign Ministers later agreed on a procedure for the phasing out of current activities and their transfer to ASEAN where appropriate.[35]

The formation of this new organ of regional cooperation was but one of the encouraging trends cited by President Johnson in a September 26 message to Congress in which he asked additional support for what had already become a favorite American project, the new Asian Development Bank. In addition to that institution's regular lending operations, the President pointed out, there was a widely recognized need to endow it with special funds from which it could provide low-interest development loans—so-called "soft loans"—for projects unsuited to financing at normal commercial rates. No funds for this purpose would be requested during the current (1968) fiscal year, Mr. Johnson explained; but he hoped that Congress would approve a U.S. contribution of up to $200 million which would be spread over the following four years and would be available only for expenditure on U.S. goods and services.[36] Such a limitation, though it would naturally reduce the attractiveness of the proposed assistance to recipient countries, was consistent with the general policy being applied in U.S. aid programs in order to reduce the pressure on the U.S. balance of payments. Since no immediate action was called for, Congress allowed the President's request to await consideration at its 1968 session.

No one would have thought of criticizing such institutions as the Asian Development Bank on the ground that they contributed nothing directly to the military security of non-Communist Asia. Their contribution was naturally of a different order. ". . . Lasting peace in Asia," the President pointed out in his message, "requires much more than resistance to armed aggression. Peace will come to stay when despair gives way to hope . . . when insurrection gives way to peaceful opportunity . . . when hunger gives way to harvests."[37] Those who felt that American policy was already becoming over-militarized as a result of Vietnam could only welcome such an emphasis. Senator Mansfield, just back from a study mission to the "Rim of Asia," appeared particularly sympathetic to any "shift from military confrontation to economic interplay throughout the Western Pacific."[38]

Yet it remained a fact that the military security of the Pacific nations was under challenge not only in Vietnam and Korea but in all the nations within range of Chinese land or missile power. The need to plan for security in the years ahead was underlined by Great Britain's announcement on July 18 of a plan to accelerate still further its military withdrawal from Singapore and Malaysia, reducing its forces there by one-half by the early 1970's and removing them altogether by the mid-1970's, with a corresponding readjustment of British commitments under SEATO.[39] Just how the resultant gap could be filled was not immediately apparent. Prime Minister Lee did not suggest that he would invite the Americans to replace the British at Singapore. What did seem obvious, however, was a growing need to review the requirements of U.S. strategy in the Pacific, including the status of the various islands taken over from Japan after World War II.

Strategic interest in the Mariannas, the Carolines, and the other island groups composing the U.S.-administered United Nations Trust

"TOMMY ATKINS IS GETTING HIS DISCHARGE PAPERS"

Yardley in *The Baltimore Sun*

Territory of the Pacific Islands had greatly waned since the early postwar years. Discussion of "Micronesia," as the territory was informally called, no longer centered on its strategic role but rather on the neglected condition of the islands' 93,000 inhabitants, the need to provide more adequately for their material and cultural needs, and their prospects for achieving self-government or independence in line with the philosophy governing all U.N. trust arrangements. President Johnson, during 1967, obtained congressional authorization to double the territory's annual budget—to $35 million—and also proposed the establishment of a commission to make recommendations looking toward a plebiscite on the territory's future not later than June 30, 1972.[40] Though Congress appropriated far less than the authorized amount and failed to act on the proposed commission, no evidence developed in Washington of any strong desire to retain the islands on strategic grounds.

Quite different was the situation with respect to the Ryukyu and Bonin Islands, two insular groups in which Japan had retained "residual sovereignty" while according full powers of administration to the United States under the San Francisco Peace Treaty concluded in 1951. Although Japan had long sought the return of these islands to its own jurisdiction, the United States had as steadfastly insisted that American control—especially at the great base of Okinawa in the Ryukyus—was essential to the defense of free world interests. With Japanese self-confidence increasing and other bilateral issues waning in importance, the Okinawa problem had gradually emerged as the greatest single irritant in U.S.-Japanese relations. Although the United States had attempted to placate Japanese (and Okinawan) feeling by various adjustments in its economic and administrative policies, the enlargement of the war in Vietnam and the concurrent growth of Chinese strategic capabilities had convinced American military men that they must retain essential control of the Ryukyus for some time to come.

This conflict between American and Japanese views continued to preoccupy both governments during 1967, largely overshadowing a second issue growing out of Japan's reluctance to admit American investment on equal terms. Discussions between Japanese and American scholars were dominated by the Okinawa question,[41] which was excluded with difficulty even from the September deliberations of the cabinet-level Joint U.S.-Japan Committee on Trade and Economic Affairs.[42] Months in advance of Premier Sato's departure for Washington, where he planned to hold his second meeting with President Johnson in mid-November, it was apparent that Okinawa would be the most important as well as the most delicate subject on the two leaders' agenda.

Determined as he was to obtain concessions on the Okinawa problem, the Japanese Prime Minister did not leave for Washington with empty hands. It was in his power to give important political support to President Johnson by endorsing U.S. policies in the Pacific and, if he so chose, in Vietnam as well. Such support he did in fact provide in surprisingly liberal measure, both in the official communiqué on his talks with the President and in a November 15 address to the National Press Club. His visits to eleven nations in Asia, Mr. Sato declared, had convinced him that U.S. efforts in Vietnam "were well understood and appreciated by the governments and peoples of Asian countries."[43] Reporting widespread support in Southeast Asia "for free world efforts to cope with Communist intervention and infiltration," he even expressed the view that "reciprocal action should be expected of Hanoi for a cessation of the bombing of North Vietnam."[44]

Mr. Sato was too good a diplomat to reveal how far he was satisfied with the reward he received for these declarations. He did *not* get back Okinawa and the Ryukyus; nor did he win any promise to return them to Japan by a definite date. All he could obtain on this point—apart from the establishment of a new advisory committee to help reduce economic and social barriers between the Ryukyus and Japan proper—was an agreement by the President to "joint and continuous review" of the question, "guided by the aim of returning administrative rights . . . to Japan." Concerning the Bonin Islands, which were strategically less important, the Japanese Prime Minister obtained somewhat better results in that the President agreed to the holding of immediate consultations looking toward their early restoration to Japan—the understanding being that Japan would gradually assume much of the responsibility for the defense of the area and that the United States "would retain . . . such military facilities and areas [in the Bonins] . . . as required in the mutual security of both countries."[45]

Only time and future developments could reveal how far this compromise would prove acceptable to Japanese opinion, and how far it would mollify the rising opposition in Japan to the Vietnam war as well as the continuance of the U.S.-Japan Security Treaty. Unofficially, Mr. Sato appears to have gained the impression that the United States would be unlikely to relinquish Okinawa until such time as Japan itself was in a position to assume the defense responsibilities the United States had hitherto exercised in the interests of both countries. For Japan to assume such responsibilities would, however, quite obviously require a revolution in Japanese attitudes concerning the maintenance of armed forces, perhaps even concerning the role of nuclear weapons in modern defense. Such a revolution might perhaps come eventually, but was still only in its beginnings in 1967.

Defense problems in Korea were of a different order, since here the forces of Communism and the "free world" were already in direct and hostile confrontation and minor military clashes and acts of infiltration—in which the Communist North Koreans invariably appeared to be the aggressors—were of almost daily occurrence. Incidents involving armed infiltrators from North Korea, Ambassador Goldberg later told the Security Council, actually increased from a mere 50 in 1966 to 566 in 1967, while the number of soldiers and civilians killed by these infiltrators increased from 35 to 153.[46] Although South Korea's armed forces of 600,000 substantially outnumbered the North Korean active force of 365,000 (excluding militia), it was not surprising under such circumstances that the Seoul government should have felt unable to augment the 45,000 combat troops it had previously sent to Vietnam. Its proposal early in August to send an additional 3,000 (and ultimately as many as 15,000) reservists to Vietnam in order to free more U.S. and Korean troops for combat duty there[47] was itself a more positive response to U.S. appeals than had been heard from any other allied government except that of South Vietnam itself.

A more immediate concern for the United States and South Korea was to ensure that the existing military demarcation line between North and South Korea was adequately protected. The United States, in addition to holding a section of the truce line with two divisions of its own troops, had recently renewed its promise to support the Korean Armed Forces at adequate levels and to underwrite their modernization "as rapidly as legislative and budgetary limitations will permit."[48] As a further deterrent to hostile infiltration, the United States was understood to be building an electronic security barrier along its section of the armistice line; and there was talk (as in Vietnam) of extending it along the whole length of the Korean Demilitarized Zone.[49]

The political defense of South Korean interests was closely involved with the attitude of the United Nations, which had supported the collective resistance to Communist aggression in Korea in 1950, had been a party to the armistice agreement of 1953, and, through periodic resolutions of the General Assembly, had continued to approve the stationing of U.N. forces in South Korea to assist in its defense. In recent years, the Communist states and their sympathizers had regularly proposed to the General Assembly that this United Nations mandate be terminated. The Assembly, by small majorities in which the United States was invariably conspicuous, had as regularly re-affirmed its desire for a unified, independent, and democratic Korea and approved the continued presence of U.N. forces until this condi-tion was realized or the South Koreans themselves requested with-drawal of the troops.

Procedure at the 1967 General Assembly ran true to precedent. There was the usual wrangle about inviting the two Korean govern-ments to join in the debate—an invitation that the North Koreans invariably scorned because of their refusal to recognize U.N. authority to deal with the Korean problem. In due course, the usual resolutions looking toward the termination of U.N. responsibilities were defeated, and the U.S.-supported resolution reaffirming established U.N. atti-tudes was adopted on November 16 by the unimpressive majority of 68 to 23, with 26 abstentions.[50] The Korean issue, it appeared, was doomed to stagnate for another year unless the growing aggressiveness of the North Koreans should give the rise to some emergency in the meantime.

38 : Diplomacy in High Gear

American support for the consolidation of non-Communist Asia was obviously motivated by broader considerations than those derived from the immediate struggle in Vietnam. At the same time, officials charged with defending the Vietnam commitment were understand-ably prone to depict this local anti-Communist effort as a matter of the widest regional significance. Secretary Rusk, for instance, was not a subscriber to the so-called "domino theory," which held that the fall of a country like South Vietnam to Communism must neces-sarily entail the fall of its neighbors; yet his remarks about "a billion Chinese . . . armed with nuclear weapons" were equally insistent on Vietnam's decisive importance to the peace of Asia and the Pacific. Vice-President Humphrey, too, related "the aggression of North Vietnam" directly to the general threat from "militant, aggressive Asian Communism, with its headquarters in Peking, China."[51]

Though frequently derided within the United States, such views were taken with the utmost seriousness in other Asian and Pacific countries—and not merely in those contributing troops to Vietnam.[52] Both Premier Sato and various heads of nonaligned Asian governments were beginning to voice remarkably similar opinions. Prime Minister Lee of Singapore, who visited the United States in October, was more forthright than ever in urging perseverance in Vietnam and warning against the dangers of withdrawal.[53] Prime Minister Souvanna Phouma of Laos, another October guest, was even more categorical. "We are grateful that you came to Indochina to help us survive," he said at a White House dinner. ". . . If tomorrow South Vietnam became Communist, all that would be left for us to do would be simply to pack up and go."[54] Vice-President Humphrey gathered similar impressions in the course of an eleven-day Southeast Asian tour that centered in Malaysia and Indonesia and left him deeply encouraged by "the appreciation of the American effort in Vietnam." Asian leaders, Mr. Humphrey reported, had told him that "were we to abandon our role in Asia . . . they would be under immediate pressure to come to terms with the militant, aggressive Asian Communism which they have resisted twenty years."[55]

In no other part of the world was U.S. policy currently receiving such plaudits, even from friendly officials speaking off the record. Small wonder that President Johnson and Secretary Rusk, in looking over the foreign policy achievements of 1967, saw major significance in the progress of East Asia and the Pacific. With 25 days of 1967 still to run, Secretary Rusk ticked off the following major developments:

"—Political, economic, and social progress in most of the non-Communist countries—in some, with dramatic speed.

"—Further easing of some long-standing international tensions: for example, between Indonesia and its neighbors and between Japan and the Republic of Korea.

"—Further advances in regional and subregional cooperation.

"—Further strengthening of our relations with all but one of the non-Communist nations of the area [presumably Cambodia].

"—Continuing difficulties within Communist China.

"—Rising confidence in the future in the non-Communist nations."

"If anyone doubts that our stand in Vietnam has been a major contribution to these highly favorable developments over a vast area," Mr. Rusk added, "let him go there and talk with responsible government officials. . . . Behind the shield which we have helped to provide, a new Asia is arising."[56]

Tragedy as well as triumph awaited the Pacific nations, for the "new Asia" was about to gain its first martyr. Australian Prime Minister Holt, in a premiership of less than two years' duration, had been the instrument of an historic reorientation affecting both Australia's own affairs and those of the Asian and Pacific region generally. Under Holt's leadership, Australia had for the first time entered fully into the stream of regional life and given it a quality and a momentum it would otherwise have lacked. No one but President Johnson himself was more closely identified with the new and positive trend in Asian-Pacific affairs.

Prime Minister Holt disappeared and was presumably drowned on December 17 while swimming off an Australian beach. His removal signified no change in the general direction of Australian policy, which was temporarily taken over by John McEwen of the small Country party. Yet the extinguishing of so luminous a personality was bound to make itself felt well beyond Australia's territorial limits. President Johnson immediately announced his intention of flying halfway round the world to attend the memorial services. A similar resolve was promptly voiced both by Commonwealth leaders such as New Zealand Prime Minister Keith J. Holyoake and by the leaders of allied countries like Thailand, the Philippines, Taiwan, South Korea, and South Vietnam.

The commemoration of the Australian leader thus became the occasion for an even larger gathering of Pacific statesmen than the Manila conference of 1966. The absence of any fixed agenda left ample room for informal, bilateral contacts such as those held by President Johnson with his South Vietnamese opposite.[57] Running through all the ceremonies and meetings, the President later reported, was a sense "not only of our personal loss but of our common bonds. The spirit of Harold Holt, the spirit of the new Asia, was powerfully alive among those who gathered to pay tribute to his memory."[58]

The spirit of the new Asia was destined to encounter further shocks from a variety of directions. As President Johnson returned to Washington on December 24, after brief stops in Thailand, South Vietnam, Pakistan, Italy, and the Vatican, the U.S. Atomic Energy Commission revealed that Communist China had just carried out its seventh atmospheric nuclear test, this one a low-yield detonation that was later classified as an unsuccessful hydrogen bomb test. Likewise on Decem-24, a Cambodian diplomatic note to the United States illuminated a mounting danger that the Vietnam war might spread to new sections of Southeast Asia.

Cambodia's Prince Sihanouk had been a vigorous dissenter from the recent pro-American trend in Southeast Asia. While neighboring statesmen lauded the United States for holding back the Communist tide, Prince Sihanouk had been having his own troubles with domestic Communists and had even been compelled to suppress by force a Chinese-supported attempt to set up a "Red Guard" government in Cambodia's Battambang Province. At the same time, the Prince had continued to denounce the Americans for their alleged aggressive purposes and disregard of Cambodian sovereignty, particularly in frontier areas. Early in November, he had used the occasion of a private visit from Mrs. Jacqueline Kennedy to renew his complaints against the United States and demand a formal pledge of respect for Cambodia's borders as the price for reestablishing the diplomatic relations he himself had broken off in 1965.[59] This was a price the United States would have had difficulty in paying if only because the exact location of Cambodia's borders was in dispute between Cambodia and South Vietnam. But meanwhile tension between Cambodia and the United States was rapidly increasing as the result of clear indications that Vietcong and North Vietnamese military units were using Cambodian territory in connection with their operations against U.S. and South Vietnamese forces in adjacent areas of South Vietnam. The discovery of a good-sized Vietcong camp in a Cambodian border zone was only one item in a mounting array of evidence that Cambodia's neutrality was being systematically violated in a way that greatly endangered the lives of American and allied soldiers.

Although Prince Sihanouk refused to credit such evidence, allied military authorities appeared convinced that something must soon be done. Discussion in military circles focused mainly on the possibility of authorizing "hot pursuit" of enemy forces into Cambodia and, perhaps, imposing some kind of "quarantine" to interrupt the supplies that were said to be reaching the Communists through the Cambodian port of Sihanoukville. Reluctant to authorize such drastic steps before more peaceful methods had been exhausted, the United States on

December 4 addressed a note to Cambodia expressing its deep concern and willingness to cooperate in any reasonable way of meeting the problem—e.g., through more effective inspection of Cambodian frontier areas by the tripartite International Control Commission set up in 1954.[60] Cambodia, however, still chose to ignore the real issue and treated the American note as a virtual invasion threat. Repeating its sweeping denial of the American allegations, its note of December 24 insisted that any military operations launched against it would be opposed with all the forces at its disposal.[61] Not only would Cambodia fight to the last man, Prince Sihanouk declared; it would also appeal for Soviet and Chinese help and would call for volunteers from such "friendly" countries as China, North Korea, and Cuba.[62]

While other Washington officials studied the possibilities of military action to eliminate the enemy "sanctuaries" in Cambodia, the State Department continued to insist on its preference for international measures in support of Cambodia's efforts to maintain neutrality. In a further note to Cambodia on December 25, the United States expressed its willingness to offer material assistance to the International Control Commission, including the loan of two helicopters, to increase that body's mobility and capability for independent surveillance.[63] While waiting to reply to this offer, which was accepted on January 8, 1968,[64] Prince Sihanouk undertook to reduce the intensity of the dispute by a notable "clarification" of his earlier remarks. There might, after all, have been a few inconsequential violations of Cambodian territory by Vietcong "freedom fighters," he conceded. Cambodia, he added, would not necessarily oppose limited "hot pursuit" actions by American forces in remote areas, although it could under no circumstances tolerate incursions by the South Vietnamese. He also offered to receive a personal envoy if President Johnson cared to send one.[65]

Other Southeast Asian countries were also likely to be engulfed if the war were to be expanded beyond its previous limits. Laos and Thailand already claimed to feel the weight of increased Communist pressure. Laotian authorities asserted late in December that operations by North Vietnamese units in their country transcended the normal seasonal pattern and had assumed the character of a "general offensive."[66] Thailand was reinforcing its border with Laos because of a suspicious concentration of North Vietnamese, Thai insurgents, and Laotian Communists and tribesmen.[67] Even if such manifestations should turn out to be a false alarm, they involved an appreciable diversion of energy and attention from the great tasks of regional construction that were still in their initial stages. They illustrated the kind of perils that could still undo the majestic design to which the United States and its Pacific partners had pledged their efforts.

8 : Latin American Standoff

Nineteen sixty-seven was a year of more talk than action in Western Hemisphere affairs. In contrast to much past experience, the 20 Latin American countries got through the year with no important wars, invasions, popular upheavals, or military coups and only scattered episodes of guerrilla fighting. Signs of revolutionary ferment remained ubiquitous as the Latin American nations and the new English-speaking states of the Caribbean pursued their often tumultuous course toward economic expansion and social justice. The revolutionary incitements of Castro's Cuba continued to present a threat to certain Latin American governments and a challenge to the basic principles of the Alliance for Progress, President Kennedy's grand design for peaceful economic and social transformation in the Americas. For the most part, however, such threats were confined within tolerable limits. Most hemisphere governments could thus devote such attention as was left over from their internal problems to plans for perfecting their political association and meeting the economic and social challenges of the coming decades. The year's most memorable event was the meeting of American Presidents that took place in April at Punta del Este, Uruguay, and, at President Johnson's urging, approved plans for the establishment of a Latin American common market by 1985.

39 : Political Uncertainties

The idea of a Presidential meeting to inject new life into the faltering, six-year-old Alliance for Progress had first been ventilated in April 1966 by the then President of Argentina, Arturo U. Illia. Soon afterward, President Illia had been deposed by a military coup and Argentina had fallen under a military dictatorship of repellent aspect and ultraconservative tendency. This unforeseen development had seriously delayed the plan for a presidential meeting and, at one time, had seemed likely to kill it altogether. But President Johnson's support of the plan had helped to overcome the reservations expressed by some of the Latin American governments, and the time and place of the meeting were eventually fixed at a special meeting of American Foreign Ministers in February 1967.[1] Even after that date, however, conditions in some Latin American countries made it uncertain whether their chiefs of state would attend and, if so, what attitude they would adopt.

One country that would definitely not be represented at Punta del Este was Cuba, whose government had in effect been read out of the inter-American system as far back as 1962. Cuba, at that time, had been a major source of tension in the hemisphere and beyond because of its subversive activities against other American governments and its close association with the U.S.S.R., its partner in the famous "missile confrontation" that took place in October of that year. Since 1962, tension over Cuba had waned appreciably. Premier Castro, though he persisted in his announced aim of spreading revolution in the Americas, had made clear his refusal to take orders from either the U.S.S.R. or the rival Communist regime in China. The United States, while committed to a long-term effort to bring down the Castro regime through the cumulative effects of economic and political pressure, no longer thought in terms of military action against Cuba and, since 1962, had even discouraged attempts by Cuban exiles to organize military expeditions against their homeland. At the beginning of 1967, for example, U.S. agents broke up a force of several dozen Cubans, Haitians, and Americans who had gathered in the Florida Keys with the apparent purpose of launching an invasion of Haiti and going on from there to attempt the "liberation" of Cuba.

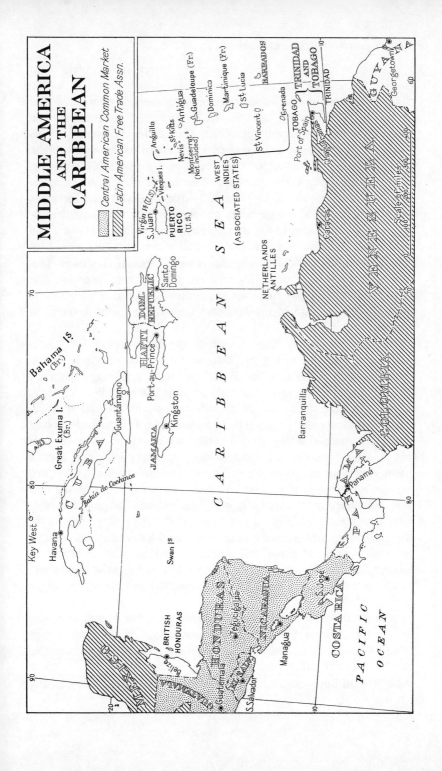

In spite of its unwillingnes to support direct action against the Castro regime, the United States remained keenly sensitive to the dangers created by Cuba's support of revolutionary efforts directed against the governments of other Latin American countries. Cuban spokesmen were contemptuous of the Alliance for Progress, with its emphasis on economic and social reforms carried out in a democratic spirit. The only real cure for the deep-rooted ills of Latin America, in the Cuban view, was violent revolution by the dispossessed classes. Ernesto (Ché) Guevara, the bearded Argentine who had for years been Castro's closest collaborator, was the sponsor of a body of revolutionary doctrine that had acquired semiofficial status in Havana and purported to adapt the theories of Fanon and the experience of Chinese and Vietnamese revolutionists to the special conditions prevailing in Latin America. Guerrilla struggles of the type that had brought Castro himself to power, according to this theory, were the most efficacious form of revolutionary activity for Latin America as a whole.

Guevara himself was out of sight at the beginning of 1967, presumably attempting to put his theories into practice in one of the areas deemed ripe for revolution. Cubans had been gaining experience in revolutionary enterprises not only in Latin America but in Africa, where they were closely identified with the nascent "liberation movement" based on the Congo (Brazzaville) and Tanzania. In recent months, Cuba had also provided considerable support to small-scale but tenacious guerrilla movements which had cropped up in several Latin American countries. One of these, in the Peruvian Andes, had been effectually suppressed; others continued to smolder as the new year got under way. Venezuela was intermittently plagued by saboteurs and terrorists acting in the name of a Cuban-supported movement known as the "Armed Forces of National Liberation." Colombia, too, was a scene of occasional ambushes and guerrilla incidents. In Guatemala there was terrorism of both leftist and rightist inspiration; but here as elsewhere such activity appeared on the whole to be declining.

A more alarming portent was the discovery in late March of a new, apparently Cuban-supported guerrilla movement in the remote lowlands of southeastern Bolivia. Ché Guevara himself was rumored to be the leader of this group, which appeared to number no more than 60 men but presented a problem the Bolivian Army was clearly

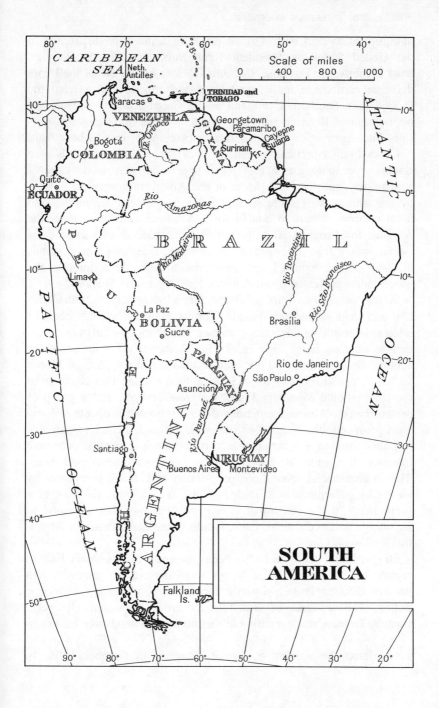

CARIBBEAN
SEA

Neth.
Antilles

Caracas

TRINIDAD and
TOBAGO

VENEZUELA

Georgetown
Paramaribo
Cayenne
Surinam
Fr. Guiana

Bogotá

R. Orinoco

GUYANA

COLOMBIA

Quito

ECUADOR

ATLANTIC

Rio

Amazonas

B R A Z I L

P E R U

Rio Madeira

Rio Tocantins

Rio São Francisco

Lima

La Paz

BOLIVIA

Sucre

Brasília

PARAGUAY

Rio de Janeiro

São Paulo

PACIFIC

Asunción

ARGENTINA

Rio Paraná

OCEAN

Santiago

C H I L E

URUGUAY

Buenos Aires   Montevideo

O C E A N

Falkland
Is.

**SOUTH
AMERICA**

Scale of miles

0   400   800   1000

ill-equipped to deal with. Urgent pleas for arms were dispatched to the United States by President René Barrientos Ortuño, Bolivia's chief executive. In response, the United States on the eve of the Punta del Este conference made available five Rangers, drawn from the U.S. Army's Southern Command in the Canal Zone, to instruct the poorly trained Bolivian troops in jungle warfare and countersubversion. Such instruction would naturally take some time to bear fruit.

Other Latin American countries would be exposed to perils of a similar order as long as hardship and deprivation remained as prevalent as they were in 1967. Most of the American governments were by this time making some attempt to promote social, economic, and fiscal reforms, if only to qualify for U.S. grants and loans under the Alliance for Progress. But the quality and success of these efforts varied widely from one country to another. Internal political trends in some cases supported and in others ran directly counter to the general aims professed by all Alliance for Progress participants.

Argentina's new military government, headed by General Juan Carlos Onganía, had earned few plaudits for its political performance—its interest in restoring democracy seemed less than nil—but was nevertheless winning fairly high marks in Washington for its economic actions, among them a 40 per cent devaluation of the peso on March 13 which paved the way for a $400 million stabilization credit from the International Monetary Fund, the United States, and a group of private banks. Although opinions differed about the country's long-term prospects, the military regime with its fundamental indifference to public opinion was better able to cooperate with outside economic interests than more democratic Argentine governments had been. Thus a controversy over the expropriation of U.S. oil companies by an earlier government was settled on the eve of Punta del Este as a preliminary to the enactment of a new, liberal oil law designed to encourage renewed foreign participation in the exploitation of Argentina's oil wealth.

Brazil, since 1964, had also been governed by a military-backed regime which, despite some lapses from democratic principle, had earned U.S. applause primarily for its anti-inflationary economic policy. The architect of Brazil's new order, President Humberto Castello Branco, was preparing at the moment to hand over his extensive powers to a military colleague, Arthur da Costa e Silva, who had been elected by a joint session of Congress in October 1966. In advance of his successor's inauguration on March 15, Castello Branco took pains to safeguard his own work by extracting congressional approval of a new constitution and press law which together provided for a strong executive and a considerable degree of immunity from public criticism. President-elect da Costa e Silva, who received general pledges of U.S. support on a preinaugural visit to the White House, chose "social humanism" as the theme of his administration and promised on assuming office to provide government "for the people" even if the latter should withhold their approval.[2]

Chile's popularly elected President, Eduardo Frei Montalva, was a more progressive thinker—his phrase, "revolution in freedom," crystallized the whole philosophy of the Alliance for Progress—but also a more vulnerable politician. Frei's plans for economic advance in Chile, centering on a government partnership with the U.S.-developed copper industry and on extensive reforms in landownership, had conjured up a powerful coalition of opposing interests on both Left and Right. On January 17, these elements inflicted a bitter humiliation on the chief executive when the Senate voted to refuse him permission to leave the country for a scheduled meeting with President Johnson. Some weeks later, a sharp defeat of Frei's Christian Democratic party in municipal elections continued the "cutting down to size" of a leader who at one time had symbolized the democratic, reformist principle in Latin American affairs as vividly as Castro symbolized the principle of revolutionary violence.

Most of the smaller South American countries had their own problems to compete for attention with the forthcoming presidential meeting. Uruguay, after a disheartening fifteen years of government by National Council, returned on March 1 to a one-man presidential system and, it was hoped, an era of greater economic realism under the leadership of retired General Oscar Diego Gestido. Paraguay was rounding out its thirteenth year of quasi-dictatorship under President Alfredo Stroessner, whose rule had been barren of great achievements but currently appeared to be veering in a somewhat more democratic direction. Peru and Ecuador, both of which had known military dictatorship in the recent past, were again enjoying the blessings of democratic government, although both countries were rather sharply at odds with the United States as the result of their attempts to monopolize Pacific fishing rights to a distance of 200 miles from their shores.[3] This issue would not prevent the attendance of the Peruvian and

Ecuadorean chief executives at Punta del Este, but was among the factors that would contribute to the emergence of Ecuador's Interim President, Otto Arosemena Gómez, as a focus of anti-U.S. dissidence at the presidential meeting. Colombia, too, was much irritated against the United States at the moment because of an economic controversy which had led to the deferment of U.S. development credits and was adjusted only on the eve of the Punta del Este conference.

Among the Central American and Caribbean countries, only Nicaragua confronted urgent internal problems in advance of the Punta del Este sessions. Ten years after the assassination of President Anastasio Somoza, Nicaraguan politics continued to revolve around the predominant economic and political position held by members of the late dictator's family. One of his sons, Luis A. Somoza DeBayle, had already served a term as President, and another, Major General Anastasio Somoza DeBayle, was elected to the presidential office on February 5, 1967—not before the opposition candidate had provoked an abortive rising in which he vainly attempted to enlist the support of the military in forcing "honest" elections. In spite of a professed devotion to constitutional government, the new President-elect had not hitherto been highly regarded in the hemisphere, and had some difficulty in securing an appointment with President Johnson on a post-election visit to the United States. The illness and death of his brother Luis in April offered a convenient excuse for not appearing at Punta del Este, where Nicaragua was represented by its outgoing chief executive.

The presidential election held in El Salvador on March 5 occasioned fewer sensations, and the victory of the "official" candidate, Colonel Fidel Sánchez Fernández, promised a continuation of the cautiously progressive policies initiated by President Julio Adalberto Rivero. The other Central American republics, Honduras, Costa Rica, and Guatemala, had all held presidential elections within the past year or two. Panama, where a new election was due in 1968, was also temporarily quiescent as all political factions awaited the outcome of negotiations with the United States on the future of the Canal Zone, undertaken on President Johnson's initiative in the wake of the serious disorders of 1964.

Mexico presented few major problems for U.S. policy, despite its insistence, alone among the American governments, on maintaining diplomatic relations with Cuba. The forward-looking economic and social policies of President Gustavo Díaz Ordaz and his administration had earned repeated commendation from President Johnson, and the joint development projects on which the two governments were engaged had been cited as models for the rest of the hemisphere. Mexico had also taken a leading role in the negotiation of the Treaty for the Prohibition of Nuclear Weapons in Latin America, which was signed by fourteen Latin American states in Mexico City on February 14 and became known as the Treaty of Tlatelolco.[4] Although the United States was sympathetic to the treaty's proclaimed objective, a variety of technical and political considerations prevented it from offering complete endorsement;[5] and the cautious attitude of other nuclear powers whose cooperation was required left some doubt as to when the treaty could actually go into effect.

Among the insular republics of the Caribbean, the Dominican Republic exhibited a heartening (if relative) measure of stability after its tragedy of civil war and U.S. intervention in 1965. Haiti, completing a somber decade under President François Duvalier's police-state rule, remained the pariah of the hemisphere, a dismal example of retrogression and abuse that violated every inter-American precept. Concern for his personal safety would have sufficed in itself to explain Dr. Duvalier's avoidance of the Punta del Este meeting, to which he sent a special representative.

More forward-looking developments were occurring among the English-speaking Caribbean countries, for which the 1960's had been a period of transition to independent nationhood within the British Commonwealth. Trinidad and Tobago, independent since 1962, had gone so far as to apply for admission to the Organization of American States, and were to be represented at Punta del Este by Prime Minister Eric Williams. Barbados, whose independence was only a few weeks old, had also expressed a desire for O.A.S. membership. Less eager to participate in the inter-American grouping were Jamaica, where a new generation of political leadership was coming on the scene with the retirement of Prime Minister Sir Alexander Busta-mante, and Guyana, immersed as always in its perennial feud between the Negro adherents of Prime Minister Forbes Burnham and the left-ist, East Indian opposition led by Dr. Cheddi B. Jagan.

Great Britain's remaining Caribbean territories, with one or two exceptions, were also achieving quasi-independence in a new political grouping known as the West Indies (Associated States), in which

British responsibility would henceforth be limited to the fields of defense and foreign affairs. St. Kitts, Nevis, and Anguilla joined in adopting the new status in February and were followed in quick succession by Dominica, St. Lucia, Grenada, Antigua, and St. Vincent. Only Montserrat preferred to stay aloof from the new arrangement, whose halfway character gave rise to some criticism in the U.N. Committee of 24 on Colonialism[6] but was thought by Britain and the United States—and, apparently, the islanders themselves—to embody the best available compromise between colonial subordination and the hazards of outright independence.

40 : Punta del Este and After

Much advance planning preceded the meeting of American Presidents at Punta del Este. Like every inter-American gathering, the encounter presented the United States with dangers as well as opportunities. It would afford an excellent chance to encourage other American governments to take constructive action toward Alliance for Progress goals—land reform, tax reform, educational and administrative reform, new housing, encouragement of private investment, participation in binational and regional development projects. But there would also be a danger that the other American governments might, as at previous conferences, "gang up" on the United States and overwhelm it with demands for quite different things—grants and loans for development and, above all, preferential access to the U.S. market for their export products.

That most Latin American governments were convinced of their need for such advantages had been made plain on innumerable occasions. Yet these were precisely the kind of benefits that the United States could least easily grant—at least in the desired measure—in view of its heavy financial commitments outside of Latin America and its strong objection to preferential trading arrangements as a matter of economic principle. Since the advent of the Alliance for Progress, the United States had greatly increased its grants and loans for Latin American economic development, which had lately been running at a rate of $1 billion a year. On the matter of special trade concessions, however, it had continued to maintain that trade preferences were inherently undesirable and that a solution for Latin America's problems should rather be sought in a generalized reduction of trade barriers through such arrangements as those currently under negotiation in the Kennedy Round.

To assist in parrying the unacceptable proposals advanced at every inter-American gathering, the United States had long ago formed the habit of arming itself with some dramatic proposal of its own which, over and above its intrinsic merits, would demonstrate good will and yet demand no major U.S. outlays or policy changes. One year, attention would be directed to the potentialities of atomic energy as a factor in economic development; the next, to the need for projects to benefit the common man; the third, to the importance of multinational projects. In 1967, it might have seemed appropriate to choose as a theme the urgent need for curbing Latin America's explosive rate of population growth. This, however, remained a delicate subject in Latin America. Instead, the United States elected to focus on the alleged necessity of establishing a Latin American common market analogous to the European Common Market that had worked such wonders for its participants within the past decade.

Admittedly, conditions in most parts of Latin America were vastly different from those in industrialized Western Europe. Yet informed Latin Americans already recognized the importance of reducing and, eventually, eliminating man-made barriers to trade in order to promote freer exchange of their products and further the growth of large-scale industrialization and regional specialization in what might, perhaps, eventually become a mass market of continental scope. More than half the Latin American countries—ten South American states and Mexico—were already moving hesitantly in this direction as members of the Latin American Free Trade Association (LAFTA). More rapid progress had been made by the five comparatively underdeveloped nations that made up the Central American Common Market. The establishment of an all-Latin American common market that would absorb the two existing organizations would undoubtedly give rise to some complex technical problems; yet it seemed to many a worthwhile enterprise even though it sidestepped the more immediate preoccupations obsessing most Latin American governments. From the U.S. point of view, it had the special advantage of putting the responsibility for action where it properly belonged, in Latin America rather than in Washington.

Secretary Rusk secured at least a qualified assent to the common market principle at a meeting of the American Ministers of Foreign Affairs which was convened in Buenos Aires in mid-February to fix the date, site, and agenda of the meeting of Presidents. Also on the program of the Chiefs of State, it was agreed, would be the question of eliminating unnecessary military expenditure in Latin America, a matter of considerable concern to the United States in view of recent indications that some of the Latin American governments were reverting to an old habit of spending money on arms that could be better applied to development. *Not* approved for the Presidents' agenda was an Argentine proposal looking toward the establishment of a new inter-American defense organ controlled by the military establishments of the nations involved. Apart from its doubtful necessity, a plan that was put forward by Argentina and supported by Brazil could not have failed to arouse mistrust on the part of other governments that were unsympathetic to military dictatorship and hesitated even to sit down with the Argentine regime.

The authority that sanctioned these preliminary decisions was technically known as the Eleventh Meeting of Consultation of the Ministers of Foreign Affairs of the American Republics, which had been convened for the express purpose of guiding the preparations for the Presidential meeting.[7] Concurrently, the same Foreign Ministers had also been holding a separate series of meetings in Buenos Aires under the more dignified name of the Third Special Inter-American Conference. The purpose of this latter assemblage was unrelated to the Punta del Este meeting. Its task was to complete a far-reaching revision of the Charter of the Organization of American States with a view to bringing the inter-American system into line with developments since the organization was first constituted in its existing form in 1948. Prepared and reviewed by a succession of O.A.S. bodies during 1966, the Protocol of Amendment to the Charter[8]— or "Protocol of Buenos Aires," as it came to be called—redefined the scope of the organization and gave increased emphasis to its responsibilities in the economic, scientific, and educational fields. In addition, it undertook to remold the basic structure of the O.A.S. by equipping it with a General Assembly that would meet every year and would complement the organization's existing Permanent Council as well as the Inter-American Economic and Social Council and a new Council for Education, Science, and Culture.

Unanimously approved on February 27 by representatives of the 20 participating countries,[9] these changes would not actually go into effect until two-thirds of the O.A.S. governments had ratified them. (President Johnson recommended ratification in a message sent to the Senate on June 12,[10] but that body took no action during the 1967 congressional session.) Meanwhile, new members could be admitted to the organization under a special procedure which had been devised in 1964 and was utilized for the first time on February 23 when representatives of the governments assembled in Buenos Aires held still a third meeting—this one a special session of the O.A.S. Council—to approve the application of Trinidad and Tobago. Officially, that country's admission as the 22nd O.A.S. member state would become effective on June 12 with the deposit of its instrument ratifying the O.A.S. Charter.

Still other steps would have to be taken before the American Presidents could actually proceed to Punta del Este for their three-day meeting, now set for April 12-14. Detailed documentation must still be drawn up by a special inter-American committee—Lincoln Gordon, the outgoing Assistant Secretary of State for Inter-American Affairs, was the U.S. representative—and subjected to last-minute review by the Foreign Ministers. In the course of these discussions, the United States made one significant concession with respect to the proposed Latin American common market. The original hope in Washington had been that a functioning common market might be established by 1980, thus making the 1970's a "decade of Latin American integration" as the 1960's had been the decade of the Alliance for Progerss. This timetable proved unacceptable to other governments, however, and the target date for completion of the common market was quietly advanced from 1980 to 1985.

Such a relaxation of the time schedule did not in itself ensure that the establishment of a common market would actually be agreed upon at the presidential level—still less that the agreement, if made, would be vigorously implemented. Amid the talk of measures to be taken by the Latin American states in common, the Latin American governments had not lost sight of their desire for trade concessions and other benefits from the United States. If Washington wanted a common market, it would clearly have to offer persuasive inducements—not only general pledges of moral and financial support, but specific commitments relating to Latin American trade and development. What kind of offers would President Johnson bring to Punta del Este as his contribution to the success of the meeting?

The answer did not lie entirely in the President's hands, since it was Congress that held the purse-strings as well as the power to regulate foreign commerce. Apparently misjudging the extent to which influential congressional leaders already dissented from his methods of conducting foreign policy, the President decided early in March to seek support from Congress for the stand he proposed to take at Punta del Este by requesting its "guidance and counsel"—in other words, its approval of increased expenditures—in advance of his departure for the meeting. In a message of March 13, the President asked the Congress to authorize an increase of up to $1.5 billion (or $300 million a year) in U.S. financial assistance to Latin America over the next five years.[11] These amounts would be in addition to the $624 million economic aid program for Latin America that the President had already recommended for the fiscal year 1968.

The unexpectedly hostile reaction to this proposal was to place the President in a position almost as embarrassing as that of his Chilean colleague who had been refused permission to visit the United States. In the House, the presidential proposal was endorsed with no more grumbling than usually accompanied requests for funds. In the Senate, it ran into the strongest kind of oppostion within the Foreign Relations Committee, less because of the money involved than because of the feeling of Chairman Fulbright and others than Congress was being "pressured" into acting as a "rubber stamp" in a matter requiring close and careful deliberation. Unable to obtain a satisfactory congressional resolution, Mr. Johnson was presently forced to drop the project. In an attempt to create a favorable atmosphere for the conference, he concentrated his energies thereafter on an informal, two-day meeting and barbecue for a group of Latin American diplomats and their wives who flew to Texas on March 31 to enjoy the hospitality of the LBJ Ranch.

Mr. Johnson was still relying heavily on his personal charm when he arrived at Punta del Este a few days later. The idea of combining the meeting with a presidential tour of selected Latin American countries had been abandoned in view of the likelihood of anti-U.S. demonstrations in some of the countries visited and of hurt feelings in those passed over. But all of the American Chiefs of State were on hand to greet the President in Punta del Este except for Duvalier of

"AMIGOS!"

Peb in *The Philadelphia Inquirer*

Haiti and Barrientos Ortuño of Bolivia, who had stayed away not because of the guerrilla outbreak in his country but to show his dissatisfaction with the O.A.S. attitude on a long-standing frontier dispute with Chile. Apart from Arosemena of Ecuador, who was apparently smarting over a recent cut in U.S. aid, all of the leaders present seemed most amiably inclined; and Mr. Johnson took full advantage of the opportunity for private converse with each of them. This exercise alone, it was later claimed, paid ample dividends in the later refusal of the Latin American countries to vote against the United States in U.N. discussions of the Middle East crisis.

An equal tact and good feeling was apparent in the restrained behavior of the assembled leaders as they approached the formal business of the conference. Making every effort to avoid dominating the proceedings, President Johnson repeatedly stressed the importance of Latin American initiative in scheduling the conference and making it a success. Mindful of Mr. Johnson's recent rebuff by the Senate, the other Presidents—except Arosemena—refrained from pressing for additional U.S. aid and showed respectful appreciation for such minor benefits as the visitor was able to offer. Among them were increased U.S. assistance in agriculture, education, science, and communications; additional support of the International Coffee Agreement; a promise to seek additional "soft loan" funds for the Inter-American Bank; and major increases in food allotments for school lunches.[12]

These, however, were minor matters as compared with the central question of trade preferences for Latin American exports. The Latin American Chiefs of State were still waiting to hear what, concretely, the United States was prepared to do in the trade field to justify the far-reaching undertakings it sought from them in regard to the proposed common market. On this point, Secretary Rusk had been unable to satisfy his fellow Foreign Ministers and only President Johnson could speak the decisive word.

President Johnson did not announce the preferential treatment for Latin American exports to the United States that some of his auditors had been hoping for. He did, however, give notice of an innovation in trade policy that was to prove important in both a Latin American and a global context. This was his acceptance, in principle at least, of the idea that trade preferences might be extended on a temporary basis by the industrialized countries as a group to the less developed countries as a group. "We are ready," Mr. Johnson said, "to explore with other industrialized countries—and with our own people—the possibility of temporary preferential tariff advantages for all developing countries in the markets of all industrialized countries."[13] The United States, in other words, would consider making special concessions for the exports of developing countries on condition that the other industrialized countries did the same. Such a plan, presumably, would call for important changes in the practice of the European Economic Community, which already gave preferential treatment to the exports of France's and Belgium's former colonies in Africa. This openly discriminatory arrangement on the part of the European countries was much resented in Latin America and had been the subject of fruitless representations by the United States to its E.E.C. friends. Under President Johnson's new proposal, these Common Market preferences would presumably be superseded by a general preference system under which the Latin American countries would be given access to the Common Market area on equal terms with their African competitors.

Although there was no assurance that the explorations proposed by President Johnson would turn out favorably, his announcement sufficed to ensure the approval of the major documents drawn up for signature at Punta del Este. In a "Declaration of the Presidents of America" and an appended "action program,"[14] the Latin American Chiefs of State resolved "to create progressively, beginning in 1970, the Latin American Common Market, which should be substantially in operation in a period of no more than fifteen years." They also pledged themselves to lay the physical foundations for economic integration through multinational projects, and to put forth new efforts in the fields of agriculture and food production, education and health, and the harnessing of science and technology for the benefit of their peoples. To the satisfaction of the United States, they even assumed a commitment to "eliminate unnecessary military expenditures." Before the conference adjourned, the Declaration was signed by everyone except the President of Ecuador, who still seemed to feel that he had more to gain by flouting the United States than by conciliating it.

"In my judgment, this has been an exceedingly valuable conference," said President Johnson as the sessions concluded on April 14. Secretary Rusk considered the Latin Americans' decision to move toward a common market "perhaps the most important decision they will have made since they became independent states." Sol M. Linowitz, the new U.S. Representative to the O.A.S., saw the conference as heralding new life for the Alliance for Progress and "a new era of common understanding in the Americas." But all agreed that the real test would come as the participating nations began to put their resolutions into practice. "The first phase of the Alliance has been a success by any realistic standard," said President Johnson. "The second phase is now underway." That phase, he warned, would require "a fierce—a stubborn—dedication to those undramatic day-to-day attainments that are the sinews of economic and social progress."[15]

A series of inter-American meetings in the following months attested both the variety of the tasks confronting the American nations and the difficulty of maintaining the sense of dedication the President had called for. First in the series was the annual meeting of the Governors of the Inter-American Bank, held in Washington in late April. In its six years of operation, that much lauded institution had authorized just over $2 billion in development loans as well as $82 million in technical assistance loans and grants. Encouraged by President Johnson's promise at Punta del Este to seek additional funds for the Bank's "soft loan" operations, the Governors decided at their Washington meeting to recommend a $1.2 billion increase in the institution's Fund for Special Operations for the period ending in 1971. Of this amount, the United States itself proposed to contribute $900 million over the next three years. Although Congress subsequently authorized the increase on recommendation of the President,[16] the effect of its action was somewhat dimmed by a demand for a special audit of the Bank's operations that seemed to impugn the competence of President Felipe Herrera and his staff.[17]

More discordant sounds arose from the biennial meeting of the U.N. Economic Commission for Latin America, held in Caracas in early May and attended by Great Britain, France, the U.S.S.R., and other industrialized countries. In contrast to the restraint displayed by their superiors at Punta del Este, the Latin American spokesmen at Caracas showed few inhibitions in denouncing the trade policies of the Western industrialized nations as restrictive, discriminatory, and unfair to Latin America.[18] By this time it was evident that the Kennedy Round negotiations in Geneva would provide few benefits for the developing countries, while it would obviously be many months before President Johnson's idea of generalized tariff preferences could bear fruit.

The sense of discouragement concerning trade policy persisted when delegates of the American nations met in June in Viña del Mar, Chile, for another economic review under the auspices of the Inter-American Economic and Social Council. The main task of this meeting, at which the United States was represented by Covey T. Oliver, the newly designated Assistant Secretary of State for Inter-American Affairs, was the drafting of more detailed development plans to implement the guidelines agreed upon at Punta del Este. The principal achievement was the formation of a number of liaison and working groups to deal with the varied aspects of Latin American integration, among them the technically difficult task of coordinating the development of the Latin American Free Trade Association (LAFTA) and the Central American Common Market.[19]

Through the summer, additional meetings continued at every level. A first contact between LAFTA and Central American representatives took place at the end of July. LAFTA Foreign Ministers agreed a month later to set up a coordinating committee to negotiate the proposed merger and to try to bring in the Caribbean countries as well as the Central Americans. In September, delegates and observers from sixteen Latin American countries attended a six-day "family planning" congress in Caracas that disclosed unexpected support for measures to check the dizzying growth of Latin American population. In Washington, meanwhile, Congress was not sparing the Alliance for Progress as it began its annual campaign to trim the foreign aid allotment below the President's estimates. Like other aspects of U.S. overseas policy, the Alliance was beginning to feel the backwash of the Vietnam commitment as well as the mounting disorders on the home front. A controversy about arms sales to developing countries[20] was also threatening the Latin American sections of the aid program, the details of which would not be settled until much later in the year.

Set against these negative portents were indications that some features of the Alliance for Progress might be taking a firmer hold than in the past. Eleven of the Latin American countries, it was asserted, had by this time equaled or surpassed the 2.5 per cent per capita growth rate set out as a general standard of performance in 1961. A number of them, moreover, appeared less hostile than formerly to the private foreign investment which, whatever the scale of governmental loans and grants, would continue to carry the main burden of Latin American development. Investment by Latin Americans themselves was said to be exceeding the target for the first time. "As we meet here this evening, we cannot claim victory for the Alliance," President Johnson told a group of prize-winning Latin American high school students who had gathered at the Pan American Union in Washington to observe the sixth anniversary of the enterprise on August 17. "We can only say 'so far, so good'—progress is being made, though the shining legacy that we would leave to our young remains to be delivered." Perseverance, Mr. Johnson emphasized, was the key to success; and he promised that despite reverses the United States would persevere, convinced that "what happens in the Western Hemisphere, what happens in North and South America, will point the way ultimately to a more tranquil, more just, more fruitful world for all people."[21]

41 : Challenge from the Far Left

What enterprises had Latin America's revolutionary forces been engaged on while the American governments—except for Cuba—were laying the groundwork for peaceful Latin American integration? Like the revolutionary forces in the world at large, the foes of the established order in Latin America had been divided among themselves, and their division was growing sharper as the issue of violent versus nonviolent methods of political and social change was thrust into the foreground by the actions of the Castro regime and its admirers. Latin America offered its own variation on the world-wide conflict between moderate and radical trends that had divided the international "camp of Socialism" into pro-Soviet and pro-Chinese factions. Here as elsewhere, the "moderate" line was that espoused by the Soviet Union, the Eastern European countries, and the Communist parties under Soviet influence. In contrast to other areas, however, the most important challenge to this "moderate" line in Latin America emanated not from Peking but from Havana.

Soviet policy in Latin America in recent years had been far from "revolutionary" in the traditional meaning of that term. In line with the approved doctrine of "peaceful coexistence among states with different social systems," the efforts of the U.S.S.R. and its Eastern European associates had been directed not toward overthrowing Latin American governments but rather toward collaborating with them in developing diplomatic, trade, and cultural ties and expanding economic and technical cooperation. In harmony with this approach, the long-established Communist parties of Venezuela, Chile, Uruguay, and other Latin American countries had embraced a moderate course of action designed to advance their interests by peaceful methods and, in many cases, even by joining their efforts with those of "progressive bourgeois elements." This cautious approach had, however, proved far from congenial to the partisans of armed struggle and revolutionary violence who drew their inspiration from the special brand of revolutionary activism developed in Cuba under the leadership of men like Castro and Guevara. Some of these elements had split off from the regular Communist parties; others had grouped themselves under a socialist label, or had avoided party affiliations altogether and identified themselves with one or other of the direct action groups that were operating in Latin America with Cuban encouragement and support.

Premier Castro, who had never hesitated to voice his disagreements with Peking or Moscow, openly avowed these differences toward the end of March in a blistering denunciation of Latin America's established Communist parties for their alleged lack of principle, their readiness to establish ties with the ruling "oligarchies," and their inhibiting influence on rural-based guerrilla movements of the type that Ché Guevara had advocated and was even then initiating in Bolivia.[22] Increasingly, the absent Guevara was becoming the object of a Cuban "personality cult." In April, the Cuban press began to publicize a long and turgid article in which Guevara foretold the victory of the current revolutionary struggles in Latin America and throughout the world. "How bright and near the future would look," Guevara wrote, "if two, three, many Vietnams were to flower on the surface of the globe, with their quota of death and their immense tragedies, their daily heroism, their repeated blows against imperialism, and the compulsion on the latter to disperse its forces under the scourge of the growing hatred of the peoples of the world!"[23]

Although Guevara's presence with the Bolivian guerrillas had not yet been confirmed, it seemed fairly evident that this small rising represented a conscious attempt to put his theories into practice in the hope of igniting a wider insurrectionary movement. New evidence of the ties between the Bolivian insurgency and the revolutionary center in Havana would shortly come to light with the capture by the Bolivian Army of a young Frenchman, Régis Debray, who was known as a friend of Castro and as the author of a book, *Revolution Within the Revolution?,*[24] which had earned him a place among contemporary theorists of revolutionary violence. "Insurrectional activity is today the No. 1 political activity," Debray had written. Although he insisted that he was in Bolivia merely as a journalist—his mission, he later asserted, had been to find and interview Guevara—the circumstances of Debray's capture were not free from suspicion and he was held for trial in spite of representations from President de Gaulle and numerous other public figures.

While the Bolivian Army pursued its futile attempts to round up

Guevara's little band of guerrillas, Venezuela angrily made known on May 12 that it, too, had come under renewed attack from Cuba with the landing of a twelve-man guerrilla force that allegedly included eight Cuban-trained Venezuelans and four Cubans, three of them Army officers. Protesting that it could no longer tolerate such harassment, to which it had repeatedly been exposed in the past, Venezuela demanded that the O.A.S. take vigorous action. Representatives of the American Foreign Ministers accordingly assembled in Washington on June 19 to begin another of their Meetings of Consultation, this one the twelfth in the series. A committee of investigation, dispatched to Venezuela to verify the charges, reported a few weeks later that Cuba was in fact continuing to give moral and material support to the Venezuelan guerrilla and terrorist movement. "The recent series of aggressive acts against Venezuela," the committee reported, was part of a "continuing policy of persistent intervention in the internal affairs of other American states by fostering and organizing subversive and terrorist activities in their territories."[25]

This Cuban-supported revolutionary activity was loudly praised in Peking[26] but aroused no favorable echoes in Moscow, which viewed the Castro regime's external policies with an increasingly jaundiced eye. Castro's insistence on promoting armed revolutions, Latin American Communist leaders maintained, were directly harmful to local Communist interests. The Venezuelan Communist party, for instance, was trying to form a popular front, not to provoke a civil war. "We are neither adventurers who despise the legal ways of struggle, nor are we for positions of opportunism," said Uruguay's Communist leader in an open disavowal of Castro's position.[27] Initially, the U.S.S.R. appears to have made an attempt to straddle the issue. An article in *Pravda* on May 21 contained measured praise for both peaceful and "sharper" methods in Latin America.[28] Within another few weeks, however, the situation had reached a point where a more explicit dissociation from Castro's attitude apparently seemed warranted.

This, it will be remembered, was the period when policy differences within the Soviet leadership were apparently being brought to a head by the war in the Middle East and the subsequent Central Committee meeting in Moscow, which was followed by a reaffirmation of the "moderate" Soviet line in connection with Kosygin's visit to New York and his meetings with President Johnson at Glassboro.[29] How far the Cuban problem may have been touched upon at Glassboro is not publicly known. But events in Cuba itself were by this time moving toward a climax with the approach of a long-heralded revolutionary assembly which was due to open in Havana at the end of July. An outgrowth of the Afro-Asian-Latin American "Tricontinental Congress" held in the Cuban capital in January 1966, this new meeting would be concerned primarily with Latin America but was expected to become a rallying point for left-wing and revolutionary groups from all over the hemisphere.

This was the situation in which Premier Kosygin undertook his surprise visit to Havana immediately following his talks with President Johnson. What passed between the Soviet and Cuban Premiers in the course of Kosygin's four-day visit on June 27-30 was not directly disclosed, but all the evidence indicated that the Soviet leader had counseled a slowdown in Cuban revolutionary efforts and warned that the U.S.S.R. did not intend to support "wars of liberation" in Latin America.[30] Whether or not this advice was influenced by anything President Johnson had said at Glassboro, it formed an interesting parallel to the words of caution the Kremlin was issuing to the U.A.R. and other Arab states in the aftermath of their defeat by Israel.

Castro would seem to have understood the Soviet leader's message but, as on many previous occasions, to have elected not to follow Soviet advice. With the eyes of revolutionary zealots everywhere turned on Havana, the situation presumably seemed to him to call for an intensification, not a toning down, of Cuba's revolutionary fervor. Addressing a huge audience at Santiago de Cuba on July 26, the Cuban leader broadened his country's revolutionary commitment even as he admitted that its base of support had narrowed. Cuba's task, he declared, was to aid all the world's oppressed peoples, including the "black fighters" of the United States—and to do so even under an alleged threat of attack by "the North American imperialist." In countering what he described as U.S. aggressive designs, Castro added, Cuba would have to rely on her own resources, for her "friends"— presumably meaning the U.S.S.R.—were too far away to help effectively.[31] As if to confirm the Soviet disavowal of Castro's revolutionary efforts, *Pravda* republished four days later a complaint by the head of the Chilean Communist party against the Cuban leader's "adventurism" and harmful meddling in the revolutionary affairs of other Latin American countries.[32]

This exchange of courtesies took place at a moment when delegates to the "First Conference of the Organization of Latin American Solidarity," or OLAS, were already assembling in Havana. The split in the revolutionary movement, with the resultant aloofness or hostility of the regular Communist organizations in a number of Latin American countries, made this gathering a good deal less representative than its sponsors had intended. The Argentine, Brazilian, and Venezuelan Communist parties did not attend at all; in other cases, mere splinter groups undertook to represent their countries' "revolutionary forces." Pro-Chinese groups, moreover, were deliberately excluded in line with Castro's attempts to elaborate a specifically Cuban form of Communism that would stand apart from the Russian and Chinese versions. As the OLAS meeting opened on July 31, the 164 delegates from 27 countries and territories—plus assorted observers and guests—seemed less a "solidarity conference" than a conventicle of extreme Left sectaries.[33]

All the more reason, presumably, to underline the radically revolutionary outlook of those who did attend and to reaffirm their commitment to armed struggle and animosity toward the United States. The absent Ché Guevara was elected honorary president of the congress; Stokely Carmichael was produced as evidence of the link between the Latin American revolution and the "revolutionary struggle" of U.S. Negroes.[34] The wave of summer rioting in Detroit and other U.S. cities had been a windfall that Castro and the other organizers of the conference were not slow to exploit. Nothing could have better illustrated their thesis that the whole American continent was gripped by revolutionary feeling and that armed violence was the only answer to the oppressive conditions that weighed upon the masses in North and South America alike. A resolution of one of the committees of the congress hailed the struggle of the black people of the United States against their "aggressors," declared that the people of Latin America regarded it as a part of their own struggle, and exhorted U.S. Negroes to intensify their revolutionary action and reinforce their fraternal relations with the peoples of Asia, Africa, and Latin America.[35]

The emphasis on armed struggle that pervaded the work of the congress was not entirely uncontested. Some representatives of the "legal," pro-Soviet Communist movement were present and put up a vigorous, though ultimately unsuccessful, fight against the condemnation of "certain Socialist countries" for providing economic and technical aid to "oligarchies" and "dictatorships." They also forced a compromise on the text of the final declaration adopted by the congress before its adjournment on August 10. Even in its watered-down form, however, this document declared that it was the right and duty of the Latin American peoples to make revolution; that revolutionary armed struggle was the "fundamental line" of the revolution in Latin America; and that guerrilla warfare was the most effective way of unleashing and developing the revolutionary struggle in most Latin American countries.[36]

The United States and the other American governments were unwilling to let such incitements pass unchallenged. Even before the congress met, the American Foreign Ministers had appointed a special committee to keep an eye on its activities. The congress had hardly got under way before this watchdog group reported that its proceedings amounted to "a further step in the efforts of Communism and other subversive forces in the hemisphere to promote, support, and coordinate guerrilla, terrorist, and other subversive activities directed against established governments." Here, said the committee, was additional testimony to "the efforts of the government of Cuba to control and direct these subversive activities in our hemisphere." Such a conclusion, coming on top of the evidence of Cuban involvement in the Venezuelan disorders, was judged serious enough to warrant the personal attendance of the Foreign Ministers at a further session of the Twelfth Meeting of Consultation, which was accordingly set to reconvene in Washington on September 22.[37]

Contrary to what might have been expected, the Havana congress was followed not by a fresh outburst of guerrilla activity but by a decline in activity already under way. Guerrilla groups operating or attempting to operate in Bolivia, Venezuela, and Nicaragua now appeared to be meeting with serious reverses.[38] These indications did not, however, affect the determination of most other American governments to proceed with some form of disciplinary action against Cuba. Still less were they deterred by the objections of the U.S.S.R., which chose to ignore the criticisms of its own attitude at Havana and appeared to be returning, somewhat half-heartedly, to a pro-Cuban line. Denouncing an alleged intensification of the "anti-Cuban campaign" in the United States and some Latin American countries, the U.S.S.R. in a mid-September statement reaffirmed its promise of "every assistance and support in [Cuba's] struggle for its freedom and independence and for the right to follow the path chosen by the Cuban people."[39]

Such statements, in Secretary Rusk's opinion, misrepresented the real nature of the Cuban problem. "The reason for our policy of isolating Cuba under its present government," Mr. Rusk reminded his fellow Foreign Ministers at the reconvened Meeting of Consultation, "is not its internal system but Castro's policies of promoting and assisting subversion and terrorism in the other countries of the hemisphere and of maintaining military arrangements with an extracontinental power." The evidence of such subversion and intervention, the Secretary of State pointed out, was not confined to the formal reports of O.A.S. investigating bodies. Only the day before, Bolivia's representative had electrified the other Foreign Ministers with a slide show and other evidence indicating that Ché Guevara—now beardless —was personally leading the guerrilla operations in his country. "The task in front of us is a very simple one," Mr. Rusk said. "It is to make it clear to Castro that these activities must stop."[40]

In the past, the United States had usually been well in advance of Latin American opinion on the Cuban issue. This time, it found itself in something of a middle position as compared with the anti-Castro zeal displayed by right-wing and military governments like those of Nicaragua, Bolivia, and Argentina. The most useful actions the American governments could take, Secretary Rusk suggested, would be to condemn and denounce Cuba's actions and policies, seek international support in maintaining the isolation of the Castro regime, intensify coastal and frontier vigilance, and intensify cooperation among neighboring countries, particularly those most affected by the "Castro Communist threat."[41] The United States did not, however, give support to any idea of armed intervention against Cuba, nor did it endorse renewed proposals to set up an inter-American general staff or political defense committee within the O.A.S.

A tightening of the Cuban quarantine thus became the central feature of the resolution which the Foreign Ministers adopted on September 24. Again condemning Cuba's acts of aggression and intervention, the Meeting of Consultation urged friendly outside countries to restrict their contacts with Cuba; called for an Afro-Asian boycott of the tricontinental solidarity organization; expressed concern at the support of Cuba by outside (i.e., Communist) powers; and recommended that O.A.S. member countries intensify their over-all vigilance and, in particular, undertake a partial boycott of vessels trading with Cuba.[42] A further U.S. proposal calling for a blacklist of firms trading with Cuba was not adopted. Mexico, moreover, refused to sign the key resolution, although it supported a separate proposal to acquaint the United Nations with the way in which Cuba had been flouting the U.N. principle of nonintervention.[43]

"It seems to me that we have had a very good meeting indeed, demonstrating the solidarity and unity of the hemisphere," said Secretary Rusk. Hailing the "virtual unanimity" achieved on the Cuban question, Ambassador Linowitz declared that the Castro regime had received not a "slap on the wrist" but "a chop on the arm."[44] Castro himself, however, chose to dismiss the new O.A.S. sanctions as a "ridiculous farce"; and there were others who wondered how far they could really tighten hemisphere security in view of the undeveloped state of most countries' defenses against subversion.[45]

Even without the aid of the new O.A.S. resolutions, it was plain by this time that the guerrilla campaigns of 1967 were approaching an inglorious close. The insurgent group in Bolivia had quite obviously lost the initiative and now sought only to avoid capture as it penetrated deeper into the jungle. On October 9, Bolivian military authorities announced that Ché Guevara himself had been killed in a clash the previous day. Later reports left no doubt that it had indeed been Guevara and that he had in fact been killed, although there remained a strong presumption that he had been slaughtered some hours after being taken prisoner. Two members of the Central Committee of the Cuban Communist party allegedly perished with him.

Guevara's ignominious end not only sealed the fate of the Bolivian venture but seemed to call in question the whole idea of guerrilla operations as an effective revolutionary technique in Latin America. The Guevara experiment had no more "caught on" in Bolivia than similar attempts had caught on in Venezuela or other Latin American countries. Instead of firing the imagination of the indigent rural population, the spark had sputtered and gone out. With Guevara's death, moreover, the insurrectionary cause had lost its most appealing figure, just as the death of the Congolese Patrice Lumumba a few years earlier had deprived the cause of extremist nationalism in Africa of one of its most effective symbols.

Yet it would have been premature to equate this setback with a collapse of the threat of revolutionary violence. In some ways, Guevara dead might be a more potent figure than Guevara living. Acknowledging that he had disagreed with his associate in some particulars, Premier Castro gave evidence of planning to intensify the Guevara cult in much the way that Lumumba's backers had sought to manipulate that leader's image in a continuing assault on "colonialism and neocolonialism." The very mystery surrounding Guevara's death assured him a certain posthumous notoriety, while the fate of Régis Debray, who was soon to be sentenced by a Bolivian military court to 30 years' imprisonment, would lend the revolutionary cause an added measure of respectability in the eyes of intellectuals the world over. The world-wide prestige already attached to anti-U.S. revolutionary sentiments appeared to many observers to find reflection at this time in the award of the Nobel Prize for literature to Miguel A. Asturias, a Guatemalan writer and diplomat whose political outlook had already gained him the U.S.S.R.'s Lenin Peace Prize.

The abysmal poverty and unrest prevailing along the backbone of South America would meanwhile continue to harbor a potential for new revolutionary outbreaks. Efforts to improve conditions in this whole area were getting under way with the establishment of a multinational Andean Development Corporation in which Chile, Colombia, Peru, Ecuador, and Venezuela intended to join forces in line with the regional integration philosophy projected at Punta del Este. But it remained a question whether such efforts, here or elsewhere in Latin America, could bear fruit in time to head off new explosions of revolutionary violence.

Guevara's fiasco did nothing to improve the cold relations between Cuba and the U.S.S.R. Castro, in fact, appeared determined that not only the Soviets but the world at large should know the extent of his dissatisfaction with Moscow's attitude. Instead of going in person to the U.S.S.R.'s November anniversary celebration or sending President Osvaldo Dorticós Torrado, the Cuban Premier chose a lowly Minister of Health to head the Cuban delegation. No Cuban representative attended the Kremlin diplomatic reception on November 6, nor did Castro send any congratulatory message to the Soviet leaders. In conversation with foreign visitors, he freely expounded his differences with the U.S.S.R. on guerrilla tactics, on Communist trade with Latin American countries, and even on the Soviet policy of relying on "material incentives" as a stimulus to production.[46] Late in the year it was reported that some 40 pro-Soviet Communists had actually been jailed in Cuba in consequence of their opposition to Castro's insurgency program.[47]

In insisting on the right to determine its own policy, Cuba was merely availing itself of the same freedom of action that had already been seized by Yugoslavia, Rumania, and other members of the "camp of Socialism." Castro's moves were perhaps bolder in the sense that Cuba, in addition to its absolute dependence on Soviet economic support, was doomed to occupy an exposed strategic position in the very shadow of the United States. On the other hand, the Cuban leader could presumably count on Moscow's unwillingness to desert him completely if only because the Soviet leaders would fear to see him move into the Chinese Communist camp. As for his theories of revolution, their ultimate proof or disproof would depend not only on the attitude of the disaffected peoples in the hemisphere but also on the success of the other American governments in carrying out the pledges they had lately renewed at Punta de Este.

42 : Local Thunderstorms

For most American governments, the implementation of the Punta del Este decisions was but one among many ongoing preoccupations. The fact that no Latin American country experienced a violent change of government in 1967 might conceivably be interpreted as a sign that the political environment in Latin America was improving in spite of revolutionary incitements from Havana. Yet several Latin American countries experienced a measure of domestic travail that thrust the questions discussed at Punta del Este far into the background. New problems also arose to trouble the common life of the inter-American family and of the Caribbean neighbors who were more and more becoming a part of it.

One of the most curious episodes of these months was the near-disruption of the new West Indian Associated State of St. Kitts-Nevis-Anguilla. Incensed at finding themselves subjected to the administrative jurisdiction of St. Kitts, Anguillan leaders declared their island independent on May 30, got the decision ratified by a referendum of the 6,000 inhabitants, rejected a compromise solution worked out at a Commonwealth conference in Barbados, and repeatedly though vainly sought diplomatic recognition by the United States. Not until December did the Anguillans resign themselves to a compromise settlement involving the designation of a British administrator to look after their interests within the three-island federation. In the meantime the situation had been complicated both by differences between Anguillan leaders and by charges that U.S. financial interests were attempting to exploit the situation for their own advantage. True or not, such allegations illustrated the unplanned yet often violent impact of private U.S. activities on the life of neighboring areas. A somewhat comparable situation existed in the British-ruled Bahamas, whose first all-Negro government, installed at the beginning of the year, showed great uneasiness about the influence exercised by U.S. gambling interests in economic and even political affairs.

The emergence of new self-governing entities in areas where British influence had formerly been paramount was already modifying the political complexion of the hemisphere as well as the linguistic and cultural balance within the O.A.S., to which both Trinidad and Tobago and Barbados were admitted in the course of the year. The implication of such trends for the United States, it was announced, was to be examined in depth over the coming months by a special presidential study group led by Milton Barall.[48] Such a study would presumably be unable to ignore the problems of the United States' own dependency of Puerto Rico, where a referendum held on July 23 disclosed a strong majority in favor of maintaining the existing "Commonwealth" status but failed to satisfy either the advocates of U.S. statehood or the much smaller group that clamored for outright independence.

Another aspect of the U.S. position in the Caribbean that remained subject to great uncertainty concerned the future status of the Panama Canal, still tied up in protracted diplomatic discussions that also involved a plan to construct a second, sea-level canal in Panamanian or adjacent territory. Apparently hoping to strengthen the political position of Panamanian President Marco A. Robles, the United States and Panama announced on June 26 that three separate but related treaties dealing with these issues had been drawn up and currently awaited governmental approval.[49] The texts, however, were not made public for fear of nationalist repercussions in Panama, where political temperatures were rising in anticipation of the presidential elections scheduled for May 12, 1968. As autumn advanced it became evident that nothing further could be accomplished before the elections, and that the U.S. commission appointed to study alternative routes for the proposed sea-level waterway would also require more time to complete its task.

The United States' relations with Mexico continued to present a heartening contrast to the uncertainties encountered in dealings with more southerly neighbors. These two countries, said President Johnson as he welcomed President Díaz Ordaz on a visit to the White House on October 26, respected each other's rights and approached their transitory differences in such a spirit of compromise and good will that their relations were now "closer than they have ever been in the history of our two Republics." This gratifying if scarcely novel assertion was amply borne out in the course of the Mexican leader's visit, which found him agreeing with President Johnson on a nine-point "action program" for dealing with common problems, warning the U.S. Congress against the dangers of reviving protectionism, and accompanying his host to the U.S.-Mexican border for ceremonies marking the final transfer to Mexican jurisdiction of the El Chamizal territory formerly located in El Paso, Texas.[50]

This display of mutual good will contrasted sharply with the humiliation the United States had lately experienced at the hands of Ecuador, where President Arosemena's anti-U.S. feelings had failed to abate in the months since Punta del Este. In a speech to the American school in Guayaquil, U.S. Ambassador Wymberley DeR. Coerr had taken issue with Arosemena's criticisms of the Alliance for Progress and U.S. policy in terms that the State Department found "reasoned" and "nonpolemical" but were construed by Ecuador as "public, open criticism" of the President. In consequence, Ecuador demanded on the weekend of October 8 that the Ambassador be recalled within 48 hours. Bowing to traditional diplomatic practice, the United States complied immediately, expressing "genuine sorrow" over "this manifestation of lack of understanding and of confidence in the Alliance for Progress."[51] A few weeks later, Washington agreed to the establishment of a joint committee to renegotiate current and planned loans to Ecuador and eliminate features that country found distasteful.[52]

Relations with Peru were also somewhat chilled at this period as a result of policy differences exacerbated by Peruvian nationalism and internal politics. In pursuance of its view that Latin American countries ought not to waste their resources on expensive items of military equipment, the United States had intervened with Great Britain during the summer to dissuade it from selling Peru six old-fashioned Canberra bombers that country had been seeking for several months. Peru, however, instead of deferring to the superior wisdom of the United States, had turned to France and arranged to purchase a dozen of that country's ultramodern, supersonic Mirage-V fighter-bombers.[53] President Fernando Belaúnde Terry, it appeared, had been under heavy military pressure to strengthen the Air Force despite a mounting economic crisis that had led among other things to a devaluation of the sol on September 1. Yet Belaúnde's own political standing was also growing increasingly precarious. The outlook for a country which, at one time, had seemed destined for high honors under the Alliance for Progress was further clouded toward the end of the year by the filing of exorbitant financial claims against the U.S.-owned International Petroleum Company, an old bugbear of Peruvian nationalism.[54]

Chile went through a sharp internal crisis in November as the result of cabinet and trade-union opposition to an anti-inflationary plan devised by President Frei that involved the withholding of part of a planned wage increase. Five persons were killed in a general strike against the plan on November 23. Not long afterward, the government suffered a new political setback in the election of a Communist-supported opposition figure to fill a key vacancy in the Senate. Tired of trying to govern against the combined opposition of Left and Right, President Frei began to talk of trying to broaden his political base by taking in the leftist parties despite their well-advertised lack of enthusiasm for the Alliance for Progress.

Uruguay was another country whose continued internal turmoil belied such hopes as had accompanied the recent inauguration of President Gestido. Inflation and popular unrest increased from week to week, yet Gestido delayed asserting his authority until October, when the threat of a general strike afforded an opportunity to remodel his cabinet and institute much-needed stabilization measures. Like other Latin American countries, Uruguay suffered a new blow in the devaluation of the British pound, which was followed by a readjustment of the exchange values of various Latin American currencies. Before Gestido's new stabilization program could begin to show results, the President himself succumbed to a heart attack and died on December 6. His successor, Jorge Pacheco Areco, lost no time in beginning negotiations for a U.S. credit as well as new trade agreements with the U.S.S.R. and other Communist countries. He also took stern measures against leftist newspapers that followed the Castro line in objecting to Soviet economic ties with "bourgeois" countries.[55]

A matter of wider concern in Latin America and the United States was a growing furor over arms policy, the direct result of Peru's purchase of French jets and a parallel deal by Argentina involving 50 modern French tanks. Apart from its annoyance over this French intrusion into hemisphere concerns, the United States deplored a trend that ran directly counter to the Punta del Este pledge to "eliminate unnecessary military expenditures" and apply all available resources to development. U.S. authorities still insisted that there was no "arms race" in Latin America, that the Latin American countries were merely trying to modernize their obsolete military establishments, and that military expenditure in Latin America was less than in any other part of the world.[56] Yet there was no denying that the arms disease was spreading. Brazil, it was said, was also in the market for supersonic aircraft and was eager to purchase 20 Northrop F-5 tactical fighters, hitherto unavailable to Latin American countries as a matter of U.S. policy. To add to the administration's embarrassment, Congress was already in an uproar over the discovery that the United States had been financing a limited amount of arms sales in the hemisphere through special credits negotiated by the Pentagon and underwritten by the Export-Import Bank.[57]

New policies to deal with this complex situation seemed clearly necessary; but the interested elements of the U.S. Government were not of one mind about the kind of policy required. One approach much favored in Congress called for a straight reduction in funds for military assistance to Latin America. These funds, however, were already severely limited and thus represented only a small part of the problem. Wary of any scheme that smacked of U.S. coercion, State Department officials preferred the idea of getting the Latin American governments to assume the major responsibility themselves and try to relate their arms spending to development needs through the annual review procedure of the Alliance for Progress.[58] There remained, however, the possibility that Latin American governments would insist on making substantial arms purchases even if Congress, or the Alliance for Progress authorities, failed to approve. In such cases, Washington would naturally prefer that its friends should at least get the most suitable equipment, and that the United States—rather than France or Britain—should get the sales. In line with this thinking, it was disclosed in mid-October that the United States had already relaxed its previous ban on supersonic jet sales in Latin America and would no longer object if individual Latin American governments wished to negotiate with the manufacturer of the F-5.[59]

Such news afforded little cheer to those in Congress who were already upset about the whole subject of U.S. arms policy in the developing world and were beginning, perhaps illogically, to reappraise their attitude not merely toward arms aid but toward foreign aid in general. Uneasiness about these matters played a part in the year-end congressional revolt which ultimately resulted in the smallest foreign aid appropriation since the beginning of the program. Not content with reducing direct military assistance to Latin America to a mere $75 million for the next fiscal year, Congress inserted in the Foreign Assistance Act of 1967 a special provision denying all development or food aid to countries that diverted aid funds to military purchases or used their own funds for unnecessary military expenditures.[60] These restrictions were further tightened in the subsequent Foreign Aid Appropriation Act, which explicitly barred direct aid for sophisticated weapons systems (such as missile systems and jet aircraft) and directed that if underdeveloped countries spent their own money on such systems, an equivalent amount should be deducted from U.S. economic assistance.[61]

Curbing the good together with the bad, Congress also reduced its appropriation for the peaceful activities of the Alliance for Progress to the lowest level since the start of that program. In March, the legislature had failed to act on President Johnson's request for an increase in Alliance funds in advance of Punta del Este. By November, it had reduced the authorization of new money for the fiscal year 1968 from the $643 million recommended by the President to $578 million. This figure, in turn, was further reduced to $469,330,000 in the funds actually appropriated in December.

Those who saw such actions as a body blow to the Alliance for Progress had further cause for low spirits in the unhappy condition of the O.A.S., which was going through an internal crisis that pointed up its growing inadequacy to the tasks the member states had imposed upon it. Particularly serious difficulties had developed with respect to the election of a new Secretary-General to succeed José A. Mora of Uruguay, whose term would expire in May 1968. Initially, the outstanding candidate was former President Galo Plaza Lasso of Ecuador, whose abilities and independence of mind were highly valued both in the United States and elsewhere. Señor Galo Plaza's very reputation, however, may have damaged his chances by making him look too much like a U.S. or "big-power" candidate. Other aspirants were also in the field, and a solid bloc of Central American states threw its support to Eduardo Ritter Aislán of Panama, who was also backed, with some disregard for protocol, by members of the O.A.S. bureaucracy. After a series of inconclusive balloting sessions, the choice of a new Secretary-General had to be put over into 1968.

Concurrently, a series of administrative mishaps, among them the dismissal of an O.A.S. official for improper political activity and another for financial irregularities, emphasized the deficiencies of the organization's administrative standards and the need for vigorous reforms if its prestige was to recover. In conjunction with the political strains in many parts of the hemisphere, the conflicts over arms policy, the widespread discouragement over what was beginning to look like an actual slowdown in economic progress, and the resentment provoked by the latest U.S. aid cutbacks, such disarray within the O.A.S. was bound to accentuate the sense of general letdown that had followed the momentary exhilaration of Punta del Este.[62]

Months earlier, Senator Dirksen had summarized his views on the Alliance for Progress in the sarcastic question, "Where is the alliance? Where is the progress?"[63] In some respects the question seemed even more pertinent in December than it had in January. Ambassador Linowitz, it is true, insisted that Latin America stood on the verge of a tremendous boom like that of the United States in the late nineteenth century. Assistant Secretary Oliver saw the hemisphere as inspired by "a new pride and a new hope for a better future." Secretary Rusk continued to contrast the forward-looking agreement reached at Punta del Este with the "sharp reverses" encountered by "Castro's efforts to promote guerrilla warfare and subversion in the Western Hemisphere."[64] Castro and his friends were obviously not doing very well at the moment; yet it seemed that the non-Marxist nations would also have to improve their performance if the revolution already under way in the Americas was to retain the imprint of their inherited standards and values.

9 : Attention: The World

Twenty-two years had elapsed, in 1967, since the historic day on which the United States had joined with 50 others among the world's older nations to create an international organization aimed at eliminating war and establishing conditions in which peace could flourish. Announcing the annual observance of United Nations Day on October 24, President Johnson declared with pride that the United States, during those 22 years, had "faithfully honored its commitments to the world body, in pursuit of a just and lasting peace." Mr. Johnson did not deny, however, that the record of the organization fell short of the hopes that had accompanied its foundation. "The United Nations," he pointed out, "has no magic formula for solving the increasingly complex problems of our revolutionary age. Its failures have disheartened those who saw in it the only hope for peace in a world torn by strife. Yet despite those failures, it has achieved much that could not have been achieved without it. It remains the symbol, and the standard, of man's desire to turn away from ancient quarrels and make peace with his neighbor."[1]

Though involved in every phase of the world's concerns from peace-keeping to the preservation of ancient monuments, the United Nations and its family of associated agencies had never been able to assume the full responsibility for channeling the strains and stresses of a world in movement. As President Johnson himself remarked in

336

another connection during 1967, "Our investment in the United Nations, and its various agencies and special programs, *supplements other activities* undertaken to preserve, protect, or promote a wide range of national interests."[2] Spokesmen for almost any one of the 122 states enrolled as U.N. members at the beginning of 1967 could have said the same. The United Nations had, or could create, facilities for dealing with practically any international problem, global or local, political, economic, social, legal, scientific or technical. The employment of these facilities, in any given instance, depended not merely on their availability but on the judgment of the interested parties as to how far their use was likely to further the particular national interests at stake.

The nature and extent of U.N. involvement in world affairs was thus extremely uneven. On the problems of the Middle East, its role had been central if not decisive. In the Far East, similarly, it had set important precedents by its resistance to Communist aggression in Korea in 1950-53, but had since that time been scarcely more than an interested bystander. On questions like disarmament and the emancipation of colonial territories it had proved more effective in passing hortatory resolutions than in swaying the policies of nations. Even a matter of such general interest as the promotion of economic development in Asia, Africa, and Latin America was only partially handled within a U.N. framework. Any realistic examination of the problems that involved the United Nations in the 1960's must thus invoke a kind of "bifocal" vision encompassing activities outside the U.N. as well as within it.

43 : The U.N. and World Politics

It is easy to realize why the United States, in President Johnson's phrase, regarded the United Nations as supplemental rather than central to its own foreign policy. Like most of the constituent nations, the United States had seen a need for an organization like the United Nations but, at the same time, had been reluctant to concede decisive powers to an instrumentality whose future behavior it could not be sure of controlling within acceptable limits. That had been its reason for insisting, like the other great powers, on the right to veto substantive decisions by the Security Council, a right on which it still continued to rely even though it had never felt compelled to make use of it in practice. As time went on, moreover, this initial feeling of reserve had been reinforced by the realization that the American viewpoint in the United Nations was becoming a minority viewpoint and that the United States was increasingly outnumbered by members who entertained a radically different view of the world situation and its requirements, as well as the responsibilities of the world organization in meeting them. In the early years of the United Nations, the preferences of the United States and its friends had been seriously challenged only by the six delegations of the Soviet bloc—joined, on occasion, by a few of the Asian nations—and had normally been upheld by large, Western-oriented majorities. But the gradual increase in U.N. membership to well over twice its original number, including many former colonial territories in Asia and Africa, had decisively shifted the balance of opinion and voting power within the General Assembly. With the expansion of the Security Council from eleven to fifteen members in 1966, a similar change had become apparent in that body, although the great powers continued to retain essential control though the retention of the rule of unanimity. The outlook of the Secretariat had also shifted with the selection of U Thant of Burma, an outspoken foe of "colonialism" and "cold war" policies, to succeed the more Western-minded Dag Hammarskjold of Sweden after the latter's death in 1961.

The majority among the newer U.N. members had found far more to criticize than to support in the attitude of the United States and its more influential friends. Few new states had seen any reason to support a policy that was obviously more concerned with countering Communist initiatives than with speeding the emancipation of colonial peoples or providing funds for developing countries. Their expressions of dissatisfaction had been supported as a matter of course by the Communist members and, in many cases by Latin American and even some Western countries. The Western group itself had become increasingly divided in recent years over such difficult issues as the representation of China in the world organization and the financing of U.N. peace-keeping operations. France, under Gaullism, had taken as individualistic a stand in U.N. affairs as in the other affairs of the Western community.

As a result of these trends, there were by the mid-1960's few significant U.N. questions on which the United States could count on majority support for its own viewpoint, and a great many on which it could be certain in advance that it would be outvoted. This state of affairs had bred a natural hesitancy to confront the United Nations with matters in which U.S. interests were heavily engaged—particularly when, as in the case of Vietnam, the U.N. gave little evidence of being able to take effective action at all. Not only had American authorities become increasingly doubtful about the U.N.'s capacity to handle issues of special interest to the United States. They had also voiced concern about a growing tendency on the part of some of the newer members, particularly African states, to override the elementary rules of legality and parliamentary procedure in their zeal to give effect to their particular viewpoint. The late Adlai E. Stevenson had warned against this tendency as early as 1963, and Ambassador Goldberg, as Mr. Stevenson's successor, saw fit to issue a similar warning early in 1967.[3]

Such differences help to explain the fact that despite repeated efforts over the years, the United Nations had never been able to equip itself with effective means for carrying out its primary task, the maintenance of international peace and security. The original idea of establishing regular military forces under the Security Council had proved unrealizable, mainly as the result of differences between the United States and the U.S.S.R. Lacking a permanent international force, the organization had repeatedly been compelled to create emergency international forces on the spur of the moment to deal with dangerous situations of the sort that had developed in the Middle East in 1956-57, the Congo in 1960, and Cyprus in 1964. Attempts to place this vital function on a firmer, more permanent basis had been set at naught by the refusal of the U.S.S.R., France, and some other countries to acknowledge the legality of the operations in question—or to concede their obligation to help pay for them, in accordance with the requirements of the Charter as interpreted by the International Court of Justice. These disputes had virtually immobilized the United Nations for a prolonged period in 1964-65 during which the organization had been brought close to bankruptcy as a result of the heavy financial obligations incurred during the Congo operation.

By 1967, the financial pressures had eased to some extent despite the continued failure of the U.S.S.R. and France to pay their past assessments or come forward with substantial voluntary contributions, as they had at one time appeared to intend. But the political differences on the peace-keeping question appeared as intractable as ever as the 33-nation Special Committee on Peace-keeping Operations, first established by the General Assembly in 1965, resumed its search for a method of financing future peace-keeping efforts should the need arise. In a series of meetings that continued from February to May, the committee failed to agree on anything of importance except that it would need additional time to carry out its task. The U.S.S.R. did renew its proposal to assist U.N. finances with a voluntary contribution of unstated size; but it hedged the offer by making it contingent on parallel action by the United States. Having already met its regular assessments for peace-keeping purposes and made substantial voluntary contributions in addition, the United States quite refused to make any new commitment before the Soviet Union had acted.[4]

Such was the state of the dicussion when the General Assembly convened on April 21 in its Fifth Special Session, the primary purpose of which was to provide for the future of South West Africa.[5] In view of the disagreements among the major countries, there was little the Assembly could do about the peace-keeping question except to hear the opposing views and, in a resolution adopted on May 23, renew its appeal for voluntary contributions and ask the Special Committee to continue its work and report progress in the fall.[6] By the time this resolution was adopted, the peace-keeping function had been dealt a further blow by Abdel Nasser's insistence on the removal of the U.N. Emergency Force from the Egyptian-Israeli armistice line.[7] The subsequent course of the Middle East crisis did nothing to compensate for this setback; indeed, the Committee of 33 reported in September that it had been unable to go on with its studies at all in view of the preoccupation of the U.N. membership with other matters.[8] The only practical advantage flowing from the liquidation of UNEF would be the saving of some $14 million a year in a financial situation which, U Thant reported in September, remained "precarious" even though "not immediately critical."[9]

The Middle East war did equally little to enhance the U.N.'s wider reputation as an instrumentality for peace. With the United States and the U.S.S.R. committed to opposite aims in the Middle Eastern situation, the Security Council could neither prevent the outbreak of fighting nor get the fighting stopped until Israel had achieved its objectives and was ready to halt of its own accord. Still less was the Security Council able to give timely guidance concerning the requirements for a peaceful settlement; and the General Assembly, subsequently convened on Soviet initiative in its Fifth Emergency Special Session, was also unable to take a coherent stand on the major issues.[10] Only the essentially nonpolitical efforts of the U.N. Truce Supervision Organization and the U.N. Relief and Works Agency for Palestine Refugees (UNRWA) were pursued with a modicum of success during the troubled postwar months.

Later in the year, the United Nations was to exert a more effective influence in the Greek-Turkish crisis over Cyprus, where the major powers were not directly at odds and the U.N. peace-keeping presence in the form of UNFICYP, the U.N. Force in Cyprus, was not directly challenged. Although the Security Council and other U.N. agencies played only a supplemental role in the solution of the November crisis, the concept of a continued and even expanded role for UNFICYP (which, unlike UNEF, was financed entirely by voluntary contributions from the United States and others) was central to the entire arrangement.[11]

In dealing with these issues, the U.N. at least attempted to meet the responsibilities imposed by its own charter. Quite different was the experience with Vietnam, an even more dangerous conflict in which the United Nations as an organization could play no fruitful role at all in view of such factors as the direct involvement of the United States, the Soviet commitment in support of North Vietnam, and Hanoi's refusal to recognize U.N. competence in a matter originally regulated by the Geneva Conference of 1954. Although the United States had acted as early as February 1966 to place the Vietnam issue on the agenda of the Security Council, repeated consultations since that date had disclosed no prospect of a fruitful discussion, and this negative outlook was to be confirmed late in 1967 by Ambassador Goldberg's soundings pursuant to the U.S. Senate resolution of November 30.[12]

Its inability to deal effectively with the Vietnam issue had not, of course, prevented the United Nations from becoming deeply involved in all the controversies arising from U.S. action there. U Thant, who claimed to see analogies between the Vietcong struggle and the American war of independence,[13] had not only been active "on a personal basis" in exploring the possibilities for negotiation but had become more and more outspoken in his condemnation of the bombing and other aspects of U.S. policy.[14] Although such strictures did little to promote good feeling between the United Nations and the American Government, they reflected a point of view that was obviously shared in greater or less degree by the vast majority of U.N. members. Seldom, in fact, had the United States appeared so isolated on a major issue in an organization it had done so much to bring into being and keep alive.

Disarmament and arms control was another area of vital U.N. responsibility, and one in which the possibility of progress had usually been directly dependent on the measure of agreement prevailing between the United States and the U.S.S.R. As in the peace-keeping field, the search for practical arms limitation measures had been entrusted by the General Assembly to smaller and more specialized bodies. Chief among them was, of course, the Eighteen-Nation Disarmament Committee, whose search for agreement on a nuclear non-proliferation treaty has been reviewed in an earlier chapter.[15] In addition, the U.N. Committee on the Peaceful Uses of Outer Space had been given important responsibilities for discouraging warlike activities as well as promoting peaceful cooperation beyond the earth's atmosphere. Having successfully completed the negotiation of the general treaty on outer space that was to come into force in October 1967,[16] the Space Committee had gone on to other tasks which will be considered later in this chapter.

Of livelier interest to many U.N. members was the organization's long-standing crusade against "colonialism" and the related phenomenon of racial discrimination, or *apartheid,* as practiced in South Africa and the territory under its administration. Pressed with more ardor than results, this campaign had reached a high point in the 1966 Assembly resolution revoking South Africa's mandate over South West Africa and providing for U.N. administration of that territory pending its early accession to independence.[17] This action, however, had manifested the practical weaknesses of the U.N. as well as the emotional fervor of many of its members. Even with its mandate revoked, South Africa still remained in control of the South West African territory. There seemed no practical way of dislodging it except by the use of force; and the major powers that might conceivably have been able to employ sufficient force for the purpose were plainly quite unwilling to do so. As already noted, this state of affairs completely frustrated the efforts of the special U.N. committee charged with devising "practical means" of administering South West Africa during the transition to independence, and likewise prevented the adoption of an effective resolution at the Assembly's Special Session in the spring of 1967.[18] Here again, the United States with its commitment to "dialogue" and peaceful procedures was quite unable to meet the desires of the anticolonial majority that insisted on prompt and decisive action.

The fight against colonialism was carried forward between sessions of the General Assembly by the 24-nation Special Committee established in 1961 to press for implementation of the Declaration on the Granting of Independence to Colonial Countries and Peoples.[19] As in previous years, this committee continued throughout 1967 its vigorous criticism of the actions and policies of colonial powers in a host of non-self-governing territories that ranged from Gibraltar and the British colonies in the Caribbean and the Indian Ocean to Guam, American Samoa, and the Portuguese, French, and British possessions in Africa. Also as in previous years, the United States and Great Britain attempted to resist the prevailing impetuosity but were regularly and overwhelmingly outvoted by a majority made up of anticolonial and Communist nations. The high point of the committee's 1967 activities was a visit to Africa for meetings in the Congo, Zambia, and Tanzania. Its most significant contribution to anticolonial doctrine was a harsh indictment of the foreign interests that were alleged to be impeding decolonization in Southern Africa and other territories under colonial administration.[20]

While the effectiveness of this anticolonial agitation was difficult to prove, the number of territories actually subject to colonial domination continued to shrink as new states shook off the last vestiges of foreign, primarily British, rule. The former British-administered territories of Botswana, Lesotho, and Barbados had acceded to independence and joined the United Nations in 1966. Aden and the South Arabian Federation, not content with London's promise of independence by early 1968, were already getting ahead of the British timetable and would in fact achieve independence as the People's Republic of Southern Yemen on November 30, 1967.[21] Six British West Indian territories, as already noted, combined in 1967 to form a new self-governing federation called the West Indies (Associated States).[22] Promised full independence for 1968 were Britain's Indian Ocean colony of Mauritius, its African protectorate of Swaziland, and the U.N. Trust Territory of Nauru, a Pacific island with a population of 3,100 that was jointly administered by the United Kingdom, Australia, and New Zealand.

Nauru's accession to independence would leave the United Nations with responsibility for only two remaining Trust Territories of its original total of eleven. One of these was Australian-administered New Guinea, the other the U.S.-administered Strategic Trust Territory of the Pacific Islands.[23] While the Trusteeship Council and the Committee of 24 continued to press for independence for these and other non-self-governing territories, U Thant was already worrying about the proliferation of "microstates" whose limited area, population, and resources raised doubts about their suitability for full membership in the international community. With minor exceptions, all new countries thus far had been voted into the United Nations as a matter of course. In the introduction to his annual report, U Thant suggested that it might in future be preferable to establish other forms of association for "microstates" which would give them the benefits of membership without saddling them with disproportionate burdens and responsibilities.[24]

Promotion of respect for human rights and fundamental freedoms was another U.N. area in which American policy and practice diverged from majority preferences. Despite its strong commitment in support of human rights at home and abroad, the United States had always been in two minds about the U.N.-sponsored attempt to ensure the exercise of basic human rights by embodying them in international treaties. Individual Americans had played a leading role in this effort; but the executive branch and, still more, the Senate had been profoundly hesitant to associate the United States with the results. The Convention on Genocide,[25] a product of unofficial American initiative, had been awaiting Senate approval since 1949 and no longer appeared to have the slightest prospect of ratification. President Kennedy, in 1963, had sought Senate approval for three further conventions dating from the mid-1950's that dealt respectively with the abolition of slavery, the abolition of forced labor, and the political rights of women.[26] Yet it was not until February 1967 that Ambassador Goldberg was invited to appear before the Foreign Relations Committee to develop the case for ratification. Urging that action on the three conventions be completed in time for the 1968 observance of International Year for Human Rights, Mr. Goldberg pointed out that the

United States already guaranteed the rights in question to its own citizens and, in ratifying, would merely be helping to project its own values on a wider scale.[27] On recommendation of the Foreign Relations Committee, the Senate later voted unanimous approval of one of the three conventions— the Supplementary Convention on the Abolition of Slavery, the Slave Trade, and Institutions and Practices Similar to Slavery—which accordingly became binding on the United States as from December 6, 1967. But the Foreign Relations Committee declined to recommend the conventions on forced labor and the political rights of women on the ground that they involved domestic matters.[28]

In view of its urgent need for Senate support on the space treaty and the U.S.-Soviet Consular Convention, the administration made no move during 1967 to associate the United States with more recent U.N. human rights conventions. The International Convention on the Elimination of all Forms of Racial Discrimination, adopted by the General Assembly in 1965[29] and signed by the United States on September 28, 1966, was not submitted to the Senate during 1967. Nor did the United States disclose whether or not it would eventually sign the International Covenant on Economic, Social and Cultural Rights and the International Covenant on Civil and Political Rights, both adopted by the General Assembly with American support on December 16, 1966.[30] U Thant, in the introduction to his annual report, expressed the hope that the forthcoming observance of Human Rights Year would provide a new stimulus toward bringing these recent conventions into effect. Countries that might think of holding aloof because of the guarantees of human rights incorporated in their domestic legislation, he said, "should realize that their active participation in this United Nations long-term effort is also an important part of their contribution to international solidarity and to the efforts to attain the Charter objectives of peace, economic and social cooperation and the harmonization of the action of nations."[31]

44 : The Expanding Environment

With the increasing membership of the international community had gone a parallel increase in the scope of its interests. At the founding of the United Nations in 1945, the responsibilities of the world organization had been limited for all practical purposes to the habitable earth. The term "global," in those days, had defined the utmost reach of the international imagination. Twenty-two years later, the expansion of man's horizons had already done away with such arbitrary limitations and carried the international interest into the boundless reaches of the universe. Concurrently, the nature and potentialities of the earth itself were being subjected to an intensive reexamination that likewise projected the community interest into new areas, new elements, and new forms of activity.

Two types of international concern ran parallel throughout this broad process of scientific investigation and technological innovation, which, in the aggregate, was revolutionizing both man's knowledge of his environment and his own place in it. One such concern was the need for new definitions of national rights and responsibilities at a time when governments and their citizens were rapidly extending their activities outside the traditional areas of national sovereignty. The other concern arose from the increasingly self-evident need for international cooperation in curbing the hazards and exploiting the opportunities, both scientific and practical, that accompanied this activity and, in many cases, transcended the potentialities of any one government.

The Antarctic Treaty of 1959,[32] with its dual emphasis on the reservation of Antarctica for peaceful purposes and on the promotion of scientific cooperation on a basis of freedom of scientific investigation, had represented a pioneering effort to satisfy this twofold interest in a single international compact. Later experience under the treaty bore ample testimony to the success of this experiment. Early in 1967, for example, a routine inspection by the United States of Antarctic stations maintained by other parties to the treaty gave evidence that even the U.S.S.R., despite its strong resistance to any form of outside inspection on its own territory, was fully conforming to the spirit and provisions of the international regime established for Antarctica.[33]

In setting up its Committee on the Peaceful Uses of Outer Space, the U.N. General Assembly had opted for a somewhat similar approach that bracketed the legal with the scientific aspects of space activity. But though the guiding principles elaborated for outer space since 1959 were not dissimilar to those inspiring the Antarctic Treaty, their implementation had proved much more difficult. Arising in part from the inherent uncertainties attendant on man's first ventures outside the earth's atmosphere, these difficulties also reflected the persistently competitive nature of the "space race" between the United States and the U.S.S.R.

The fruits of ten years' effort to define the international interest in space were not, however, by any means inconsiderable. On the legal side, a really substantial achievement had been recorded of late with the negotiation of the already mentioned Treaty on Principles Governing the Activities of States in the Exploration and Use of Outer Space, Including the Moon and Other Celestial Bodies.[34] This epoch-making document, as previously noted, was opened for signature in January 1967, approved by both the U.S. Senate and the Supreme Soviet of the U.S.S.R., and signed by some 84 nations up to the time of its entry into force on October 10, 1967.[35] Admittedly, the provisions of the "Treaty on Principles" were not sufficiently comprehensive to preclude all forms of military activity in space, and the United States had gone ahead with its plans for a military "Manned Orbiting Laboratory" (MOL) and a multiwarhead "space bus" even while the Soviet Union was pressing the development of its "Fractional Orbital Bombardment System" (FOBS).[36] Nevertheless the treaty represented a bold beginning that would, among other things, preclude the advancement of claims of sovereignty in space as the race to the moon and other celestial bodies intensified.

The record on scientific cooperation in space was less impressive. Although the United States and its non-Communist friends collaborated on a wide variety of space projects, there had thus far been little real cooperation between the United States and the U.S.S.R. The programs of both of these space giants were still essentially geared to competition, not cooperation; and neither the vaguely worded American invitations to cooperate nor the costs and difficulties of a competitive approach had yet sufficed to modify this trend appreciably. The setbacks and disappointments encountered by the space powers during 1967 were, however, of an unusually serious nature. Three American astronauts—Virgil I. Grissom, Edward H. White, 2nd, and Roger B. Chaffee—were killed when their simulated Apollo spacecraft burned on the launching pad on January 27. Soviet cosmonaut Vladimir M. Komarov lost his life on April 24 on reentry from a manned orbital flight, the U.S.S.R.'s first in two years. Among the indications of a slackening momentum in space enterprises were

a subsequent slowdown in the U.S. lunar program and the postponement, on Soviet initiative, of a U.N. Conference on the Exploration
and Peaceful Uses of Outer Space that was to have met in Vienna in
September 1967.[37] Although the United States persisted in its proclaimed intention of landing men on the moon in 1969-1970 and
carried out a number of spectacular preliminary missions,[38] its over-
all space effort was increasingly hampered by waning public and
congressional interest and by successive budget cuts that would particularly affect the planetary space flights envisaged for the 1970's.
The budgetary allotment for fiscal year 1968, for which President
Johnson originally recommended an appropriation of $5.05 billion,
was ultimately set as low as $4.6 billion, and there were indications
that still heavier cuts would be imposed in the following fiscal year.

Such troubles perhaps encouraged President Johnson to renew his
standing invitation to the U.S.S.R. to join the United States in cooperative space ventures. In a message on communications policy sent
to Congress on August 14, the President particularly urged the Soviet
Union and its Eastern European associates to join the 58-nation International Telecommunications Satellite Consortium (INTELSAT),
owner of the rapidly expanding global communications system inaugurated in 1965 with the launching of the Early Bird satellite.[39] In a
broader context, the President renewed past offers of cooperation in
his ceremonial remarks on the entry into force of the new space treaty.
Although the first decade of the space age had "witnessed a kind of
contest," Mr. Johnson said, the next decade "should increasingly
become a partnership—not only between the Soviet Union and
America, but among all nations under the sun and stars."[40]

Occasional comments by Soviet space scientists gave the impression
that they were well aware of the advantages to be gained from cooperation with their principal rivals and would be glad to orient their
work in that direction. For the time being, however, Moscow maintained an air of secrecy as it proceeded with the launching of its
"Cosmos" satellites—over 50 of them, many presumably with military uses, in 1967 alone—and other phases of its ongoing program.
Although the 50th anniversary of the Bolshevik Revolution was
marked by no new "space spectacular," the U.S.S.R. did achieve an
important "first" with the landing of an instrumented capsule on
Venus on October 18 at a time when the American Mariner 5, flying
past at a planned distance of 2,500 miles, was independently gathering data about the same planet.

With the Treaty on Principles completed and the Vienna space conference postponed to 1968, the U.N. Space Committee and its Legal Subcommittee had by this time turned their attention to two additional tasks involved in drawing up a general code of behavior for outer space. One of these was the elaboration of an agreement on liability for damages incurred as a result of outer space activities; the other, the drafting of an agreement setting forth the obligations of states to assist distressed astronauts and, in the event of unscheduled landings, to return astronauts and space objects to their countries of origin. The latter enterprise was the less difficult of the two. Under some prodding from the General Assembly, the Space Committee held a special meeting in mid-December to approve the text of an agreement on the return of astronauts which was forwarded to the Assembly in time for unanimous endorsement on the final day of its 22nd Regular Session.[41]

It was not only in new fields like space that mankind's burgeoning activities seemed increasingly in need of regulation. Use of the oceans had also been expanding to a degree that already outdistanced the legal principles laid down at the two U.N. Conferences on the Law of the Sea in 1958 and 1960.[42] Disputes over fishing rights, unlicensed broadcasting from the high seas, and pollution of the marine environment were among the wide variety of subjects that inspired concern in 1967. In March, the wreck of the tanker *Torrey Canyon* in the Scilly Isles and the resultant discharge of tons of oil along the Cornish and French coasts dramatically focused attention on the hazards involved in man's expanding but often irresponsible use of the high seas.

The United States, in addition to its long-standing support for international agreements regulating fishing rights and practices,[43] displayed increasing interest in cooperation in the field of oceanography and, by extension, in systematic efforts "to develop the seas for the benefit of mankind."[44] Following up earlier policy pronouncements, President Johnson in January 1967 appointed a Commission on Marine Science, Engineering, and Resources, headed by Julius Adams Stratton, to "develop, encourage, and maintain a coordinated, comprehensive, and long-range program in marine science for the benefit of mankind."[45] Vice-President Humphrey, reporting further in a speech of July 29, renewed the U.S. pledge to cooperate with both advanced and less developed countries and announced that the Navy's navigation satellite system would be made available to assist civilian navigation.[46]

These were small steps in relation to the magnitude of oceanic problems, and the path of international cooperation was not always smooth. In March, the U.S.S.R. announced that it intended to open its northern sea route along the Siberian coast to the vessels of all nations;[47] but in August the United States felt compelled to abandon a proposed scientific voyage around the Arctic Ocean by two Coast Guard icebreakers because of Moscow's assertion that the intended route would violate Soviet territorial waters. Though Washington rejected this contention as wholly contrary to international law,[48] the United States itself was not inclined to act precipitately in extending international authority in maritime matters. The administration and interested members of Congress reacted coolly to an announcement that Malta intended to propose to the General Assembly a treaty that would reserve the use of the ocean floor for peaceful purposes, vest jurisdiction in an international agency, and allocate most of the financial benefits of exploiting the sea bed to less developed countries. The United States, it was asserted, had no intention of supporting such a far-reaching proposal at so early a stage but would favor careful study of the whole issue under U.N. auspices—a procedure later endorsed by the General Assembly.[49]

This multiplication of new international interests was not entirely favorable to older projects which, whatever their intrinsic merits, tended to be thrust into the background and in some cases to suffer from dwindling enthusiasm and support. Cooperation in the peaceful uses of atomic energy, perhaps the most exciting international venture of the mid-1950's, had long ago ceased to stir the public imagination despite the solid work that still went forward under the International Atomic Energy Agency, Euratom, and other auspices. A somewhat comparable fate now threatened to overtake two projects enthusiastically launched by the Johnson administration as recently as 1965 but now, it seemed, increasingly unlikely to come up to initial expectations.

One such project was the "water for peace" program that President Johnson had announced in October 1965, at a time of mounting concern over the insufficiency of available supplies of pure water to meet the needs of the coming decades. The United States, Mr. Johnson had declared at that time, stood ready to "contribute its share of the resources needed for an international crash program" aimed at providing "water for all humanity."[50] Eighteen months later, this presidential concept had dwindled remarkably. An Interdepartmental Committee on Water for Peace, after looking into the matter on behalf of the

President, reported in April 1967 that world-wide efforts in the field of water development were clearly not keeping pace with the need. As to the question of international financing, however, the committee offered only the blunt statement that nations and regions desiring to respond to their water problems "must undertake this responsibility themselves."[51] The exuberance of 1965 seemed largely forgotten as representatives of 94 nations gathered in Washington in May for an International Water for Peace Conference growing out of the President's original initiative. Avoiding any reference to "crash programs," the President now confined himself to advocating a modest "network of water resource centers." Secretary Rusk, in turn, offered the un-electrifying announcement that his department was establishing a special Water for Peace Office to coordinate U.S. activities in this field.[52]

A similar loss of scale and momentum occurred in connection with the intensified international effort in education that President Johnson had announced with even greater fanfare in the fall of 1965. The rather meager fruits of this initiative had been the passage by Congress of an International Education Act in 1966 and the scheduling for 1967 of an International Conference on the World Crisis in Education, which met in Williamsburg, Virginia, in October under the chairmanship of President James Perkins of Cornell University. Deploring the fact that international assistance to education was declining at a time when the educational needs of the developing nations were greater than ever, the conference endorsed a proposal from President Johnson (later approved by the General Assembly) that the United Nations be asked to schedule a World Education Year.[54] Unwilling to stop with this largely symbolic gesture, however, the conference went on to urge that the level of international aid to education be doubled from its estimated current rate of $1 billion a year. Great as the need undoubtedly was, such a proposal had little chance of being acted upon at a time when the United States and other wealthy nations were struggling with heavy military costs as well as balance-of-payments problems and currency difficulties.

Cooperation in the domain of pure and applied science was in some ways easier than cooperation with a political bearing. Scientists of many nations had worked together in the observance of the International Geophysical Year (1957-58) and the International Year of the Quiet Sun (1965-66), and plans were currently being drawn for a five-year International Biological Program as well as a two-year Global Atmospheric Research Program to back up the World Weather Watch established under the auspices of the World Meteorological Organization.[56] The participation of Soviet scientists and agencies in many of these activities encouraged the hope that cooperation might ultimately become the normal procedure in a world which, in 1967, was still so deeply rent by East-West animosities.

45 : Decade of Discouragement

Virtually everyone agreed, in the 1960's, that more rapid economic and social progress in the less developed countries was vital to the attainment of international peace, security, and prosperity. "We know," said President Johnson in his 1967 foreign aid message, "that in the long run, the wealthy nations cannot survive as islands of abundance in a world of hunger, sickness, and despair."[57] "Development is the new name for peace," wrote Pope Paul VI in one of the chapter headings of his encyclical *Populorum progressio,*[58] a major policy document issued in March 1967 that placed the full authority of the Catholic Church behind the basic U.N. objective of promoting "social progress and better standards of life in larger freedom."

Moved by such convictions and spurred by the clamor of the less developed countries themselves, the General Assembly had voted in 1961 to designate the 1960's as the United Nations Development Decade—a time, so it was intended, of intensified effort by all concerned to accelerate the progress of the developing countries toward self-sustaining economic growth and social advancement.[59] By the end of the decade, it had been agreed, aggregate national income in the developing countries should be growing at the rate of at least 5 per cent a year. As a means to this end, the economically advanced countries had been urged to provide their less favored associates with the equivalent of 1 per cent of their combined national incomes in the form of international assistance and capital for development.

The Development Decade was nearly two-thirds over in 1967, and most authorities agreed that the situation in the developing countries was not improving as had been hoped. Gains there had undoubtedly been, in both material and psychological terms. Some authorities now placed the annual rate of growth in the developing countries as high as 5 per cent, population growth at 2.5 per cent, and per capita growth at a not too unfavorable 2.5 per cent. Paul G. Hoffman, Administrator of the U.N. Development Program, spoke of a "rising tide of common sense" in the economic policies of the developing nations, a shift to more realistic planning, and an abatement in the doctrinaire resistance to private investment as the main instrument of development.[60] Yet the over-all picture was scarcely reassuring in either statistical or human terms. "We are not winnning the war on want," U Thant wrote in the introduction to his annual report. "The opportunity gap for many, if not most, individuals and nations in the world is growing wider. Inequality is increasing. Each week more and more people suffer the degradation of an economic and social injustice which is needless, and they know it."[61]

How had it come about that in spite of intensive efforts by many countries, the Decade of Development was by now beginning to be called the Decade of Discouragement or, worse still, the Decade of Disappointment? Neither the developed nor the developing nations could be assigned exclusive responsibility. The emerging nations, U Thant conceded, "are far from doing all they honestly could and all that they must. The industrialized nations, for their part, must awaken from the apathy accompanying their affluence to the realities of the world around them, to the epochal ferment in which they are involved. . . . Assistance from the advanced nations to the developing nations should be increased without delay, doubled, then tripled in as few years as possible."[62] The drastic nature of this recommendation suggested how seriously the problem was viewed at U.N. Headquarters.

The economic factors behind this sense of disillusionment were easily identified. The flow of resources from developed to developing countries had consistently fallen short of expectations. The trade of the developing countries, in turn, had failed to earn sufficient foreign funds to provide an adequate margin for investment after other foreign obligations were met. At the same time, population in many countries of the "third world" had been expanding at a rate that ran close behind the increase in productivity and thus diverted resources from development to consumption without perceptibly increasing the latter. Efforts to come to grips with the problem of population growth had, thus far, remained hesistant and largely ineffective. Scarcely less indecisive had been the drive to expand the developing countries' agricultural production, which was lagging behind population growth in a way that threatened catastrophic shortages unless production could be rapidly expanded in the coming decades.

American leadership in the theory and practice of international development had been established as early as 1949, the year of President Truman's celebrated Point Four program. But the general aim of U.S. development policy—to bring the developing countries to the "take-off point" that would mark the beginning of self-sustaining economic growth—remained far from accomplishment in most instances. The striking successes achieved in such countries as Iran, Taiwan, and South Korea had been the exception, not the rule. The United States itself, moreover, had faltered in the pursuit of its international development objectives in recent years. Increasingly preoccupied with the war in Vietnam and its own balance-of-payments problem, it had progressively reduced the share of its growing national wealth that was allocated to development needs. "The combined value of our economic and food aid," President Johnson noted in his 1967 foreign aid message, "is less than seven-tenths of 1 per cent of our national income, only slightly more than the average for all advanced countries. We devote smaller shares to foreign assistance than such countries as France and Belgium."[63]

The failure of most developed countries to meet the over-all investment target could be readily documented from the reports of the United Nations and the Development Assistance Committee of the O.E.C.D. (Organization for Economic Cooperation and Development).[64] In 1965, the total outflow of development capital from D.A.C. member countries had been measured at $10.3 billion; in 1966, it failed to expand and was suspected of having actually declined because a small increase in net official assistance had been offset by an apparent decline in private investment.[65]

Unsuccessful in expanding their development contribution through existing channels, the major capital-exporting nations had been even less inclined to subsidize the new United Nations agencies established at the insistence of the developing countries to promote industrialization and distribute increased amounts of development capital. The U.N. Development Program, a long-established activity focused mainly on technical cooperation, did collect a record $183 million in pledges of assistance at its annual fund-raising conference in October.[66] But efforts to obtain voluntary contributions for the new U.N. Industrial Development Organization (UNIDO) and the U.N. Capital Development Fund, whose establishment the Western nations had strongly resisted in the first place, were spectacularly unsuccessful.[67]

Even the International Bank for Reconstruction and Development (I.B.R.D.), a mainstay of the international development effort for more than two decades, reported increasing difficulty in raising funds for its operations despite the attractive, "banker's" terms on which its obligations were offered. More serious was the virtual exhaustion of the resources of the I.B.R.D.'s soft-loan affiliate, the International Development Association. Originally set up on U.S. initiative in 1960 to provide development loans on easier terms than were available through the World Bank itself, the I.D.A. by mid-1967 had made loans of $1,694 million and had only $97 million left in unobligated resources. Anticipating the need to replenish I.D.A.'s coffers, if possible on a larger scale than before, World Bank President George D. Woods had urged the developed nations to raise their future contributions to a level of $1 billion a year, of which the United States was asked to contribute $400 million.

The most serious difficulty with this proposal was not the amount of money involved but the unwillingness of the United States to promise action that might adversely affect its already precarious balance of payments. In an attempt to compromise the issue, the United States announced in April 1967 that it would be prepared to make a substantial donation to I.D.A. over a three-year-period, but only on condition that something over half its contribution be spent within the United States itself. Though consistent with the current trend in U.S. aid policies, this proviso ran counter to I.D.A.'s policy of favoring development purchases in the cheapest market. It was also unacceptable to other potential contributors, who reasoned that if the United States was entitled to insist on "tied" purchases, they should be similarly privileged.[68] The issue was not resolved at the September meeting of the World Bank and Fund in Rio de Janeiro, which was soon followed by the disclosure of Mr. Woods' impending retirement. The need to replenish I.D.A.'s resources would clearly be one of the most urgent problems confronting Secretary of Defense McNamara when he moved from the Pentagon to the World Bank early in 1968.

Even a substantially increased flow of capital assistance could provide only a minor part of the resources the developing countries needed to finance their economic growth. Four-fifths of these countries' foreign exchange expenditures came from the proceeds of their own international trade; and here, too, the situation of most developing countries was difficult and unsatisfactory. The world trade boom of the 1950's and 1960's had largely passed these nations by. Their share in total world exports had markedly declined, and though their earnings on what they did export had increased of late, this gain had been largely offset by payments of principal and interest on their foreign indebtedness. The net result had been to leave them with a strong sense of grievance against the industrialized countries, which were widely felt to be exploiting them in a "neocolonialist" spirit and, in effect, enriching themselves at their poorer neighbors' expense.

This sense of grievance had been much in evidence at the first U.N. Conference on Trade and Development (UNCTAD), held in Geneva in 1964, where pressure from the 77 participating less-developed countries had led to the establishment of UNCTAD as a permanent U.N. agency with special responsibility for promoting the economic interests of developing nations. A second UNCTAD conference, designed to plan new forward steps in trade and development, was scheduled to meet in New Delhi early in 1968, and was deemed certain to see a renewal of the developing countries' campaign for more generous treatment. It had been the hope of the United States and other industrialized countries that the complaints of the developing countries would by that time have been at least partially assuaged by trade concessions growing out of the Kennedy Round negotiations in Geneva. These hopes, however, were largely disappointed by the actual results of the Kennedy Round, which, as announced in May 1967, offered comparatively few benefits to the developing countries; nor did the latter find much to applaud in the subsequent agreement of the Western countries on the creation of new I.M.F. "special drawing rights."[69]

The irritation of the developing countries at what seemed to them a consistent bypassing of their interests reached explosive force at a 71-nation conference held in Algiers in October for the specific purpose of preparing a common position for the forthcoming New Delhi meeting. For the first time, the demands of the developing countries for more favorable trading conditions and more development capital on easier terms were vigorously set forth in a formal policy declaration known as the "Charter of Algiers of the Economic Rights of the

Third World."[70] The demands themselves were already familiar. What was new was the fact that well over half the countries of the world were able to agree on a statement as comprehensive in scope as it was urgent in tone.

The industrialized countries, less numerous but more powerful, had also to prepare their positions for the New Delhi conference. While the developing nations were meeting in Algiers, an O.E.C.D. working group had been conferring in Paris about the trade of developing countries and, in particular, about the plan for generalized tariff preferences that President Johnson had spoken of at the meeting of American Presidents in Punta del Este. As already noted, the United States was strongly opposed to granting special tariff concessions to the Latin American countries, as the latter had been demanding. Nevertheless, the President had mentioned at Punta del Este a possibility of trying to increase the export earnings of the developing countries *as a group* through the granting of "temporary tariff advantages for all developing countries by all industrialized countries."[71] After further exploration of this idea in the months since Punta del Este, the United States had gone to the Paris meeting with the hope of securing its adoption as official Western policy.

This modification in what had been an historic opposition to all types of preferential trade arrangements had not been motivated exclusively by altruistic concerns. In part it was also directed against the existing system of trade preferences that linked the Western European countries, particularly the United Kingdom and France, with their former colonies in Africa and elsewhere. These "North-South" preferences were distasteful to the United States for a number of reasons. They threatened to divide the world as a whole into competing trade blocs. They discriminated against Latin America, which, thus far, was not included in any preferential system. Furthermore, the "reverse preferences" granted by many developing countries to their European trading partners discriminated against the United States itself by limiting its access to the markets of the developing world. Rather than try to retaliate by setting up its own discriminatory preference system in the Western Hemisphere, the United States preferred to aim at a nondiscriminatory system in which the preferences would be extended to all developing countries on an equal basis and, at the same time, the "reverse preferences" for European countries would be eliminated.[72]

Like earlier U.S. initiatives on behalf of the developing countries, this plan found only limited favor with other members of the 21-nation O.E.C.D. In principle, the idea of temporary generalized tariff advantages for developing countries proved generally acceptable— but only for their manufactured and semimanufactured products, not for their more important raw material exports. A number of European nations, moreover, were strongly opposed to abandonment of their "reverse preferences" in the developing world. Disagreement on this point, unresolved in the special O.E.C.D. committee, persisted at the Paris session of the O.E.C.D. Council on November 30-December 1. Despite their failure to reach accord on the central issue, however, all O.E.C.D. members agreed that the work of the special group should provide a common basis for action in UNCTAD and elsewhere and that they should make every effort to ensure the success of the New Delhi conference.[73]

A more familiar device in the trade field was the use of so-called commodity agreements designed to stabilize the market for particular products through joint action by importing and exporting countries. The International Wheat Agreement and the International Sugar Agreement were both extended during 1967, as was the 1962 Arrangement Regarding International Trade in Cotton Textiles, which sought to regulate the growth in textile exports from developing to indus-trialized countries. The International Coffee Agreement, widely re-garded as one of the most successful of such commodity arrangements, also continued in operation, although a dispute about the rapid growth of Brazilian soluble coffee exports to the United States cast some temporary doubt on the prospects for its renewal in 1968. Efforts to conclude an international cocoa agreement, initiated under U.N. auspices in 1963, continued during 1967 but had not yet suc-ceeded as the year ended.[74]

The expansion of world agricultural production and food supplies was another area in which the United States had taken important initiatives but had failed thus far to enlist the full support of its partners in Europe and elsewhere. Almost all authorities acknowl-edged the urgency of achieving increased production and better dis-tribution of agricultural products to meet the needs of the expanding world population. Many were the predictions of famine and disaster if mankind failed to use effectively the scientific resources now avail-able for dealing with this problem. Action, however, still lagged behind analysis, and the United States had thus far achieved at best a very limited success in inspiring its partners to join it in a truly effective anti-hunger campaign. Emergency food assistance for India, for example, had been conceived in Washington as a genuinely multinational effort but had ended up as virtually an American operation, one in which even India itself had been slow to make the decisive moves toward agricultural reform that the United States thought necessary.[75]

The United States had somewhat greater success in securing the adoption as part of the Kennedy Round arrangements of an international grain agreement that would serve the interests of the developing countries as well as the major producing nations. While failing to obtain a guarantee of continued access to the European Common Market for its own grain exports, it did procure agreement on the principles of an International Grains Arrangement which, in addition to setting new price ranges for world trade in wheat, would provide the developing countries with a gift of 4.5 million tons of grain (or cash equivalent) in each of the next three years. Forty-two per cent of this amount was to be provided by the United States itself, with the balance coming from European countries, Canada, Australia, and Japan.[76] As signed by the United States on November 8 (subject to ratification after Senate approval), the new arrangement would enter into force on July 1, 1968 and would supersede the International Wheat Agreement at that time.[77]

U.S. policy in international food matters was naturally conditioned to some extent by the state of agriculture at home. After trying for many years to restrict agricultural production in order to slow the build-up of unsalable surpluses, the United States had made an important change of policy in 1966 in authorizing an increase in wheat plantings to meet increased needs at home and overseas. This tactic, however, was again reversed in 1967, a year when the maintenance of domestic farm prices was felt to take precedence over the expansion of production to feed the hungry in other countries. Through much of the year, the "Food for Freedom" program was implemented with what some interested observers considered a notable lack of vigor; and an expansion of food exports on special terms that was authorized in October seemed largely motivated by a desire to buoy the domestic market in a preelection year.[78] Those who saw inconsistencies in preaching a war on hunger while reducing wheat acreages and food aid shipments could reflect on President Johnson's statement that nearly $16 billion in U.S. farm products shipped to 116 countries since 1954 had "meant the difference between life and death for millions all around the world."[79]

Central to any plan for the alleviation of world hunger was the need to find some way of coping with the mounting population increase, particularly in developing countries. If existing rates of increase continued unchecked, U.N. demographers calculated, the world population would increase from an estimated 3,365 million in mid-1966 to double that number by the year 2005. Most lay authorities considered it self-evident that widespread use of artificial birth control would be no less essential than increased material production in establishing a long-range equilibrium between people and resources; and the continued silence of the Pope on this critical issue diminished the applause for his otherwise comprehensive statement on development problems. Outside of ecclesiastical circles, the case for "family planning" was clearly gaining increased acceptance, and programs in this area were now openly going forward under both U.S. and U.N. auspices. Indicative of the changing climate of world opinion was the presentation to U Thant in December 1967 of a Declaration on Population, signed by the heads of state or government of 30 countries representing one-third of the world's population, which declared the opportunity for family planning to be a basic human right directly related to the U.N. goals of development, peace, and individual dignity.[80]

In the long run, a combination of family planning and increased agricultural productivity might somehow stave off the threat of quiet catastrophe that overhung the planet in 1967. That the immediate outlook still remained critical was emphasized by the Food and Agriculture Organization in an annual survey revealing that per capita food production in the developing countries had actually declined over the past decade. Increased self-help as well as vastly increased international assistance would be needed if the developing countries were to carry out the necessary revolution in their agricultural policies, declared India's B. R. Sen, Director-General of F.A.O. and a leader of opinion on world food problems.[81] A. H. Boerma of the Netherlands, Administrator of the U.N.-F.A.O. World Food Program, was selected at F.A.O.'s biennial Conference in Rome to carry on the work that Mr. Sen had been engaged on during the past eleven years.

New personalities were coming to the fore in various sectors of the international economic front. In addition to the changes in F.A.O. and the World Bank, Eric Wyndham White was preparing to retire as Director-General of the GATT organization and would soon be turning over his responsibilities to Olivier Long of Switzerland. In the O.E.C.D., Willard Thorp had completed his term as Chairman of the Development Assistance Committee and was to be succeeded by another American, Edwin M. Martin. It was not through any lack of dedication and skill on the part of these international civil servants that the 1960's thus far had been a decade of discouragement; nor could their successors be expected to change the situation in any essential way within the limitations set by existing governmental attitudes. The chances of any fundamental improvement during the balance of the 1960's would clearly depend on the action of the governments, old and new, that had so solemnly pledged their efforts to realize the goals of the Development Decade and of the U.N. Charter itself.

46 : The 22nd General Assembly

Few indeed were the items of international business that escaped the attention of the U.N. General Assembly. That body's regular annual sessions, traditionally beginning in the third week of September, still represented the nearest approximation to the "town meeting of the world" envisaged by the founders of the United Nations. As we have already noted, the Assembly broke its normal rhythm to hold two special sessions in the earlier part of 1967, the first devoted primarily to South West Africa and the second to the emergency situation in the Middle East. Both of these matters appeared again, together with a diversified list of other international concerns, on the 94-item agenda of the 22nd Regular Session, which convened in New York on September 19 and continued into the night of December 19-20 before adjourning subject to recall in the spring of 1968.

Not since the sudden death of Dag Hammarskjold in 1961 had the Assembly begun its autumn session amid such dismaying circumstances as those attendant on the escalating conflict in Vietnam and the warlike conditions still smoldering in the Middle East. The international situation, wrote U Thant in the introduction to his annual report, released on the Assembly's opening day, had not only failed to improve in the past year but had deteriorated considerably. Violence and threats of violence were on the increase throughout the world, the Secretary-General declared, and the United Nations itself was again confronted with a "crisis of confidence" as a result of its failure to grapple more effectively with the problems of peace-keeping and finance, disarmament, the Middle East, *apartheid* and colonialism, and economic and social development.[82] Abdul Rahman Pazhwak, the Assembly's outgoing President, was equally somber. "If fools and folly rule the world," the Afghan diplomat declared at the opening day ceremonies, "the end of man in our time may come as a rude shock, but it will no longer come as a complete surprise."[83]

In spite of these expressions of concern, the Assembly's opening formalities were not entirely lacking in indications of a hopeful and conciliatory spirit. The overwhelming vote by which Rumanian Foreign Minister Corneliu Manescu was elected President of the 22nd Session showed how far the world had moved from the "cold war" atmosphere of the early U.N. years, when representatives of Communist countries had automatically been debarred from such high office. His countrymen, Manescu observed in accepting the Assembly's mandate, had learned that to be respected one must show respect, and that the best way to get the rules of international life applied was for everyone to observe those rules strictly with regard to others. The small and medium-sized countries, Manescu suggested, had a special vocation to speak up for morality, legality, and the improvement of bilateral relations and to work for an atmosphere conducive to the solution of major problems.[84]

However conscientiously the smaller countries might seek to apply these precepts, the results of the Assembly's deliberations would still depend in even wider measure on the attitudes of the United States, the U.S.S.R., and the other great powers. Ambassador Goldberg struck a characteristically conciliatory note in his opening address to the Assembly on September 21. "In serving the cause of a just and peaceful world, we are not permitted the luxury of being easily discouraged," said the U.S. Representative.[85] Foreign Minister Gromyko, in his address next day, took a more polemical line. Denouncing the U.S. "policy of international brigandage" in Vietnam and elsewhere, the Soviet spokesman followed his government's customary procedure in submitting for Assembly discussion a brace of proposals that seemed designed primarily to embarrass the United States and its allies.[86] One of these initiatives, described in an earlier chapter, involved the conclusion of a convention banning the use of nuclear weapons, a project the United States had strong if rather complicated reasons for opposing.[87] The other called for accelerated work on an old U.N. project, the drafting of a definition of aggression. According to Soviet sources, such a definition was urgently needed in order to curb the increasingly frequent use of armed force "for committing acts of aggression against sovereign states and for suppressing peoples fighting against colonialism and for their freedom and independence"[88]—an obvious, if tendentious, reference to actions by the United States, Portugal, and other Western countries.

Acceptance of these insidious proposals as originally framed would have meant that a majority of U.N. members had become so predisposed against the United States that they had lost the faculty of distinguishing between the reality of American actions and their misrepresentation by Soviet propaganda. The tone of the Assembly's general debate, in which the policies of the United States came in for heavy criticism from many directions, might well have suggested that such a process was occurring and that the United States had come to be regarded as a generally noxious element in international life. The balance of forces in the U.N. had changed, Soviet delegate Nikolai T. Fedorenko asserted early in the session; the 22nd General Assembly "has, in effect, become a trial of the aggressor, a just trial of a system which generates ruthless wars, violence and bloodshed."[89]

Yet when Gromyko's proposals and other controversial issues were eventually put to the vote, it became apparent that the United States still retained sufficient influence in the Assembly to blunt its rival's "cold war" initiatives and, in many if not all cases, to mobilize an adequate majority in support of its own viewpoint. Many of the smaller powers were reluctant to antagonize either the United States or the U.S.S.R., and hedged their votes accordingly. Gromyko's call for a convention banning the use of nuclear weapons was thus watered down into a resolution endorsing the principle of a nuclear ban but making no definite provision for its implementation.[90] The demand for a speeded-up definition of aggression gave rise to floods of Soviet-inspired propaganda but likewise failed, in the end, to win Assembly endorsement. Eventually the matter was entrusted to a 35-nation special committee with instructions to consider the question in all its aspects and report to the Assembly at its next regular session.[91]

On other aspects of the disarmament problem, the United States and the U.S.S.R. agreed more often than they differed. As already noted, the most important undertaking in this field, the completion of a nuclear nonproliferation treaty, had been held up primarily by differences between the United States and its own allies in regard to the arrangements for inspection and control. No agreement on this matter having been reached during the Assembly session, the Soviet and American delegations joined in supporting a resolution in which the Assembly urged the Eighteen-Nation Disarmament Committee to continue its work and report back by March 15, 1968 so that arrangements could be made to reconvene the 22nd Session.[92]

A similar measure of U.S.-Soviet agreement facilitated the Assembly's work on outer space. In two resolutions unanimously adopted on November 3, the Assembly requested the Committee on the Peaceful Uses of Outer Space to continue its work, and called for general support of the U.N. Conference on the Exploration and Peaceful Uses of Outer Space, now definitely scheduled to meet in Vienna in August 1968.[93] Weeks later, at its closing session on December 19, the Assembly was able to vote unanimous approval of the Agreement on the Rescue and Return of Astronauts, recently completed by the Outer Space Committee, and to ask that group to perfect the pending agreement on space liability in time for consideration at the 23rd Session.[94] Still another manifestation of U.S.-Soviet agreement on a noncontroversial item was a resolution supporting plans to schedule a Fourth International Conference on the Peaceful Uses of Atomic Energy in 1970 or 1971.[95]

Matters involved in current East-West politics inevitably produced more disagreement, though here too the United States could generally muster adequate if scarcely overwhelming support for its point of view. To the relief of many who remembered the frustrations of the recent Emergency Session, the Assembly did not again involve itself with the issues of peace in the Middle East. The initiative in this area was left to the Security Council, whose efforts culminated in the resolution of November 22 and the appointment of Ambassador Jarring as U.N. representative to assist the parties in coming to agreement.[96] The only important action on Middle East affairs by the Assembly was the adoption of a pair of U.S.-supported resolutions renewing past appeals for aid to Palestine refugees and displaced persons.[97]

As in past years, support for the U.S. position proved thinnest on political questions relating to the Far East. The resolution reaffirming the U.N. stand on Korea, for instance, carried by a bare 68 votes to 23, with 26 abstentions.[98] Even less impressive, though quite sufficient for the purpose, were the votes by which the Assembly upheld for still another year the U.S. contention that Communist China was unqualified for representation in the United Nations.

The voting strength of those U.N. members who favored the admission of the Peking regime to U.N. representation had never been proportionate to their zeal. Up to 1967, the annual resolution calling for admission of the People's Republic of China and the expulsion of "the representatives of Chiang Kai-shek" had never mustered more than 47 votes out of a U.N. membership of well over 100. The high point of the pro-Peking effort thus far had been the tied vote of 47 to 47 (with 20 abstentions) by which this proposal had failed in 1965—a figure well short of the two-thirds majority which the Assembly, under U.S. prompting, had declared essential for any change in the representation of China. With mainland China in the throes of its "Cultural Revolution" and even the U.S.S.R. giving only perfunctory support for the "restoration" of its U.N. "rights," the pro-Peking vote had actually fallen in 1966, to 46 in favor with 57 opposed and 17 abstentions. In the new vote taken on November 28, 1967, the vote in favor of Chinese Communist representation declined again to 45, this time with 58 delegations opposed and 17 abstaining. Concurrently, the Assembly reaffirmed the importance of the question of Chinese representation—and hence the necessity of a two-thirds majority for any change—by voting 69 to 48 (with 4 abstentions) in favor of the annual U.S. resolution to this effect.[99] In addition, the Assembly buried for the second successive year an Italian proposal, supported by the United States, to authorize a special study of the whole question of Chinese representation with the object of finding an equitable and practical solution.

On the almost equally explosive issue of U.N. peace-keeping operations, the 22nd General Assembly came no closer to agreement than its predecessors. With the outlook for future peace-keeping efforts dimmed by the lack of an agreed financing formula, the persistent failure of France and the U.S.S.R. to pay over their half-promised "voluntary contributions" condemned the organization to continued financial weakness as well. The only encouraging development of the 22nd Session was a new emphasis on the potentialities of the special military contingents that Canada and some other member states had already earmarked for U.N. service. In the introduction to his annual report, U Thant suggested that it would be useful to make a basic study of the problems and possibilities relating to such "standby" forces.[100] The Assembly, in asking the Special Committee on Peacekeeping Operations to continue its work and report progress by July 1, 1968, did not specifically endorse this suggestion. It did, however, ask the Special Committee to study matters related to facilities, services, and personnel that member states might provide for peacekeeping operations.[101] U.S. sources expressed the hope that such a study might at long last "provide the needed traction to move ahead in this area."[102]

Another recommendation of the Secretary-General on which no action was taken during the 22nd Session was his proposal that the criteria for membership in the United Nations be reexamined with a view to limiting the admission of "microstates" and offering them more suitable forms of association.[103] The only action in this matter was a letter from Ambassador Goldberg to the President of the Security Council suggesting that that body's long dormant Committee on the Admission of New Members be reactivated to study the question.[104] In the meantime, the admission of the smallish though hardly microscopic state of Southern Yemen on December 14[105] increased the membership of the United Nations to 123. Noting the prospective advent of still another new country—which, however, appeared to have its eye on associate status rather than full U.N. membership—the Assembly voted to terminate the trusteeship agreement for Nauru effective with the coming into force of that territory's independence on January 31, 1968.[106]

The birth of Southern Yemen cleared the United Nations agenda of one long-standing and prickly "colonial" issue, hitherto known as the Aden question. Plenty of other colonial problems remained, however, and it was in this area that the Western governments—including the United States—were most consistently denounced and outvoted by a sizable coalition of African, Asian, and Communist states. The Assembly's sharply worded resolutions on colonialism and racial discrimination in Southern Africa—South West Africa, Southern

Rhodesia, the Portuguese territories, and South African *apartheid*—
have been described in an earlier chapter. On each of these issues,
the United States made clear its opposition to the evils that had
aroused the Assembly's anger. On none of them, however, did it
feel able to support the impetuous and "unsound" methods advocated by the majority of U.N. members. In the words of an official
U.S. commentary, all of these resolutions "called for sweeping measures within the sphere of the Security Council—measures which have
little prospect of implementation. Such impractical demands only
serve to diminish the prestige of the General Assembly."[107]

Almost equally incompatible with U.S. views were the greater part
of the resolutions adopted at the suggestion of the Special Committee
of 24 on Colonialism, whose bias in favor of instant emancipation
regardless of circumstances had long been the despair of responsible
officials in Washington, London, and other Western capitals. Few of
the world's remaining dependent territories were overlooked in a
series of Assembly resolutions, adopted by substantial though varying
majorities, insisting on the rights of indigenous inhabitants and demanding the prompt abrogation of colonial rule.[108] In addition, the Assembly
adopted two omnibus resolutions in the colonial field, one deploring
the activities of foreign financial interests in colonial territories[109] and
the other denouncing the policies of the colonial powers, calling for
the liquidation of military bases in colonial territories, and urging
support of "national liberation movements."[110]

Somewhat less heat arose from the Assembly's discussion of economic issues, in which the United States was often in the minority but
did occasionally manage to give a constructive lead. Noticeable amid
the stream of resolutions demanding increased support of economic
development[111] were two that called for coordination and review of
food aid programs and set a $200 million target for voluntary con-
tributions to the World Food Program of the United Nations and the
Food and Agriculture Organization for 1969 and 1970.[112] (The
United States pledged up to $100 million of this total in commodities,
shipping services, and cash.)[113] Acting on President Johnson's recent
suggestion to the educational conference at Williamsburg, the Assembly provisionally designated 1970 as International Education Year.[114]
On motion of the Netherlands, it also took preliminary steps toward
proclaiming the 1970's a second U.N. Development Decade and
laying out an international development strategy for that period.[115]

Proceedings in the social and humanitarian field were also less inharmonious than in some previous years, although persistent disagreement in the Assembly's Third Committee prevented final action on a number of pending projects.[116] The principal achievement in this area was the unanimous approval of a Declaration on the Elimination of Discrimination Against Women, which stated in effect that discrimination against women should be eliminated.[117] The attempt to draft a Convention on the Elimination of Religious Intolerance— a counterpart to the Convention Against Racial Discrimination adopted in 1965—became bogged down in arguments about Soviet anti-Semitism and other matters and had to be held over to the next session. Likewise deferred for future consideration were a draft convention and declaration on freedom of information and a plan to name a U.N. High Commissioner for Human Rights. Having previously designated 1968 as International Year for Human Rights, the Assembly adopted a somewhat controversial resolution dealing with arrangements for an International Conference on Human Rights that was to convene in Tehran in April.[118] The procedural recommendations advanced by African and Communist delegations suggested an intention to use the occasion primarily for the mounting of a new offensive against South African *apartheid*.

Two of the Assembly's principal actions in the legal field, the establishment of a committee on defining aggression and the approval of the agreement on aid to astronauts, have been noted earlier. A third achievement of some significance was the adoption of a Declaration on Territorial Asylum aimed at strengthening the guarantees available to persons fleeing from persecution. Largely at the instance of the United States, the Assembly also passed a resolution deploring departures from the international rules on diplomatic status and urging respect for diplomatic privileges and immunities.[119] Malta's proposal concerning the status of the ocean floor, which was treated as a political rather than a legal issue, gave rise to the unanimous decision to set up an *ad hoc* committee to study the problems involved and report to the next session.[120]

Completing the Assembly's agenda were the administrative and budgetary questions involved in the U.N.'s day-to-day management. In adjusting the scale of financial assessments for member states for the next three years, the U.S. share was reduced from 31.91 to 31.57 per cent of a regular budget which, for 1968, was fixed at a total of

$140,430,950. In the interests of more effective financial planning, the Assembly also requested that future budgetary estimates be projected over a two-year rather than a one-year period.[121] A problem of some significance in the administrative area grew out of the recurrent demands by the Soviet Union and others that the staff of the Secretariat should more adequately reflect the geographic diversity of the U.N. membership. To the usual resolution offering general endorsement of this objective, France succeeded in adding a policy statement—viewed without enthusiasm by the United States—which aimed at encouraging staff members to make more use of the French language.[122] A second matter of general interest concerned U Thant's plans for reorganization and streamlining of the top level of the Secretariat. After acquainting the Assembly with his intentions, the Secretary-General announced that ten of his principal aides, including Ralph J. Bunche of the United States, were being promoted to the new rank of Under-Secretary-General while other officials in the top echelon would in future bear the title of Assistant Secretary-General.[123]

No one showed disproportionate enthusiasm over these accomplishments as the Assembly prepared to adjourn until spring. Though not primarily the fault of the Assembly, the U.N.'s failure to come to grips with the Vietnam problem was seen by many delegations as a derogation from what might have been the organization's role in such a critical year. Nor had the Assembly itself accomplished anything that could be compared in importance with the space treaty approved in 1966. Disappointed in its hope of endorsing a nuclear nonproliferation treaty, it had also failed to resolve the peace-keeping question, shied away from the issues of the Middle East, and been reduced to futile adjurations in its attempt to assert U.N. authority over South West Africa. Weighed against these negative items, the record of positive achievement was creditable but scarcely very impressive: an agreement on space rescue, declarations on the rights of women and the right of asylum, a committee on the sea bed, and a series of resolutions reaffirming well-known viewpoints on disarmament, colonialism, and economic development.

Noting that international conditions during the session had remained far from favorable to its work, Assembly President Manescu could at least find words of praise for the atmosphere of industry and cooperation that had characterized the session. The unusually large number of resolutions adopted by consensus, he suggested, offered a practical demonstration of the value of seeking solutions through consultation.[124] Ambassador Goldberg admitted to both encouraging and discouraging impressions as he reviewed the organization's experience in recent months. The United Nations, he noted, had shown some capacity for emergency action in conflict areas like the Middle East and Cyprus; but it had developed little capacity for dealing with "the underlying grievances and pressures from which these conflicts erupt." "The world community must make real peace settlements to relieve these pressures," Mr. Goldberg warned. "This is the major future challenge to the United Nations—and hence to us, its members, who hold the U.N.'s fate in our hands."[125]

10 : Foreign Policy in a "Sick Society"

"The Great Society has become a sick society." Such was the un-varnished judgment of Senator Fulbright in an address at Honolulu on August 8 that was to stand out among the attempts to characterize the American scene in 1967. "Abroad," the Senator declared, "we are engaged in a savage and unsuccessful war against poor people in a small and backward nation. At home . . . our cities are exploding in violent protest against generations of social injustice. America, which only a few years ago seemed to the world to be a model of democracy and social justice, has become a symbol of violence and undisciplined power. . . . Far from building a safe world environment for American values, our war in Vietnam and the domestic deterioration which it has aggravated are creating a most uncongenial world atmosphere for American ideas and values."[1]

Not all Americans would have painted their country's situation in the summer of 1967 in quite such lugubrious colors. The Senator from Arkansas, some of his countrymen might have suspected, had been carried away by his inveterate distaste for the "cold war," his deep distrust for what he had called the "arrogance of power," his growing alarm about the effects of the war in Vietnam, and his mounting personal disagreements with President Johnson. Yet few Americans would have denied that the Senator's lamentations had a basis in fact. Many of them would have accepted his fundamental thesis that the United States, under the combined impact of war abroad and mounting unrest at home, was going through a crisis as grave as any in the past century.

Even President Johnson had ceased, by 1967, to insist that the United States was a nation in flourishing health. Amid his reiterations of firmness in Vietnam and his statistical recitals concerning the national wealth and the administration's antipoverty programs, the President himself gave evidence at times of feeling that something had gone wrong with the United States and that the nation had become involved in a perilous labyrinth whose exit was yet to be discovered. In common with many of his countrymen, moreover, Mr. Johnson displayed occasional impatience at the obtuseness, or worse, of those who refused to see the national problems as he saw them. Feelings of frustration, irritation, and intolerance were seldom absent from the discussion of public affairs in 1967. There was no single act of irrational violence that could be compared with the assassination of President Kennedy in 1963 or of Dr. Martin Luther King and Senator Robert Kennedy in 1968. Yet the atmosphere that permitted such deeds was sensible to all and deeply disquieting to many who had the nation's interests at heart.

An orderly diagnosis of this national malady, if such is the correct term, would clearly lie beyond the range of a study devoted to American foreign relations. Yet no examination of American foreign policy in 1967 can fail to take account of a distemper whose very causes lay partly in the foreign policy area and whose effects were felt in every branch of international affairs. By no means is it suggested that all the manifestations of American foreign policy in 1967 exhibited a pathological tinge. For the most part, foreign policy lumbered along with about the usual speed, imagination, and effectiveness. Yet the over-all impression, especially at those points where foreign policy was most directly influenced by national attitudes, is undeniably one of increasingly divided counsels, waning self-confidence, and diminishing capacity to control the course of events at home or abroad.

47 : National Fever Chart

The war in Vietnam, with its rising casualties, inflationary economic impact, and indeterminate prospects, would have sufficed by itself to awaken sharp internal antagonisms of the sort the nation had already experienced as recently as the Korean war period of 1950-53. But the war in Korea, conducted under the banner of the United Nations and directed against what was generally regarded as a clearcut case of military aggression, had occasioned no such widespread and active dissent as was now made manifest in large and disorderly protest demonstrations, sporadic draft evasion and resistance, and, on a different plane, the withdrawal of large numbers of young people to the dream world of the "hippies." All wars, no doubt, exert a less than wholesome influence on the nations involved in them. The Vietnam venture differed from other wars in that it repelled and antagonized the very group whose idealism and sense of commitment had helped to sustain the constructive endeavors of American foreign policy throughout the past generation.

To the gnawing uneasiness over Vietnam were added the growing strains within the body of American society, the problems of rural poverty, urban deterioration, rising crime rates, and, above all, the racial discontents that were brought so sharply into focus by the July riots. Here, too, the idealism of the earlier civil rights agitation appeared to be evaporating as the dream of a racially "integrated" society was shredded by white intransigence while moderate Negro leaders were challenged by "black power" advocates and prophets of violence. The feelings of tension and hostility associated with the changing character of the racial struggle exacerbated the divisive effects of the war and militated against a rational approach to either the problems of Vietnam or the problems of urban America.

As already indicated, the combined effect of the war and the July riots was to pose with a new urgency the question of national priorities which had been implicit since the beginning of the Vietnam involvement. The need for massive programs of urban renewal, housing, education, and the like had never seemed more obvious; yet the prospects for undertaking them, given the demands of the war and the indifference or outright hostility of influential segments of congressional and public opinion, had seldom appeared more unfavorable. President Johnson continued, as in the past, to insist that the nation was able to provide for both its domestic and its foreign needs. To assert the contrary, he said in the autumn of 1967, was "just pure bunk." Secretary of Defense McNamara took a similiar view. It was a "myth," he suggested, "that we cannot simultaneously wage war against aggression abroad and a war against poverty, urban decay and social injustice here at home." The question, according to him, was one of will power and readiness to make the necessary sacrifices.[2]

As a practical matter, however, the attempt was not to be made. The tendency of President Johnson's recommendations from August onward was to accord continued priority to the war effort and, if anything, diminish still further the share of expediture allotted to domestic programs. Those who felt with Senator Fulbright that the nation was being weakened by "a grotesque inversion of priorities" continued to demand a scaling down of the military effort in the interest of a more "balanced" foreign policy and a more adequate response to domestic needs. Yet the majority in Congress and the nation appeared to take a contrary view and to favor, if anything, an outright reduction in domestic expenditures—especially if the growing costs of the war were to necessitate an increase in taxes such as the President had been urging ever since January.

The revulsion against current foreign policy was not, however, confined to those who opposed the war in Vietnam and urged a stronger attack on the nation's domestic ills. It also included many who were "hawkish" on Vietnam and disinclined toward large domestic expenditures. For many members of Congress, the Vietnam commitment was merely the latest and most glaring in a series of foreign enterprises—undertaken, in most cases, on presidential initiative and often without congressional approval—whose combined effect had been a gross "overextension" of American power and a dangerous "overcommitment" of American resources. Put forward mainly by men of internationalist traditions like Senators Fulbright and Mansfield,[3] the doctrine of "overcommitment" had a natural appeal for legislators of more isolationist tendency who, while they might favor strong action in Vietnam, were congenitally hostile to foreign aid, East-West trade, and similar policies with which the administration had long been identified.

The result of this convergence of attitudes was the appearance, particularly within the Senate, of a curious "hawk-dove" coalition whose members differed strongly on Vietnam but agreed in opposing the general trend of U.S. policy and in working to limit its scope. One manifestation of this neo-isolationist trend, as it was sometimes called for want of a better term, was the strong resistance in Congress to any involvement in the war in the Middle East or, later, in the internal disturbances in the Congo and Nigeria. Another manifestation, less easily explained on rational grounds, was the unusually ruthless cutting of the foreign aid program on which Congress engaged at intervals right up to the time of its adjournment in mid-December.

Behind the resistance to specific aspects of the administration's foreign policy was a more general feeling of helplessness and frustration in face of the President's commanding influence and power of initiative in relation to Vietnam and, indeed, to the whole question of war or peace in the contemporary world. The growth of presidential power in foreign affairs in recent decades, which had found perhaps its most striking manifestation in the Vietnam commitment and the increasingly far-reaching actions taken to implement it, was alarming to Senator Fulbright and others on both practical and constitutional grounds. Nearly all congressional actions relating to foreign affairs in 1967 could be read at least in part as an attempt—constructive in some cases, much less so in others—to reassert congressional authority and restore a more equitable balance in the policy-making process. Such feelings did not prevent the Senate from eventually approving the Consular Convention with the U.S.S.R. and the treaty on outer space. They did, however, assert themselves repeatedly in the pre-ratification debates on those treaties as well as in more routine legislative actions relating to foreign affairs.

The most direct attack on this problem was a proposed Senate resolution, first put forward by Senator Fulbright on July 31, which sought to limit the administration's power to make foreign commitments on its own responsibility and declared in effect that the only valid "national commitments" were those in which Congress participated through a treaty or other legislative instrumentality. It is true that this far-reaching formula fell short of general approval even within the Senate Foreign Relations Committee. Yet Senator Fulbright's conviction that there was a need for further restraints on administration action was continuously reinforced by the attitude of the administration itself, particularly its habit of citing the so-called Southeast Asia or "Tonkin Gulf" resolution of 1964[4] as justification for its actions in Vietnam. (Under-Secretary of State Katzenbach, testifying before the Fulbright committee in August, scandalized his senatorial audience by going so far as to call the Southeast Asia resolution the "functional equivalent" of a declaration of war.)[5] As a contribution to public discussion, the Foreign Relations Committee eventually approved a watered-down version of the "national commitment" resolution and an accompanying report decrying "the dangerous tendency toward executive supremacy in foreign policy in recent years."[6] But with the attention of Senate critics so largely focused on questions of Vietnam strategy and tactics, consideration of the larger constitutional issue was put over to 1968.

Outside the halls of Congress, the legislative revolt against the presidential conduct of foreign affairs was matched by a growing rejection of the national foreign policy by substantial sections of the public. A sense of alienation from the government and its processes, and of incomprehension or anger at the actions taken in its name, began to find expression not merely in assertions of a contrary viewpoint but in open, personal disrespect for the President and members of his administration. Americans had always felt free to criticize their government, but rarely had they felt the impulse to deride and scorn it as many of them did in 1967. President Johnson, whose public approval rating as measured by the Gallup Poll declined from 47 per cent in January to 38 per cent in October, was widely if erroneously accused of basing all decisions on a crass desire for reelection in November 1968—a date whose approach was felt in all political quarters as leaders of both parties sought ways of accommodating their views about the war to the dictates of party politics.

Contributing to the lack of respect for the national government was a widespread feeling that its members had become hopelessly addicted to prevarication and even to outright trickery and deceit. The "credibility gap," noted with such dismay in 1966, had by 1967 become so thoroughly assimilated into the national outlook that administration statements, whether dealing with "progress" in Vietnam or with other matters, were discounted almost as a matter of course. This feeling of governmental obtuseness in ethical matters was immensely stimulated by the disclosure in February, initially by the "anti-establishment" *Ramparts* magazine, that the Central Intelligence Agency had for years been providing clandestine financial support to student and intellectual organizations, both national and international, that had been identified with the liberal and anti-Communist cause in the "cold war" confrontations with Communist-influenced organizations, mainly during the 1950's.[7]

Undertaken in accordance with policies established by the National Security Council and continued in effect under four Presidents (usually without the knowledge of the organization assisted), this activity could be defended on the ground that no alternative sources of financial backing had been available at the time the arrangements were made.

C.I.A. support, in the words of Under-Secretary Katzenbach, had "enabled many far-sighted and courageous Americans to serve their country in times of challenge and danger to the United States and the free world."[8] Yet the clandestine involvement of a secret intelligence agency like the C.I.A. in matters pertaining to freedom of the mind was bound to create a deeply unfavorable impression in intellectual circles at home and abroad. The ensuing international scandal could be compared in intensity, if in no other respect, with that aroused by the trial and conviction of Soviet writers Sinyavsky and Daniel a few months earlier. Vice-President Humphrey, an experienced defender of administration policies, referred to the affair as "one of the saddest times, in reference to public policy, our government has had."[9]

In the midst of the uproar engendered by these disclosures, the President set up a special three-man panel (Under-Secretary Katzenbach, Secretary of Health, Education, and Welfare John W. Gardner, and C.I.A. Director Richard Helms) to formulate new policies aimed at protecting the independence and integrity of the educational community while ensuring that American private organizations were able to play their "proper and vital role" in the world. In accordance with the recommendations of this group, steps were presently taken to discontinue covert Federal assistance to educational or private voluntary organizations, and secret C.I.A. funding was declared terminated by the end of the year. As an alternative, the Katzenbach group recommended the establishment of a new "public-private" mechanism that could openly channel public funds into meritorious overseas activities; but the year closed without agreement on the form, financing, or scope of such an organization.[10]

In an attempt to deal with a related source of friction and criticism, new guidelines were laid down late in the year to regulate the conduct of government-sponsored research on foreign areas by universities and other private institutions.[11] Yet necessary as they undoubtedly were, such corrective steps could make little positive contribution to the government's programs in international educational and cultural affairs. The new impetus President Johnson had sought to impart in this area had slackened noticeably under the influence of Vietnam, although the work of the Williamsburg conference and the plan for an International Education Year[12] held out the hope of a revival of interest if war conditions eventually abated.

In its domestic impact, the C.I.A. scandal offered fresh stimulus to the mounting agitation among the dissident intellectuals, peace marchers, draft resisters, and racial activists associated with what was loosely known as the "New Left." Bound together more by dislike of things as they were than by agreement on positive goals, the adherents of this dissident trend were far from constituting a unified force. A significant if transitory rift in the "peace" movement occurred in June as a result of the Middle East war, in which some peace militants forgot their antiwar sentiments in their enthusiasm for Israel. In September, a further splintering occurred at a conference on "New Politics" at which a Negro militant group seized control in much the same belligerent spirit that Stokely Carmichael had lately manifested at the OLAS conference in Havana.[13]

Such differences among the dissenters did nothing to temper their ever-mounting rancor against the government, which reached tumultuous expression on October 21 in the Washington "peace" rally organized by the National Mobilization Committee to End the War in Vietnam. "From dissent to resistance" was the favored slogan of the predominantly youthful demonstrators involved in this affair, whose unsuccessful attempts to invade the Pentagon focused world-wide attention on their antiwar and antigovernment sentiments. A comparable, though minor, disturbance occurred in New York on November 14 when Secretary Rusk arrived to deliver an unexceptionable address on "The Political Future of the Family of Man."[14] President Johnson, contrasting "responsible dissent" with "storm-trooper bullying," suggested at his November 17 news conference that "some of the things that are taking place in this country" were "extremely dangerous to our national interest" and "not very helpful to the men that are fighting the war for us." The President himself began to confine his public appearances to times and places where no such disturbances were to be expected.

The seriousness of such manifestations could easily be exaggerated. Most of the nation's 200,000,000 inhabitants were still going about their normal occupations, untouched or only remotely influenced by the disorder on home and foreign fronts. Yet there were responsible observers who could suggest that the nation was suffering "a kind of national nervous breakdown," a "third trauma" or "depression of the national spirit" as intense as those associated with the Civil War and the Great Depression of the 1930's.[15] On even the most optimistic interpretation, the national mood invited comparison with the psychic disturbances remembered from the era of Senator Joseph R. McCarthy in the 1950's. Nor was it more conducive than the McCarthy atmosphere to the pursuit of a steady-handed and well-ordered foreign policy. The wonder was, perhaps, that the effect on established national policies was not even more damaging.

48 : Turning Point in Defense

One reason for the limited international impact of America's domestic turmoil may be found in the constitutional division between the executive branch, with its basic responsibility for the day-to-day conduct of foreign relations, and the Congress, with its special mandate to provide appropriations and other tools of foreign policy over the longer range. Congress was no less sensitive to the national mood than the administration, and distinctly unhappy about its inability to exert a more potent influence on day-to-day policy. But since its attempts at self-assertion were mainly confined within the framework of its legislative responsibilities, they were more suited to circumscribing the administration's range of action in later years than to swaying its course in 1967.

Traditionally, national defense had been the area in which really basic differences between Congress and the administration were least prone to occur. Chary as they were of spending the taxpayers' money on overseas projects, the House and Senate could usually be counted on to approve substantially whatever the administration thought needed to assure a strong defensive military posture. Indeed, the tendency in Congress had usually been to go beyond the administration in calling for bombers, nuclear-powered ships, and other weapons that were recommended by one or another of the uniformed services but were thought unnecessary by the civilian heads of the defense establishment.

This tendency to outrun administration views persisted vigorously during 1967, particularly with respect to the alleged need for prompt deployment of an effective antiballistic missile system. But there was also evidence of a contrary tendency that arose directly from the prevalent disagreement with the administration's course in Vietnam and the consequent urge to attach restrictive conditions to legislative actions in both defense and other fields. In authorizing the expenditure of an extra $4,548 million for defense purposes during the fiscal year 1967, for example, Congress attached a special policy declaration which, in its original form, had been intended to limit the scope of American military action in Vietnam. At a later stage, however, it was amended in such a way as to express "support for our fighting men" as well as interest in a negotiated settlement.[16] (The $4,548 million was part of a supplemental defense appropriation of $12,196,520,000 for fiscal 1967 which the President had requested in January and which became law in April.)[17]

In estimating its defense and defense-related expenditures for the new fiscal year 1968, the administration had originally submitted an over-all figure of $76.8 billion in which were included $2.3 billion for atomic energy programs, $0.8 billion for military assistance, and $72.3 billion for the Department of Defense. Although the total exceeded previous "peacetime" military budgets, it nevertheless reflected important self-imposed limitations. The $21.9 billion requested for support of military operations in Southeast Asia, for example, would clearly not allow for any major expansion of the ground war in Vietnam, and the over-all strength of the Armed Forces in Vietnam and elsewhere was scheduled to increase only slightly, to a total of 3,464,000 at the end of the fiscal year. The existing force of 934 intercontinental and 512 submarine-launched ballistic missiles was to remain approximately unchanged, while the bomber force of 680 aircraft was to be reduced by the elimination of one wing of B-52's; and no provision was made for the development of a "follow-on" bomber for the period when the B-52 and B-58 would have become obsolete. Finally, as already noted, the budget made no provision for deployment of the Nike-X antiballistic missile system pending the outcome of discussions with the U.S.S.R. about a possible mutual limitation of A.B.M. deployments.[18]

These and other features of the defense program had their critics in Congress as well as in the defense establishment, whose uniformed heads were encouraged to speak their minds in the congressional hearings devoted to the annual defense procurement authorization law,[19] the Department of Defense Appropriation Act,[20] and the military construction authorization and appropriation bills for the 1968 fiscal year.[21] A feature common to these running controversies was the sharp divergence between the views of Secretary McNamara, the budget-minded civilian head of the Defense Department, and the service chiefs and their congressional supporters. Mr. McNamara's opposition to a new strategic bomber, and to the prompt deployment of an A.B.M. system, had been bitterly criticized, as was his insistence on the development of the still untried F-111 fighter-bomber as an all-purpose aircraft designed to meet the needs of all three services. Still another long-standing McNamara project which had generated intense opposition was a proposed merger of the Army Reserve and National Guard, which Congress had taken great pains to prevent and which was finally dropped in June 1967 in favor of a less far-reaching reorganization plan.[22]

Manpower policy was complicated in 1967 not only by the continuing military deployment in Europe and the growing demands of the Vietnam theater, where U.S. forces had been building toward an authorized level of 480,000, but also by the prospective expiration of the Selective Service law and the existence of wide divergences of opinion as to whether any draft would be needed in future and, if so, how it should be organized. Spokesmen for the "peace movement," and some others, were opposed to any draft at all; but studies by a National Advisory Commission and other qualified groups had unanimously concluded that a purely voluntary system would not produce sufficient manpower to implement current military policies. In a message to Congress on March 6, the President accordingly recommended a four-year extension of the expiring act, with certain modifications in procedure which included the use of a "fair and impartial random selection system"—i.e., a lottery—and priority induction for the youngest (nineteen-year-old) draft-eligible group.[23] These recommendations, with the exception of the lottery, were generally if unenthusiastically approved by Congress in time to keep the Selective Service System operating without interruption.[24]

This matter having been provisionally settled, Congress continued working on its major task of completing the basic Defense Department Appropriation Act for the new fiscal year. As signed by the President on September 30, it carried a total of $69.9 billion—$1.6 billion below the President's January estimate for this major segment of the defense program—and was accompanied by a number of unwelcome provisions concerning which the President registered a mild complaint. Among them was the prohibition on foreign construction of wooden-hulled minesweepers which caused such irritation in the

United Kingdom because of its impact on British-American military sales arrangements.[25]

In the meantime, the broader defense picture was being substantially modified both by developments in Vietnam and by indications that the United States and the Soviet Union stood at the threshold of a new round in the nuclear-missile race. On August 3, the President had sent to Congress his special message announcing that the ceiling on U.S. forces in Vietnam was being raised from 480,000 to 525,000, warning that defense expenditure in fiscal year 1968 might exceed the January budget estimate by as much as $4 billion, and renewing his appeal for an anti-inflationary tax increase.[26] It was at this same period, moreover, that the President apparently overrode the judgment of his Defense Secretary and yielded to the advice of his uniformed counselors in authorizing a major extension of the bombing of military targets in North Vietnam.[27]

A rejection of Mr. McNamara's views on still another critical issue apparently lay behind the decision to deploy a "light" antiballistic missile network, ostensibly directed against a possible Chinese missile attack, which was announced by the Secretary of Defense himself in his San Francisco speech of September 18.[28] This decision, as already noted, appeared to have been aimed in considerable part at stilling domestic demands for a large-scale A.B.M. deployment to match the Soviet A.B.M. network. Yet its effectiveness as a sop to A.B.M. advocates in the United States was doomed to remain uncertain in view of multiplying indications that the U.S.S.R., in addition to its A.B.M. deployment, was engaged on a large-scale expansion and diversification of its offensive missile capability even while it refused to meet the United States for discussions of a mutual limitation on missiles of both offensive and defensive types.

More sensational than the further news of Moscow's reported "fractional orbital bombardment system" (FOBS), announced by Secretary McNamara on November 3,[29] was the disclosure late in November that Mr. McNamara himself would be leaving the Defense Department as soon as the new budget for the fiscal year 1969 had been prepared and presented to Congress. President Johnson's reasons for dispensing with the services of this extraordinary man, months before the opening of the new political campaign, were not revealed. Mr. McNamara's departure to take up a post at the International Bank would undoubtedly remove a point of friction from the

the U.S. governmental scene, but it would also deprive the admin-istration of the man who had been its most potent instrument in the reshaping of defense policy and organization throughout the 1960's. In his seven years at the Pentagon, Secretary McNamara had been a zealous opponent of waste and inefficiency in all its forms, even to the point of opposing activities and weapons that others thought essential to the national defense.

Nowhere had this bent been more apparent than in the resistance of the Secretary of Defense to the build-up of atomic striking forces beyond the needs of deterrence as he saw them. It was senseless, Mr. McMamara had argued, to insist on nuclear "superiority" to the U.S.S.R. at a time when the whole idea of superiority had been drained of meaning by the development of more and more complex weapons; just as it was futile to engage in the competitive deployment of antimissile systems that would magnify defense expenditures on both sides without increasing real security on either. While some Americans had found this reasoning oversophisticated, effective chal-lenges had been few at a time when the United States enjoyed *de facto* nuclear superiority and the Soviet A.B.M. system was still in the devel-opment stage. The real test of Mr. McNamara's views would be more likely to come at a time when the Russians were actively challenging the U.S. superiority and when Mr. McNamara would no longer be on hand to defend his opinions.

49 : The Dollar in Danger

Fears for the military security of the United States were not a major element in the national anxiety syndrome of 1967. A much more constant source of apprehension had to do with the continuing rise in prices, the precarious state of the national balance of payments, and the increasingly insecure position of the dollar in the national and world economy. Uneasiness on these points ranked close behind the war in Vietnam and the tension in the cities as a source of worry to both government and public.

These anxieties were not without a paradoxical side when viewed in relation to the prodigious growth and productivity of the American economy in the postwar years and particularly in the 1960's. "We have now enjoyed six years of unprecedented and rewarding prosperity," President Johnson recalled in his 1967 State of the Union message; and the prospect at that time seemed to be for more of the same. Gross national product, or the total production of goods and services, had advanced by 5½ per cent in 1966, to a preliminary figure of $740 billion. For 1967, the President and his Council of Economic Advisers anticipated another generally prosperous year, with a further 6½ per cent increase in G.N.P. to around $787 billion.[30] Not all of this continuing growth could be considered "real," however, since a substantial part of it reflected the upward trend in price levels that had been evident through most of the period since World War II. Consumer prices had risen by 3.3 per cent in 1966 alone, the largest annual increase in nearly a decade; and a further increase of perhaps 2.5 per cent was thought likely in 1967. To the extent that this inflationary trend continued unchecked, the purchasing power of the dollar would be reduced and its domestic and international standing impaired.

Among the varied causes of this inflationary trend was the war in Vietnam, which, as already noted, was by this time absorbing more than $20 billion a year in direct military expenditure as well as substantial additional sums for economic aid and similar purposes. Since a part of this money was spent outside the United States and unmatched by any corresponding inflow on the credit side, the Vietnam war had also become a factor in prepetuating the chronic deficit in the U.S. balance of payments.

Balance-of-payments problems long predated the Vietnam build-up, however. Through almost the entire postwar period, the United States had been spending more abroad than it took in from abroad—mainly, it is true, for purposes that were considered highly laudable—and had been gradually losing gold as foreign dollar-holders exchanged some of their dollar earnings for gold at the fixed price of $35 an ounce. In accordance with its international commitments, the United States thus far had scrupulously met this demand from its abundant if dwindling gold reserves. At the end of 1966, these reserves still totaled $13,235 million, although the greater part of this amount was (until 1968) required by law to be retained as backing for paper money in circulation. If the trend continued long enough, however, the United States would obviously be unable to meet the demand for gold at the established price level and would be compelled to modify its gold-buying policies, thus presumably reducing the value of the dollar on international markets just as inflation was reducing its value at home. Given the central position of the dollar in international trade and finance, such action could be expected to result in a period of financial instability as damaging to the United States as it would be to other nations.

Efforts to alleviate this situation and avert its worst consequences had been initiated in the later years of the Eisenhower administration and had been continued and intensified under Presidents Kennedy and Johnson. While helping to keep the annual deficit within tolerable limits, such efforts had failed thus far to eliminate it entirely because of the continuing large outflows of U.S. investment capital and military, foreign aid, and tourist expenditures. These factors had more than offset the substantial surplus earned by the United States in its foreign trade, which amounted to $3.8 billion in 1966 and even more in earlier years. As measured on the familiar "liquidity" basis, the over-all balance-of-payments deficit was still reckoned at $1,335 million for 1965 and $1,357 million for 1966 (corrected figures).[31]

Complete elimination of the deficit, many observers believed, would require far-reaching policy revisions of a sort the United States had thus far been unwilling to contemplate—drastic curtailment of overseas military deployments, the adoption of a "tight money" or high interest policy at home, and/or a shift of policy on the matter of fixed exchange rates. Thus far, the administration had preferred to limit itself to a policy of exhortations and limited expedients, among them a "voluntary" program to restrict U.S. investment in other developed countries, an "interest equalization tax" designed to lessen the attractiveness of investment in foreign securities, a reduction in the duty-free allowance for U.S. tourist purchases, and a requirement that most foreign aid funds be spent within the United States.

The interest equalization tax, first enacted in 1964, was due to expire in the summer of 1967, and Congress, acting on the President's request, eventually extended it for a period of two more years.[32] A more drastic presidential recommendation, with important implications for both the domestic economy and the balance of payments, had been Mr. Johnson's request in January 1967 for a 6 per cent surcharge on corporate and individual income taxes for the duration of the Vietnam emergency.[33] An anti-inflationary tax increase, by limiting the rise in domestic prices, would tend to keep U.S. exports competitive in world markets and reverse the recent downward trend in the trade surplus. By convincing the world that the United States was seriously determined to put its finances in order, it would also tend to strengthen confidence in the dollar and discourage any inordinate demand for gold.

As matters turned out, however, there was to be no tax increase during 1967. A perceptible economic slowdown in the first quarter of the year made Congress reluctant to act and occasioned disagreement even among the experts. By August, the economy was moving forward again and the nation, despite congressional disinclination to allocate additional funds for urban renewal programs, was confronted with the prospect of a greatly enlarged budgetary deficit as a result of the growing Vietnam commitment and other factors. In his supplementary budget message of August 3, the President accordingly renewed his appeal for a tax surcharge—now set at 10 per cent rather than 6 per cent—in the interests of avoiding such evils as "a ruinous spiral of inflation . . . , brutally higher interest rates . . . , an unequal and unjust distribution of the cost of supporting our men in Vietnam, [and] a deterioration in our balance of payments by increasing imports and decreasing exports."[34] Congress, however, was unconvinced by these rather lurid warnings and still hesitated to act unless and until it was assured that the administration would do its bit by sharply curtailing expenditures on nonmilitary programs.

Concern for long-term balance-of-payments equilibrium had also heightened the U.S. interest in the Kennedy Round of tariff negotiations, particularly in so far as they had held out a hope of expanded trade with other industrialized countries in the European Common Market and elsewhere. But though strongly favorable in principle to mutual tariff reductions "across the board," the United States had refused to bargain for lower tariffs on a considerable range of products and, as we have seen, had been unable—pending action by the Congress—to promise any modification in the system of valuing certain chemical imports for tariff purposes on the basis of the American selling price (A.S.P.) in preference to the normal valuation based on export value. While assuring continued protection for a number of U.S. industries, this stand also helped to limit the scale of the mutual concessions agreed upon in the final stages of the Kennedy Round. Nevertheless the President could hail the "solid record of achievement" at Geneva as "unmatched in world trade history for its constructive and beneficial results." Thanks to the principle of reciprocity on which the United States had insisted, Mr. Johnson declared, "Our consumers will benefit by lower import costs. Our export industries will benefit by greater market opportunities abroad."[35]

Implementation of the Geneva tariff cuts would not require congressional action, since they were covered by authority already voted by Congress in the Trade Expansion Act of 1962.[36] The only further action needed was a presidential proclamation, issued in December, which provided for phased tariff reductions by the United States beginning January 1, 1968.[37] Other sections of the Kennedy Round agreement would, however, require congressional concurrence. Participation in the new International Grains Arrangement would require the advice and consent of the Senate. In addition, Congress would have to pass a law repealing the American selling price system if the United States was to get the benefit of the conditional reductions on chemical tariffs that formed a part of the Geneva compromise. Finally, the President gave notice late in the year of his intention to send to Congress a general Trade Bill which, in addition to repealing the A.S.P., would modify the Adjustment Assistance Program for firms and workers hurt by foreign competition and "provide authority that will enable us to make further progress in promoting world trade."[38]

The need for a definition of U.S. trade policy for the period beyond the Kennedy Round had long been recognized and had already been the subject of important nonofficial studies.[39] For the administration, President Johnson had announced that once the Kennedy Round was out of the way, Special Representative Roth would head a long-range policy study that would focus on improving the trade position of the less developed countries as well as further reduction of trade barriers between industrialized nations.[40] The immediate need, Ambassador Roth told a congressional committee in July, was a period of "review and reflection" while the Kennedy Round results were being digested. Accordingly, he said, the administration was not contemplating "any further major initiative in trade liberalization in the immediate future," but for the present was asking only for the repeal of the A.S.P. and continuing authority to make certain technical tariff adjustments.[41]

An interim trade bill along these lines would presumably have been submitted to Congress in the fall of 1967 had not that body already been so deeply engaged with the question of a tax rise. The mood of Congress, however, had been far from favorable to such initiatives. Protectionist sentiment, inspired in part by the concessions negotiated at Geneva, had been on the increase and had been spreading through the legislative branch at the very time the administration—using authority voted by Congress in the past—was engaged on its most far-reaching venture in trade liberalization. The textile industry, as usual in good times and bad, was clamoring for more effective protection against foreign competition. New voices were also joining the protectionist chorus. Steel producers, for example, were beginning to call for special protection against rising imports. Within the administration, Secretary of Agriculture Orville L. Freeman was echoing farmers' demands for a reduction of dairy imports. Such a reduction was in fact ordered by the President at the end of June[42] in what looked like a departure from the liberal spirit behind his earlier decision to reduce tariffs on watches and sheet glass.[43]

This protectionist drive gained redoubled force with the announcement of the Kennedy Round results, which had concentrated on reciprocal tariff reduction but did nothing to restrict the resort to import quotas and other nontariff barriers. By early fall, proposals had been introduced in Congress involving the imposition of quota restrictions on a wide variety of imported products, ranging from steel to strawberries. There was even talk of an "omnibus" quota bill imposing quantitative restrictions "across the board." Mr. Roth and others expressed the fear that such actions might undo the whole achievement of the Kennedy Round.[44] Acknowledging the seriousness of the threat, President Johnson designated a team of five cabinet members to fight the new trend in testimony before the Senate Finance Committee.

Foreign countries were also heard from. Japan, the Latin American nations, the European Economic Community, and others registered formal protests and hinted at the likelihood of retaliatory action should the United States attempt to restrict their legitimate trade. Forty such protests or warnings—some of them perhaps inspired by the State Department itself—were reported by Under-Secretary Katzenbach. Mexican President Díaz Ordaz, in Washington for a state visit, carried his appeal directly to the Congress in his address to a joint session on October 27. President Johnson himself implied that he would veto any quota bill that Congress might pass.[45] Strongly backed by private foreign trade groups, this show of resistance sufficed to ward off the threat of congressional action in 1967, but many predicted a more determined protectionist offensive in 1968.

Since import restriction would almost certainly result in a limitation of exports as well, it seemed an unpromising course of action so far as rectification of the balance of payments was concerned. Partly because of a slowdown in business activity in Europe, American exports were already failing to sustain the administration's hopes for a marked improvement in the trade surplus. Figures for the full year 1967 would later indicate that exports had increased by 5.3 per cent and imports by 5 per cent, to $30.9 billion and $26.8 billion respectively. The resultant trade surplus of $4.1 billion was $300 million better than the 1966 figure but remained lower than in any other year since 1959.[46]

A more potent factor in what turned out to be a near-disastrous year from the balance-of-payments standpoint was the growing loss of international confidence that affected both the pound and the dollar and produced the international financial crisis of late 1967. Ironically, this crisis followed hard on the heels of the constructive agreement among the major Western nations concerning the creation of a new international reserve unit in the form of "special drawing rights" on the International Monetary Fund. The purpose of that agreement, as already explained, was to create more orderly conditions for the expansion of world trade in the future. As such, it represented an important success for American foreign policy, despite the far-reaching modifications to which the original American plan was subjected before its approval by the Group of Ten and the I.M.F.[47] The agreement's immediate sequel, however, was a financial tempest that shook the existing international monetary system to its foundations.

An earlier chapter has traced the major stages of this international financial crisis—the growth of Britain's deficit, the devaluation of the pound on November 18,[48] the subsequent conversions of dollars into gold, and the almost desperate attempts by the United States to bolster confidence in the dollar by proclaiming its determination to maintain the existing gold-dollar relationship and by eliciting gestures of solidarity from the central bankers of countries participating in the London gold pool.[49] In terms of current gold and capital movements, these efforts were only partially successful. The U.S. loss of gold in December alone amounted to $900 million; for the year as a whole, a net loss of $1,170 million reduced the total gold stock at the year's end to $12,065 million.[50] The over-all balance of payments also deteriorated sharply during the same period. The deficit of $1,850 million in the final quarter of the year, as measured on a liquidity basis, substantially exceeded the full-year deficit incurred in 1966. The balance-of-payments deficit for 1967 as a whole was eventually reckoned at $3,575 million on a liquidity basis—nearly three times the 1966 figure—or $3,400 million on an "official reserve transaction" basis.[51]

Other elements in the balance of payments made their contribution to these unsatisfactory results. Net outflows of capital, for example, increased during 1967 despite good observance of the voluntary program of investment curbs that had been in effect since 1965 and was renewed for another year on November 16.[52] A more weighty psychological factor in the year-end flight from the dollar was the continued refusal of Congress to enact a tax increase. Virtually every qualified observer agreed that the failure to raise taxes was the strongest factor lessening international confidence in the ability and will of the United States to cope with its financial difficulties.

Congressional opposition to a tax surcharge, centering in the House Ways and Means Committee headed by Representative Wilbur D. Mills, was grounded not in unconcern for the balance of payments but in a feeling that retrenchment should be a two-way process involving not only increased taxes but reduced expenditure as well. Various formulas were put forward as the price the administration might suitably be asked to pay for a tax increase: a reduction of government spending by 5 per cent, by 3 per cent, by $5 billion, or by $9 billion over a two-year period. Renewing his appeals in the wake of the British devaluation, the President promised maximum efforts toward government economy and eventually ordered Federal departments and agencies to cut their expenditures in the current fiscal year by some $2.6 billion, over and above the $1.5 billion already cut by Congress in passing the various appropriation bills. More than this the administration apparently felt it could not do without inflicting unwarrantable damage on existing foreign and domestic programs. Its efforts, however, were not enough to satisfy the relevant committeemen, who announced in the midst of the gold crisis that further consideration of a tax increase would be put over to the next session. By that time, the situation would have been materially altered by the stringent new program of mandatory balance-of-payments restraints that was to be announced by President Johnson on the first day of 1968.[53]

The economic policy record for 1967 was not entirely negative. Gross national product, at $785 billion, came close to the January estimate, although consumer prices also rose by 3.1 per cent and real economic growth amounted to only 2.6 per cent, a significant decline from the 6 per cent average growth rate maintained during the 1962-66 period. Abroad, the successful completion of the Kennedy Round and the agreement on special drawing rights were achievements of no mean order. At bottom, however, the success of these arrangements and, in a wider sense, of American world policy as a whole would still depend on "keeping competitive," avoiding inflationary wage and price increases, and limiting those activities that increased the dollar outflow without contributing to the realization of national aims.[54]

50 : Cutting Foreign Aid

The economy mood in Congress found other outlets besides the resistance to a tax increase. The crest of the economy wave in November and December 1967 coincided with the final stages in the mutilation by Congress of the foreign aid program for the fiscal year 1968. Since most foreign aid funds were already being spent within the United States, congressional reductions and other changes in the program made no significant contribution to curbing the payments deficit. In terms of their foreign policy impact, however, they claim a place among the national debacles of the year.

Even in their original form, the President's recommendations concerning foreign aid fell short of the minimum estimates of those who looked at world development problems from a global rather than a national, budgetary standpoint. U Thant was by no means the only public figure who considered the current level of development outlays by the wealthier nations to be far too low. Responsible Americans like David Rockefeller of the Chase Manhattan Bank advocated a doubling of the annual assistance by industrialized to developing countries.[55] Vice-President Humphrey was another who deplored the fact that the developed countries as a group were devoting no more than 7/10 of 1 per cent of their gross national product to development assistance.[56]

American foreign aid proposals, however, were tailored not to what the developing nations could usefully absorb, but to what Congress seemed likely to grant. For fiscal year 1968, the over-all foreign aid budget was set by the President at $3,126 million, including $596 million for military assistance and $2,530 million for economic aid through the Agency for International Development (AID). Described by AID Administrator William S. Gaud as a "tight or bikini-type budget," the $2,530 million figure was nevertheless substantially more than the President had asked or Congress had appropriated the year before. Although the total foreign aid request was rightly asserted to be the smallest in the history of the aid program, the major reductions were accomplished on the military side of the program by shifting the costs of military assistance to Vietnam, Thailand, and Laos to the budget of the Department of Defense. In addition to foreign aid proper, the President's January budget also included separate allocations of $1,772 million for the Food for Freedom Program, $104 million for the International Development Association, and $124 million for the Peace Corps.[57]

A number of policy innovations were recommended by the President in the subsequent foreign aid message of February 9[58] in which he also indicated how the bulk of the proposed economic development funds were to be allocated—$624 million to Latin America, $758 million to the Near East and South Asia, $195 million to Africa, and $812 million to East Asia, including $550 million for Vietnam. Self-help, Mr. Johnson said, should be the first of the basic principles to be written into the new Foreign Assistance Act—self-help and a multilateral or "burden-sharing" approach to foreign aid that would put the emphasis on economic development undertakings of regional scope and would accord highest priority to investment in agriculture, health, and education. Funds for programs in these areas, he said, accounted for over $1 billion of his request.[59]

These principles were not in themselves objectionable to the Congress, which eventually incorporated most of them in the preamble to the Foreign Assistance Act of 1967,[60] the authorizing measure that laid down broad guidelines for the aid program and established ceilings for the subsequent appropriation. Congress, however, had never been enthusiastic about voting large sums for foreign aid, and its misgivings were reinforced in 1967 by growing uneasiness about the general trend of U.S. policy in Vietnam and elsewhere. Unable to influence the administration's course by direct means, members of the Senate Foreign Relations Committee and other congressional bodies took to expressing their disagreement by putting obstacles in the way of its foreign aid plans. An early instance of this tendency, described in a previous chapter, was the Senate's refusal to honor President Johnson's March 13 request to authorize up to $1.5 billion in extra aid funds for Latin America in advance of the Punta del Este conference.[61] Following his return from Punta del Este, where he had given additional pledges of U.S. support for Latin American economic development, the President sent to Congress a budget amendment designed to accomplish some of the same purposes by increasing the fiscal year 1968 allotment for Latin America by $400 million.[62] Of this amount, the Congress would ultimately approve a special contribution of $300 million to the Inter-American Development Bank while rejecting a proposed $100 million increase in direct support of the Alliance for Progress.

As the whittling down of the President's over-all request began to gather momentum, a new distraction arose with the disclosure in July that certain funds ostensibly appropriated for economic development in the past had actually been used to help finance the sale of arms to Latin American and other developing countries. The details of these complicated transactions, which involved primarily the Defense Department and the Export-Import Bank and apparently had totaled as much as $1.5 billion in the past two fiscal years, were difficult to establish with precision, but it was apparent that they had been facilitated by the use of a so-called "revolving fund" established under previous foreign aid legislation.[63]

As with the earlier disclosures concerning C.I.A. financing of educational organizations, there was room for honest differences of opinion about the usefulness and propriety of the deals in question. Admitting that arms expenditure by less developed countries was undesirably high, the State Department insisted that there were instances, as in the Middle East and Latin America, in which it was nevertheless essential to facilitate arms acquisitions in order to prevent the development of regional imbalances or local threats to security.[64] Most members of Congress took a less elaborate view. Not only were arms build-ups in developing countries bad in themselves,

"SOME SUPERSONIC WARPLANES, SOME MONEY TO PAY FOR THEM——AND, OH YES, SOME FOOD FOR THE PEASANTS"

Herblock in *The Washington Post*

they reasoned, but the concealment of the U.S. Government's role in such transactions was unconscionable. In psychological if not in logical terms, the discovery provided a further justification for the mutilation of the aid program that was already in progress and was to be further accentuated as the season advanced.

Disagreements about just how far to go in trying to block such arms transactions in the future were largely instrumental in delaying the passage of the Foreign Assistance Act until early November. Eventually, after prolonged debate, it was decided that the so-called "revolving fund" should be eliminated by June 30, 1968 and, in addition, that no form of assistance should be provided in future to countries that diverted U.S. aid to military expenditure, broke relations with the United States, or dealt with North Vietnam. Made wary by the Vietnam experience, Senator Fulbright also secured the inclusion in the authorization law of a special stipulation to the effect that the furnishing of assistance did not imply a commitment to use the U.S. Armed Forces for the defense of any foreign country. In working out these provisions, Congress also made liberal preliminary cuts in the administration's money request, reducing the total funds available for appropriation from $3,126 million to $2,850 million.[65] "I regret to say that the Foreign Assistance Act of 1967 reduces the margin of hope to the danger point," said President Johnson as he signed the measure on November 15. "I urge each member of Congress to search his own mind and his own heart before he joins in any effort to erode these vital programs still further."[66]

Seldom had a Presidential admonition been more timely, for the appropriations committees of the two houses were already engaged in making much sharper reductions in the actual appropriation that would be incorporated in the Foreign Assistance and Related Agencies Appropriation Act, 1968. By the time the two houses reached final agreement on this measure on December 15, the administration's defeat had become a rout. Funds provided for economic assistance, including administrative expenses, were reduced to a bare $1,895,635,000; military assistance was cut to $400,000,000; the total for the two together was reduced to $2,295,635,000. Strict limitations, amounting in some cases to virtual prohibitions, were also placed on aid to the United Arab Republic, Communist countries, and countries dealing with Cuba or North Vietnam; and there were also special restrictions on aid to underdeveloped countries that spent money on sophisticated weapons systems.[67] This travesty of his original program elicited no statement from President Johnson when he signed the measure on January 2, 1968, halfway through the fiscal year for which it purported to provide.

Also included in the appropriation measure were the allotments for other aid-related activities which the President had mentioned in his January budget and subsequent communications. The Peace Corps was granted $107.5 million of the $124 million originally requested to support the efforts of some 16,000 volunteers in 53 countries and one territory.[68] As authorized by earlier legislation, $104 million was made available to fulfill an earlier, three-year commitment to the International Development Association, though this would do nothing to alleviate I.D.A.'s current financial difficulties.[69] As already mentioned, a drastic reduction in funds for the Alliance for Progress was offset in part by the appropriation of $300 million as the first installment in a three-year build-up of the Inter-American Bank's Fund for Special Operations.[70]

A parallel request for soft-loan funds for the Asian Development Bank—the President, in his message of September 26, had suggested a contribution of $200 million over a four-year period—was not included in the financial plan for fiscal year 1968 and was accordingly not acted upon by Congress at the 1967 session.[71] Also left over to the new year, mainly because of the arms-sale controversy, was a bill to extend the life of the Export-Import Bank for five years from June 30, 1968 and to increase its lending authorization from $9 billion to $13.5 billion. In its preliminary work on this measure, which was passed early in 1968, Congress struck sharply at the President's "bridge-building" policy toward the Communist world by forbidding the Eximbank to lend funds toward setting up the proposed Fiat automobile plant in the U.S.S.R.[72]

The role of food aid in U.S. policy, and the related emphasis on curbing population growth in developing countries, have been noted in earlier chapters. Although the Food for Freedom program continued to suffer from a lack of firm direction during 1967, the United States did ring up two important achievements in this area in the programming of emergency food aid to India[73] and in the inclusion within the Kennedy Round agreements of an International Grains Arrangement that would, among other things, provide 13.5 million tons of grain to less developed countries over a three-year period.[74] World food problems, as the President and others had often pointed out, were an area in which there was an obvious need for multinational efforts involving both food-surplus and food-deficit countries. Thus far, the United States had had but limited success in trying to mobilize its friends of the developed world for a concerted attack on the problem of world hunger—or, for that matter, on other aspects of international development problems. Even in a genuinely multilateral development effort, however, the United States would undoubtedly be expected to display more continuity of purpose than had been apparent in some aspects of its own aid story for 1967.

51 : "We Shall Ride the Tiger"

It is difficult not to catch in the legislative history of the 1967-68 foreign aid program an echo of the harsh and even violent spirit that characterized so many of the public events of 1967. Congress could not have been expected to remain entirely unaffected by a seasonal trend which, though described in different terms by different observers, was generally conceded to be the reverse of constructive. To John Gardner, Secretary of Health, Education, and Welfare, the nation was afflicted during the latter half of 1967 by "a kind of negativism—a grumbling, complaining mood" that affected both the domestic and the foreign sectors. Senator Mansfield discerned a sense of "unease and frustration" which, he felt, reflected such diverse influences as the war in Vietnam, unrest in the cities, a months-old copper strike in the West, and "the rise of the younger generation, expressing themselves as most young generations do." Senator Fulbright, more drastically, continued to assert that America was being corrupted by the war, betraying its own traditions, and turning itself into a "militarized society."[75] What all of them appeared to agree upon was that the nation was currently in a poor condition to deal objectively with the problems before it.

This sense of anger and malaise pervaded all developments on the national scene, not only the intensifying debate on Vietnam but the radicalization of "New Left" opposition, the revolt against administration economic programs, and the rising ferment of political activity in anticipation of the 1968 elections. Subconsciously, at least, the harassed President might well have had more than Vietnam in mind when he arose to toast Prime Minister Lee of Singapore at a White House dinner on October 17. "Mr. Prime Minister," the President said, "you have a phrase in your part of the world that puts our determination very well, I think. You call it 'riding the tiger.' You rode the tiger. We shall."[76] The British-educated Prime Minister, who may well have recalled the limerick about the young lady from Niger, refrained from any such jocose reference on the public record.

It was inevitable in a preelection year that discussion of the war and other national issues should increasingly become entwined with the shaping of positions for the coming electoral test. Virtually everyone assumed that President Johnson would be the Democratic candidate for reelection, and that he would use the occasion to seek national endorsement for his policy of "keeping faith" with the Saigon government and avoiding either abandonment or all-out war in Southeast Asia. Mr. Johnson's growing tendency to stress the element of American national interest in the Vietnam involvement appeared to bear out these expectations. There were many who disagreed with this approach; yet the over-all impact of Vietnam on the political scene was nothing if not confusing. Vietnam, at bottom, was a national rather than a partisan issue. The fact that the war was being conducted by a Democratic administration assured it neither the united support of Democrats nor the united opposition of Republicans. Both parties were divided by the war in much the same way as was the nation as a whole.

If anything, support for the war had generally appeared firmer on the Republican than on the Democratic side. Senate minority leader Dirksen had almost invariably supported the President's position, often in direct disagreement with majority leader Mansfield. Former Vice-President Nixon, a leading aspirant for the Republican nomination in 1968, was circumspectly hawkish about the war, as was Governor Ronald Reagan of California, another presidential hopeful. Governor George Romney of Michigan, in contrast, had initially supported the President's stand in almost every detail but had become increasingly interested in promoting peace negotiations and exploring prospects for a neutralization of Southeast Asia. Other Republicans like Governor Nelson A. Rockefeller of New York and Senator Thruston B. Morton of Kentucky also seemed increasingly inclined toward dissociation from the war as conducted by the Johnson administration.

Among Democratic politicians, the administration's war policy had few if any prominent defenders except for Vice-President Humphrey and the President himself. The Southern Senators and congressmen who called for heavier bombing of North Vietnam had never been regarded as presidential aspirants, and their agitation was frequently drowned out by Senator Fulbright's antiwar pronouncements, Senator Mansfield's unwearied appeals for negotiation, and the anti-White House arguments of Senator Robert Kennedy and his adherents. But Senator Kennedy was the only member of this critical trio who had been widely thought of as a presidential possibility, and he had repeatedly disclaimed any intention of challenging President Johnson for the 1968 nomination.

There was, however, a fourth Democratic Senator, Eugene J. McCarthy of Minnesota, who had also emerged as a vigorous critic of the administration's course in Vietnam and, by mid-autumn of 1967, was even calling for the resignation of Secretary Rusk and urging the Democrats to repudiate the Johnson war policy in advance of the election. Disclaiming "peace at any price" sentiment and calling for "an honorable, rational and political solution of this war," Senator McCarthy announced on November 30 that he himself would enter the Democratic primaries in at least four states in order to promote an open debate on the issues raised by the war and challenge the administration's seeming pursuit of military victory regardless of cost.[77] It was the President's own party that thus gave birth to the first open and explicit challenge to his basic policy in Southeast Asia.

The dwindling of political support for Mr. Johnson's position was matched by a degree of attrition within the President's official family, partly as the result of normal turnover but partly, it seemed, as a reflection of discontent with the high priority assigned to military operations in Vietnam. Secretary Rusk, whom no one accused of disagreeing with the President's policy, had stuck doggedly to his difficult post, and few significant changes had occurred thus far at subordinate levels of the State Department and Foreign Service. Among the major ambassadorial posts, Mr. Bunker's replacement of Governor Lodge as Ambassador to Saigon was the only important change until Ambassador Charles E. Bohlen returned from Paris in December to succeed Foy D. Kohler as Deputy Under-Secretary of State for Political Affairs.

At the Assistant Secretary of State level, similarly, there had been no political significance in such changes as the appointment of Covey T. Oliver to succeed Lincoln Gordon in charge of Inter-American

Affairs soon after the Punta del Este conference. By November, however, the atmosphere had changed. The resignation at that time of Charles Frankel as Assistant Secretary of State for Educational and Cultural Affairs was widely ascribed to a feeling that official emphasis on Vietnam had undermined the effectiveness of the government's international educational and cultural programs.[78]

Much more sensational were the reports that Ambassador Goldberg was thinking seriously of relinquishing his post as U.S. Representative to the United Nations. Although the reasons for Mr. Goldberg's disenchantment were not publicly disclosed, the difficulty of defending the U.S. course in Vietnam—and, still more, of enlisting the U.N. in the cause of peace in that country—could obviously not have failed to contribute to it. Mr. Goldberg himself admitted that his greatest personal "disappointment and frustration" in two and one-half years' service at the U.N. had arisen from his inability to find a way of involving the organization in a constructive role in Vietnam peacemaking.[79]

Secretary McNamara's impending departure from the government, made known by the President on November 27, was not overtly connected with Vietnam, yet it was bound to stand out as a supreme example of official gravitation away from the position upheld by the President with the support of Secretary Rusk and members of the White House staff. Widely regarded at one time as the architect of "McNamara's war," the Secretary of Defense had in recent months come to be looked upon as something of an administration "dove," particularly so far as the bombing of North Vietnam was concerned.[80] In the absence of convincing explanations of his departure, unofficial speculation gave more weight to supposed disagreements on Vietnam and on antimissile defenses[81] than to the challenge of the new position Mr. McNamara would be taking up as President of the World Bank.

Rising criticism of the war, waning support within the administration, threats to the dollar, opposition to the tax rise, mangling of the foreign aid program, these and other whips of fortune had as yet had no perceptible effect on President Johnson's determination to persevere along the established lines. Reviewing the foreign policy developments of recent months—the regional consolidation in Asia, the agreements on trade and finance, the progress toward nuclear nonproliferation, the Punta del Este conference, the U.N. resolution on the Middle East, the avoidance of war over Cyprus—the President could still assert that 1967 had been "a year of rather remarkable constructive achievements . . . despite the struggle in Vietnam."[82] "Peace will come—I am convinced of that," he told the A.F.L.-C.I.O. national convention at Bal Harbour, Florida, on December 12. "But until peace does come, I will continue, with the support of our loyal, determined people, to hold the line that we have drawn against aggression—and to hold it firm and to hold it steady."[83]

Holding the line against aggression did not, in the President's mind, preclude occasional modifications in the formulation of U.S. terms for a commencement of negotiations. Mr. Johnson's February letter to Ho Chi Minh had, as we have seen, been followed in September by the enunciation of the "San Antonio formula," in which the conditions for a halt in the bombing of North Vietnam were significantly relaxed.[84] A week after the President's Bal Harbour speech came his further suggestion that the South Vietnamese regime take the initiative in starting "informal talks" with representatives of the National Liberation Front—a suggestion which, as already noted, was sharply rejected by President Thieu and consigned to at least temporary oblivion at the two leaders' meeting in Canberra.[85] Yet despite their lack of immediate results, these presidential initiatives would seem in retrospect to have accelerated the momentum toward peace negotiations that was to lead in due course to a reformulation of North Vietnam's conditions for talks[86] and, ultimately, to the cessation of bombing of most parts of North Vietnam on April 1, 1968.

Mr. Johnson's globe-girdling, pre-Christmas flight to attend the memorial services for Australian Prime Minister Holt[87] was the year's last and most spectacular exercise of the barnstorming proclivities the President had manifested on such earlier trips as those to Guam and Punta del Este. Covering a distance of 27,000 miles in 112 hours, the American Chief Executive conferred with Asian and Pacific leaders in Australia, visited American troops in Thailand and South Vietnam, held an airport conference with President Ayub Khan at Karachi, met with Italian Government leaders in Rome, visited Pope Paul VI at the Vatican, and returned to the White House to broadcast a Christmas Eve message recounting the events of his journey, reaffirming the national desire for peace, and praising "the bravery of the human spirit and the compassion of the human heart and the power of life to triumph over pain and darkness."[88]

It would not be the happiest of Christmas seasons for a people that had already given nearly 16,000 of its sons to "hold the line that we have drawn against aggression" and could look forward to no early release from either foreign or domestic travail. Yet even now there was evidence from the public opinion polls that a majority of the nation regarded the war as a national obligation, however unpleasant, and that the President's own popularity had recovered to a point—47 per cent, as measured by the Gallup Poll—no lower than at the beginning of the year.[89]

A more fundamental question about American attitudes, though it was one that defied statistical analysis, concerned the nation's ability to retain its self-possession and its "cool" amid the uncertain hazards of the time. The issue was well posed in a statement on Far Eastern policy commissioned by the Freedom House Public Affairs Institute and released December 29. "In the final analysis," this statement declared, "the most basic challenge confronting us today is to learn how to live with insecurity without succumbing to panic or extremism. Despite our most ardent desires, we shall not be able to 'solve' many of the crucial problems that confront us in any rapid or final fashion. This is particularly true in the field of foreign policy. One response to such a situation is to pretend that the problems do not exist by withdrawing from them, and in this manner buying psychological solace for the moment at tremendous subsequent cost. Another is to overreact in an effort to reach a quick, simple and final solution.

"It is more difficult to pursue complex, incremental policies, having made careful calculations as to the full range of alternatives and the relative importance of the particular issue or region to us and to the world.

"Such policies place a premium upon knowledge, skill and patience. They do not satisfy our New Left or our Old Right. They are not in accord, moreover, with some of our cultural traditions. However, they do accord with the nature of our times—and with the future. And they are not beyond our capacities provided we recognize the stakes involved and summon the will to undertake them."[90]

Chronology of Major Events

N.B. Italicized references are to sections of the text which provide additional information or background data.

An asterisk (*) opposite the name of a country indicates that one or more high-level contacts with the President of the United States will be found listed under "The United States."

A dagger (†) indicates that additional entries will be found under "The United Nations."

1 : THE UNITED STATES

MAJOR TREATIES AND AGREEMENTS

Entered into force:

Jan. 12 (for U.S.). Agreement for Facilitating the International Circulation of Visual and Auditory Materials of an Educational, Scientific and Cultural Character, done at Lake Success July 15, 1949 (Beirut agreement; TIAS 6116).[1]

Feb. 5. Treaty of Amity and Economic Relations with Togo, signed at Lomé Feb. 8, 1966 (TIAS 6193).[1]

July 16. 1967 Protocol for the Further Extension of the International Wheat Agreement, 1962, open for signature at Washington May 15-June 1, 1967 (TIAS 6315).[1] *Sec. 45.*

[1] The initials TIAS refer to the Treaties and Other International Acts Series published by the Department of State.

Oct. 1. Protocol Extending the Arrangement Regarding International Trade in Cotton Textiles of Oct. 1, 1962, done at Geneva May 1, 1967 (TIAS 6289).[1] *Sec. 45.*

Oct. 10. Treaty on Principles Governing the Activities of States in the Exploration and Use of Outer Space, Including the Moon and Other Celestial Bodies, opened for signature in Washington, London, and Moscow Jan. 27, 1967 (TIAS 6347).[1] *Secs. 19, 44.*

Dec. 6 (for U.S.). Supplementary Convention on the Abolition of Slavery, the Slave Trade, and Institutions and Practices Similar to Slavery, done at Geneva Sept. 7, 1956. *Sec. 43.*

Ratified:

Mar. 31. Consular Convention between the U.S. and the U.S.S.R., signed at Moscow June 1, 1964. *Sec. 19.*

Sept. 22. Consular Convention between the U.S. and France, signed at Paris July 18, 1966. Ratifications exchanged Dec. 7, 1967; enters into force Jan. 7, 1968.

Oct. 24. Treaty of Amity and Economic Relations with Thailand, signed at Bangkok May 29, 1966.

Ratification advised by Senate:

Dec. 6. Protocol for the further prolongation of the International Sugar Agreement of 1958, done at London Nov. 14, 1966. *Sec. 45.*

Signed:

Feb. 27. Protocol of Amendment to the Charter of the Organization of American States (Protocol of Buenos Aires), signed at Buenos Aires. *Sec. 40.*

June 30. Geneva (1967) Protocol to the General Agreement on Tariffs and Trade, and related agreements, done at Geneva June 30, 1967. Proclaimed Dec. 16, 1967; enters into force Jan. 1, 1968. *Secs. 24, 49.*

Nov. 8. International Grains Arrangement, 1967: Wheat Trade Convention and Food Aid Convention, open for signature at Washington Oct. 15-Nov. 30, 1967. *Secs. 24, 45.*

PRESIDENTIAL TRAVELS

Mar. 19-21. The President visits Guam for conferences on the war in Vietnam. *Sec. 7.*

Apr. 10-15. The President visits Punta del Este, Uruguay for the conference of American Presidents, returning by way of Paramaribo, Surinam. *Sec. 40.*

Apr. 23-26. The President attends the funeral of Dr. Konrad Adenauer and confers with Chancellor Kurt Georg Kiesinger and other Western leaders in Bonn, Germany. *Sec. 23.*

May 25. The President visits Montreal and Ottawa and confers with Canadian Prime Minister Lester B. Pearson.

Oct. 28. The President visits Ciudad Juárez, Mexico, with Mexican President Gustavo Díaz Ordaz. *Sec. 42.*

Dec. 19-24. The President visits Australia for memorial services for Prime Minister Harold Holt (Dec. 21-22) conferring with Asian leaders and returning via Thailand (Dec. 22-23), South Vietnam, Pakistan, Italy, and the Vatican (Dec. 23). *Secs. 10, 38, 51.*

PRESIDENTIAL VISITORS

Following is a list of the principal conferences held by President Johnson with visiting heads of state or government (in Washington unless otherwise noted):

Jan. 26—President-elect Arthur da Costa e Silva, Brazil. *Sec. 39.*

Feb. 9-10—King Hassan II, Morocco. *Sec. 29.*

Feb. 13-14—Emperor Haile Selassie I, Ethiopia. *Sec. 29.*

Mar. 14—Prime Minister Il Kwon Chung, Republic of Korea. *Sec. 37.*

Mar. 20-21—Premier Nguyen Cao Ky and Chief of State Nguyen Van Thieu, Republic of Vietnam (at Guam). *Sec. 7.*

Mar. 28—Prime Minister Muhammad Hashim Maiwandwal, Afghanistan.

Apr. 3-4—President Cevdet Sunay, Turkey.

Apr. 7—President-elect Anastasio Somoza DeBayle, Nicaragua. *Sec. 39.*

Apr. 20—Prime Minister Keith Holyoake, New Zealand.

May 9—Vice-President and Prime Minister C. K. Yen, Republic of China. *Sec. 35.*

May 25—Lord Casey, Governor-General of Australia.

June 1—Prime Minister Harold Holt, Australia. *Sec. 35.*

June 2—Prime Minister Harold Wilson, United Kingdom.

June 8—President H. Kamuzu Banda, Malawi.

June 17-18—Prime Minister Harold Holt, Australia (at Camp David, Md.). *Sec. 35.*

June 22—Premiers Jens Otto Krag, Denmark and Aldo Moro, Italy.

June 23, 25—Chairman Aleksei N. Kosygin, U.S.S.R. (at Glassboro, N.J.). *Secs. 4, 7, 14, 20, 41.*

Aug. 15-16—Chancellor Kurt Georg Kiesinger, Federal Republic of Germany. *Sec. 25.*

Aug. 17—President Felix Houphouet-Boigny, Ivory Coast.

Aug. 22-23—Muhammad Reza Shah Pahlavi, Iran. *Sec. 15.*

Sept. 11—King Constantine [II], Greece, *Sec. 27.*

Sept. 18-19—President Giuseppe Saragat, Italy.

Sept. 22—Prime Minister Leabua Jonathan, Lesotho.

Sept. 26—President Hamani Diori, Niger.

Sept. 27—Prime Minister Jens Otto Krag, Denmark.

Oct. 4—Prime Minister Giorgio Borg Olivier, Malta.

Oct. 10—Lt. Gen. Joseph A. Ankrah, Ghana.

Oct. 13—Prime Minister Hugh Lawson Shearer, Jamaica.

Oct. 17—Prime Minister Lee Kuan Yew, Singapore. *Secs. 38, 51.*

Oct. 20-21—Prime Minister Souvanna Phouma, Laos. *Sec. 38.*

Oct. 24—President Ahmadou Ahidjo, Cameroon.

Oct. 26-28—President Gustavo Díaz Ordaz, Mexico (in Washington and El Paso, Texas). *Sec. 42.*

Nov. 1—King Mahendra Bir Bikram Shah Deva, Nepal.

Nov. 8—King Hussein I, Jordan. *Sec. 16.*

Nov. 14-15—Premier Eisaku Sato, Japan. *Sec. 37.*

THE CONGRESS

Jan. 10-Dec. 15. The 90th Congress holds its First Session and adopts the following major enactments affecting foreign affairs (with Public Law numbers and dates of presidential approval):

P.L. 90-5, Mar. 16—Authorizing supplemental defense appropriations for FY 1967 (S. 665). *Sec. 48.*

P.L. 90-7, Apr. 1—Supporting emergency food assistance to India (H.J. Res. 267). *Sec. 34.*

P.L. 90-8, Apr. 4—Supplemental Defense Appropriation Act, 1967 (H.R. 7123). *Sec. 48.*

P.L. 90-22, June 5—Defense procurement authorization for FY 1968 (S. 666). *Sec. 48.*

P.L. 90-40, June 30—Military Selective Service Act of 1967 (S. 1432). *Sec. 48.*

P.L. 90-56, July 26—Atomic Energy Commission Authorization, FY 1968 (H.R. 10918).

P.L. 90-59, July 31—Extending the interest equalization tax (H.R. 6098). *Sec. 49.*

P.L. 90-67, Aug. 21—National Aeronautics and Space Administration Authorization, FY 1968 (S. 1296). *Sec. 44.*

P.L. 90-88, Sept. 22—Authorizing increased contributions to the Inter-American Development Bank (H.R. 9547). *Secs. 40, 50.*

P.L. 90-96, Sept. 29—Department of Defense Appropriation Act, 1968 (H.R. 10738). *Sec. 48.*

P.L. 90-110, Oct. 21—Military Construction Authorization Act, 1968 (H.R. 11722). *Sec. 48.*

P.L. 90-131, Nov. 8—National Aeronautics and Space Administration Appropriation Act, 1968 (H.R. 12474). *Sec. 44.*

P.L. 90-133, Nov. 8—Departments of State, Justice, and Commerce, the Judiciary, and Related Agencies Appropriations Act, 1968 (H.R. 10345).

P.L. 90-137, Nov. 14—Foreign Assistance Act of 1967 (S. 18722). *Sec. 50.*

P.L. 90-147, Nov. 20—Public Works and Atomic Energy Commission Appropriation Act, 1968 (H.R. 11641).

P.L. 90-175, Dec. 5—Peace Corps Act Amendments (S. 1031). *Sec. 50.*

P.L. 90-180, Dec. 8—Military Construction Appropriation Act, 1968 (H.R. 13606). *Sec. 48.*

P.L. 90-249, Jan. 2, 1968—Foreign Assistance and Related Agencies Appropriation Act, 1968 (H.R. 13893). *Sec. 50.*

OTHER DEVELOPMENTS

Jan. 27. Astronauts Virgil I. Grissom, Edward H. White, 2d, and Roger B. Chaffee are killed as fire sweeps their Apollo spacecraft during a simulated launching. *Sec. 44.*

July 24. Federal troops are made available to quell Negro riots in Detroit, Mich. *Sec. 1.*

Sept. 20. John Charles Daly, Jr., succeeds John W. Chancellor as Director of the Voice of America.

2 : THE COMMUNIST WORLD

THE SOVIET BLOC

Feb. 8-10. The Foreign Ministers of the Warsaw Pact countries meet in Warsaw.

Apr. 24-26. Leaders of European Communist parties confer in Karlovy Vary, Czechoslovakia. *Sec. 19.*

June 9. Communist leaders of Bulgaria, Czechoslovakia, German Democratic Republic, Hungary, Poland, the U.S.S.R., and Yugoslavia meet in Moscow and pledge support to the Arab states in their conflict with Israel. *Sec. 14.*

July 11-12. Government and party leaders of seven Communist nations (including Yugoslavia but excluding Rumania) confer in Budapest on the Middle East situation. *Sec. 15.*

Dec. 19-21. Leaders of eight Communist nations (including Rumania) confer in Warsaw on the Middle East. *Sec. 22.*

THE U.S.S.R.*

Apr. 24. Col. Vladimir M. Komarov is killed in an accident to the spacecraft Soyuz 1. *Sec. 44.*

June 23, 25. Premier Aleksei N. Kosygin, in New York to attend the U.N. General Assembly, meets with President Johnson at Glassboro, N.J. *Secs. 4, 7, 14, 20, 41.*

Nov. 7. The 50th anniversary of the Bolshevik Revolution is celebrated in Moscow and throughout the U.S.S.R. *Sec. 22.*

"GERMAN DEMOCRATIC REPUBLIC"

July 2. Elections for a new Volkskammer and regional councils result in complete victory for candidates of the Communist-dominated National Front. Prime Minister Willi Stoph presents a new Ministerial Council July 14.

HUNGARY

Mar. 19. Candidates of the Patriotic People's Front win 99.7 per cent of the popular vote in general elections.

Apr. 14. Jenö Fock succeeds Gyula Kállai (assumed office June 30, 1965) as Chairman of the Council of Ministers, and Pál Losonczi succeeds István Dobi (first elected Aug. 15, 1952) as President of the Presidium of the National Assembly.

RUMANIA

Dec. 9. The Grand National Assembly elects Communist party Secretary-General Nicolae Ceausescu as President of the State Council, succeeding Chivu Stoica (elected Aug. 21, 1965). *Sec. 22.*

YUGOSLAVIA

May 16. President Josip Broz Tito (first elected Jan. 14, 1953) is reelected by the Federal Assembly to a new 4-year term.

For Far Eastern Communist countries see "East Asia and the Pacific."

For Disarmament see "The United Nations."

3 : THE WESTERN NATIONS

THE NORTH ATLANTIC TREATY ORGANIZATION

Mar. 30. The Supreme Headquarters Allied Powers Europe (SHAPE) leaves Rocquencourt, France and is established Mar. 31 at Casteau, Belgium. *Sec. 25.*

June 13-14. The North Atlantic Council holds its spring ministerial meeting in Luxembourg. *Sec. 25.*

Oct. 16. NATO's civilian headquarters is formally opened in Brussels following closure of the Paris headquarters. *Secs. 25, 28.*

Dec. 13-14. The North Atlantic Council meets in ministerial session in Brussels and approves plans for increased political cooperation. *Sec. 28.*

ORGANIZATION FOR ECONOMIC COOPERATION AND DEVELOPMENT

July 19-21. The Development Assistance Committee holds its 6th high-level meeting in Paris. *Sec. 45.*

Nov. 30-Dec. 1. The O.E.C.D. Ministerial Council holds its 7th annual meeting in Paris. *Secs. 28, 45.*

THE EUROPEAN COMMUNITIES

May 11. The United Kingdom applies for membership in the European Economic, Coal and Steel, and Atomic Energy Communities. *Sec. 24.*

May 29-30. The heads of state and/or government of the six member nations holds a commemorative meeting in Rome. *Sec. 24.*

July 6. Jean Rey (Belgium) assumes office as President of the merged commissions of the three communities. *Sec. 24.*

THE GROUP OF TEN

Aug. 26. Representatives of the Group of Ten nations agree in London on a contingency plan for the creation of special drawing rights in the International Monetary Fund. *Sec. 24.*

CANADA*

Mar. 5. Governor General George P. Vanier (inducted Sept. 15, 1959) dies and is succeeded Apr. 17 by Roland Michener.

DENMARK*

Dec. 15. The cabinet of Premier Jens Otto Krag (Social Democratic, formed Nov. 28, 1966) resigns.

FRANCE

Mar. 5, 12. The Gaullist Union for the New Republic barely retains its majority in elections to the National Assembly. *Sec. 23.*

Apr. 1. The government headed by Prime Minister Georges Pompidou (nonparty; assumed office Nov. 28, 1962) resigns. Pompidou forms a new government Apr. 7.

June 5. A nuclear device is tested at France's Pacific proving ground. Further tests are carried out June 27 and July 2.

GERMAN FEDERAL REPUBLIC*

Apr. 19. Ex-Chancellor Konrad Adenauer dies and receives a state funeral Apr. 25. *Sec. 23.*

Aug. 15-16. Chancellor Kurt Georg Kiesinger meets with President Johnson in Washington. *Sec. 25.*

ITALY*

MALTA*

NETHERLANDS

Feb. 15. The Catholic People's and Labor parties lose seats in elections to the Second Chamber.

Apr. 3. Petrus J.S. de Jong (Catholic People's party) takes office as head of a right-of-center coalition government.

PORTUGAL†

SWITZERLAND

Oct. 29. The four-party coalition wins a new four-year term of office in elections to the National Assembly.

UNITED KINGDOM*

June 2. Prime Minister Harold Wilson meets with President Johnson in Washington.

Nov. 18. The exchange rate of the pound is lowered from $2.80 to $2.40. *Sec. 26.*

THE VATICAN*

For Greece, Turkey, and Cyprus see "The Near and Middle East."

4 : THE NEAR AND MIDDLE EAST

GREECE* (*Sec. 27*)

Mar. 30. The caretaker government of Ioannis Paraskevopoulos (took office Dec. 22, 1966) resigns. Panayotis Kanellopoulos (National Radical Union) takes office Apr. 3 as head of a new one-party cabinet.

Apr. 21. The Kanellopoulos government is overthrown by a military coup led by Lt. Gen. Gregory E. Spandidakis, Col. George Papadopoulos, and Brig. Gen. Stylianos Patakos. Constantine V. Kollias (nonparty) is named Premier.

Dec. 13. The King goes into exile following an unsuccessful attempt to overthrow the junta. The government is reorganized with Lt. Gen. George

Zoitakis as Regent, Col. Papadopoulos as Premier, and Brig. Patakos as Deputy Premier.

TURKEY*

CYPRUS† (*Sec. 27*)

PALESTINE PROBLEM†

May 19. The mission of the U.N. Emergency Force established in 1957 is terminated at the request of the U.A.R. *Sec. 12.*

May 22. U.A.R. President Gamal Abdel Nasser announces the closure of the Gulf of Aqaba to Israeli vessels and those carrying strategic cargoes to Israel. *Sec. 12.*

June 5. Heavy fighting begins between Israel on one side and the U.A.R., Jordan, and Syria on the other. The Suez Canal is closed by the U.A.R. June 6 as Cairo and other Arab capitals sever relations with the U.S. and (where applicable) the U.K. A cease-fire between Israel and Jordan is announced June 7. *Sec. 13.*

June 8. The U.A.R. and Syria announce conditional acceptance of a cease-fire. Fighting ceases on the U.A.R. front June 9 but continues on the Syrian front until June 10. *Sec. 13.*

(See further "The United Nations.")

ARAB STATES

Aug. 29-Sept. 1. The heads of state or representatives of 12 Arab nations (minus Syria) confer in Khartoum. *Sec. 15.*

IRAQ

May 10. President Abdel Rahman Arif installs a new cabinet with himself as Premier.

July 10. Lt. Gen. Taher Yahya succeeds President Arif as head of a new cabinet.

JORDAN*

Mar. 4. Sherif Hussein ibn Nasser succeeds Wasfi-al-Tal (assumed office Feb. 13, 1965) as Prime Minister.

Apr. 15. Elections are held for a new Parliament. Saad Jumaa is designated Premier Apr. 23.

Aug. 1. Saad Jumaa is asked to form a new cabinet.

Oct. 7. Bahjat al-Talhouni heads a new cabinet.

KUWAIT

Jan. 25. Kuwait Nationalist supporters of the royal family win a majority in elections to the National Assembly.

PEOPLE'S REPUBLIC OF SOUTHERN YEMEN†

Nov. 30. The British-ruled Federation of South Arabia becomes independent as the People's Republic of Southern Yemen, with Qahtan al-Shaabi as President. *Sec. 17.*

UNITED ARAB REPUBLIC

June 9. President Gamal Abdel Nasser announces his resignation but retracts it in deference to the wishes expressed by the National Assembly. *Sec. 13.*

YEMEN

Nov. 5. President Abdallah al-Salal (assumed office Oct. 31, 1962) is removed by a military coup as Abdul Rahman al-Iryani is named Chairman of the Presidential Council and Mohsen al-Aini becomes Premier. The new cabinet is installed Nov. 6. *Sec. 17.*

Dec. 18. Premier al-Aini resigns and Maj. Gen. Hassan al-Amri is asked to form a war cabinet. *Sec. 17.*

IRAN*

Oct. 26. Shah Muhammad Reza Pahlavi (acceded Sept. 16, 1941) and Empress Farah are crowned in Tehran. *Sec. 15.*

5 : SOUTHERN ASIA

AFGHANISTAN*

Oct. 11. The cabinet of Premier Muhammad Hashim Maiwandwal (assumed office Nov. 6, 1965) resigns. The appointment of Noor Ahmad Etemadi as Premier is announced Nov. 1.

INDIA (*Sec. 34*)

Feb. 15-21. The Indian National Congress loses heavily in the fourth general elections to national and state assemblies.

Mar. 12. Indira Gandhi (Congress party; assumed office Jan. 24, 1966) is unanimously elected to a new five-year term as Prime Minister. The new government is sworn in Mar. 13.

May 6. An electoral college elects Vice-President Zakir Hussain (Congress party) to succeed Sarvepalli Radhakrishnan (same party; assumed office May 13, 1962) for a five-year term as President starting May 13.

PAKISTAN*

NEPAL*

6 : EAST ASIA AND THE PACIFIC

SOUTHEAST ASIA TREATY ORGANIZATION

Apr. 18-20. The SEATO Council holds its 12th annual meeting in Washington with France not participating. *Secs. 7, 35.*

Apr. 21-22. The ANZUS Council holds its 16th meeting in Washington. *Secs. 7, 35.*

July 5-7. The Asian and Pacific Council (ASPAC) holds its second ministerial meeting in Bangkok. *Sec. 37.*

Aug. 8. The Association of Southeast Asian Nations (ASEAN) is formed by Malaysia, Singapore, Thailand, the Philippines, and Indonesia in a meeting at Bangkok. *Sec. 37.*

Aug. 28-29. The ministerial meeting of the Association of Southeast Asia (ASA) in Kuala Lumpur decides on a procedure for phasing out ASA activities and their transfer, where appropriate, to the Association of Southeast Asian Nations (ASEAN). *Sec. 37.*

Dec. 17. Prime Minister Harold Holt (Liberal; assumed office Jan. 26, 1966) disappears while swimming. Deputy Prime Minister John McEwen (Country party) becomes Prime Minister Dec. 19. *Sec. 38.*

Apr. 1. A new constitution calling for an elected chief executive and bicameral legislature is promulgated.

Sept. 3. Lt. Gen. Nguyen Van Thieu, Chief of State, and Premier Nguyen Cao Ky are elected President and Vice-President, respectively, for a four-year term. Elections to the Senate are held Sept. 3, and to the House of Representatives Oct. 22. *Secs. 8, 10.*

Oct. 31. Messrs. Thieu and Ky are inaugurated as President and Vice-President respectively. Nguyen Van Loc is appointed Premier. *Sec. 10.*

Feb. 13. U.S. bombing of North Vietnam resumes after a six-day pause coinciding with a lunar new year truce in ground fighting. *Sec. 6.*

Mar. 20. President Johnson confers with U.S. and South Vietnamese leaders at Guam. *Sec. 7.*

Apr. 20. Representatives of the seven nations participating in the anti-Communist resistance in Vietnam confer in Washington. *Sec. 7.*

Sept. 29. President Johnson offers a new formula for a halt in bombing in a speech at San Antonio, Texas. *Sec. 9.*

Dec. 21. President Johnson confers in Canberra with President Thieu of South Vietnam. *Sec. 10.*

Dec. 29. North Vietnam's conditions for peace talks are restated by Foreign Minister Nguyen Duy Trinh. *Sec. 10.*

CAMBODIA (*Secs. 10, 38*)

Apr. 30. The cabinet of Lon Nol (elected Oct. 18, 1965) is dismissed and replaced May 3 by a new cabinet under Son Sann.

LAOS*

Jan. 1. A new parliament is chosen in general elections.

THAILAND*

INDONESIA (*Sec. 35*)

Feb. 22. President Sukarno (assumed office 1949) delegates all governmental authority to General Suharto, Minister of Defense and Chairman of the Cabinet Presidium.

Mar. 12. General Suharto succeeds Sukarno as Acting President with all executive powers retroactive to Feb. 22.

SINGAPORE*

REPUBLIC OF CHINA*† (*Sec. 35*)

"PEOPLE'S REPUBLIC OF CHINA"†

June 17. Communist China detonates its first hydrogen bomb. *Sec. 36.*

Dec. 24. The seventh Chinese Communist atmospheric test is carried out in the Lob Nor area. *Sec. 38.*

(For details of the "Great Proletarian Cultural Revolution" see Sec. 36.)

JAPAN*

Jan. 29. The Liberal Democrats retain an absolute majority in elections to the House of Representatives. *Sec. 35.*

Feb. 17. Premier Eisaku Sato (Liberal Democrat; elected Nov. 9, 1964), assumes the Premiership for the second time.

Sept. 13-15. The Joint U.S.-Japan Committee on Trade and Economic Affairs holds its 6th meeting in Washington. *Sec. 37.*

Nov. 14-15. Premier Sato confers with President Johnson in Washington. *Sec. 37.*

REPUBLIC OF KOREA*†

May 3. President Chung Hee Park (Democratic Republican party; assumed office May 16, 1961) is reelected for a 4-year term beginning July 1. *Sec. 35.*

June 8. The Democratic Republican party retain its majority in elections to the National Assembly which are marked by widespread violence and irregularities. *Sec. 35.*

7 : AFRICA

GENERAL

June 6. A 15-year East African Cooperation Treaty, establishing an East African Community effective Dec. 1, is signed in Kampala by the Presidents of Kenya, Tanzania, and Uganda. *Sec. 33.*

Sept. 11-14. The Assembly of Heads of State and Government of the Organization of African Unity holds its 4th session in Kinshasa. *Sec. 30.*

CAMEROON*

DEMOCRATIC REPUBLIC OF THE CONGO†

June 24. President Joseph D. Mobutu promulgates a new constitution following its approval by a popular referendum held June 4-14. *Sec. 30.*

DAHOMEY

Dec. 17. The government of President Christophe Soglo (assumed power Dec. 22, 1965) is ousted by a military coup and supplanted by a military revolutionary committee with Maj. Maurice Kouandété as Chairman. Lt. Col. Alphonse Alley is named Head of State Dec. 21 with Maj. Kouandété as Prime Minister.

ETHIOPIA*

FRENCH SOMALILAND (*Sec. 33*)

Mar. 19. A French-sponsored referendum elicits a majority vote in favor of continued association with France.

June 13, 21. The renaming of French Somaliland as French Territory of the Afars and Issas is approved by the French Parliament.

GABON

Mar. 19. President Léon M'ba (elected Feb. 1961) is reelected in presidential and parliamentary voting in which only the ruling party presents candidates.

Nov. 28. President M'ba dies and is succeeded Dec. 2 by Vice-President Bernard-Albert Bongo.

GHANA*

IVORY COAST*

LESOTHO*

LIBYA

July 1. Premier Hussein Mazek (assumed office Mar. 20, 1965) resigns and is succeeded by Abdelkader al-Bedri.

Oct. 25. Premier al-Bedri resigns and is succeeded by Abd al-Hamid Bakush as head of a new cabinet.

MALAWI*

MOROCCO*

July 6. Dr. Mohamed Benhima is appointed Premier to succeed King Hassan II (assumed office June 8, 1965).

NIGER*

NIGERIA

May 30. The Eastern Region declares its independence as the Republic of Biafra. Military operations are begun by the Federal Government in July and continue throughout the year. *Sec. 30.*

PORTUGUESE AFRICA† (*Sec. 31*)

SIERRA LEONE

Mar. 17. The Sierra Leone People's party loses its majority in elections to the House of Representatives. Martial law is declared Mar. 21 after Siaka Stevens (All People's Congress) is inducted as Prime Minister to replace Sir Albert Margai (Sierra Leone People's party; assumed office Apr. 29, 1964).

Mar. 23. The civilian government is overthrown by a military coup and supplanted by an 8-man National Reformation Council of which Lt. Col. Andrew Joxon-Smith is named Chairman Mar. 27.

SOMALI REPUBLIC (*Sec. 33*)

June 10. Abdirashid Ali Shermarke is elected by the National Assembly to a six-year term as President, assuming office June 30 as successor to Aden Abdulla Osman (elected July 6, 1961).

July 10. Mohammed Haji Ibrahim Egal is designated Prime Minister to succeed Abdirazak Haji Hussein (assumed office Aug. 1964).

SOUTH AFRICA†

Feb. 28. Theophilus Ebenhaezer Dönges (National party) is chosen by an electoral college to succeed Charles R. Swart (same party) for a 7-year term as President beginning May 31.

May 31. The inauguration of President-elect Dönges is canceled because of illness and President of the Senate Jozua F. Naudé becomes acting head of state.

SOUTHERN RHODESIA† (*Sec. 31*)

SOUTH WEST AFRICA† (*Sec. 32*)

SUDAN

May 15. Premier Saddiq al-Mahdi (Umma party; elected July 27, 1966) loses a confidence vote, resigns, and is succeeded May 26 by Mohammed Ahmed Mahgoub (Umma party) as head of a coalition cabinet.

Jan. 13. The government of President Nicholas Grunitzky (elected May 5, 1963) is overthrown in a military coup led by Lt. Col. Etienne Eyadema.

Apr. 14. Col. Eyadema proclaims himself President, dissolves the National Reconciliation Committee, and installs a new government.

8 : INTER-AMERICAN AFFAIRS

ORGANIZATION OF AMERICAN STATES

Jan. 24. The 11th Meeting of Consultation of Ministers of Foreign Affairs of the American Republics opens a first period of session in Washington.

Feb. 15-27. The Third Special Inter-American Conference meets in Buenos Aires and approves a Protocol of Amendment to the O.A.S. Charter. *Sec. 40.*

Feb. 16-26. The 11th Meeting of Consultation of Ministers of Foreign Affairs holds a second period of session in Buenos Aires and approves an agenda for the meeting of Chiefs of State of American Countries. *Sec. 40.*

Feb. 23. The admission of Trinidad and Tobago as the 22nd member state of the O.A.S. is approved at a special meeting of the O.A.S. Council in Buenos Aires. Trinidad and Tobago signs the O.A.S. Charter Mar. 13 and deposits its ratification June 12. *Sec. 40.*

Apr. 8-11. The 11th Meeting of Consultation of Ministers of Foreign Affairs holds a third period of session in Punta del Este, Uruguay. *Sec. 40.*

Apr. 12-14. The American Chiefs of State meet in Punta del Este and approve the formation of a Latin American common market by 1985. *Sec. 40.*

June 19. The 12th Meeting of Consultation of American Foreign Ministers convenes in Washington and unanimously approves an inquiry into Venezuelan charges against Cuba. *Sec. 41.*

Sept. 22-24. The 12th Meeting of Consultation of Ministers of Foreign Affairs resumes in Washington and votes further measures against Cuban-based subversion. *Sec. 41.*

Oct. 4. The admission of Barbados as the 23rd O.A.S. member state is unanimously authorized by the O.A.S. Council. Barbados deposits its ratification of the O.A.S. Charter Nov. 15. *Sec. 42.*

DENUCLEARIZATION TREATY†

Feb. 14. The Treaty of Tlatelolco, banning nuclear weapons in Latin America and the Caribbean, is signed by 14 Latin American countries in Mexico City. *Secs. 21, 39.*

LATIN AMERICAN FREE TRADE ASSOCIATION

Feb. 8. Bolivia becomes the 11th member of LAFTA.

Aug. 28-30. The LAFTA Foreign Ministers meet in Asunción and agree on preliminary steps toward establishment of the Latin American common market. *Sec. 40.*

ORGANIZATION OF LATIN AMERICAN SOLIDARITY

July 31-Aug. 10. The First Conference of the Organization of Latin American Solidarity (OLAS) is held in Havana. *Secs. 1, 41.*

BRAZIL*

Mar. 15. Arthur da Costa e Silva (elected Oct. 3, 1967) succeeds Humberto Castello Branco (inaugurated Apr. 15, 1964) for a 4-year term as President. *Sec. 39.*

EL SALVADOR

Mar. 5. Col. Fidel Sánchez Fernández (National Conciliation party) is elected to a 5-year presidential term beginning July 1 as successor to President Julio Adalberto Rivera. *Sec. 39.*

JAMAICA*

Feb. 21. The Jamaica Labor party retains its majority in elections to the House of Representatives.

Feb. 27. Donald Sangster (Jamaica Labor party) succeeds Sir Alexander Bustamante (same party) as Prime Minister.

Apr. 11. Prime Minister Sangster dies and is succeeded by Hugh Shearer (Jamaica Labor party).

MEXICO* (*Secs. 39, 42*)

NICARAGUA*

Feb. 5. Maj. Gen. Anastasio Somoza DeBayle (National Liberal party) is elected to a 5-year term as President beginning May 1 as successor to President Lorenzo Guerrero-Gutiérrez (took office Aug. 3, 1966; same party). *Sec. 39.*

URUGUAY

Mar. 1. The National Council system of government inaugurated in 1952 is terminated with the inauguration of Gen. Oscar Diego Gestido (Colorado party) for a 5-year term as President. *Sec. 39.*

Nov. 6. President Gestido dies and is succeeded by Vice-President Jorge Pacheco Areco. *Sec. 42.*

9 : THE UNITED NATIONS

MEMBERSHIP

Dec. 14. The membership is increased from 122 to 123 by the admission of Southern Yemen. *Secs. 17, 46.*

SECURITY COUNCIL

Following is a list of major Security Council actions and decisions, with resolutions numbers and votes:

RES/233 (1967), June 6. Calling for an immediate cease-fire in the Near East (unanimous). *Secs. 13, 14.*

RES/234 (1967), June 7. Demanding a cease-fire at 2000 hours GMT (unanimous). *Secs. 13, 14.*

RES/235 (1967), June 9. Demanding that hostilities between Israel and Syria cease forthwith (unanimous). *Secs. 13, 14.*

RES/236 (1967), June 12. Calling for observance of the cease-fire in the Near East (unanimous). *Sec. 14.*

RES/237 (1967), June 14. Calling for humanitarian treatment of prisoners and civilians (unanimous). *Sec. 14.*

RES/238 (1967), June 19. Extending the stationing of the U.N. Force in Cyprus for six months ending Dec. 26, 1967 (unanimous). *Sec. 27.*

RES/239 (1967), July 10. Opposing foreign assistance to mercenaries in the Democratic Republic of the Congo (unanimous). *Sec. 30.*

RES/240 (1967), Oct. 25. Demanding cessation of prohibited military activities in the Middle East (unanimous). *Sec. 16.*

RES/241 (1967), Nov. 15. Calling on Portugal to end any assistance to mercenaries operating against the Congo (without objection). *Secs. 30, 31.*

RES/242 (1967), Nov. 22. Requesting the Secretary-General to designate a Special Representative for the Middle East (unanimous). *Sec. 16.*

RES/243 (1967), Dec. 12. Recommending Southern Yemen for U.N. membership (unanimous). *Secs. 17, 46.*

RES/244 (1967), Dec. 22. Extending the stationing of the U.N. Peace-keeping Force in Cyprus for three months ending Mar. 26, 1968 (unanimous). *Sec. 27.*

GENERAL ASSEMBLY

Apr. 21-June 13. The Assembly holds its Fifth Special Session under the presidency of Abdul Rahman Pazhwak of Afganistan and adopts the following resolutions and decisions:

2248 (S-V), May 19. Providing for a U.N. Council and Commission to administer South West Africa (85-2-30). *Sec. 32.*

2249 (S-V), May 23. Requesting the Special Committee on Peace-keeping Operations to continue its work (90-1-11). *Sec. 43.*

2250 (S-V), May 23. Postponing conference on outer space to 1968 (without objection). *Sec. 44.*

June 13. Electing a Council and a Commission to administer South West Africa. *Sec. 32.*

June 17-Sept. 18. The Assembly holds its Fifth Emergency Special Session under the Presidency of Abdul Rahman Pazhwak of Afghanistan and adopts the following resolutions and decisions:

2252 (ES-V), July 4. Appealing for assistance to refugees in the Middle East (116-0-2). *Sec. 14.*

2253 (ES-V), July 4. Opposing any alteration in the status of Jerusalem (99-0-20). *Sec. 14.*

2254 (ES-V), July 14. Reiterating views on Jerusalem (99-0-18). *Sec. 14.*

2256 (ES-V), July 21. Temporarily adjourning the session (63-26-27). *Sec. 14.*

2257 (ES-V) Sept. 18. Referring the Middle East issue to the 22nd Regular Session (unanimous).

Sept. 19-Dec. 19. The Assembly holds the first part of its 22nd Regular Session in New York under the presidency of Corneliu Manescu of Rumania and adopts the following resolutions, among others (with votes):

2258 (XXII), Oct. 25. Commending report on effects of atomic radiation (unanimous).

2260 (XXII), Nov. 3. Requesting Committee on Peaceful Uses of Outer Space to continue its work (unanimous). *Sec. 46.*

2261 (XXII), Nov. 3. Calling for support of Conference on Outer Space (unanimous). *Sec. 46.*

2262 (XXII), No. 3. Calling for use of force in Southern Rhodesia (92-2-18). *Sec. 31.*

2263 (XXII), Nov. 7. Proclaiming Declaration on Elimination of Discrimination Against Women (unanimous). *Sec. 46.*

2269 (XXII), Nov. 16. Reaffirming U.N. views on Korea (68-23-26). *Secs. 37, 46.*

2270 (XXII), Nov. 17. Reaffirming views on Portuguese territories (82-7-21). *Sec. 31.*

2271 (XXII), Nov. 28. Reaffirming that any proposal to change the representation of China is an important question (69-48-4). *Sec. 46.*

2274 (XXII), Dec. 4. Asking increased support for economic development (76-0-9).

2275 (XXII), Dec. 4. Asking increased resources for International Development Association (unanimous).

2276 (XXII), Dec. 4. Requesting easing of terms for development assistance (87-0-0).

2280 (XXII), Dec. 4. Appealing for increased resources for U.N. Development Program (81-0-6).

2286 (XXII), Dec. 5. Welcoming treaty for prohibition of nuclear weapons in Latin America (82-0-28). *Sec. 40.*

2287 (XXII), Dec. 6. Providing for conference on law of treaties (89-0-1).

2288 (XXII), Dec. 7. Deploring activities of foreign financial interests in colonial territories (91-2-17). *Sec. 46.*

2289 (XXII), Dec. 8. Urging further study of a prohibition on use of nuclear weapons (77-0-29). *Secs. 21, 46.*

2290 (XXII), Dec. 8. Establishing targets for world food program (without objection). *Sec. 46.*

2291 (XXII), Dec. 8. Fixing scale of assessments for 1968-70 (76-4-5). *Sec. 46.*

2294 (XXII), Dec. 11. Continuing Office of High Commissioner for Refugees through 1973 (106-0-0).

2295 (XXII), Dec. 11. Deferring consideration of Draft Declaration on Religious Intolerance (106-0-0). *Sec. 46.*

2296 (XXII), Dec. 12. Supporting Second U.N. Conference on Trade and Development (unanimous).

2300 (XXII), Dec. 12. Requesting continued studies of multilateral food aid (90-1-13). *Sec. 46.*

2302 (XXII), Dec. 12. Deploring British policy in Oman (72-18-19). *Sec. 17.*

2305 (XXII), Dec. 13. Envisaging a second U.N. Development Decade (102-0-0). *Sec. 46.*

2306 (XXII), Dec. 13. Provisionally designating 1970 as International Education Year (102-0-1). *Secs. 44, 46.*

2307 (XXII), Dec. 13. Reiterating condemnation of *apartheid* (89-2-12). *Sec. 32.*

2308 (XXII), Dec. 13. Continuing Special Committee on Peace-keeping Operations (96-1-5). *Sec. 46.*

2309 (XXII), Dec. 13. Envisaging a fourth atoms-for-peace conference (86-0-4). *Sec. 46.*

2310 (XXII), Dec. 14. Admitting Southern Yemen to U.N. membership (by acclamation). *Secs. 17, 46.*

2312 (XXII) Dec. 14. Adopting Declaration on Territorial Asylum (unanimous). *Sec. 46.*

2321 (XXII), Dec. 15. Associating U.N. Capital Development Fund with U.N. Development Program (75-8-12).

2324 (XXII), Dec. 16. Condemning trial of 37 South West Africans (110-2-1). *Sec. 32.*

2325 (XXII), Dec. 16. Calling for South African withdrawal from South West Africa (93-2-18). *Sec. 32.*

2326 (XXII), Dec. 16. Reiterating views on colonialism (86-6-17). *Sec. 46.*

2330 (XXII), Dec. 18. Establishing Special Committee on Defining Aggression (90-1-18). *Sec. 46.*

2332 (XXII), Dec. 18. Urging observance of International Convention on Elimination of Racial Discrimination (106-2-2).

2333 (XXII), Dec. 18. Deferring consideration of U.N. High Commissioner for Human Rights (75-22-15). *Sec. 46.*

2335 (XXII), Dec. 18. Commending UNICEF (unanimous).

2336 (XXII), Dec. 18. Deferring consideration of freedom of information (unanimous). *Sec. 46.*

2337 (XXII), Dec. 18. Asking ratification of human rights conventions (112-0-0).

2339 (XXII), Dec. 18. Supporting International Conference on Human Rights (74-3-37). *Sec. 46.*

2340 (XXII), Dec. 18. Commissioning study of peaceful uses of sea-bed and ocean floor (99-0-0). *Secs. 44, 46.*

2341 (XXII), Dec. 19:
   A. Calling for support of UNRWA (98-0-3).
   B. Calling for support of displaced persons in Middle East (105-0-0). *Secs. 16, 46.*

2342 (XXII), Dec. 19:
   A. Commending report on effects of nuclear weapons (113-0-1).
   B. Requesting report on general disarmament (113-0-1). *Sec. 21.*

2343 (XXII), Dec. 19. Calling for suspension of nuclear weapon tests (103-1-7). *Sec. 21.*

2344 (XXII), Dec. 19. Requesting report on eliminating military bases in Asia, Africa and Latin America (105-0-13).

2345 (XXII), Dec. 19. Commending agreement on rescue of astronauts (115-0-0). *Secs. 44, 46.*

2346 (XXII), Dec. 19:
   A. Requesting report on nuclear nonproliferation (112-1-4).
   B. Approving a conference of non-nuclear-weapon states (110-0-8). *Secs. 21, 46.*

2347 (XXII), Dec. 19. Terminating trusteeship for Nauru (unanimous). *Sec. 46.*

2353 (XXII), Dec. 19. Calling for further negotiations on Gibraltar (75-19-27). *Sec. 26.*

2359 (XXII), Dec. 19:
  A. Calling for better geographic distribution of Secretariat staff (116-0-1).
  B. Supporting development of staff language skills (88-0-3). *Sec. 46.*

2363 (XXII), Dec. 19:
  A. Appropriating $140,430,950 for 1968 (102-1-4). *Sec. 46.*

2370 (XXII), Dec. 19. Requesting an annual budget planning estimate (114-0-1). *Sec. 46.*

Other General Assembly developments:

Nov. 6. Algeria, Hungary, Pakistan, Paraguay, and Senegal are elected to the Security Council for 1968-69, replacing Argentina, Bulgaria, Japan, Mali, and Nigeria.

Nov. 20. Nine states are elected to the Economic and Social Council for 1968-70.

Nov. 28. A resolution to admit the People's Republic of China to U.N. representation fails of adoption (45-58-17). *Sec. 46.*

Nov. 30. The Assembly adopts a consensus wishing Aden well on its accession to independence. *Secs. 17, 46.*

OTHER U.N. ACTIVITIES

Feb. 21-Mar. 23, May 18-Dec. 7. The Conference of the Eighteen-Nation Disarmament Committee meets in Geneva to discuss a nuclear nonproliferation treaty and other matters. *Secs. 19, 21, 46.*

SPECIALIZED AND RELATED AGENCIES

World Meteorological Organization:

Apr. 3-28. The W.M.O. holds the Fifth Meteorological Congress in Geneva and reelects David A. Davies (U.K.) as Secretary-General.

World Health Organization:

May 8-26. The 20th World Health Assembly meets in Geneva.

Food and Agriculture Organization:

Nov. 4-23. The F.A.O. holds its 14th biennial conference in Rome and elects A.H. Boerma (Netherlands) to succeed B.R. Sen (India) as Director-General. *Sec. 45.*

International Atomic Energy Agency:

Sept. 26 ff. The I.A.E.A. holds its 11th General Conference in Vienna.

International Bank and Fund:

Sept. 25-29. The Boards of Governors of the International Bank for Reconstruction and Development, the International Monetary Fund, and affiliated institutions hold their 22nd annual meeting in Rio de Janeiro and agree on a plan for the creation of special I.M.F. drawing rights. *Sec. 24.*

International Labor Organization:

June 7-29. The 51st International Labor Conference is held in Geneva.

GENERAL AGREEMENT ON TARIFFS AND TRADE (GATT)

May 15. The major participants in the 6th (Kennedy) round of multilateral tariff negotiations announce agreement on reductions of trade barriers and a multilateral food aid program. *Sec. 24.*

June 30. The multilateral agreements embodying the results of the Kennedy Round are signed in Geneva. *Sec. 24.*

Nov. 9-24. The Contracting Parties hold their 24th session in Geneva and elect Olivier Long (Switzerland) to succeed Eric Wyndham White as Director General. *Sec. 45.*

Notes

Following is an alphabetical list of periodical and serial publications cited in the notes:

Adelphi Papers (London: Institute for Strategic Studies).
Africa Report (Washington: African-American Institute).
Articles et documents (Paris: La Documentation Française).
Aussenpolitik (Freiburg: Verlag Rombach).
"Bulletin": Department of State Bulletin (Washington: U.S. Department of State).
Current Digest of the Soviet Press (Ann Arbor: Joint Committee on Slavic Studies).
Current Notes on International Affairs (Canberra: Australian Department of External Affairs).
"Documents": Documents on American Foreign Relations (volumes prior to 1952 published at Princeton: Princeton University Press, for the World Peace Foundation; volume from 1952 to 1966 inclusive published at New York: Harper & Row, for the Council on Foreign Relations). Documents cited by number only will appear in the forthcoming volume for 1967 (New York: Simon and Schuster, for the Council on Foreign Relations).
Estudios internacionales (Santiago: Instituto de Estudios Internacionales de la Universidad de Chile).
Europa-Archiv (Bonn: Deutsche Gesellschaft für Internationale Politik).
External Affairs (Ottawa: Canadian Department of External Affairs).
Foreign Affairs (New York: Council on Foreign Relations).
Foreign Policy Briefs (Washington: U.S. Department of State).
International Commerce (Washington: U.S. Department of Commerce).
International Conciliation (New York: Carnegie Endowment for International Peace).
International Herald Tribune (Paris).
Israel Digest (New York: Jewish Agency—American Section).

Journal of Inter-American Studies (Coral Gables, Fla.: University of Miami Press).

Keesing's Contemporary Archives (Bristol: Keesing's Publications, Ltd.).

Life (New York).

NATO Letter (Paris/Brussels: NATO Information Service).

New Times (Moscow: Trud).

New York Times (New York).

Notes et études documentaires (Paris: La Documentation Française).

Relazioni internazionali (Milan: Istituto per gli Studi di Politica Internazionale).

The Reporter (New York).

Soviet News (London: Press Department of the Soviet Embassy).

Speeches and Press Conferences (New York: Ambassade de France, Service de Presse et d'Information).

Survey of Current Business (Washington: U.S. Department of Commerce).

"U.N. Chronicle": U.N. Monthly Chronicle (New York: U.N. Office of Public Information).

The United States in World Affairs (volumes prior to 1967 published New York and Evanston: Harper & Row, for the Council on Foreign Relations).

Vital Speeches of the Day (Southold, N.Y.: City News Publishing Co.).

"Weekly Compilation": Weekly Compilation of Presidential Documents (Washington: U.S. National Archives and Records Service).

World Business (New York: Chase Manhattan Bank).

The World Today (London: Royal Institute of International Affairs).

Resolutions of the U.N. General Assembly, here cited by serial number and date, are published in a supplement to the *Official Records* of each session. Preliminary texts of the more important resolutions appear in the *U.N. Monthly Chronicle.*

Official transcripts of all presidential news conferences during 1967 were published in the *Weekly Compilation of Presidential Documents,* from which the quotations in the text have invariably been taken unless otherwise noted. Other documents bearing on foreign affairs often appear in both the *Weekly Compilation* and (with minor editorial differences) in the *Department of State Bulletin.* In such cases, the text appearing in the *Bulletin* has normally been used in the belief that it will be more readily available to users of this series.

All dates in the following notes refer to the year 1967 unless another year is specifically indicated.

1 : Introducing 1967

1. Frantz Fanon, *The Wretched of the Earth,* translated from the French by Constance Farrington (New York: Grove Press, Inc., 1965), p. 73. Reprinted by permission of Grove Press, Inc.; copyright © 1963 by Presence Africaine. (Fanon, a Martinique Negro born in 1925, studied medicine in France and par-

ticipated in the Algerian revolution before his death in New York in 1961).

2. Text from *U.N. Chronicle*, Oct., p. 131.

3. Denver address, Aug. 26, 1966, in *Documents, 1966*, pp. 12-18.

4. *New York Times*, Apr. 2.

5. Same, Apr. 2 and 5 and May 1.

6. For details cf. Sec. 41.

7. See further Chapter 10.

8. *International Herald Tribune*, Aug. 12-13.

9. *Documents*, no. 1; full text in *Weekly Compilation*, Jan. 16, pp. 26-39.

10. *Documents, 1962*, pp. 225-6.

11. See further Sec. 47.

12. *Statement of Secretary of Defense Robert S. McNamara . . . on the Fiscal Year 1968-72 Defense Program and 1968 Defense Budget, January 23, 1967* (U.S. Department of Defense, Press Release, Jan. 26), p. 42.

13. *Documents*, no. 1.

14. *Documents*, no. 4.

15. *New York Times*, Jan. 12 and 15; Johnson news conference, Mar. 2, in *Bulletin*, Mar. 20, p. 445; see further Chapter 4 at note 16.

16. See Chapter 2 at note 17.

17. *Documents*, no. 4.

18. James Reston in *New York Times*, Jan. 11.

19. *The United States in World Affairs, 1966*, p. 404.

20. For details see Sec. 24.

21. *New York Times*, Jan. 20.

22. Cf. Chapter 5 at note 31.

23. *New York Times*, Jan. 17 and 31.

2 : Vietnam: The Permanent War?

1. E.g., program of the National Liberation Front of South Vietnam, Dec. 20, 1960, in Marcus G. Raskin and Bernard B. Fall, eds., *The Viet-Nam Reader* (New York: Vintage Books, 1965), pp. 216-21; four-point statement of North Vietnamese Premier Pham Van Dong, Apr. 8, 1965, in *Documents, 1965*, pp. 147-9.

2. Baltimore speech, Apr. 7, 1965, in same, p. 143.

3. See especially *Documents, 1965*, pp. 144, 165-7, and 191-2; same, *1966*, pp. 194-5.

4. *Documents, 1965*, pp. 184-7 and 314; same, *1966*, pp. 207-11 and 254-60.

5. *Documents, 1965*, pp. 147-9.

6. *Documents, 1966*, p. 202.

7. Same, p. 256.

8. *The United States in World Affairs, 1966*, pp. 93-4.

9. See especially Harrison E. Salisbury, *Behind the Lines: Hanoi, December 23, 1966-January 7, 1967* (New York: Harper & Row, 1967).

10. *Documents, 1966*, p. 354.

11. State of the Union message, Jan. 10, in *Documents*, no. 1.

12. *New York Times*, Jan. 12.

12a. Joint statement, Oct. 25, 1966, in *Documents, 1966*, p. 250.

13. *New York Times*, Jan. 4 and 8; cf. note 5.

14. *New York Times*, Jan. 6.

15. Same, Jan. 11.

16. State Department statement, Sept. 18, in *Bulletin*, Oct. 9, pp. 462-3.

17. State Department statement, Mar. 21, in *Bulletin*, Apr. 10, p. 595.

18. Same as note 16; Guthrie role in *New York Times*, Mar. 23.

19. *Documents,* no. 60; earlier versions in same, *1965,* pp. 191-2; same, *1966,* pp. 194-5.
20. *Documents,* no. 61; comments in *New York Times,* Feb. 2 and 6.
21. News conference, Feb. 20.
22. *New York Times,* Feb. 5-7.
23. Same, Sept. 18 and 19; also statement cited in note 16.
24. *Documents,* nos. 62 and 63.
25. *New York Times,* Feb. 9.
26. *Documents,* no. 62.
27. Text, with reply of Feb. 15, in same, no. 64.
28. Same as note 21.
29. *New York Times,* Feb. 14 and 15.
30. Defense Department statement, Feb. 13, in *Documents,* no. 65a.
31. *New York Times,* Feb. 15.
32. *Documents,* no. 63b.
33. Same, no. 64c.
34. Same, no. 65b.
35. Same as note 16.
36. *New York Times,* Mar. 22.
37. Same, Mar. 11; further details in *Bulletin,* Mar. 20, pp. 464-6.
38. *New York Times,* Mar. 3; *Bulletin,* Mar. 27, p. 516.
39. *New York Times,* Mar. 6.
40. Same, Feb. 21.
41. News conference, Mar. 9.
42. *Documents,* no. 67.
43. Same, no. 66; further, *Bulletin,* Apr. 17, p. 629; also *New York Times,* Mar. 29; same, Apr. 1 and 3.
44. Press conference, Mar. 28, in *U.N. Chronicle,* Apr., pp. 67-77.
45. *Documents,* no. 70.
46. Same, nos. 69 and 71.
47. *New York Times,* Mar. 21.
48. Bunker statement, May 11, in *Bulletin,* June 5, pp. 844-5.
49. News conference, Guam, Mar. 21.
50. See especially *Life,* Apr. 7, p. 44.
51. *New York Times,* Apr. 1 and 2; Rusk in *Bulletin,* May 8, pp. 727-8.
52. *External Affairs,* May, pp. 160-2; U.S. response in *Documents,* no. 74; see further *New York Times,* Apr. 17, 19, and 22.
53. Same, Apr. 12.
54. Communiqué, Apr. 20, in *Documents,* no. 86; see also Rusk statement in *Bulletin,* May 15, pp. 742-4.
55. Communiqué, Apr. 21, in *Documents,* no. 75.
56. Communiqué, Apr. 22, in same, no. 87.
57. Apr. 24 address in *New York Times,* Apr. 25; Apr. 28 address in *Documents,* no. 76.
58. News conference, May 3.
59. Statement of May 11, in *Documents,* no. 77a.
60. News conference, May 18.
61. Soviet notes in *New York Times,* June 3 and 6; U.S. notes in *Bulletin,* June 26, p. 953, and same, July 10, p. 44.
62. News conference statement, June 25, in *Documents,* no. 13.
63. Report to nation, June 25, in same, no. 12.
64. Address of July 30, in *U.N. Chronicle,* Aug.-Sept., p. 80.
65. *International Herald Tribune,* Aug. 2.
66. Press reports and news conference statements of July 12 and 13; texts in *Weekly Compilation,* July 17, pp. 1004-9 and 1011-15; July 12 text also in *Bulletin,* Aug. 7, pp. 167-70.
67. *Weekly Compilation,* July 17, p. 1008.
68. Press reports, July 21-Aug. 6; also Clifford-Taylor news conference, Aug. 5, in *Bulletin,* Aug. 28, pp. 256-60. On the Thai contribution cf. same, Dec. 11, p. 792; same, Jan. 1, 1968, p. 4.
69. Cf. introduction to Chapter 10.
70. Budget message, Aug. 3, in *Weekly Compilation,* Aug. 7, 1084-92; excerpts in *Documents,* no. 5.

71. *New York Times,* July 1; *Bulletin,* Aug. 7, pp. 170-1.
72. *New York Times,* Aug. 13 and Sept. 21.
73. News conference, Aug. 18.
74. *New York Times,* Aug. 22.
75. Cf. Sec. 36.
76. *New York Times,* Aug. 23.
77. Statement of Aug. 23 in *Soviet News,* Aug. 29.
78. *International Herald Tribune,* Aug. 24.
79. Text in *New York Times,* Sept. 1.
80. Text in same, Aug. 26; further details in same, Oct. 11.
81. News conference, Sept. 1.
82. Public Law 88-408, Aug. 10, 1964; *Documents, 1964,* pp. 216-17.
83. Cf. Sec. 47.
84. *Bulletin,* Sept. 25, p. 391; *Foreign Policy Briefs,* Sept. 25; further comments in *Weekly Compilation,* Sept. 11, pp 1256-61.
85. Text in *New Times,* Sept. 27, pp. 33-40; incomplete text in *New York Times,* Dec. 15.
86. News conference, Sept. 8, in *Bulletin,* Sept. 25, p. 390.
87. *U.N. Chronicle,* Oct., pp. 23-5.
88. Text in *Documents,* no. 115.
89. Text in *Soviet News,* Oct. 3.
90. *New York Times,* Sept. 27.
91. Cf. note 27.
92. Hendrick Smith in *New York Times,* Feb. 7 and Apr. 9, 1968.
93. *Documents,* no. 78.
94. *New York Times,* Oct. 4 and 20.
95. Rusk news conference, Oct. 12, in *Bulletin,* Oct. 30, pp. 555 and 563; Humphrey quoted in *New York Times,* Oct. 16.
96. Address of Nov. 21, in *Bulletin,* Dec. 11, p. 787; interview of Nov. 19, in *New York Times,* Nov. 20. For further details see *Bulletin,* Dec. 4, pp. 748-51; same, Dec. 11, pp. 781-8.
97. News conference, Nov. 17
98. *New York Times,* Oct. 31.

99. Cf. below at note 116.
100. *New York Times,* Dec. 6, 8, and 16.
101. Same, Nov. 3; for details see *Bulletin,* Nov. 20, pp. 667-72, and U.S. Senate, Committee on Foreign Relations, 90th Cong., 1st sess., *Submission of the Vietnam Conflict to the United Nations: Hearings* on S. Con. Res. 44 and S. Res. 180 (Washington: G.P.O., 1967), pp. 173-5 and 183.
102. *New York Times,* Nov. 4.
103. *Bulletin,* Dec. 4, p. 748.
104. S. Res. 180, 90th Cong., Nov. 30, in *Documents,* no. 79; Johnson comments at news conference, Nov. 17.
105. *New York Times,* Dec. 21; background in same, Dec. 10, 13, and 16.
106. Same, Dec. 20.
107. Same.
108. Eisenhower in same, Nov. 29; Thieu in same, Dec. 3.
109. Same, Nov. 27 and Dec. 11.
110. Cf. Sec. 38.
111. *New York Times,* Dec. 2, 3, and 7.
112. Humphrey in same, Dec. 8; McCloskey statement, Dec. 8, in *Documents,* no. 80.
113. Cf. note 85.
114. *Documents,* no. 81.
115. *New York Times,* Dec. 26.
116. Roy Reed in same, Dec. 20.
117. Same, Dec. 21.
118. Cf. Sec. 38.
119. *Documents,* no. 82.
120. *Bulletin,* Jan. 15, 1968, pp. 74-6.
121. Same, pp. 77-9; also (in part) in *Documents,* no. 83.
122. *New York Times,* Dec. 27.
123. Hanoi broadcast, Jan. 1, 1968, in *Documents,* no. 84.
124. Same.
125. W. P. Bundy, quoted in *New York Times,* Dec. 31.
126. Same, Feb. 2, 1968.

3 : Flames in the Middle East

1. *New York Times,* Feb. 8 and 20.
2. *The United States in World Affairs, 1966,* pp. 212-14.
3. *New York Times,* Jan. 3.
4. U.N. Document S/2322, Sept. 1, 1951.
5. *The United States in World Affairs, 1965,* p. 186.
6. Details in *U.N. Chronicle,* Feb., p. 13; same, Mar., pp. 17-18; same, Apr., pp. 40-2; same, May, p. 27.
7. *New York Times,* Feb. 23.
8. *Soviet News,* Apr. 4.
9. *New York Times,* May 14.
10. Same, Apr. 28.
11. Same, Jan. 16 and 17.
12. *U.N. Chronicle,* Feb., p. 10; further, *New York Times,* Jan. 25, 26, and 30.
13. *New York Times,* Apr. 24.
14. Same, May 10 and 12.
15. Address of May 22, in *New York Times,* May 26; broadcast of June 9, in same, June 10.
16. U.N. address, June 19, in *New York Times,* June 20.
17. U.N. address, June 19, distributed by Israeli Information Services, New York.
18. Condensed text in *Current Digest of the Soviet Press,* June 7, pp. 19-20.
19. Address of May 22, in *New York Times,* May 26.
20. Same; also report of Secretary-General in *U.N. Chronicle,* July, pp. 136-40.
21. See especially *U.N. Chronicle,* June, pp. 87-94; same, July, pp. 135-6.
22. U.S. aide memoire, Feb. 11, 1957, in *Documents, 1957,* pp. 258-60.
23. Details in *U.N. Chronicle,* June, pp. 6-8.
24. *American Foreign Policy, 1950-1955: Basic Documents,* vol. 2 (Department of State Publication 6446, Washington: G.P.O., 1957), p. 2237.
25. *New York Times,* May 23.
26. *Al Ahram,* quoted in *New York Times,* May 27.
27. Address of May 22, in *New York Times,* May 26.
28. Johnson in *Documents,* no. 31; Nolte in *New York Times,* May 25 and Sept. 30.
29. *New York Times,* June 10.
30. Text in *Bulletin,* June 12, pp. 871-3. For summary of Security Council meetings, May 24-31, see *U.N. Chronicle,* June, pp. 5-6 and 8-26. Further documentation is reprinted from the *Bulletin* in *United States Policy in the Near East Crisis* (Department of State Publication 8269, Washington: G.P.O., 1967).
31. *New York Times,* May 25.
32. Same, May 24.
33. Broadcast of June 9, in same, June 10.
34. James Feron in *New York Times Magazine,* Jan. 7, 1968, p. 102; also *New York Times,* June 4.
35. *New York Times,* June 2.
36. James Feron in *New York Times Magazine,* Jan. 7, 1968, pp. 102-4.
37. *New York Times,* May 28.
38. *Bulletin,* June 19, pp. 920-9.
39. *New York Times,* May 30.
40. Cf. note 43 to Chapter 4.
41. *New York Times,* June 4.
42. Same, June 3.
43. News conference, Nov. 27, in *Articles et documents,* Dec. 8, pp. 14-23; cf. note 68 to Chapter 5.
44. U.N. Document S/7916/Rev.1, in *Bulletin,* June 26, pp. 948-9; further, *U.N. Chronicle,* July, pp. 5-8.
45. Remarks of June 3 in *Weekly Compilation,* June 12, p. 829.

46. *New York Times,* June 5.
47. Max Frankel in same, June 9.
48. For analysis of both diplomatic and military aspects see especially Michael Howard and Robert Hunter, "Israel and the Arab World: The Crisis of 1967," *Adelphi Papers,* no. 41, Oct.
49. U.A.R. statement, June 6, and Nasser speech, June 9, in *New York Times,* June 7 and 10; U.S. denials in *Bulletin,* June 26, pp. 934-6 and 951; same, July 3, p. 11; *Documents,* no. 42.
50. *New York Times,* June 6 and 8.
51. U.N. Document S/RES/233 (1967), June 7, in *Documents,* no. 33; details in *U.N. Chronicle,* July, pp. 8-13 and 31-2; further, *Bulletin,* June 26, pp. 934-41 and 947-8.
52. U.N. Document S/RES/234 (1967), June 7, in *Documents,* no. 36; details in *U.N. Chronicle,* July, pp. 13-14; further, *Bulletin,* June 26, p. 948.
53. This and preceding quotation from *New York Times,* June 10.
54. U.N. Document S/RES/235 (1967), June 9, in *Documents,* no. 38; details in *U.N. Chronicle,* July, pp. 12-23; further, *Bulletin,* June 26, pp. 944-9. See also *U.N. Chronicle,* July, pp. 23-7, and *Bulletin,* July 3, pp. 3-5.
55. See notes 51, 52, 54, and 61.
56. U.S.S.R. Embassy, Washington, Press Release No. 12, June 6.
57. Rusk statement, June 5, in *Bulletin,* June 26, pp. 949-50; White House statement, June 5, in *Documents,* no. 32.
58. Drew Middleton in *New York Times,* June 8; Peter Grose in same, June 9.
59. *Documents,* no. 35.
60. James Reston in *New York Times,* June 11 (weekly review section); Max Frankel in same, June 12.

61. U.N. Document S/RES/236 (1967), June 12, in *Documents,* no. 39; details in *U.N. Chronicle,* July, pp. 23-32; further, *Bulletin,* July 3, pp. 3-5 and 11.
62. U.N. Document S/7951/Rev.2, in *Bulletin,* July 3, p. 12; Goldberg comment in same, p. 7, and *Documents,* no. 40.
63. U.N. Document S/7952/Rev.3, in *Bulletin,* July 3, p. 12.
64. *New York Times,* June 11.
65. Same, June 13.
66. Same, June 12.
67. U.N. Document S/RES/237 (1967), June 14, in *Documents,* no. 41; details in *U.N. Chronicle,* July, pp. 27-32; further, *Bulletin,* July 3, pp. 5-12.
68. *Soviet News,* June 13; *New York Times,* June 11.
69. *Soviet News,* June 13.
70. Goldberg to Thant, June 15, in *Bulletin,* July 3, pp. 12-13.
71. *The United States in World Affairs, 1960,* pp. 340-3.
72. Statement and resolution (A/L. 519) in *New York Times,* June 20. For full details on the Assembly session see *U.N. Chronicle,* July, pp. 32-81; same, Aug.-Sept., pp. 7-28; further, *Bulletin,* July 10, pp. 46-52; same, July 24, pp. 108-13; same, July 31, pp. 148-51; same, Aug. 14, 216-18. The highlights of the session are covered in *Documents,* nos. 42, 44-7, and 49-51.
73. *Soviet News,* June 27.
74. Cf. Chapter 4 at note 47.
75. *Documents,* no. 13.
76. *Documents,* no. 12.
77. *Documents,* no. 2.
78. Statement of June 20 and draft resolution (A/L.520) in *Documents,* no. 42.
79. *New York Times,* June 23.
80. Same, June 24 and 27. Details of Albanian resolution (A./L. 521) in *U.N. Chronicle,* July, p. 32.

81. Reuters dispatch in *New York Times,* June 19.
82. *Documents,* no. 43.
83. U.N. Document A/L.522, in *New York Times,* June 29; details in *U.N. Chronicle,* July, pp. 32-3.
84. U.N. Document A/L.523; details in *U.N. Chronicle,* July, p. 33; Goldberg statement, July 3, in *Documents,* no. 44.
85. General Assembly Resolution 2252 (ES-V), July 4, in *Documents,* no. 45; details in *U.N. Chronicle,* July, pp. 77-80; further, *Bulletin,* July 24, pp. 112-13.
86. Resolution 2253 (ES-V), July 4, in *Documents,* no. 46; details as above.
87. Resolution 2254 (ES-V), July 14, in *Documents,* no. 47; details in *U.N. Chronicle,* Aug.-Sept., pp. 7-21; further, *Bulletin,* July 31, pp. 148-51.
88. *Documents,* no. 48.
89. *New York Times,* July 21-22 and Sept. 19.
90. Drew Middleton in same, Sept. 19; *Pravda,* Sept. 8, in *Current Digest of the Soviet Press,* Sept. 27, pp. 20-1.
91. Resolution 2256 (ES-V), July 21, in *Documents,* no. 49; details in *U.N. Chronicle,* Aug.-Sept., pp. 22-8; further, *Bulletin,* Aug. 14, pp. 216-18. For the formal conclusion of the session see *Documents,* no. 51, and *U.N. Chronicle,* Oct., pp. 3-6.
92. Speech of July 5, in *Soviet News,* July 11.
93. *New York Times,* July 13; communiqué in *Soviet News,* July 18.
94. *U.N. Chronicle,* Aug.-Sept., pp. 3-7 and 28-30.
95. *New York Times,* July 11 and 19; Johnson in *Documents,* no. 2.
96. *Bulletin,* Aug. 7, pp. 160-1.
97. *New York Times,* July 19.
98. UNRWA figures from *New York Times,* Oct. 20. For U Thant's reports on the local situation see *U.N. Chronicle,* Aug.-Sept., pp. 30-32; same, Oct., pp. 11-13 and 104-9.
99. *International Herald Tribune,* July 24.
100. Same, Aug. 3-7.
101. *New York Times,* Sept. 2; additional details from *International Herald Tribune,* Sept. 2-3; full text in *Relazioni internazionali,* Sept. 9, p. 890.
102. *International Herald Tribune,* Sept. 2-3.
103. Same, Aug. 1.
104. *Bulletin,* Sept. 18, pp. 358-62.
105. Same, Dec. 18, pp. 825-7.
106. *New York Times,* Sept. 27.
107. Details in *Bulletin,* June 26, pp. 952-3; same, July 10, p. 41; same, Aug. 7, p. 171; same, Aug. 21, p. 229; same, Oct. 9, p. 459.
108. *New York Times,* Sept. 17, 28; same, Oct. 1, 25, 26; *Bulletin,* Nov. 13, p. 652; background in *The United States in World Affairs, 1966,* pp. 204-5 and 215-16.
109. Text, Sept. 21, in *Documents,* no. 115.
110. *New York Times,* Oct. 22.
111. U.N. Document S/RES/240 (1967), Oct. 25, in *Documents,* no. 52; details in *U.N. Chronicle,* Nov., pp. 3-9; further, *Bulletin,* Nov. 20, pp. 690-2; Rafael quoted from *New York Times,* Oct. 25.
112. *New York Times,* Oct. 31.
113. Same, Nov. 6-8.
114. U.N. Document S/8227, Nov. 7
115. U.N. Document S/8229, Nov. 7.
116. U.N. Document S/8289; details in *New York Times,* Nov. 11 and Dec. 9.
117. U.N. Document S/RES/242 (1967), Nov. 22, in *Documents,*

no. 54; details in *U.N. Chronicle,* Dec., pp. 8-19; further, *Documents,* nos. 53 and 55.
118. Press reports, Nov. 23-Dec. 11.
119. *U.N. Chronicle,* Jan. 1968, pp. 61-2.
120. General Assembly Resolution 2341 (A) and (B), Dec. 19; details in *U.N. Chronicle,* Jan. 1968, pp. 60-1.
121. *New York Times,* Dec. 14-16; further, *Israel Digest,* Dec. 29.
122. *New York Times,* Dec. 13, 14, 15, and 20.
123. Same, Dec. 23 and 25.
124. C. L. Sulzberger in same, Dec. 31.
125. *Bulletin,* Dec. 11, p. 799; Anderson talks in *New York Times,* Nov. 2, 3, and 9.
126. Same, Nov. 27.
127. Same, Dec. 24.
128. *Soviet News,* Dec. 5.
129. See note 43.
130. *New York Times,* Dec. 8; same, Feb. 16, 1968.
131. Same, Dec. 9, 13, and 22.
132. Same, Dec. 11 and 16.
133. Same, Dec. 18, 25, 27, and 31.
134. Same, Dec. 19.
135. Same, Nov. 23 and Dec. 15.
136. *Bulletin,* Dec. 25, p. 861.
137. *U.N. Chronicle,* Dec., pp. 46-9; same, Jan. 1968, p. 84; *Bulletin,* Jan. 8, 1968, p. 65.
138. Cf. Sec. 27.

4 : East-West Pause

1. Statement of Dec. 6, 1966 in *Weekly Compilation,* Dec. 12, 1966, p. 1778; statement of Nov. 10, 1966, cited in *The United States in World Affairs, 1966,* p. 399.
2. *Documents,* no. 1.
3. E.g., Harrison E. Salisbury in *New York Times,* Nov. 3.
4. *Pravda,* Feb. 16, quoted in same, Feb. 16; see further Sec. 36.
5. Text in *Documents, 1963,* pp. 130-2.
6. Text in *Documents, 1966,* pp. 391-8; signature documents in *Bulletin,* Feb. 20, pp. 266-9.
7. Cf. Sec. 3.
8. *The United States in World Affairs, 1966,* pp. 115-17, 123.
9. *New York Times,* Jan. 19.
10. *Soviet News,* Jan. 31.
11. *New York Times,* Feb. 5, Mar. 12.
12. Cf. note 15 to Chapter 1.
13. Cf. Sec. 6.
14. Communiqué in *New York Times,* Feb. 14.
15. Same, Feb. 10.
16. News conference, Mar. 2; text in *Bulletin,* Mar. 20, p. 445.
17. Thompson statement, June 13, in *Weekly Compilation,* June 19, p. 873; see also *New York Times,* Mar. 23, Apr. 8, and May 19.
18. *Documents,* no. 8; background material in *Bulletin,* Apr. 3, pp. 568-77; additional details in *U.N. Chronicle,* Mar., 14-16.
19. *New York Times,* Mar. 11.
20. *Soviet News,* May 2, pp. 57-9.
21. Press reports, April-June.
22. U.S. Senate, Committee on Foreign Relations, 90th Cong., 1st sess., *The Communist World in 1967: Hearings . . . with former Ambassador to the Soviet Union and Yugoslavia George F. Kennan, Jan. 30, 1967* (Washington: G.P.O., 1967), p. 8.
23. S. Ex. D, 88th Cong., 2d sess.; text in *Documents, 1964,* pp. 125-38.
24. *New York Times,* Jan. 21, Mar 8; additional administration statements in *Bulletin,* Feb. 13, pp.

247-50; same, Feb. 20, pp. 287-8; same, Apr. 3, p. 545.

25. S. Ex. D, 90th Cong., 1st sess.; Johnson message in *Documents*, no. 111; additional statements in *Bulletin*, Apr. 10, pp. 600-12.

26. *New York Times*, Mar. 14 and Apr. 13.

27. Cf. *Documents*, no. 112; also Sec. 44.

28. *The United States in World Affairs, 1966*, pp. 127-8; *Documents, 1966*, pp. 57-65.

29. *Bulletin*, Feb. 27, p. 334; same, Mar. 27, pp. 518-23; same, May 1, pp. 696-9; same, June 12, pp. 881-5.

30. *New York Times*, Feb. 21, Feb. 26, and Apr. 15.

31. Same, Mar. 31, Apr. 5, May 19, and July 15.

32. Same, Jan. 22, Feb. 28, and May 3; cf. Chapter 10 at note 72.

33. *Bulletin*, Feb. 27, pp. 331-2; same, Mar. 6, p. 393.

34. Same, Mar. 20, pp. 479-80.

35. *New York Times*, Apr. 12.

36. Same, Jan. 23, Feb. 8, Mar. 1 and 25, Apr. 5; also note 95, below.

37. *New York Times*, Apr. 22 and 27.

38. Svetlana Alliluyeva, *Twenty Letters to a Friend* (New York: Harper & Row, 1967).

39. Cf. Rusk comments in *Bulletin*, May 22, pp. 781-2.

40. *Pravda*, May 26, quoted in *New York Times*, May 27.

41. *New York Times*, May 18 and June 1.

42. Same, Apr. 12.

43. Same, May 11-18, May 30, and June 1.

44. Cf. Secs. 12 (Yemen) and 36 (Hong Kong).

45. Cf. Sec. 7.

46. For a detailed account of the Middle East crisis see Chapter 3.

47. See especially Harrison E. Salisbury in *New York Times*, July 12 and Nov. 3; cf. also Sec. 14.

48. Cf. Sec. 27.

49. *Documents*, nos. 10 and 13; on the Glassboro meetings see also Secs. 4, 7, and 15.

50. Cf. Sec. 41.

51. Cf. Sec. 15.

52. *Jenmin Jih Pao*, quoted in *New York Times*, June 12; Hsinhua, quoted in same, June 26.

53. Cf. Sec. 36.

54. *New York Times*, July 25-26.

55. Quoted in same, July 24.

56. Cf. Sec. 8.

57. *Documents*, no. 15; related material in *Bulletin*, Sept. 4, pp. 291-4; same, Sept. 11, pp. 315-18.

58. Statement of Aug. 24, in *Documents*, no. 14.

59. *New York Times*, Sept. 13.

60. Details in same, Sept. 15 and Oct. 1.

61. *Bulletin*, Sept. 25, p. 385.

62. *New York Times*, Sept. 10 and Oct. 9.

63. *Documents*, no. 16.

64. *U.N. Chronicle*, Oct., p. 98.

65. *Bulletin*, Oct. 23, pp. 543-5.

66. *Soviet News*, Oct. 3.

67. *New York Times*, Oct. 13.

68. Harry Schwartz in same, Oct. 22.

69. Same, Oct. 13.

70. Same, Oct. 23, 26, and 30; see also Claire Sterling, "The Soviet Fleet in the Mediterranean," *The Reporter*, Dec. 14, pp. 14-18.

71. *Documents*, no. 17.

72. *New York Times*, Dec. 14.

73. *Documents*, no. 17.

74. *New York Times*, Nov. 1, Dec. 18, 1967 and Jan. 20, 1968.

75. *Documents*, no. 18; further U.S. statement in *Bulletin*, Jan. 8, 1968, pp. 63-5.

76. *Documents*, no. 19.

77. General Assembly Resolution 2346 A (XXII), Dec. 19, in *Documents*, no. 20; details in

U.N. Chronicle, Jan. 1968, pp. 10-12.

78. Resolution 2342 (XXII), Dec. 19; details in *U.N. Chronicle,* Jan. 1968, pp. 12-13; further, *Bulletin,* Jan. 15, 1968, pp. 97-100.

79. Resolution 2343 (XXII), Dec. 19; details in *U.N. Chronicle,* Jan. 1968, pp. 13-15.

80. Resolution 2286 (XXII), Dec. 5; details in *U.N. Chronicle,* Oct., pp. 13-14; same, Nov., pp. 18-22; same, Dec., pp. 72-3; same, Jan. 1968, pp. 25-6; see further Sec. 40.

81. Resolution 2346 B (XXII), Dec. 19, in *Documents,* no. 20; details in *U.N. Chronicle,* Jan. 1968, pp. 10-12.

82. Resolution 2289 (XXII), Dec. 8; details in *U.N. Chronicle,* Dec., pp. 69-72; same, Jan. 1968, pp. 23-5; further, *Bulletin,* Jan. 1, 1968, pp. 26-30.

83. *Soviet News,* Nov. 17, supplement, p. 14.

84. Same.

85. *Soviet News,* Nov. 28 and Dec. 5.

86. Same, Jan. 2, 1968.

87. Same, Dec. 12.

88. Same.

89. U.S. note, Dec. 29, in *Bulletin,* Jan. 29, 1968, p. 155.

90. *New York Times,* Dec. 23.

91. Same, Dec. 20-21.

92. Same, Dec. 24, 1967 and Jan. 1, 1968.

93. Same, Oct. 17 and Nov. 10.

94. Same, Nov. 26, Dec. 1, 2, and 20; also *Bulletin,* Jan. 1, 1968, p. 16; same, Jan. 8, 1968, p. 67.

95. Cf. *Bulletin,* Dec. 18, p. 820.

96. Cf. Johnson interview, Dec. 19, in *Bulletin,* Jan. 8, 1968, p. 36.

97. Cf. testimony of Philip E. Mosely, reported in *New York Times,* Nov. 8.

5 : Will Success Spoil the West?

1. Cf. Sec. 27.

2. See especially *New York Times,* Jan. 6, 22, 25; same, Mar. 8; same, Apr. 3.

3. Cf. Sec. 26.

4. Cf. Sec. 25.

5. *Bulletin,* May 1, pp. 678-85.

6. Remarks of Apr. 26, in same, May 15, pp. 751-2.

7. *Speeches and Press Conferences,* No. 260A, pp. 7-11.

8. For the U.S. viewpoint see especially *Bulletin,* Feb. 27, pp. 333-4 and 338-9; same, Mar. 20, pp. 476-8; same, June 12, pp. 879-80; same, July 31, pp. 123-40.

9. White House announcement, Jan. 11, in same, Feb. 6, pp. 216-17.

10. *New York Times,* Feb. 8.

11. Wyndham White statement, May 15, in same, May 16; further, *International Commerce,* May 22, p. 2. For more detailed analysis see especially *Documents,* nos. 121 and 122; on the International Grains Arrangement, cf. Chapter 9 at note 76.

12. See Chapter 10.

13. *New York Times,* July 1.

14. *The United States in World Affairs, 1965,* p. 110; same, *1966,* pp. 181-2.

14a. For further discussion see Sec. 49.

15. *New York Times,* Jan. 8, 10, 11, 17, and 23.

16. Same, Mar. 9, 11, and 14.

17. Speech of Mar. 17, reported in same, Mar. 18; text in *Vital Speeches,* May 15, pp. 455-62.

18. *New York Times,* Apr. 7, 11-13, 16, 19, and 21; same, May 5.
19. Same, Apr. 19.
20. Same, Apr. 27.
21. Same, May 3; see further Sec. 25.
22. *New York Times,* June 22, July 19.
23. Cf. Sec. 26.
24. Cf. Sec. 25.
25. Statement of Aug. 28, in *Documents,* no. 124; see also Fowler statement in *Bulletin,* Sept. 25, pp. 393-6.
26. Group of Ten communiqué, Aug. 26, in *Documents,* no. 123; text of plan in *New York Times,* Sept. 12.
27. *International Herald Tribune,* Aug. 28.
28. I.M.F. resolution, Sept. 29, in *Documents,* no. 125; see also Fowler statement, Sept. 26, in *Bulletin,* Oct. 23, pp. 523-6; also *New York Times,* Sept. 25, 27, and 30.
29. *Statement of Secretary of Defense Robert S. McNamara . . . on the Fiscal Year 1968-72 Defense Program and 1968 Defense Budget, January 23, 1967* (U.S. Department of Defense, Press Release, Jan. 26), pp. 71-3.
30. Cf. report of Gen. Lyman L. Lemnitzer to the North Atlantic Assembly, Nov. 20, in *NATO Letter,* Jan. 1968, pp. 2-7.
31. Cf. Chapter 1 at note 22.
32. *New York Times,* Jan. 20; same, Feb. 13, 17, and 22; same, Apr. 13; same, July 31.
33. Same, Feb. 24, 28. For details see U.S. Senate, Committees on Foreign Relations and Armed Services, 90th Cong., 1st sess., *United States Troops in Europe: Hearings . . . on S. Res. 49 and S. Res. 83* (Washington: G.P.O., 1967).
34. Same, Feb. 17.

35. U.S. statement, May 2, in *Documents,* no. 23; further, *New York Times,* May 3.
36. Same.
37. Rusk in *Bulletin,* May 22, pp. 782-3; also *New York Times,* May 4.
38. Rusk as cited; also *New York Times,* July 31.
39. Cf. Chapter 4 at note 20.
40. NATO Council communiqué, Dec. 16, 1966, in *Documents, 1966,* pp. 149-55.
41. See especially *New York Times,* Apr. 21.
42. Communiqué, Apr. 7, in *Documents,* no. 22; related material in *Bulletin,* May 1, pp. 686-7; further, *Weekly Compilation,* Apr. 10, pp. 600-1.
43. *New York Times,* May 10.
44. NATO Council communiqué, June 14, in *Documents,* no. 24.
45. Address of June 20, in *Bulletin,* July 31, pp. 141-6.
46. *New York Times,* Apr. 1; same, June 14; same, July 6 and 19.
47. Especially *New York Times,* July 7.
48. Same, July 8, 13, 15, and 19.
49. *International Herald Tribune,* Aug. 12-13.
50. Joint statement, Aug. 16, in *Documents,* no. 25; related material in *Bulletin,* Sept. 11, pp. 325-9.
51. *New York Times,* Sept. 14 and 15.
52. Same, Sept. 13 and 14; Johnson statement, Sept. 30, in *Weekly Compilation,* Oct. 9, p. 1378.
53. *New York Times,* Oct. 2 and 11.
54. Cf. Chapter 4 at note 63.
55. *New York Times,* Sept. 27, 29, and 30; communiqué in *Relazioni internazionali,* Oct. 7, p. 994.
56. *New York Times,* Oct. 28; same, Nov. 6 and 12.
57. Same, Oct. 11 and 12.
58. Same as note 30.

59. Cf. Sec. 27.
60. Details in *U.N. Chronicle*, Aug.-Sept., pp. 48-59.
61. *New York Times*, Nov. 1 and 4.
62. General Assembly Resolution 2353 (XXII), Dec. 19; details in *U.N. Chronicle*, Jan. 1968, p. 82.
63. *New York Times*, Oct. 24, 25, and 30.
64. Same, Nov. 24 and 30; same, Dec. 1 and 9.
65. Statement of Nov. 18, in *Documents*, no. 126; see also Fowler statement in *Bulletin*, Dec. 11, p. 793.
66. *New York Times*, Nov. 27.
67. Same, Dec. 1.
68. Text in *Articles et documents*, Dec. 8, pp. 14-23.
69. The thesis of U.S. responsibility is developed in Stephen Rousseas, *The Death of a Democracy: Greece and the American Conscience* (New York: Grove Press, Inc., 1967).
70. *New York Times*, Apr. 26; Rusk statement, Apr. 28, in *Bulletin*, May 15, pp. 750-1.
71. *New York Times*, May 10, 12, and 17.
72. U.N. Document S/RES/238 (1967), June 19; details in *U.N. Chronicle*, July, pp. 81-7; further, *Bulletin*, July 10, pp. 52-3.
73. *New York Times*, Nov. 9-11.
74. James Feron in same, Nov. 28.
75. *Documents*, no. 27.
76. *Soviet News*, Nov. 28.
77. U.N. Document S/8266; details in *U.N. Chronicle*, Dec., pp. 3-8.
78. U.N. Document S/8248/Add.6, Dec. 3.
79. U.N. Document S/RES/244 (1967), Dec. 22; details in *U.N. Chronicle*, Jan. 1968, pp. 3-8; further, *Bulletin*, Jan. 15, 1968, pp. 95-6.
80. Cf. above at note 68.
81. *New York Times*, Nov. 29.
82. *Documents, 1962*, pp. 225-6.
83. *Documents*, no. 21.
84. Rostow in *Bulletin*, Dec. 25, pp. 876-81; communiqué in *Documents*, no. 30; see further *New York Times*, Dec. 1 and 2.
85. *Documents*, no. 127.
86. *New York Times*, Dec. 12-13.
87. Cf. Chapter 4 at note 87.
88. NATO Council communiqué, Dec. 14, in *Documents*, no. 30; further, *New York Times*, Dec. 12 and 13.
89. Annex to communiqué, in *Documents*, no. 30.
90. *New York Times*, Dec. 13.
91. Same, Dec. 19 and 20.

6 : Africa Struggles On

1. *Foreign Policy Briefs*, May 22.
2. *Documents, 1966*, pp. 298-304.
3. Cf. *Documents*, no. 91; also *New York Times*, Apr. 13 and Dec. 31.
4. *Documents*, no. 1.
5. Official text in same, no. 90.
6. *New York Times*, Jan. 28.
7. *Bulletin*, Feb. 27, pp. 328-30 and 351-2; further *New York Times*, Feb. 10-11 and Mar. 4.
8. *Bulletin*, Mar. 13, pp. 425-8; further, *New York Times*, Feb. 14-15 and 18.
9. *Bulletin*, June 26, pp. 954-9.
10. *New York Times*, Feb. 18.
11. U.N. Document S/RES/239 (1967), July 10; details in *U.N. Chronicle*, Aug.-Sept., pp. 32-9; further, *Bulletin*, July 31, pp. 151-3.
12. *New York Times*, July 10 and 12.

13. Summary in *U.N. Chronicle,* Oct., pp. 26-7.

14. *New York Times,* Sept. 14-15; more fully in R. Nagel and R. Rathbone, "The OAU at Kinshasa," *The World Today,* Nov., pp. 473-83.

15. C. L. Sulzberger in *New York Times,* Nov. 8.

16. U.N. Document S/RES/241 (1967), Nov. 15; details in *U.N. Chronicle,* Dec., pp. 20-28; further, *Bulletin,* Dec. 11, pp. 807-8.

17. State Department statement, Aug. 21, in *Bulletin,* Sept. 11, p. 320.

18. *New York Times,* Aug. 24.

19. Same, Oct. 15, 21, 27, 31, and especially Tad Szulc in same, Nov. 5.

20. Same, Sept. 15.

21. Same, Nov. 23-26.

22. U.N. Document S/RES/232 (1966), Dec. 16, 1966, in *Documents, 1966,* pp. 320-2.

23. *Documents,* no. 96; additional material in *Bulletin,* Jan. 23, pp. 146-7. For a full statement of the U.S. position see *Bulletin,* Mar. 6, pp. 366-77.

24. *U.N. Chronicle,* Oct., p. 123.

25. *New York Times,* June 14; same, July 17 and 26; *International Herald Tribune,* Aug. 3.

26. For details see especially Drew Middleton in *New York Times,* Oct. 4, and Lawrence Fellows in same, Oct. 5.

27. Same.

28. Same; also U.N. dispatch in *New York Times,* Oct. 5.

29. General Assembly Resolution 2262 (XXII), Nov. 3, in *Documents,* no. 97; details in *U.N. Chronicle,* Oct., p. 63; same, Nov., pp. 12-18; same, Dec., pp. 44-6.

30. *New York Times,* Nov. 10, 11, and 15.

31. Same, Nov. 24.

32. Same, Sept. 20, Oct. 16, and Nov. 11.

33. Same, Feb. 11 and Oct. 29; more extensive background in *Africa Report,* Nov.

34. E.g., *U.N. Chronicle,* July, pp. 103-7.

35. Same as note 16.

36. General Assembly Resolution 2270 (XXII), Nov. 17; details in *U.N. Chronicle,* Dec., pp. 35-44.

37. *New York Times,* Nov. 18.

38. General Assembly Resolution 2145 (XXI), Oct. 27, 1966, in *Documents, 1966,* pp. 309-11.

39. Same as note 5.

40. Rogers text in *Bulletin,* Feb. 20, pp. 302-5; details of Ad Hoc Committee in *U.N. Chronicle,* Feb., pp. 3-4; same, Mar., pp. 6-10; same, Apr., pp. 11-16.

41. Statement of Apr. 26, in *Documents,* no. 92; see further *New York Times,* Apr. 21 and 27 and May 11 (letter to editor).

42. General Assembly Resolution 2248 (S-V), May 19, in *Documents,* no. 93. For details see *Documents,* no. 94; *U.N. Chronicle,* May, pp. 4-10; same, June, pp. 27-37.

43. *U.N. Chronicle,* July, p. 87.

44. Same, Aug.-Sept., pp. 39-40.

45. Same, Nov., pp. 28-30; text in U.N. Document A/6822.

46. *U.N. Chronicle,* Oct., p. 124.

47. General Assembly Resolution 2325 (XXII), Dec. 16, in *Documents,* no. 95; details on this and the following resolution in *U.N. Chronicle,* Jan. 1968, pp. 62-7.

48. Resolution 2324 (XXII), Dec. 16; further details in *Bulletin,* Jan. 15, 1968, pp. 92-5.

49. Press reports, Feb. 2-9.

50. *The United States in World Affairs, 1966,* p. 262.

51. Same as note 5.

52. Resolution 2307 (XXII), Dec. 13; details in *U.N. Chronicle,*

Jan. 1968, pp. 47-50.
53. *New York Times,* Oct. 28 and Nov. 22.
54. Same, Oct. 31.
55. Resolutions 2354 and 2355 (XXII), Dec. 19; details in *U.N. Chronicle,* Jan. 1968, pp. 82-3.

56. Resolution 2356 (XXII), Dec. 19; details in same, p. 83.
57. *New York Times,* Oct. 29.
58. For details see *External Affairs,* Mar. 1968, pp. 130-5.
59. *Weekly Compilation,* Dec. 11, p. 1663.
60. *New York Times,* Nov. 1.

7 : *Around China's Rim*

1. *Documents,* no. 89.
2. *Documents,* no. 56.
3. Public Law 90-7, Apr. 1, in *Documents,* no. 57.
4. Statement of Sept. 1, in *Documents,* no. 58.
5. *New York Times,* Jan. 4, 1968.
6. Same, Dec. 31.
7. State Department statement, Apr. 12, in *Documents,* no. 59.
8. Communiqué, Oct. 4, in *Soviet News,* Oct. 10.
9. *New York Times,* June 12.
10. Same, Oct. 13.
11. *Documents,* no. 1.
12. For a fuller statement by W. P. Bundy, see *Bulletin,* Feb. 27, pp. 323-7.
13. U.S. Senate, Committee on Foreign Relations, 90th Cong., 1st sess., *Asia, the Pacific, and the United States: Hearings . . . with Former Ambassador to Japan Edwin O. Reischauer, Jan. 31, 1967* (Washington: G.P.O., 1967), p. 7. For a similar view cf. note 32.
14. For details cf. *Bulletin,* Feb. 6, pp. 193-9; same, Apr. 10, pp. 597-8; same, June 5, pp. 851-5; same, July 17, 61-4.
15. Cf. *Bulletin,* Apr. 3, pp. 548-53.
16. *Documents, 1962,* pp. 284-94.
17. For a sensitive analysis of Indonesian problems cf. Adam Malik, "Promise in Indonesia," *Foreign Affairs,* Jan. 1968, pp. 292-303.
18. *New York Times,* Feb. 7; same, Mar. 22 and 29; same, Apr. 12.

19. Robert Trumbull in same, Mar. 29; Drew Middleton in same, June 3.
20. Communiqué, May 10, and related material in *Bulletin,* June 5, pp. 846-50.
21. *New York Times,* Mar. 2; other details in *U.N. Chronicle,* Feb., pp. 33-7; same, May, pp. 42-3.
22. *U.N. Chronicle,* Feb., pp. 33-7.
23. Same, May, pp. 39-43.
24. Cf. Chapter 2 at note 54.
25. *New York Times,* May 30 and 31; cf. below at note 34.
26. Cf. *Bulletin,* June 26, pp. 960-3; further, *Weekly Compilation,* June 5, pp. 812-14.
27. Cf. Chapter 2 at note 73.
28. *New York Times,* Apr. 21 and 30.
29. Cf. below at note 51; also note 95 to Chapter 2.
30. *New York Times,* June 18.
31. Cf. Sec. 46.
32. Richard M. Nixon, "Asia After Viet Nam," *Foreign Affairs,* Oct., pp. 111-25.
33. For details see especially *Current Notes on International Affairs,* July, pp. 288-91; same, Aug., 317-24.
34. Same, pp. 325-8.
35. Same, p. 326.
36. *Documents,* no. 85.
37. Same.
38. U.S. Senate, Committee on Foreign Relations, 90th Cong., 1st sess., *The Rim of Asia: Report of Senator Mike Mansfield . . .*

*on a Study Mission to the West-
ern Pacific, Sept. 1967* (Committee print, Washington:
G.P.O., 1967), p. 14.
39. *New York Times* and *International Herald Tribune,* July 19.
40. For details cf. *Bulletin,* Apr. 10,
pp. 598-9; same, June 5, p. 865;
same, Sept. 18, pp. 363-78; also
Robert Trumbull in *New York
Times,* Oct. 30.
41. *New York Times,* Sept. 15-18.
42. Communiqué, Sept. 15, and related material in *Bulletin,* Oct.
9, pp. 451-9.
43. *New York Times,* Nov. 16.
44. Communiqué, Nov. 15, in *Documents,* no. 88; related material
in *Bulletin,* Dec. 4, pp. 742-4.
45. Communiqué, as cited. For subsequent developments cf. *Bulletin,* Apr. 29, 1968, pp. 570-1.
46. Goldberg in *New York Times,*
Jan. 27, 1968; details in *Bulletin,* Nov. 20, pp. 692-4; same,
Feb. 12, 1968, pp. 199-200.
47. *International Herald Tribune,*
Aug. 4; cf. Chapter 2 at note
68.
48. Johnson-Il Kwon Chung communiqué, Mar. 14, and related
material in *Bulletin,* Apr. 3, pp.
548-53.
49. *New York Times,* Sept. 15 and
16; same, Dec. 24; cf. Chapter
2 at note 86.
50. General Assembly Resolution
2269 (XXII), Nov. 16; details
in *U.N. Chronicle,* Nov., pp.

22-3; same, Dec., pp. 49-55;
further, *Bulletin,* Dec. 18, pp.
844-5.
51. Rusk in note 1, above; Humphrey in *New York Times,* Oct.
16.
52. Cf. note 68 to Chapter 2.
53. *New York Times,* Oct. 19 and
23; see also Johnson-Lee communiqué, Oct. 18, in *Bulletin,*
Nov. 6, p. 615.
54. Statement of Oct. 20, in *Bulletin,* Nov. 13, p. 654.
55. *New York Times,* Nov. 8 and
18; see further *Bulletin,* Dec.
11, pp. 789-92. For further statements see *Documents,* no. 78.
56. Address of Dec. 6, in *Bulletin,*
Jan. 1, 1968, pp. 3-5; cf. Johnson remarks, Dec. 4, in *Documents,* no. 6.
57. Cf. note 119 to Chapter 2.
58. Statement of Dec. 24, in *Bulletin,* Jan. 15, 1968, p. 79. For
full documentation on the President's Asian trip see same, pp.
69-78.
59. *New York Times,* Nov. 5-9; for
further discussion see Sec. 10.
60. *Bulletin,* Jan. 22, 1968, p. 124.
61. *New York Times,* Dec. 28.
62. Same, Dec. 22 and 28.
63. *Bulletin,* Jan. 29, 1968, p. 134.
64. *New York Times,* Jan. 11, 1968.
65. Same, Dec. 29.
66. Same, Dec. 1, 14, 20, 27, 28, 30.
67. Same, Dec. 30; background in
same, Oct. 20, 23; same, Dec. 2,
8.

8 : Latin American Standoff

1. Cf. note 7.
2. *New York Times,* Mar. 17; on
the U.S. visit see *Bulletin,* Feb.
13, pp. 242-4.
3. For details see *New York Times,*
Mar. 12 (p. 7E) and Mar. 17.
4. U.N. Document A/6663; summary in *Foreign Policy Briefs,*

Feb. 27. For subsequent U.S.
action see *Bulletin,* Apr. 29,
1968, pp. 554-6.
5. U.S. statement, Feb. 13, in *Documents,* no. 98.
6. *U.N. Chronicle,* Mar., pp. 25-
30; same, Apr., pp. 25-36.
7. Resolution of 11th Meeting of

Consultation, Feb. 26, in *Documents*, no. 101. For related material see *Bulletin*, Mar. 20, pp. 472-3; further, *Weekly Compilation*, Mar. 6, p. 351.

8. O.A.S. Document OEA/Ser.A/2, Add.2 (English). For summary cf. *Documents*, no. 100 and (more fully) William Manger, "Reform of the OAS," *Journal of Inter-American Studies*, Jan. 1968, pp. 1-14.

9. Final Act of the Third Special Inter-American Conference, Feb. 27, in *Documents*, no. 99.

10. *Documents*, no. 100. For U.S. ratification in April 1968 see *Bulletin*, May 13, 1968, pp. 614-16.

11. *Documents*, no. 102.

12. Johnson statements, Apr. 12-14, in *Documents*, nos. 103, 104, and 106. For additional statements see *Bulletin*, May 8, pp. 706-7; further, *Weekly Compilation*, Apr. 24, pp. 634-5.

13. Statement of Apr. 13, in *Documents*, no. 104.

14. *Documents*, no. 105. For fuller documentation see O.A.S. Document OEA/Ser.C/IX.1 (English).

15. Johnson in *Documents*, no. 106; Rusk and Linowitz in *Bulletin*, May 8, pp. 722 and 730.

16. Public Law 90-88, Sept. 22. For background see *Documents*, no. 108, and *Bulletin*, June 12, p. 887. For the appropriation see Chapter 10 at note 70.

17. *New York Times*, Sept. 21-23.

18. Juan de Onis in same, May 15; further details in *U.N. Chronicle*, June, pp. 65-8.

19. See especially Paul L. Montgomery in *New York Times*, June 25.

20. Cf. Chapter 10 at note 63.

21. *Documents*, no. 107.

22. *New York Times*, Mar. 15-16.

23. Published Apr. 16; text in *Estudios internacionales*, July, pp. 272-82.

24. Regis Debray, *Revolution in the Revolution? Armed Struggle and Political Struggle in Latin America* (New York: Monthly Review Press, 1967).

25. Final act, Sept. 24, in *Documents*, no. 110; also *New York Times*, July 27.

26. Same, May 13.

27. Same, May 10 and 18.

28. Same, May 22.

29. Cf. Chapter 4 at note 47.

30. *New York Times*, June 28-July 1.

31. Same, July 27.

32. Same, July 31.

33. For details see especially "La Stratégie révolutionnaire en Amerique Latine: De la Tricontinentale à la Conference de l'O.L.A.S.," (*Problemes d'Amerique Latine*, no. 7), *Notes et études documentaires*, no. 3453, Jan. 12, 1968, pp. 5-35. Other treatments include: (1) U.S. Senate, Committee on the Judiciary, Subcommittee to Investigate the Administration of the Internal Security Act, 90th Cong., 1st sess., *The First Conference of the Latin American Solidarity Organization: A Staff Study* (Washington: G.P.O., 1967); (2) Boris Goldenberg, "Fidel Castros Revolutionstheorie im Konflikt mit Moskau," *Europa-Archiv*, Sept. 25, 647-56; (3) Hermann P. Gebhardt, "Castro und die OLAS-Konferenz von Havana," *Aussenpolitik*, Dec., pp. 743-50; French translation in *Articles et documents*, Mar. 29, 1968, pp. 16-20.

34. Cf. Chapter 1 at note 6.

35. *Notes et études documentaires*, no. 3453, Jan. 12, 1968, p. 28.

36. Same, pp. 24-6.

37. Final Act, Sept. 24, in *Documents*, no. 110.

38. Benjamin Welles in *New York Times,* Sept. 11.
39. TASS statement in *Soviet News,* Sept. 19.
40. Statement of Sept. 23, in *Documents,* no. 109; see also Johnson statement, Sept. 22, in *Bulletin,* Oct. 16, pp. 498-9.
41. *Documents,* no. 109.
42. Resolution III, in *Documents,* no. 110.
43. Resolution IV, in same.
44. Rusk statement, Sept. 24, in *Bulletin,* Oct. 16, p. 493; Linowitz in *New York Times,* Sept. 26.
45. *New York Times,* Sept. 29-30.
46. H. L. Matthews in *War-Peace Report,* quoted in same, Dec. 21.
47. Same, Dec. 22.
48. Same, Oct. 14.
49. *Bulletin,* July 17, p. 65.
50. Same, Nov. 20, pp. 673-85.
51. Same, Nov. 6, pp. 621-2; also *New York Times,* Oct. 9.
52. *New York Times,* Oct. 26.
53. Same, Oct. 4 and 8.
54. Same, Jan. 22, 1968.
55. Same, Jan. 3, 1968.
56. E.g., Linowitz in *Bulletin,* Nov. 6, p. 619; Oliver in same, Dec. 25, pp. 871-2.
57. Cf. Chapter 10 at note 63.
58. *New York Times,* Oct. 8; Linowitz in *Bulletin,* Nov. 6, pp. 619-20.
59. *New York Times,* Oct. 12 and 18; same, Nov. 7; Oliver in *Bulletin,* Dec. 25, pp. 871-2.
60. Public Law 90-137, Nov. 14, sec. 301 (f) (4), in *Documents,* no. 119.
61. Public Law 90-249, Jan. 2, 1968, sec. 119. See further Chapter 10 at note 70.
62. Cf. Juan de Onis in *New York Times,* Dec. 23.
63. Same, Jan. 20.
64. Linowitz in *New York Times,* Dec. 8; Oliver in *Bulletin,* Jan. 1, 1968, p. 8; Rusk in same, pp. 1-2.

9 : Attention: The World

1. Proclamation, Aug. 1, in *Weekly Compilation,* Aug. 7, p. 1077.
2. Message, Mar. 9, in *Bulletin,* Apr. 3, p. 568 (emphasis supplied).
3. Stevenson in *The United States in World Affairs, 1963,* p. 320; Goldberg in Chapter 6 at note 6.
4. Details in *U.N. Chronicle,* March, pp. 10-13; same, Apr. pp. 3-11; same, May, pp. 10-18; same, June, pp. 37-42; further, *Bulletin,* Apr. 17, pp. 636-41; Soviet memorandum, Mar. 16, in *Soviet News,* Apr. 11.
5. Cf. Chapter 6 at note 41.
6. General Assembly Resolution 2249 (S-V), May 23; details in *U.N. Chronicle,* June, pp. 37 and 42-6; further, *Bulletin,* June 12, pp. 894-7.
7. Cf. Chapter 3 at note 20.
8. *U.N. Chronicle,* Oct., p. 13.
9. Introduction to annual report, in same, p. 127.
10. Cf. Sec. 14.
11. Cf. Sec. 27.
12. Cf. Chapter 2 at note 105.
13. Address of July 30, in *U.N. Chronicle,* Aug.-Sept., p. 80.
14. E.g., *Documents,* no. 77a.
15. See Secs. 19 and 21.
16. Cf. note 35, below.
17. Resolution 2145 (XXI), Oct. 27, 1966, in *Documents, 1966,* pp. 309-11.
18. Cf. Chapter 6 at note 42.
19. *Documents, 1960,* pp. 575-7; same, *1961,* pp. 516-18.

20. Details in *U.N. Chronicle,* Mar., pp. 18-30; same, Apr., pp. 19-42; same, May, pp. 20-9; same, June, pp. 51-6; same, July, pp. 89-111; same, Aug.-Sept., pp. 84-96; same, Oct., pp. 17-22; same, Nov., pp. 30-2. On Gibraltar cf. Chapter 5 at note 60.

21. Cf. Chapter 3 at note 126.

22. Cf. Chapter 8 at note 6.

23. Cf. Chapter 7 at note 40.

24. *U.N. Chronicle,* Oct., pp. 135-6.

25. *Documents, 1948,* pp. 435-8.

26. Letter of July 22, 1963, in *Bulletin,* Aug. 26, 1963, pp. 322-3; texts in same, pp. 323-8. For background cf. William Korey, "Human Rights Treaties: Why is the U.S. Stalling?" *Foreign Affairs,* Apr., pp. 414-24.

27. *Bulletin,* Mar. 27, pp. 524-9.

28. *New York Times,* Nov. 3; *Bulletin,* Dec. 18, p. 846; same, Jan. 15, 1968, p. 104.

29. *Documents, 1965,* pp. 398-412.

30. *The United States in World Affairs, 1966,* pp. 353 and 375-6.

31. *U.N. Chronicle,* Oct., p. 119.

32. *Documents, 1959,* pp. 528-35.

33. *Bulletin,* Jan. 9, pp. 71-2; same, Apr. 17, pp. 633-4.

34. Text in *Documents, 1966,* pp. 391-8.

35. Cf. Chapter 2 at notes 5 and 27; also *Bulletin,* Jan. 15, 1968, pp. 100-1.

36. Cf. Chapter 4 at notes 71 and 72.

37. Resolution 2250 (S-V), May 23; details in *U.N. Chronicle,* Mar., pp. 16-17; same, June, pp. 46-8. Cf. below at note 93.

38. For details see *Report to Congress from the President of the United States: United States Aeronautics and Space Activities, 1967* (Washington: G.P.O., 1968).

39. *Bulletin,* Sept. 4, p. 300.

40. Statement of Oct. 10, in *Documents,* no. 112.

41. Resolution 2345 (XXII), Dec. 19; text of agreement in *Documents,* no. 113; Johnson statement in same, no. 114; further details in *U.N. Chronicle,* Jan. 1968, pp. 18-23; *Bulletin,* Jan. 15, 1968, pp. 80-7. For signature of the agreement (Apr. 22, 1968) see *Bulletin,* May 13, 1968, p. 626.

42. *The United States in World Affairs, 1958,* pp. 411-13; same, *1960,* pp. 359-60.

43. Cf. *Bulletin,* Feb. 6, p. 216; same, Feb. 27, pp. 331-2; same, Mar. 6, p. 393; same, Apr. 17, pp. 635-6; same, Jan. 8, 1968, p. 67; also Chapter 4 at notes 33 and 94.

44. Johnson report, Mar. 9, in *Weekly Compilation,* Mar. 13, pp. 412-13. For background see *The United States in World Affairs, 1966,* p. 352; also E. W. Seabrook Hull, "The Political Ocean," *Foreign Affairs,* Apr., pp. 492-502; also *Bulletin,* Feb. 12, 1968, pp. 211-15; same, Apr. 22, 1968, pp. 537-42.

45. *Weekly Compilation,* Jan. 16, pp. 24-5; see also same, Mar. 13, pp. 412-13.

46. *Bulletin,* Aug. 21, pp. 227-9.

47. *New York Times,* Mar. 29.

48. *Bulletin,* Sept. 18, p. 362.

49. U.S. Senate, Committee on Foreign Relations, 90th Cong., 1st sess., *Governing the Use of Ocean Space: Hearings on S.J. Res. 111, etc., Nov. 29* (Washington: G.P.O., 1967). See further below at note 120.

50. *Documents, 1965,* p. 359.

51. *Bulletin,* May 15, pp. 758-65.

52. Same, June 19, pp. 902-7; further, same, Aug. 21, pp. 245-6.

53. *Documents, 1965,* pp. 354-6 and 435-7.

54. Johnson address, Oct. 8, in *Bulletin,* Oct. 30, pp. 569-71; cf. below at note 114.

55. *New York Times,* Oct. 9-10.

56. Same, Apr. 4 and 28; same,

Sept. 21 and Oct. 4. For general background cf. *Bulletin,* Jan. 16, pp. 90-7; same, June 19, pp. 910-17.

57. *Documents,* no. 118.

58. Text in *New York Times,* Mar. 29.

59. Resolution 1710 (XVI), Dec. 19, 1961, in *Documents, 1961,* pp. 535-8.

60. *New York Times,* Oct. 10.

61. *U.N. Chronicle,* Oct., p. 117.

62. Same, pp. 117-18.

63. *Documents,* no. 118.

64. Cf. Chapter 10.

65. D.A.C. communiqué, July 20, in *Documents,* no. 29; similarly *U.N. Chronicle,* July, pp. 118-19.

66. *U.N. Chronicle,* Nov., pp. 42-3; also *New York Times,* Oct. 10.

67. *U.N. Chronicle,* June, pp. 68-71.

68. *New York Times,* Apr. 8; same, May 2, 9, and 10.

69. Cf. Sec. 24.

70. Summary in *Keesing's Contemporary Archives,* Mar. 2-9, 1968, p. 22564; details in Markus Timmler, "Algier: Das erste Regierungstreffen der ganzen Dritten Welt," *Aussenpolitik,* Dec., pp. 725-34.

71. *Documents,* no. 104; cf. Chapter 8 at note 13.

72. *Foreign Policy Briefs,* Jan. 15, 1968; also *New York Times,* Oct. 28.

73. Communiqué, Dec. 1, in *Documents,* no. 30; see also Chapter 5 at note 84.

74. On the coffee agreement cf. *Bulletin,* Mar. 4, 1968, pp. 330-9; on commodity agreements in general, cf. same, Mar. 18, 1968, pp. 387-92.

75. Cf. Chapter 7 at note 2.

76. *International Commerce,* May 22, p. 2; *Bulletin,* July 24, pp. 100-1. For further details see *Bulletin,* May 6, 1968, pp. 590-4.

77. *Bulletin,* Nov. 27, pp. 716-17.

78. *New York Times,* June 10; same, July 27; same, Oct. 25, 27, and 28.

79. *Bulletin,* Dec. 4, pp. 762-3; see also same, Apr. 29, 1968, pp. 568-9.

80. *U.N. Chronicle,* Jan. 1968, pp. 105-6.

81. *New York Times,* Oct. 12-13.

82. *U.N. Chronicle,* Oct., pp. 93-137; for quotation see Chapter 1 at note 2.

83. *New York Times,* Sept. 20.

84. *U.N. Chronicle,* Oct., pp. 7-8. For background on the session cf. "Issues Before the 22nd General Assembly," *International Conciliation,* no. 564, Sept.; for a summary of major actions see *Documents,* no. 116. More detailed accounts appear in *U.N. Chronicle,* Oct., Nov., and Dec. 1967 and Jan. 1968.

85. *Documents,* no. 115; cf. Chapter 2 at note 88.

86. *Soviet News,* Oct. 3.

87. Cf. Chapter 4 at note 66.

88. *Soviet News,* Oct. 3.

89. *Literaturnaya Gazeta,* quoted in *Soviet News,* Oct. 31.

90. Resolution 2289 (XXII), Dec. 8; details in note 82 to Chapter 4.

91. Resolution 2330 (XXII), Dec. 18; details in *U.N. Chronicle,* Dec., pp. 57-62; same, Jan. 1968, pp. 34-41 and 117-18.

92. Resolution 2346 (XXII), Dec. 19, in *Documents,* no. 20; details in note 77 to Chapter 4.

93. Resolutions 2260 and 2261 (XXII), Nov. 3; details in *U.N. Chronicle,* Nov., pp. 27-8; same, Dec., pp. 55-7; cf. above at note 37.

94. Resolution 2345 (XXII), Dec. 19; details in note 41, above.

95. Resolution 2309 (XXII), Dec. 13; details in *U.N. Chronicle,* Jan. 1968, p. 27.

96. Cf. Chapter 3 at note 117.

97. Resolutions 2341 A and B

98. Resolution 2269 (XXII), Nov. 16; details in note 50 to Chapter 7.
99. Resolution 2271 (XXII) Nov. 28; details in *U.N. Chronicle,* Dec., pp. 28-35; further, *Bulletin,* Dec. 18, pp. 829-33.
100. *U.N. Chronicle,* Oct., pp. 101-2.
101. Resolution 2308 (XXII), Dec. 13; details in *U.N. Chronicle,* Dec., pp. 73-4; same, Jan. 1968, pp. 41-7; *Bulletin,* Jan. 1, 1968, pp. 20-5.
102. *Documents,* no. 116.
103. *U.N. Chronicle,* Oct., pp. 135-6; cf. above at note 24.
104. *Bulletin,* Jan. 29, 1968, p. 159.
105. Resolution 2310 (XXII), Dec. 14; details in note 137 to Chapter 3.
106. Resolution 2347 (XXII), Dec. 19; details in *U.N. Chronicle,* Dec., pp. 99-101; same, Jan. 1968, p. 81.
107. *Documents,* no. 116; for details see Secs. 31 and 32.
108. Details in *U.N. Chronicle,* Jan. 1968, pp. 80-3.
109. Resolution 2288 (XXII), Dec. 7; details in *U.N. Chronicle,* Dec., pp. 74-8; same, Jan. 1968, 67-70.
110. Resolution 2326 (XXII), Dec. 16; details in *U.N. Chronicle,* Jan. 1968, pp. 70-80.
111. Details in *U.N. Chronicle,* Nov., pp. 33-7; same, Dec., pp. 79-82; same, Jan. 1968, pp. 85-92.
112. Resolutions 2290 (XXII), Dec. 8, and 2300 (XXII), Dec. 12;

details in *U.N. Chronicle,* Jan. 1968, pp. 87-8.
113. *Foreign Policy Briefs,* Jan. 29, 1968.
114. Resolution 2306 (XXII), Dec. 13; details in *U.N. Chronicle,* Jan. 1968, pp. 89-90; further, *Bulletin,* Jan. 29, 1968, pp. 156-8; cf. above at note 54.
115. Resolution 2305 (XXII), Dec. 13; details in *U.N. Chronicle,* Jan. 1968, p. 89.
116. Details in *U.N. Chronicle,* Nov., pp. 37-42; same, Dec., pp. 82-9; same, Jan. 1968, pp. 90-102.
117. Resolution 2263 (XXII), Nov. 7; details in same, Nov., pp. 37-9; same, Dec., pp. 82 and 113-17.
118. Resolution 2339 (XXII), Dec. 18; details in same, Dec., p. 89; same, Jan. 1968, pp. 93-4 and 97-8.
119. Details on legal actions in same, Dec., pp. 109-12; same, Jan. 1968, pp. 117-24.
120. Resolution 2340 (XXII), Dec. 18; details in same, Jan. 1968, pp. 28-34; further, *Bulletin,* Jan. 22, 1968, pp. 125-7; cf. above at note 49.
121. Details on financial actions in *U.N. Chronicle,* Nov., pp. 50-4; same, Dec., pp. 101-6; same, Jan. 1968, pp. 106-10, 115-17.
122. Resolution 2359 (XXII), Dec. 19; details in same, Dec., pp. 107-9; same, Jan. 1968, pp. 114-15.
123. Same, Jan. 1968, p. 132.
124. Same, pp. 8-9.
125. Statement of Dec. 20, in *Documents,* no. 116.

10 : Foreign Policy in a "Sick Society"

1. Text from *New York Times Magazine,* Aug. 20, pp. 30 ff.; annotated text in *Vital Speeches,* Sept. 1, pp. 678-82.
2. Johnson in *Weekly Compilation,* Nov. 20, p. 1551; McNamara quoted by James Reston in *New York Times,* Nov. 10.

3. Cf. Chapter 1 at note 22 and Chapter 5 at note 31.
4. P.L. 88-408, Aug. 10, 1964, in *Documents, 1964,* pp. 216-17.
5. *New York Times,* Aug. 18.
6. Texts in *New York Times,* Nov. 17 and 22.
7. Details in same, Feb. 14-27.
8. Katzenbach statement, Feb. 22, in *Weekly Compilation,* Feb. 27, p. 297.
9. *New York Times,* Feb. 21.
10. Same, Feb. 16, Dec. 18, and Dec. 30; *Bulletin,* Apr. 24, pp. 665-8; same, Jan. 29, 1968, p. 145.
11. *Bulletin,* Jan. 8, 1968, pp. 55-9.
12. Cf. Chapter 9 at notes 54 and 119; also H. Taubman in *New York Times,* Mar. 8, 1968.
13. Cf. Chapter 1 at note 6.
14. Text in *Documents,* no. 3.
15. National Committee for an Effective Congress, quoted in *New York Times,* Dec. 26.
16. P.L. 90-5, Mar. 16; Johnson statement, Mar. 16, in *Weekly Compilation,* Mar. 20, p. 480.
17. P.L. 90-8, Apr. 4; background and details in *Bulletin,* Feb. 13, pp. 236-7; further, *Weekly Compilation,* Apr. 10, pp. 587-8.
18. Budget message and statement, Jan. 24, in *New York Times,* Jan. 25 (excerpts in Documents, no. 4); McNamara statement, Jan. 23, as cited in note 12 to Chapter 1.
19. P.L. 90-22, June 5.
20. P.L. 90-96, Sept. 29.
21. P.L. 90-110, Oct. 21; P.L. 90-180, Dec 8.
22. *New York Times,* June 3.
23. Message of Mar. 6, in *Weekly Compilation,* Mar. 13, pp. 385-96.
24. P.L. 90-40, June 30.
25. P.L. 90-96, Sept. 29; Johnson comment in *Weekly Compilation,* Oct. 9, p. 1378. Cf. Chapter 5 at note 52.

26. *Documents,* no. 5; cf. Chapter 2 at note 70.
27. Cf. Chapter 2 at note 80.
28. *Documents,* no. 16; cf. Chapter 4 at note 86.
29. *Documents,* no. 17; cf. Chapter 4 at note 71.
30. See especially State of the Union message (excerpts in *Documents,* no. 1) and message on the Economic Report in *Weekly Compilation,* Jan. 30, pp. 105-16 (excerpts in *Documents,* no. 117).
31. Details in *Survey of Current Business,* Mar., pp. 14-32.
32. P.L. 90-59, July 31; cf. *Bulletin,* Sept. 25, pp. 396-7.
33. State of Union message, Jan. 10, in *Documents,* no. 1; cf. Chapter 1 before note 18.
34. Full text in *New York Times,* Aug. 4; excerpts in *Documents,* no. 5.
35. Message of Nov. 27, in *Documents,* no. 122; details on the Kennedy Round in Sec. 24.
36. P.L. 87-794, Oct. 11, 1962; summary in *Documents, 1962,* pp. 496-508.
37. *Bulletin,* Jan. 15, 1968, pp. 88-91.
38. Same as note 35.
39. E.g., William Diebold, Jr., "New Horizons in Foreign Trade," *Foreign Affairs,* Jan. 1967, pp. 291-303; John W. Evans, *U.S. Trade Policy: New Legislation for the Next Round* (New York: Harper & Row, for the Council on Foreign Relations, 1967).
40. Johnson statement, Mar. 24, in *Weekly Compilation,* Mar. 27, pp. 530-1.
41. *Bulletin,* Aug. 7, pp. 173-80.
42. *Weekly Compilation,* July 3, p. 947; same, July 10, pp. 968-70.
43. Cf. Chapter 5 at notes 9 and 10.
44. *New York Times,* Oct. 6, 16, and 24.
45. Katzenbach in *New York Times,* Oct. 31; Díaz in same, Oct. 28

(cf. Chapter 8 at note 50); Johnson in same, Nov. 3.

46. Details in *International Commerce*, Mar. 4, 1968, pp. 2-7.
47. Cf. Sec. 24.
48. Cf. Sec. 26.
49. Cf. Sec. 28.
50. *New York Times*, Feb. 1.
51. Details in *Survey of Current Business*, Mar. 1968, pp. 15-36.
52. *New York Times*, Nov. 17.
53. *Weekly Compilation*, Jan. 8, 1968, pp. 20-26 (misdated Jan. 1, 1967).
54. Cf. Johnson remarks, Dec. 6, in *Documents*, no. 127.
55. *New York Times*, Apr. 19; cf. David Rockefeller, "The Case for Foreign Aid," *World Business*, May, pp. 6-9.
56. *New York Times*, May 28.
57. Budget statement and commentaries, Jan. 24, in *New York Times*, Jan. 25.
58. *Documents*, no. 118.
59. For further details see *Bulletin*, May 29, pp. 826-33; same, Aug. 14, pp. 208-15; also U.S. Agency for International Development, *Proposed Foreign Aid Program FY 1968: Summary Presentation to the Congress* (Washington: G.P.O., 1967).
60. P.L. 90-137, Nov. 14; excerpts in *Documents*, no. 119.
61. Cf. Chapter 8 at note 11.
62. *Bulletin*, June 12, p. 887.
63. See especially *New York Times*, July 23 and 31.
64. *Foreign Policy Briefs*, Nov. 6; same, Feb. 26, 1968; also Katzenbach address, Nov. 17, in *Bulletin*, Dec. 11, pp. 794-8.
65. Same as note 60.
66. *Documents*, no. 120; cf. Rusk statement, Nov. 20, in *Bulletin*, Dec. 11, pp. 801-7.
67. P.L. 90-249, Jan. 2, 1968; on military provisions cf. Chapter 8 at note 61.
68. Cf. *Bulletin*, Mar. 27, p. 529; also *Weekly Compilation*, June 5, p. 806.
69. Cf. Chapter 9 at note 68; also *The United States in World Affairs, 1965*, p. 310.
70. Cf. Chapter 8 at note 16.
71. Cf. Chapter 7 at note 36.
72. P.L. 90-267, Mar. 13, 1968, sec. 1 (c); cf. Chapter 4 at note 32.
73. Cf. Sec. 34.
74. Cf. Chapter 9 at note 76. On the Food for Freedom program cf. Chapter 9 at note 78.
75. Gardner in *New York Times*, Oct. 1; Mansfield in same, Nov. 11; Fulbright in same, Dec. 9 and 14.
76. *Bulletin*, Nov. 6, p. 614.
77. *New York Times*, Dec. 1; earlier statements in same, Oct. 17 and 27 and Nov. 3 and 10.
78. Same, Nov. 28; same, Mar. 8, 1968.
79. Same, Dec. 21; see also same, Dec. 6 and 7.
80. Cf. Chapter 2 at note 80.
81. Cf. Chapter 4 at note 68.
82. Remarks of Dec. 4 in *Documents*, no. 6; cf. also Rusk statement, Dec. 6, in *Bulletin*, Jan. 1, 1968, pp. 1-5 (quoted in Chapter 7 at note 56).
83. *Weekly Compilation*, Dec. 18, p. 1705.
84. Cf. Chapter 2 at notes 27 and 93.
85. Cf. Chapter 2 at notes 116-19.
86. Cf. Chapter 2 at note 123.
87. Cf. Chapter 7 at note 58. For full documentation see *Bulletin*, Jan. 15, 1968, pp. 69-79.
88. *Bulletin*, Jan. 15, 1968, p. 79.
89. Harris and Gallup poll results in *New York Times*, Dec. 31.
90. Excerpts in *New York Times*, Dec. 20.

Index *

* The reader should also consult the "Chronology of Major Events," pp. 403-422 above.

COUNCIL ON FOREIGN RELATIONS

OFFICERS AND DIRECTORS

John J. McCloy, *Chairman of the Board*
Henry M. Wriston, *Honorary President*
Grayson Kirk, *President*
Frank Altschul, *Vice-President & Secretary*
David Rockefeller, *Vice-President*
Gabriel Hauge, *Treasurer*
George S. Franklin, Jr., *Executive Director*

Hamilton Fish Armstrong
William P. Bundy
William A. M. Burden
Arthur H. Dean
Douglas Dillon
Allen W. Dulles
William C. Foster
Caryl P. Haskins
Joseph E. Johnson
Henry R. Labouisse

Walter H. Mallory
Bill D. Moyers
Alfred C. Neal
James A. Perkins
Lucian W. Pye
Philip D. Reed
Robert V. Roosa
Charles M. Spofford
Carroll L. Wilson

Publications

FOREIGN AFFAIRS (quarterly), edited by Hamilton Fish Armstrong.

THE UNITED STATES IN WORLD AFFAIRS (annual), by Richard P. Stebbins.

DOCUMENTS ON AMERICAN FOREIGN RELATIONS (annual), by Richard P. Stebbins with the assistance of Elaine P. Adam.

POLITICAL HANDBOOK AND ATLAS OF THE WORLD (annual), edited by Walter H. Mallory.

THE ECONOMICS OF INTERDEPENDENCE: Economic Policy in the Atlantic Community, by Richard N. Cooper (1968).

463

HOW NATIONS BEHAVE: Law and Foreign Policy, by Louis Henkin (1968).

THE INSECURITY OF NATIONS, by Charles Yost (1968).

PROSPECTS FOR SOVIET SOCIETY, edited by Allen Kassof (1968).

THE AMERICAN APPROACH TO THE ARAB WORLD, by John S. Badeau (1968).

GULLIVER'S TROUBLES, OR THE SETTING OF AMERICAN FOREIGN POLICY, by Stanley Hoffmann (1968).

U.S. POLICY AND THE SECURITY OF ASIA, by Fred Greene (1968).

NEGOTIATING WITH THE CHINESE COMMUNISTS: The U.S. Experience, by Kenneth T. Young (1968).

FROM ATLANTIC TO PACIFIC: A New Interocean Canal, by Immanuel J. Klette (1967).

TITO'S SEPARATE ROAD: America and Yugoslavia in World Politics, by John C. Campbell (1967).

U.S. TRADE POLICY: New Legislation for the Next Round, by John W. Evans (1967).

TRADE LIBERALIZATION AMONG INDUSTRIAL COUNTRIES: Objectives and Alternatives, by Bela Balassa (1967).

THE CHINESE PEOPLE'S LIBERATION ARMY, by Brig. General Samuel B. Griffith II U.S.M.C. (ret.) (1967).

THE ARTILLERY OF THE PRESS: Its Influence on American Foreign Policy, by James Reston (1967).

ATLANTIC ECONOMIC COOPERATION: The Case of the O.E.C.D., by Henry G. Aubrey (1967).

TRADE, AID AND DEVELOPMENT: The Rich and Poor Nations, by John Pincus (1967).

BETWEEN TWO WORLDS: Policy, Press and Public Opinion on Asian-American Relations, by John Hohenberg (1967).

THE CONFLICTED RELATIONSHIP: The West and the Transformation of Asia, Africa and Latin America, by Theodore Geiger (1966).

THE ATLANTIC IDEA AND ITS EUROPEAN RIVALS, by H. van B. Cleveland (1966).

EUROPEAN UNIFICATION IN THE SIXTIES: From the Veto to the Crisis, by Miriam Camps (1966).

THE UNITED STATES AND CHINA IN WORLD AFFAIRS, by Robert Blum, edited by A. Doak Barnett (1966).

THE FUTURE OF THE OVERSEAS CHINESE IN SOUTHEAST ASIA, by Lea A. Williams (1966).

THE CONSCIENCE OF THE RICH NATIONS: The Development Assistance Committee and the Common Aid Effort, by Seymour J. Rubin (1966).

ATLANTIC AGRICULTURAL UNITY: Is it Possible?, by John O. Coppock (1966).

TEST BAN AND DISARMAMENT: The Path of Negotiation, by Arthur H. Dean (1966).

COMMUNIST CHINA'S ECONOMIC GROWTH AND FOREIGN TRADE, by Alexander Eckstein (1966).

POLICIES TOWARD CHINA: Views from Six Continents, edited by A. M. Halpern (1966).

THE AMERICAN PEOPLE AND CHINA, by A. T. Steele (1966).